Striking a bargain

MANCHESTER
UNIVERSITY PRESS

Striking a bargain

Work and industrial relations in England 1815–1865

James A. Jaffe

Manchester University Press

Manchester and New York

Distributed exclusively in the USA by St. Martin's Press

Copyright © James A. Jaffe 2000

The right of James A. Jaffe to be identified as the author of this work has been asserted by him in accordance with the Copyright, Designs and Patents Act 1988.

Published by Manchester University Press
Oxford Road, Manchester M13 9NR, UK
and Room 400, 175 Fifth Avenue, New York, NY 10010, USA
http://www.man.ac.uk/mup

Distributed exclusively in the USA by
St. Martin's Press, Inc., 175 Fifth Avenue, New York,
NY 10010, USA

Distributed exclusively in Canada by
UBC Press, University of British Columbia, 6344 Memorial Road,
Vancouver, BC, Canada V6T 1Z2

British Library Cataloguing-in-Publication Data
A catalogue record for this book is available from the British Library

Library of Congress Cataloging-in-Publication Data applied for

ISBN   0 7190 4952 0 *hardback*

First published 2000

07 06 05 04 03 02 01 00   10 9 8 7 6 5 4 3 2 1

Printed in Great Britain
by Bookcraft (Bath) Ltd, Midsomer Norton

For my parents and Deborah

Contents

Acknowledgements

It may be hackneyed to acknowledge the collective nature of researching and writing any book, but such acknowledgements have only become trite because they bear an important measure of truth. There are many people to whom I owe thanks for their moral, intellectual or financial support during this project. Jeremy Black first suggested that I write this book for a series he was editing for Manchester University Press. For better or worse, the book ultimately grew beyond those boundaries, but Professor Black's initial interest is still greatly appreciated. At the Press, Jane Raistrick, Louise Edwards and Vanessa Graham have always been helpful, friendly and wise.

Much of the travel and research that went into this book was supported by the University of Wisconsin – Whitewater. An initial sabbatical term was later supplemented by several travel grants without which this book would never have appeared. Special thanks are also due to Avner Offer and the Warden of Nuffield College, whose invitation to spend two idyllic terms at Oxford allowed me to make my first serious advances in the writing of this manuscript. The staffs of many libraries and archives also deserve a great deal of credit for the final production of this book. In particular, the help of those librarians and archivists at the British Library, Corporation of London Record Office, Durham County Record Office, Northumberland Record Office and the Modern Records Centre are greatly appreciated.

Portions of this book have previously appeared in different forms in professional journals and I would like to thank their editors for permission to reproduce those sections here. Parts of Chapter 2 first appeared in *History of Political Economy*, portions of Chapter 6 in *Historical Studies in Industrial Relations* and parts of Chapter 7 in *Law and History Review*. Both Dave Lyddon and Christopher Tomlins proved to be exceptionally attentive editors and helped shape not only the sections of my work that appeared in their journals but the larger project as well.

Many people have also undertaken to read some of the chapters, sometimes in obscure and awkward forms and sometimes under obscure and awkward conditions. Early on, Michael Huberman shared his interest and enthusiasm in these topics, as Marc Steinberg has done more recently. I was very fortunate to meet up with Daniel Ernst and Melanie Nolan, both of whom deepened my understanding of industrial arbitration. Joel Wiener has always been most kind and supportive. An early presentation of some of the initial ideas of this book to the students of his seminar was more important to me than he perhaps knows. Bob Storch has shared his friendship as well as many meals with me. His enthusiasm for British history, despite the many miseries of our profession, always seemed to rejuvenate me. I am also fortunate to have Dick Yasko as a friend, colleague and teaching partner who makes going to work worthwhile. Finally, Bill Maynard and I have complained our way across two continents, dozens of professional conferences, and too many years of academia. It's still great fun.

This book is appearing during the year of my parents' fiftieth wedding anniversary. The dedication of this book to them shows, I hope, how much I owe to them. Deborah's love, confidence and support lies behind every page, and while I said nearly the very same thing in the Introduction of my first book, it is even more true now. Olwen and Max have taught me a thing or two along the way. They probably never would have imagined that many of those things would have found their way between the covers of this book.

Technique is just a means of arriving at a statement.

Jackson Pollock

Introduction

In order that the terms of a bargain may fairly represent the state of supply and demand, it is necessary not merely as the economists suppose, that the contracting parties should be equally profited by the contract made, but that they should be equally inconvenienced if it were not made. (*Manchester Gazette*, 22 January 1825)

The fate of narratives

In a justly famous article on food riots in eighteenth-century Britain, E.P. Thompson caustically attacked what he called 'the schizoid intellectual climate' of his time that allowed historians, mostly of the econometric bent, to construct a crude model of *homo economicus* as history's principal actor.[1] When seen by these historians as merely fitful events, food riots required no more than the construction of an 'eighteenth-century English collier who claps his hand spasmodically upon his stomach, and responds to elementary economic stimuli'. Yet Thompson's interest in the work of contemporary cultural anthropologists had suggested to him alternative interpretations of such events. At the same time that historians were interpreting food riots as hunger spasms, cultural anthropologists were revealing a complex and 'delicate tissue of social norms and reciprocities' that regulated the lives of indigenous peoples in other parts of the world. In contrast to the 'abbreviated view of economic man' apparent in the European economic histories of those times, these anthropologists had constructed identities for South Sea islanders that Thompson considered 'infinitely-complex'. The historians' neglect of such complexities led to Thompson's rather well-known complaint that more was known about the cargo cults of Melanesia than the eighteenth-century British collier.

To many, such a complaint may sound surprisingly hollow today. It is a complaint, of course, that in part is situated within a particular historical and cultural narrative, the nature of which has been the subject of considerable discussion and criticism during the last decade.[2] If one were to wish to do so, a critical unpacking of Thompson's observation can be made to reveal not only a particular 'master narrative' that privileges the importance of some events and actors over others, but also a pronounced 'fetishization', as some would call it, of the material over the linguistic. Thus it has been suggested that Thompson, along with many other social historians who have been influenced by his work, was trapped by an 'economy–production–industrial revolution–proletarianisation chain' of historical causation whose categories of analysis and cultural presumptions are understandable only within the context of a particular historical discourse. That discourse originated largely in the nineteenth century, and the permanence of its essential analytical constructs – class, experience and agency – is merely illusory. Not only are these constructs artificial, but they serve only to legitimate the recognition, investigation and analysis of certain forms of power relations. From this postmodern view, the 'schizoid intellectual climate' that Thompson complained of in the early 1970s can be equally turned against himself and other social historians. The essential dichotomies upon which much of social history was predicated, including the categories of pre-industrial/industrial, artisan/proletarian and moral economy/political economy, do not reflect any 'real' distinctions, it has been argued. Instead they are normative constructions that were created within and for the modernist liberal political order.[3]

Such alternative readings of Thompson's notion of class, which was controversial in and of itself, have rejected many of the heroic assumptions implicit in that article, 'The Moral Economy of the English Crowd'. Rather than link class formation to fundamental economic changes (or the experience of those changes), the creation of class through discursive construction projects has sought to undermine the primacy once placed on more 'profound' structural changes. Gareth Stedman Jones's re-reading of early nineteenth-century radical rhetoric helped to pry open this door through which have stepped, in the British case alone, Patrick Joyce, James Vernon, Dror Wahrman and others.[4] The list of French postmodernists whose work has influenced these historians is by now both obvious and redundant: Foucault, Braudillard, Lyotard, Barthes. In part, their work seeks to shape a perception of history that is premised not on the intensive examination of the material conditions of society and the experiences of its subjects, but on the extensive examination of the construction of those discourses and categories that informed and organized nineteenth-century society. More broadly, postmodernist history has sought to bring into question the very nature of the epistemological and ontological foundations of the modern Western world-view. As such, one commentator has recently written, such readings threaten to undermine the very nature of both the practice of history and the validity of 'History with a capital H'.[5]

Yet contemporary or postmodern critical analyses of Thompson's essay on food riots certainly might not be limited to those underlying assumptions concerning class formation and the 'irreducibility of experience'.[6] A further unpacking of Thompson's early complaint about the status of historical research would also reveal the privileged position he accorded to the male worker in his narrative. Decentring nineteenth-century social history away from its common focus on the male artisan, factory worker or collier has vitiated previous conceptions of labour even where other postmodern critiques have had little effect.[7] Whereas the heirs of nineteenth-century sociology may have been satisfied with an analytical category such as class, implicitly defined as male, the construction and articulation of gender as a historical category reconfigures that centrality. Gender, it has been argued, must be understood as one of the most important systems through which individuals comprehend and express their experiences.[8] Any social history of the nineteenth century needs to pay heed to its important role not only in the structuring of family and household relationships, but also in the construction of economic and employment relationships.[9] Equally important is the argument that knowing more about the eighteenth-century collier's elaboration of a gendered world might easily transform our perception of nineteenth-century social history from that of a heroic melodrama into a tragedy. Whereas earlier narratives of class had been principally progressive and emancipatory, analyses based upon gender not only qualify such assumptions but very nearly stand them on their heads.[10] While Thompson may have decried the way in which economic historians decapitated the English labourer and left him as a disembodied stomach, traditional social history narratives may be equally condemned for their failure to recognize the 'fatal flaws of misogyny and patriarchy'.[11]

Those 'modernist' assumptions that potentially underlay much social history, including the economic and experiential foundations of class or the gendered nature of citizenship, are further evident in Thompson's reference to the Melanesians. The success of his irony here – that British historians knew more about South Sea islanders than they did about eighteenth-century English colliers – is dependent in part upon the juxtaposition of the savage and the civilized. Such a linguistic effect would be difficult if not impossible to employ after postcolonial studies had questioned not only the universalization of Western values and standards but also the important ways in which Western identities themselves were articulated in a colonial context.[12] Both the discursive and power relations that are inherent in the articulation of the 'authentic native' have successfully laid bare the extent to which such formulations obscure and confound rather than reveal identities.[13]

The gift relationship

My point here is not to heap more blame upon Thompson, who, like materialist social history generally, has not been left undefended.[14] Indeed few historians have been as bold (or as foolhardy, depending upon one's perspective) as Patrick Joyce or Joan Scott in seeking to abandon materialism altogether. Most of those who have sought to come to terms with any one of the varieties of the 'linguistic turn', a convenient but confusing shorthand, have attempted to square the postmodern circle by adopting some of its critical postures, particularly discursive analysis, at the same time as seeking to explicate these approaches in the context of specific historical and material developments.[15] Keith Jenkins has called these historians the 'undecided or nuanced others', even though such categorizations would seem to be anathema to the postmodernist agenda itself.[16] Indeed a recent collection of essays has sought to remind us that linguistic and discursive analysis has a distinguished lineage among British social historians: one need only remember that Asa Briggs's essay on the language of class in the nineteenth century was published as far back as 1960.[17] Perhaps one of the advantages of such a critical approach, however, is the extension of social-historical research projects into the contextualization of important languages, images or texts, although it can be argued that these concerns themselves are quite traditional ones.[18] Indeed several social historians have recently drawn attention to the traditionalism inherent in many postmodern history projects.[19]

However, I raise the spectre of postmodernism not because I believe its methodology has proven to be preferable to 'modernist' social history, but because along with feminist and postcolonial studies it has served to revivify a perception of history that is both contingent and reciprocal, and these are approaches that are critical to this book.[20] In the hands of some historians, such discursive analyses can be made to evaluate how linguistic practices and formulas both reflected and transformed the material world at the same time as material changes contested and transformed linguistic practices.[21] In the early chapters of this book on the political economy of collective bargaining and on trade union ideology some of these issues will be addressed, although in the case of political economy I explore what appears to be a limit-case of the usefulness of discursive analysis. Yet some historians' engagement with the 'linguistic turn' has, and I think rightly so, also served to re-emphasize approaches to the conceptualization of the historical process that avoid the dangers of teleology. Rather than adopt any triumphalist or melodramatic 'metanarratives', such as class formation or the rise of industrial capitalism, at their best these new hybrid approaches may help emphasize history's contingencies and reciprocities, the ways in which things and ideas mutually reinforce, transform, contest and adapt to one another. Indeed, if one were bold enough, these perceptions might even be termed 'dialectical'. Both their discursive and materialist manifestations are important elements in what follows.

It is in this light that I think it might be possible to look again at Thompson's essay on bread riots and salvage something of significant value. Of course, this essay has often been understood to be about much more than just bread riots. As the title proclaims, it was about nothing less than the 'moral economy of the English crowd in the eighteenth century'. The subsequent adoption of the term 'moral economy' in many branches of the social sciences has had the effect of considerably expanding and sometimes diluting the author's intended meaning. Indeed 'moral economy' has become so common that Thompson later felt it necessary to restate his original premises and to evaluate some of the term's subsequent adaptations.[22] In his own estimation, Thompson offered the term almost solely in the context of 'confrontations in the marketplace over access (or entitlement) to "necessities" – essential food'.[23] However, he did not appear to be averse to the subsequent adoption of more 'capacious' definitions of the term so long as 'moral economy' continued to express an understanding of the extent to which economic and social relations within eighteenth-century communities were regulated according to non-monetary norms and the concomitant threats posed to those norms by the monetization and rationalization of the market.[24]

Underlying Thompson's more restricted definition of 'moral economy' was a significantly more generous explanation of the nature of the social relationship between the gentry and the working population of England during the eighteenth century. He later described the gentry's control as primarily a form of cultural hegemony whereby 'the larger outlines of power, station in life, [and] political authority appear to be as inevitable and irreversible as the earth and the sky'.[25] Despite the potential weaknesses of the term 'cultural hegemony', both from the perspective of postmodern discursive analysis and the more quotidian techniques of the exercise of power in the parish or locality,[26] in practice Thompson deployed the term in a quite agile manner. As the bread riots essay makes clear, Thompson emphasized the extent to which the relationship between the gentry and what he later labelled 'the plebs' was a reciprocal and contingent one: 'The forms of action which we have been examining', he concluded, 'depended on a particular set of social relations, a particular equilibrium between paternalist authority and the crowd'.[27] In a later article, he likened this relationship to the way in which iron filings were distributed between two poles when they were magnetized. This 'field-of-force' image, with the plebs at one pole and the aristocracy and gentry at the other, has the advantage of illuminating not only the antagonisms that existed between the gentry and plebs but also the forces of reciprocity and mutual obligations that bound them together.[28] Thus Thompson described the relationship between the gentry and the plebs as 'reciprocal ... tipping now one way, now the other.... Grossly unequal as this relationship was, the gentry nevertheless needed *some* kind of support from "the poor", and the poor sensed that they were needed.'[29] Although Thompson specifically preferred to describe this as a 'moral economy', he acknowledged that a term such as 'dialectical asymmetrical reciprocity' was roughly equivalent albeit deadening.[30] And while it is true, as some have complained, that this model is 'bi-polar' – in the sense that it leaves out any significant role for the emerging middling classes – and the 'field-of-force' metaphor itself is not exceptionally compelling, I might add, Thompson's 'bargaining between unequal social forces' and the 'patrician/plebs equilibrium' are two of the most prominent themes taken up and significantly extended in this book.[31]

Of course, postmodernists will have already smelled the foul air of materialism and representationalism and it would be foolish to defend myself against such charges. What this book does try to do is to investigate the contingencies and reciprocities that helped to constitute the social world of the early nineteenth-century artisan and shopfloor worker. And while I have adopted much from Thompson's reading of the eighteenth-century moral economy, there is much that I have had to eschew or amend as well. Clearly, one of the most obvious distinctions between Thompson's approach and the one offered here is this study's periodization. Thompson repeatedly emphasized that the reciprocities he thought were inherent in the eighteenth century's societal 'field-of-force' ruptured and snapped in the 1790s. For Thompson, the beginning of the nineteenth century witnessed a 'structural reordering of class relations and ideology', by which he appears to have meant the birth of class in its modern industrial form.[32] The old moral economy, he indicated, was eroded by the expansion of new marketing practices, downward pressure upon wages and the creation of new forms of organization and protest. More significantly, this eighteenth-century moral economy collapsed under the combined weight of the gentry's heightened fears of sedition that became associated with crowd actions during the revolutionary years and the ideological legitimization of the repression of the crowd in defence of the 'free' market that was offered by the new doctrines of political economy.[33]

The work presented here, however, seeks to extend the recognition and understanding of the importance of reciprocities and equilibria both horizontally into the urban and rural artisanal milieu and vertically into the nineteenth century. It may be true that some of those older, rural reciprocities were snapped during the crises of the years of war with France, but new forms of reciprocity were simultaneously being created and other older forms continued to survive. Recent research on the crowd, for example, has already had the effect of expanding our notions of the extent of its actions, revealing both its urban political manifestations and its persistent patriotism and xenophobia.[34] Yet such reciprocities and equilibria were not limited to crowd events. Particularly when the focus of inquiry is shifted away from the gentry–pleb relationship in the countryside or urban crowd activities and directed toward the shopfloor and the wage relationship between employers and employees in the artisanal trades, then similar reciprocities – similar 'fields of force' – become apparent. One purpose of this book, therefore, is to analyse the asymmetries, contingencies and reciprocities that acted among both urban artisans and rural manufacturing labourers during the early and mid-nineteenth century. Indeed I hope to show that even within the context of grossly unequal work relationships such 'traditional' forms of reciprocity survived and reproduced themselves. Obviously, this claim is not meant to deny that exploitation could or did occur. It is, however, meant to emphasize my argument that both economic and cultural influences functioned to attach webs of reciprocal obligations to the wage relationship that bound ostensibly 'free' labourers to their employers. In a different context, Adrian Randall deployed the term 'industrial moral economy' to describe the set of ideas and assumptions that workers brought to the employment relationship.[35] I would like to extend our understanding of that phenomenon by examining the fields of force that regulated those relationships on the shopfloor.

The persistence and reproduction of reciprocities can be traced to a variety of sources. In some instances, they survived due to the existence and promise of certain social or political institutions whose purpose was to mitigate antagonisms and resolve disputes. Such was the case, I believe, for arbitration and mediation during the first half of the nineteenth century, although even here the poles that defined the ultimate deployment of power in the 'field of force' were noticeable. More significantly, however, the work relationship itself reproduced forms of reciprocity, many of which have been the subject of significant debate in other disciplines but, I believe, have been rather unsatisfactorily analysed in their historical context. A good deal of the historical research in this area has been unduly focused on what has come to be called 'factory paternalism', which itself denotes a rather static technique of control as opposed to a dynamic relationship characterized by authority, obligation and reciprocity. In order to excavate shopfloor relationships during the period under study more thoroughly, I have often had to rely upon the case study method, an approach whose limitations are obvious. However, it is hoped that by linking this approach to broader research themes and analyses, the significance of reciprocities within an unequal relationship in the workplace will become apparent.

During the course of these 'excavations', I have relied heavily upon the work of a number of researchers in a variety of fields other than history, some of whose work may at first appear to be slightly incongruous with one another. While Thompson's notion of a social 'field of force' is a useful and important application of the concept of reciprocities, I also feel that the image of a 'field of force' is often an inadequate metaphor to describe these phenomena. Instead I have adopted here the notion of 'the gift relationship', a concept that I feel more satisfactorily expresses the contingent nature of social and cultural relations during this period. While the origins of this term lay in the field of cultural anthropology, it has been successfully applied to a number of different disciplinary contexts. According to Marcel Mauss, the gift relationship was meant to be understood as a 'system of total services' in which, contrary to utilitarian notions of an autonomous sphere of economics, the act of exchange was not limited merely to goods.[36] Instead, all 'economic' exchanges were also exchanges of honour, credit and reputation. Nonetheless, the gift relationship positively promoted the circulation of goods because one of its essential elements was the concomitant obligation to reciprocate. Thus the gift relationship was in part an exchange of goods, but it was also an exchange of both immaterial values and mutual obligations. Such reciprocities need not be an equitable exchange nor need they take place between social or economic equals. In fact, contrary to assumptions implicit in both political economy and the Anglo-American laws of contract,[37] the gift exchange can serve not only to express but also to reinforce fundamentally unequal obligations and relationships rather than to obfuscate or mystify them.

What might this archaic notion of exchange tell us about early industrial labour? I argue below that such a 'holistic' notion of exchange more satisfactorily describes workplace relations than the more common economistic one. On the shopfloor, workers not only possess the 'gift' of skill, considered in the early nineteenth century to be a form of property,[38] but they also retain a degree of discretion over exactly how much labour they prefer to release to their employers in the form of work. This discretionary portion of a worker's labour-power is often released only in the context of reciprocal obligations. This, I believe, is the essence of the origins of the trade union notion of 'a fair day's work for a fair day's pay'. Yet, as this famous dictum also implies, the employment relationship is a moral exchange as much as it is an economic one because notions of fairness are compounds of a variety of different moral standards. Therefore, as several chapters try to show, the employment relationship in the early nineteenth century also involved the exchange of honour, reputation and credit at the same time as it entailed a web of obligations upon both employers and employees.

Thus the approach taken in this book is strongly interdisciplinary. But these borrowings are not limited solely to cultural anthropology. I have taken much, for example, from the work of George Akerlof, an economist who has adapted the concept of the gift relationship to explain the reciprocities inherent in the structure of work.[39] Similarly, Avner Offer's recent attempt to locate the gift relationship in its socio-historical context helped to provide an even more comprehensive view of this phenomenon.[40] Much of this book is also based upon concepts drawn from industrial relations research. Attempts to explain the nature of this shopfloor 'gift relationship' have long been an important aspect of industrial relations research, especially among those who adopted the methodology of the shopfloor study, although they rarely, if ever, used the term 'gift' to describe the phenomenon they were studying. For them, shopfloor relations have often been characterized by 'games' or informal 'effort bargains' that mediated the relationship between employees and their supervisors. The works of Wilhelm Baldamus, Michael Burawoy, Tom Lupton and Donald Roy have been particularly influential in this area of research.[41] However, these forms of reciprocity, I argue below, are easily encompassed within the analytical framework of the gift relationship precisely because they are similarly based on concepts of reciprocities and mutual obligations. Finally, in examining the nature of reciprocities on the shopfloor, I have also attempted to employ some of the insights that may be derived from modern game theory in order to explicate more fully the bargaining relationship between shopfloor workers and their employers. Michael Huberman's work on the Lancashire cotton industry first brought my attention to this potentially fruitful line of inquiry,[42] and it led me to Robert Wilson's work on bargaining and the exchange of reputations, which offers fascinating insights into how perceptions affect performance and commitments.[43] The gift relationship, as I have said, equally involves the exchange of intangibles such as honour and reputation, and it is in this light that Wilson's work on game theory can be used to help explain and analyse reciprocities on the early industrial shopfloor.

Moral economy/moral discourses

The notion of reciprocity on the industrial or manufacturing shopfloor is not entirely unknown among historians, of course. Patrick Joyce has long been a champion of its importance and his 'linguistic turn' has only served to emphasize the importance he attaches to expressions of mutuality and reciprocity in working-class discourse. That he should do so in the context of a determined effort to break the dominance of class in the historiography of the nineteenth century should not be surprising.[44] However, it is somewhat more surprising to find Joyce asserting the importance of moral economy theories even though in his hands the term has become transfigured into postmodern 'moral discourses of labour'. Indeed a close reading reveals many obvious similarities between the uses and meanings of Thompson's 'moral economy' and Joyce's 'moral discourses'. In his study of early nineteenth-century trade union discourse, for example, Joyce argues that working-class leaders expressed an essentially moralized and customary view of society and social relationships which was a legacy of the 'moral economy' of the previous century. The language of labour, he writes, was characterized by 'corporate, reciprocal, "commonwealth" visions of society' and articulated a desire for 'a harmonious world of production encompassing master and man, in which both sides would live up to their responsibilities'.[45] In other words, 'moral categories of custom' were more in evidence than the economic categories of interests and the market.[46] And rather than express an economistic, class-view of society, Joyce argues, labour's vision was 'to moralise employment relations through the conception that there were mutualities of right and obligation obtaining between master and man'.[47] By the second half of the nineteenth century, Joyce sees more evidence of the unions' adoption of the languages of political economy and the market. However, this language remained circumscribed by labour's moral vision, which accepted competition but only when it was fair, and valued the market but only when it was moralized.[48]

The debate over whether labour's moral economy of the market ultimately served to incorporate the working class into the capitalist order or remained a source of working-class egalitarianism need not detain us here.[49] Suffice it to say that, as I argued in an earlier book, working-class leaders often spoke not in the language of class but in the languages of religion, fair play and reciprocity.[50] Indeed it was exceedingly common to find trade unionists reiterating what must have appeared to be common-sense notions of fairness and reciprocity very often derived from Christian principles. Thus the injunctions to 'do unto others' and 'love thy neighbour' entailed the notion that a moral society was based upon work relationships that were both equitable and reciprocal. Still, it is important to ask whether the recognition of a shared discourse, such as Christian mutualism, is a sufficient foundation upon which to deny the importance of economic experience as a valid category of analysis. Robert Gray, for one, acknowledges that the language of mutuality could connote a negotiative stance but, in the case of factory reform, could also be used to mobilize resistance against violators of the community's moral codes.[51] In fact, in the case of the Durham and Northumberland coal-miners, definitions of fairness (as in 'fair play') and freedom (as in 'free markets') were the essential matters in dispute during the great strike of 1831–32 and the social lines that demarcated conflicting definitions were essentially economic ones: rich against poor, workers against masters, miners against managers. The attempts to resolve these disputes reveal that while many terms of discourse were shared by the masters and the unions, the ways in which these discursive projects were applied to everyday industrial relations were significantly at odds with one another. The miners' construction of a free market, for example, was significantly at odds with the mine-owners' perception of the same thing.[52] Indeed, as James Scott has shown, a shared normative discourse does not necessarily preclude either the strategic deployment of language to legitimate a claim or alternative constructions of experience couched in a common discourse.[53]

Still, as Joyce recognizes, the trade unions' discursive endeavour to 'moralize' the market – to make the market fair and its workings reciprocal – explicitly acknowledged not only the market's existence (even if the market is only an ideological construct itself, as Thompson was at pains to argue) but also its ultimate legitimacy. And this, I would suggest, was not necessarily a reflection of the success of political economy's market discourse, the failures of which are discussed in Chapter 1, but the way in which market mechanisms came to be understood and expressed through the prism of their shopfloor relationships. During this period, work was often understood as a 'system of total services', a gift relationship. The unequal nature of employment in which masters were separate from servants formed the common-sense background for the comprehension of work as an exchange relationship rather than a production relationship. Such an understanding of work was particularly appropriate to a time when artisanal labour was still an essential element of production and management exhibited no great willingness or eagerness to seize control of the shopfloor. These circumstances may also help to explain why workers and working-class ideologues showed such a pronounced affinity for anti-capitalist theories based upon inequitable exchange rather than those based upon exploitation through production. While some autodidacts, such as Thomas Hodgskin, may have drawn upon elite scientific theories, and others, such as the London compositors, drew upon republican themes, the discourse of exchange (both moral and economic) not only structured the understanding of their experiences but also incorporated a set of explanations and assumptions that both reflected and validated that experience. These topics will be broached in Chapter 2.

In a very important sense, therefore, contrary to Joyce's assumption, it is not entirely necessary to insist upon the appeal of 'custom' in order to comprehend the persistence of such discourses of reciprocities. The language of exchange maintained its purchase among nineteenth-century artisans and labourers not because it expressed the legacy of a nostalgic past or an imagined community but because it continued to offer in part a coherent contextualization of the employment experience.[54] It would be a further mistake, as I have just noted, to confuse the meaning of a discourse that emphasizes reciprocity and mutuality with the denial of the contemporary recognition of the structural conflicts between employers and their employees. Recent attempts to emphasize the cooperative aspects of industrial relations during this period seem to me to be too willing to dismiss both the languages and the experiences of the structural inequalities of the employment relationship.[55] Labour's vision of society may well have embraced 'socially inclusive' images but at the same time it reflected a world in which work relations were nearly always unequal, often unfair, and distinctly asymmetrical.[56] This is what Tommy Hepburn, the Durham and Northumberland miners' leader of the early 1830s, meant when he explained at a rally that the union 'wanted an agreement [with the owners], but, at the same time, they wanted one-half of that agreement to be of their own making'.[57] Alastair Reid rightly identifies this craft union rhetoric as being concerned with harmonious relations between masters and men but not at the cost of subservience.[58]

These two elements of work – reciprocity and asymmetry – are essential to an understanding of labour's role in Britain's social history. To emphasize one at the cost of neglecting the other often results both in an inability to comprehend the context in which social and work relationships operated and in the failure to understand fully the complex combination of moral benevolence and moral outrage that informed labour's discourse and labour action. It is these elements that constitute the analytical core of what I have to offer here.

Notes

1 E.P. Thompson, 'The Moral Economy of the English Crowd in the Eighteenth Century', *Past and Present*, no. 50 (1971), pp. 76–136, reprinted in *Customs in Common* (London: Merlin Press, 1991).

2 On Thompson's work, especially *The Making of the English Working Class*, see the contributions to Harvey J. Kaye and Keith McClelland, eds, *E.P. Thompson: Critical Perspectives* (Philadelphia: Temple University Press, 1990). Particularly influential contributions to the more general debate have included Patrick Joyce, 'The End of Social History?', *Social History*, vol. 20: no. 1 (January 1995), pp. 73–91; Geoff Eley and Keith Nield, 'Starting Over: The Present, the Post-modern and the Moment of Social History', *Social History*, vol. 20: no. 3 (October 1995), pp. 355–64; Geoff Eley, 'Is All the World a Text?: From Social History to the History of Society Two Decades Later', in T. McDonald, ed., *The Historical Turn in the Human Sciences* (Ann Arbor: University of Michigan Press, 1996); as well as the works of William Sewell, Joan Scott and Gareth Stedman Jones, among many others. A useful guide to and survey of postmodernist and linguistic theory is provided by S. Best and D. Kellner, *Postmodern Theory: Critical Interrogations* (New York: Guildford Press, 1991).

3 Joyce, 'The End of Social History?', p. 83; Patrick Joyce, 'Refabricating Labour History; or, From Labour History to the History of Labour', *Labour History Review*, vol. 62: no. 2 (Summer 1997), pp. 147–52; James Vernon, 'Who's Afraid of the Linguistic Turn?: The Politics of Social History and its Discontents', *Social History*, vol. 19: no. 1 (January 1994), pp. 87–8.

4 G. Stedman Jones, *Languages of Class: Studies in English Working Class History, 1832–1982* (Cambridge: Cambridge University Press, 1983); James Vernon, *Politics and the People: A Study in English Political Culture, c. 1815–1867* (Cambridge: Cambridge University Press, 1993); Patrick Joyce, *Democratic Subjects: The Self and the Social in Nineteenth-Century England* (Cambridge: Cambridge University Press, 1994); and Dror Wahrman, *Imagining the Middle Class: The Political Representation of Class in Britain, c. 1780–1840* (Cambridge: Cambridge University Press, 1995).

5 Keith Jenkins, 'Introduction', in Jenkins, ed., *The Postmodern History Reader* (London: Routledge, 1997), pp. 1–30.

6 The phrase is John Toews's from his 'Intellectual History after the Linguistic Turn: The Autonomy of Meaning and the Irreducibility of Experience', *American Historical Review*, vol. 92: no. 4 (October 1987), pp. 879–907.

7 Too great a distinction between feminism and postmodernism is obviously unwise, but I employ it here solely for heuristic purposes. On the interconnectedness of the two as well as the varying response of the former to the latter, see Kathleen Canning, 'Feminist History after the Linguistic Turn: Historicizing Discourse and Experience', *Signs*, vol. 19: no. 2 (1994), pp. 368–84.

8 Joan Wallach Scott, *Gender and the Politics of History* (New York: Columbia University Press, 1989).

9 Sonya Rose, *Limited Livelihoods: Gender and Class in Nineteenth-Century England* (Berkeley: University of California Press, 1992), pp. 1–21.

10 Anna Clark, *The Struggle for the Breeches: Gender and the Making of the British Working Class* (Berkeley: University of California Press, 1995), p. 271.

11 Clark, *Struggle for the Breeches*, p. 271.

12 Mrinalini Sinha, *Colonial Masculinity: The 'Manly Englishman' and the 'Effeminate Bengali' in the Late Nineteenth Century* (Manchester: Manchester University Press, 1995) is a particularly interesting example of this approach.

13 The *locus classicus* of postcolonial analysis is Edward Said, *Orientalism* (New York: Vintage, 1978). A useful introduction to postcolonial theory is Padmini Mongia, *Contemporary Postcolonial Theory: A Reader* (London: Arnold, 1996).

14 Bryan D. Palmer's *Descent into Discourse: The Reification of Language and the Writing of Social History* (Philadelphia: Temple University Press, 1990) is one of the most prominent defences.

15 The works of Rose and Canning cited above articulate this position, for example. See also Judith R. Walkowitz, *City of Dreadful Delight: Narratives of Sexual Danger in Late-Victorian London* (Chicago: University of Chicago Press, 1992).

16 Jenkins, ed., *Postmodern History Reader*, p. 24.

17 See the editors' Introduction to John Belchem and Neville Kirk, eds, *Languages of Labour* (Aldershot: Ashgate, 1997), pp. 1–3.

18 Richard Price, 'Postmodernism as Theory and History', in Belchem and Kirk, eds, *Languages of Labour*, pp. 26–9; John Belchem, 'Reconstructing Labour History', *Labour History Review*, vol. 62: no. 3 (Winter 1997), pp. 318–23.

19 See, for example, Price, 'Postmodernism as Theory and History', as well as John Belchem, '"An Accent Exceedingly Rare": Scouse and the Inflexion of Class', in Belchem and Kirk, eds, *Languages of Labour*, p. 99.

20 Price rightly notes, however, that postmodern theory itself is antithetical to contextualization and reciprocities. See Price, 'Postmodernism as Theory and History', p. 27.

21 A somewhat similar view is expressed in Marc W. Steinberg, 'Culturally Speaking: Finding a Commons between Post-structuralism and the Thompsonian Perpsective', *Social History*, vol. 21: no. 2 (May 1996), pp. 193–214. Several of the contributions to Belchem and Kirk, eds, *Languages of Labour*, exemplify this perspective as well.

22 Thompson, *Customs in Common*, ch. 5.

23 Thompson, *Customs in Common*, p. 337; see also pp. 260–2. On this aspect of the moral economy, see the valuable contributions in Adrian Randall and Andrew Charlesworth, eds, *Markets, Market Culture and Popular Protest in Eighteenth-Century Britain and Ireland* (Liverpool: Liverpool University Press, 1996).

24 Thompson, however, appears to have been reluctant to see the term applied in vague or ill-defined ways, especially if 'moral economy' became synonymous with concepts such as tradition or custom. Thompson, *Customs in Common*, pp. 337–44.

25 Thompson, *Customs in Common*, p. 43.

26 See the helpful review by Peter King, 'Edward Thompson's Contribution to Eighteenth-Century Studies: The Patrician–Plebeian Model Re-examined', *Social History*, vol. 21: no. 2 (May 1996), pp. 215–28. The most persuasive

argument against idealist interpretations of hegemony is that of James Scott, *Weapons of the Weak: Everyday Forms of Peasant Resistance* (New Haven: Yale University Press, 1985), ch. 8.

27   Thompson, *Customs in Common*, p. 249.
28   E.P. Thompson, 'Eighteenth-Century English Society: Class Struggle Without Class?', *Social History*, vol. 3: no. 2 (May 1978), p. 151, and *Customs in Common*, pp. 72–4, 343–4.
29   Thompson, *Customs in Common*, p. 95.
30   Thompson, *Customs in Common*, p. 344.
31   Thompson, *Customs in Common*, pp. 95, 343; see also E.P. Thompson, 'Patrician Society, Plebeian Culture', *Journal of Social History*, vol. 7 (1973–74), pp. 382–405.
32   Thompson, *Customs in Common*, pp. 95–6.
33   Thompson, *Customs in Common*, pp. 246–52.
34   See, for example, Nicholas Rogers, *Whigs and Cities: Popular Politics in the Age of Walpole and Pitt* (Oxford: Clarendon Press, 1990); Linda Colley, *Britons: Forging the Nation, 1707–1837* (New Haven: Yale University Press, 1992); and Kathleen Wilson, *The Sense of the People: Politics, Culture and Imperialism in England, 1715–1785* (Cambridge: Cambridge University Press, 1995).
35   Adrian Randall, 'The Industrial Moral Economy of the Gloucestershire Weavers in the Eighteenth Century', in John Rule, ed., *British Trade Unionism, 1750–1850: The Formative Years* (London: Longman, 1988), pp. 29–51.
36   Marcel Mauss, *The Gift: The Form and Reason for Exchange in Archaic Societies*, trans. W.D. Halls (1950; New York: W.W. Norton & Co., 1990).
37   I am referring here to the relatively restricted notions of autonomy and freedom that came to dominate law and economics in the nineteenth century. See William M. Reddy, *Money and Liberty in Modern Europe: A Critique of Historical Understanding* (Cambridge: Cambridge University Press, 1987), pp. 64–81; and P.S. Atiyah, *The Rise and Fall of Freedom of Contract* (Oxford: Clarendon Press, 1979), especially ch. 14.
38   John Rule, 'The Property of Skill in the Period of Manufacture', in P. Joyce, ed., *The Historical Meanings of Work* (Cambridge: Cambridge University Press, 1987), pp. 99–118.
39   George A. Akerlof, 'Labor Contracts as Partial Gift Exchange', *Quarterly Journal of Economics*, vol. 97: no. 4 (November 1982), pp. 543–69.
40   Avner Offer, 'Between the Gift and the Market: The Economy of Regard', *Economic History Review*, vol. 50: no. 3 (1997), pp. 450–76.
41   Particularly important were works such as W. Baldamus, *Efficiency and Effort: An Analysis of Industrial Administration* (London: Tavistock, 1961); Michael Burawoy, *Manufacturing Consent: Changes in the Labor Process under Monopoly Capitalism* (Chicago: University of Chicago Press, 1979); Donald Roy, 'Quota Restriction and Goldbricking in a Machine Shop', *American Journal of Sociology*, vol. 57: no. 5 (March 1952), pp. 427–42; and T. Lupton, *On the Shop Floor: Two Studies of Workshop Organization and Output* (Oxford: Pergamon Press, 1963).
42   Michael Huberman, *Escape from the Market: Negotiating Work in Lancashire* (Cambridge: Cambridge University Press, 1996).

43 Robert Wilson, 'Reputations in Games and Markets', in Alvin E. Roth, ed., *Game-Theoretic Models of Bargaining* (Cambridge: Cambridge University Press, 1985).

44 Perhaps unfortunately, discourse in this case is relatively narrowly conceived as 'bodies of utterance of a relatively formal, public sort, often associated with institutions'. Patrick Joyce, *Visions of the People: Industrial England and the Question of Class, 1840–1914* (Cambridge: Cambridge University Press, 1991), p. 17.

45 Joyce, *Visions of the People*, pp. 91, 102.

46 Joyce, *Visions of the People*, pp. 90–1.

47 Joyce, *Visions of the People*, p. 100.

48 Joyce, *Visions of the People*, pp. 114–16. Several of these themes were first mooted in a series of exchanges that took place between Joyce and Richard Price in the pages of *Social History*. See Richard Price, 'The Labour Process and Labour History', *Social History*, vol. 8: no. 1 (January 1983), pp. 57–75; Patrick Joyce, 'Labour, Capital and Compromise: A Response to Richard Price', *Social History*, vol. 9: no. 1 (January 1984), pp. 67–76; Richard Price, 'Conflict and Co-operation: A Reply to Patrick Joyce', *Social History*, vol. 9: no. 2 (May 1984), pp. 217–24; Patrick Joyce, 'Languages of Reciprocity and Conflict: A Further Response to Richard Price', *Social History*, vol. 9: no. 2 (May 1984), pp. 225–31.

49 See K. McClelland, 'Time to Work, Time to Live: Some Aspects of Work and the Re-formation of Class in Britain, 1850–1880', in Joyce, ed., *Historical Meanings of Work*, pp. 180–209, in contrast to Alastair J. Reid, 'Old Unionism Reconsidered: The Radicalism of Robert Knight, 1870–1900', in Eugenio F. Biagini and Alastair J. Reid, eds, *Currents of Radicalism: Popular Radicalism, Organised Labour and Party Politics in Britain, 1850–1914* (Cambridge: Cambridge University Press, 1991), pp. 214–43.

50 James A. Jaffe, *The Struggle for Market Power: Industrial Relations in the British Coal Industry, 1800–1840* (Cambridge: Cambridge University Press, 1991), chs 6–7.

51 Robert Gray, 'Languages of Factory Reform in Britain, c. 1830–1860', in Joyce, ed., *Historical Meanings of Work*, pp. 152–4.

52 Jaffe, *Struggle for Market Power*, pp. 161–4, 179–85.

53 Scott, *Weapons of the Weak*, ch. 6.

54 In a related vein, Iorwerth Prothero suggests that unequal exchange theory was a generally accurate analysis of the economic experience of many artisans in the period; see *Artisans and Politics in Early Nineteenth-Century London: John Gast and His Times* (1979; London: Methuen, 1981), pp. 332–6; Rule, 'The Property of Skill', p. 117.

55 This is perhaps an unintended outcome of the extremes to which Joyce and Price were pushed in the 'conflict vs. co-operation' debate, but the emphasis upon work as a benign cooperative endeavour is beginning to find its way into the textbooks. For example, Roderick Floud, in an otherwise excellent economic history of the nineteenth century, maintains that the dominance of small-scale production and the personal nature of management must have been accompanied by generally congenial relations between employers and employees. See *The People and the British Economy, 1830–1914* (Oxford:

Oxford University Press, 1997), pp. 113–14.

56 'Socially inclusive' is the term used by Joyce, *Visions of the People*, p. 113.
57 *Newcastle Chronicle*, 23 June 1832.
58 Reid, 'Old Unionism Reconsidered', p. 227.

1

The hidden abode: industrial relations and the failure of economic discourse

Demand and supply are not physical agencies which thrust a given amount of wages into the labourer's hand without the participation of his own will and actions. The market rate is not fixed for him by some self-acting instrument, but is the result of bargaining between human beings – of what Adam Smith calls 'the higgling of the market'. (J.S. Mill, *Principles of Political Economy*, 1865)

In 1825, William Chippendale, a master cooper from London, was called to testify before the House of Commons Select Committee on the Combination Laws. According to Francis Place, that ubiquitous working-class radical, the formation of the committee was largely the result of the efforts of William Huskisson, President of the Board of Trade, who had come under significant pressure from numerous employers' groups to revive some aspects of the recently repealed Combination Laws.[1] Especially prodigious lobbying efforts were exerted at the time to place witnesses before this new committee, despite the fact that, again according to Place, working-class representatives often faced significant obstacles toward this end. It is likely that Chippendale himself was selected to testify precisely because his trade was in the midst of an industrial dispute and his testimony would lend support to the employers' efforts to impose greater legislative controls upon trade unionism.

Chippendale's testimony nonetheless contains some curious remarks, several of which are in obvious conflict with what many historians think they know about industrial relations during the early nineteenth century. He was asked, for example, whether there were uniform piece-rates throughout the London coopers' trade, to which he answered that there were. This was unexceptional. But when he was then asked how these rates were fixed, he replied: 'By the masters meeting the journeymen'. Chippendale went on to explain that during the current dispute such meetings had not yet taken place, although, he said, 'we mean to do it, to endeavour to bring them [the journeymen coopers] to reason, and tell them "whatever grievances you have, we will remedy"'.[2]

Such remarks were in part special pleading, of course. They were likely to have been intended to suggest that the repeal of the Combination Laws in 1824, by permitting the growth of trade unions, had disrupted the 'natural' and harmonious relations between masters and men. However, there is significant evidence that such collective bargaining meetings, if we can use that term, while not necessarily harmonious, were neither fanciful nor especially uncommon. As early as 1813, there appears to have been a price list for London coopering 'unanimously agreed between Masters and Journeymen, at the George and Vulture Tavern, Cornhill', according to a handbill saved in the Place Papers.[3] Indeed another handbill published several years later recalls that at the time of Chippendale's remarks in 1825, 'numerous Meetings were held between the masters and men'. The author of the handbill, A Journeyman Cooper, asserts that the masters entered into these negotiations in bad faith and 'they kept them haggling for six weeks, when the men were so disgusted at their shuffling and ungentlemanly conduct, that they (and not the masters) declined all further communication on the subject'.[4]

At first sight, these references to such negotiated settlements and prolonged collective bargaining may appear to many historians to be unique or unusual. However, evidence from other trades of the same era reveal similar apparent anomalies. Twelve years after the coopers' bargaining sessions, for example, evidence culled from the records of the Society of Operative Stone Masons illustrates that even in the highly contentious building trades negotiation and bargaining were common elements of industrial relations.[5] To take just one case, in 1837 a former union member turned subcontractor in Cardiff had reduced the piece-rates for granite masons on a job building a canal.[6] Upon being informed of the rate reduction and the apostasy of the mason/subcontractor, the national union executive, James Rennie, wrote to the subcontractor 'animadverting on his conduct'. Shortly thereafter, Rennie received a reply from the principal contractor, who accepted full responsibility for imposing the rate cut. The contractor, however, did offer to allow a delegate from the masons' union to investigate the matter and Rennie duly accepted the assignment. Upon arriving in Cardiff and examining the situation, however, he found that the masons themselves bore part of the responsibility for the rate cut because they had failed to regulate their work satisfactorily by allowing 'some of the members to earn in seven or eight days what would be considered in any part of the kingdom fair wages for a fortnight'. The national union had long maintained its opposition to piece-rates in any case and Rennie took this opportunity to convince the local lodge to accept payment by the day instead. As Rennie reported: 'I then waited on the contractor, and found he was rather inclined to continue the piece-work at the reduced prices, but, after several conferences, he finally agreed to employ the men by the day at the wages requested'.

Such meetings and conferences seem to violate our preconceptions of what industrial relations were like in the early nineteenth century. In particular, they violate the notions that negotiations were rarely if ever an aspect of industrial disputes, that industrial relations, if there were any, were conducted only at arm's length, and that neither employers nor workers possessed the experience, will or desire to conduct bargaining sessions. As Eric Hobsbawm indicated long ago, the first half of the nineteenth century was a period during which workers 'learned the rules of the game', but it was a game that really only began in earnest with the transition after 1850 from the unwilling to willing wage-bargain, as he described the coagulation of legal, political and economic changes that ushered in the second half of the century.[7] However, if one looks for it, evidence of such meetings and negotiations can be found not only in the London coopering trade or among Cardiff building workers but in industrial and manufacturing sectors as disparate as coal-mining, weaving, printing, shipbuilding and numerous other artisanal occupations of the late eighteenth and early nineteenth centuries. Indeed this book is an attempt to analyse and make sense of just such meetings and I will argue in ensuing chapters that workers and employers necessarily met together, negotiated, compromised and even colluded together at the same time as there were strikes, lock-outs, victimization and state repression. To recognize this is not necessarily to assert that industrializing Britain was a 'kinder and gentler nation', to use a recent American president's words and a comment I was once offered at a graduate seminar. It is, however, part of an attempt to uncover the 'field of force', the asymmetrical and dialectical 'gift' relationship, that circumscribed and constituted early nineteenth-century industrial relations between partners of notably unequal power and legal standing.

Considering such a project, a critical reader might be led to wonder not only whether there is enough evidence to support such a contention but, even if there is such evidence, why and how such forms of bargaining and negotiation became so thoroughly obscured and neglected over the past century and more. On the issue of evidence, I will have to ask the reader to suspend judgement until Chapter 3, where such an analysis begins in earnest. On the issue of neglect, however, I have more to say presently. As we shall see, some of the responsibility undoubtedly must be borne by those early Victorian novelists whose 'social realism' created a world in which stories of good and evil, right and wrong, the powerful and the powerless, came to narrate the social history of the era.[8] However, equally responsible were those narratives constructed by nineteenth-century economic and political theorists whose stories similarly obscured, marginalized or omitted consideration of such problems, and which will be the focus of the remainder of this chapter. Interestingly enough, several of the eighteenth-century Physiocrats, in particular Turgot and Necker, appear to have recognized the importance of negotiations and bargaining for the determination of wages and even to have located the source of subsistence wages in the 'vast disparity of power between employers ... and waged workers'.[9] This tradition was echoed, as one might expect, in the work of Adam Smith, but disappeared from the literature soon thereafter. Its disappearance, ironically, left a profound impression upon our understanding of early industrial social and labour relations. It is therefore with the failures of economic theory, and in particular with the failures of political economy and early socialist discourse, that I would like to begin.

Wage bargaining and the classical economists

The classical economists of the late eighteenth and early nineteenth centuries never developed an adequate theory of wages and hence rarely recognized the existence of wage bargaining whether in its collective or individual form.[10] This may appear somewhat surprising at first, especially since Adam Smith had apparently posited an important role for bargaining in the determination of wages in *The Wealth of Nations*. Yet as was typical of that important book, Smith's observations with regard to wage bargaining were only one of a number of reflections he made concerning the recompense of labour. More importantly for the nineteenth century, Smith's successors became absorbed by the macroeconomic question of the role of the 'wage fund' in the determination of wages in the short term, that is, the amount of pre-accumulated capital that was available to support labour during production.[11] As such, it has been argued that the political economists never developed a theory of wages at all, but only a theory of the determinants of the demand for labour.[12] In addition, by the second quarter of the nineteenth century, the second of the two principles commonly associated with classical wage theory, the so-called 'iron law of wages', by definition ignored pay bargaining since that theory was principally concerned with the long-term determination of wages in relation to population.

The classical economists have thus left little evidence that they adequately recognized or understood the nature of the labour market in the early nineteenth century. For economic and social historians of the period, this has had the unfortunate effect of fostering an inference that since the classical economists did not recognize wage bargaining in their contemporary labour markets then it was unlikely to have existed, or at least it was not one of the market's regular features. Consequently, there have been awkward attempts to account for the apparent advent of wage bargaining, collective or otherwise, around the middle of the nineteenth century. Perhaps none of these have been so awkward as the notion proposed by W.H. Hutt, the conservative economist who argued in general that trade unions were inimical to working-class prosperity and whose works were revived during Lady Thatcher's premiership. He suggested that wage bargaining developed only after John Stuart Mill among others had debunked the wage-fund theory. This freed employers from the ideological stranglehold that had assumed that any outlay on wages was subtracted from the limited funds available for capital accumulation. It is, to say the least, a rather unlikely contention that the writings of this small group of philosophers and academics had such a profound impact on the labour policies of British business leaders.[13]

It is nevertheless true that for many historians, economists and industrial relations specialists wage bargaining only came into existence after the middle of the nineteenth century and principally was associated with the transition of capitalism to a more mature stage as well as the working class's learning of the 'rules of the game'. Specialists from as varied academic and political backgrounds as those possessed by V.L. Allen, Hugh Clegg or E.J. Hobsbawn characterized industrial relations during the early period, however, as perfunctory at best. What 'relations' there were primarily consisted of arm's-length communication through notices or placards, which upon the appearance of any resistance to the demand was almost immediately followed by the deployment of the strike or lock-out weapon.[14] The superb historian Richard Price has aptly adopted the industrial relations term 'autonomous regulation' to describe this state of affairs.[15] According to this perception, forms of bargaining or mutual negotiation were not part of the industrial relations system of the early nineteenth century because neither employers nor workers recognized the legitimacy of the other to participate in decisions over pay, hours, working conditions, or other aspects of the terms of employment. Indeed bargaining, it also has been argued, was antithetical to customary attitudes toward skill which arrogated the right to regulate rates of pay exclusively to craft workers.[16]

Yet Adam Smith did identify the existence of wage bargaining, even though, as E.H. Phelps Brown noted, he did not directly acknowledge that it occurred collectively.[17] More than his successors, Smith appears to have appreciated the fact that employment relations were contractual and that as such they involved a degree of negotiation. His analysis of waged labour, in fact, is premised upon the argument that 'the common wages of labour, depends everywhere upon the contract usually made between those two parties, whose interests are by no means the same. The workmen desire to get as much, the masters to give as little as possible.'[18] However, Smith's only substantive account of the wage bargaining process itself occurs in the context of his discussion of the inverse correlation between wages and the price of provisions. Here Smith argued that wages tended to rise in years of cheap food and to fall in years of high prices largely because the price of provisions determined the size of the wage fund. That is, a smaller proportion of the wage fund was available to hire labourers in years of high prices than low.[19] Interestingly, and unlike his successors, Smith viewed the existence of the wage fund as a precipitant of wage bargaining not a necessary preclusion to it. Thus Smith wrote that when the price of provisions was high, 'more people want employment than can easily get it; many are willing to take it [employment] upon lower terms than ordinary, and the wages of both servants and journeymen frequently sink in dear years'. Conversely, when the price of food was low, 'the demand for servants increases, while the number of those who offer to supply that demand diminishes'. Smith concluded that 'masters of all sorts, therefore, frequently make better bargains with their servants in dear than in cheap years, and find them more humble and dependent in the former than in the latter'.[20]

Smith understood, therefore, that some form of wage bargaining was an elemental aspect of the labour market even though he believed that the bargaining process was constrained within limits imposed upon it by the wage fund. However, Smith further recognized that the wage fund was not the only obstacle faced by workers because the wage bargaining process was further distorted not only by the masters' tendency to obstruct it but also the workers' tendency to override it. Smith's account of and opposition to masters' combinations is well known and referred to frequently by both historians and economists. Indeed his analysis here clearly presages the work of many post-Marshallian writers on the glaring inequities of a competitive labour market.[21] It is less well appreciated, however, that Smith's reason for emphasizing the existence of masters' combinations was not only because they created an imbalance in the labour market but also because such organizations subverted the wage bargaining process, a process that he believed should have been inherent in the labour contract. Smith, therefore, tied his judgement that wages depended on a contract between parties of opposing interests to the stipulation that the parties were neither of equal power nor of equal standing before the law.[22] Without parity at the bargaining table, as it were, workers were forced to have 'recourse to the loudest clamour, and sometimes to the most shocking violence and outrage' to try to attain their goals.[23] It is only in this context that Smith then discussed the employers' 'tacit, but constant and uniform combination, not to raise the wages of labour'; how, in the event of a dispute, masters were able to combine more easily because they were fewer in number and could hold out much longer because they possessed a greater supply of stocks; and how, for the masters, the law 'authorises, or at least does not prohibit their combinations, while it prohibits those of the workmen'.[24]

Many of Smith's most prominent followers saw fit to ignore these observations and to concentrate instead on what came to be known as the 'wage-fund theory' and the 'iron law of wages'. It might not be too unfair to lay a good portion of the blame for such a turn away from the examination of the functionings of the labour market at the feet of David Ricardo, whose most important work, *On the Principles of Political Economy and Taxation*, was first published in 1817. Both Ricardo's theory of wages and, more importantly, his theory of value ultimately served to ignore and deny the significance of any analysis of how wages were settled under the conditions of the early industrial labour market.

At first glance, Ricardo's theory of wages might seem to offer some hope of just such an analysis. Labour, he argued, has both a natural price and a market price. The natural price of labour is 'that price which is necessary to enable the labourers, one with another, to subsist and to perpetuate their race, without either increase or diminution', while its market price is 'the price which is really paid for it, from the natural operation of the proportion of the supply to the demand'.[25] Such a distinction is, of course, derived from Smith's observations concerning commodity prices.[26] Yet whereas Smith argued that the natural price of commodities varied inversely to the rate of wages, and consequently was led to investigate the significance of asymmetrical power in the labour market, Ricardo asserted that it was commodity prices that determined wages and not *vice versa*.

In Ricardo's view, there was a long-term tendency for the market price of wages to rise. This may occur because of the more extensive use of capital, in which case the market price of labour would rise in tandem with the rising price of food, clothing, and the like. Or, wages may rise due to the more intensive use of capital, in which case the use of machinery would reduce the price of necessities while sustaining the demand for labour.[27] In either case, the general rise in the market wages of labour would not necessarily denote an improvement in real income. Such an improvement depended instead upon the extent to which the natural price of necessities rose more slowly than wages. As is well known, Ricardo was not at all sanguine about such a prospect. As society progressed, population increases would slow the rate of the advance of wages relative to the rate of capital accumulation. The price of necessities, however, would continue to advance. Money wages thus would continue to rise 'but they would not rise sufficiently to enable the labourer to purchase as many comforts and necessaries as he did before the rise in the price of those commodities'.[28] As a result, presaging his discussion of profits, Ricardo predicted that the condition of workers would deteriorate, the profits of the manufacturer would fall, but both the real and money value of rent would rise.[29]

Ricardo's argument that declining real wages were essentially a function of the adverse operation of the markets for land, labour and capital, moreover, was a fundamental tenet of his theory of value. The initial proposition of Ricardo's first section of the chapter on value submitted that 'the value of a commodity, or the quantity of any other commodity for which it will exchange, depends on the relative quantity of labour which is necessary for its production, and not on the greater or less compensation which is paid for that labour'.[30] Such an emphasis was necessary because Ricardo sought to establish the proportional quantities of labour embodied in any commodity as the only adequate measure of exchangeable value. To do this, all other measures, including those suggested by Adam Smith, had to be rejected. In particular, this meant clearing up Smith's 'logical muddle' whereby value had been defined in at least three different ways in the early chapters of the *Wealth of Nations* and both labour and corn recommended as suitable units of measure.[31] Ricardo's *Principles of Political Economy* therefore began by asserting that the quantity of labour realized in commodities regulated their exchange value and continued by discarding either corn or the cost of labour as suitable measures of exchange value.

Although the subsequent sections of the chapter discuss the ways in which capital affects value, and hence really undermines a purely labour theory of value, the effect of Ricardo's theorem was to dismiss out of hand the necessity of analysing the functioning of the labour market. Unlike Smith, whose cost-of-production theory posited labour costs as a fundamental element of exchangeable value, Ricardo's labour-quantity theory dispensed with the element of labour costs altogether because, in his view, wages merely acted according to the laws of the market and thus did not form a component portion of value. That is, since wages were determined by supply and demand they logically could not be employed analytically as an invariable measure of exchange value. Moreover, as Joseph Schumpeter pointed out, Ricardo's theorem was valid only in perfect equilibrium.[32] Obviously, under such conditions, imperfections in the labour market, monopolistic practices, and bargaining effects became irrelevant. Ricardo's sole reference to such phenomena was an aside in the chapter on wages: 'Like all other contracts, wages should be left to the fair and free competition of the market, and should never be controlled by the interference of the legislature'.[33] This hardly compares favourably with Smith's discussion of contracts and the labour market in the *Wealth of Nations*. Ironically, therefore, part of the influence of Ricardo's labour-quantity theory of value was to help defer the theoretical recognition of labour's quotidian circumstance in the market for nearly half a century.

However unique the formulation of the labour-quantity theory of value may have been, Ricardo's indifference toward the functioning of the contemporary labour market was shared subsequently by most orthodox political economists. For example, Thomas Malthus's *Principles of Political Economy*, first published in 1820, adhered much more strictly to Smith's supply-and-demand model of wages but did so nevertheless to the detriment of any analysis either of the labour contract or the imperfections of the labour market. In fact, it might be argued that Malthus should bear an equal portion of the blame for the classical economists' failure to analyse wage bargaining adequately. In particular, Malthus was certainly guilty of infecting others with what Schumpeter called the 'Ricardian Vice', namely 'the habit of establishing simple relations between aggregates that then acquire a spurious halo of causal importance, whereas all the really important (and, unfortunately, complicated) things are being bundled away in or behind these aggregates'.[34]

Malthus's *Principles* emphasized that wage variations were the result of the relationship between the supply and demand for labour and the supply and demand for commodities within the limits of the wage fund.[35] Several of

Smith's qualifications regarding wage determination, such as the five circumstances affecting wage differentials, were unequivocally dismissed by Malthus because in his view they reflected mere supply-and-demand differentials.[36] Imperfections in the labour market, even those attributed to workers' combinations, were ignored completely. Instead, Malthus stressed the extent to which the habits of the working class affected their subsistence as well as the factors that influenced the growth of the wage fund.

In the *Principles*, Malthus was particularly concerned to qualify, if not rebut, the generally favourable attitude toward high wages that Smith had exhibited in the *Wealth of Nations*. Malthus wrote that the social effect of high wages was contingent upon the degree of civil and political liberty in any society. Thus, in a society such as England, liberty inculcated a sense of security and respect necessary for the development of prudential habits, which in turn would delay present gratification for the sake of future rewards. In England, high wages therefore led to a higher standard of living. The fate of Ireland, on the other hand, revealed an alternative to such a rosy outlook on high wages. There, an oppressed people, lacking both education and self-respect, used the higher real wages afforded by the introduction of the potato to marry early and raise large families. As a result, higher real wages in Ireland only contributed to the immiseration of the lower classes.[37]

While the particular habits of certain people may allow them to take advantage of high wages, Malthus reasoned, these habits of course do not determine the movement of wages. The movement of wages is determined instead by the growth of the wage fund, defined by him as the total value of capital or revenue that employs labour.[38] Any addition to the capital of a country was also an addition to its wage fund, which in turn added to the demand for labour. It is apparent that Malthus considered the wage fund to be subject to inflationary pressures by the debasement of bullion and the like. However, he considered increases in the value of the fund due to price inflation both 'less durable and less effective' in sustaining the demand for labour than increases in the powers of production through the accumulation of capital.[39] Once again, therefore, Malthus led us back to a perspective in which labour is an aggregate function and the explanation of the movement of wages denies the analytical legitimacy of wage bargaining or labour market 'imperfections'.

Interestingly, this tendency to disembody labour and create an abstraction of the labour market that characterized the works of Ricardo and Malthus was a bit less extreme in the works of some of the more pedestrian classical economists. J.R. McCulloch, for example, was one of the more astute observers of the functioning of the labour market, even though he was at the same time one of the leading exponents of the wage-fund theory and thus also sought theoretical refuge in the prison house of aggregations.[40] However, unlike Ricardo and Malthus, McCulloch directed a portion of his attention directly to the evolution of forms of employment contracts in the labour market. He recognized, for example, the increased prominence of piece-work in the economy and, in fact, welcomed it. The extension of piece-work, he argued, could bring about the high-wage economy that both he and Smith championed by harnessing the engine of enlightened self-interest to the workers' subordinate social position. To McCulloch, piece-work was an impartial and equitable form of wage payment that 'admits of no partiality on the part of the masters, and of no pretence or shirking on the part of the employed'.[41] Moreover, McCulloch, like some members of the Society of Operative Stone Masons, viewed piece-work as a potential avenue of social advancement whereby a worker could undertake larger jobs by acting as a principal or subcontractor.[42] Such contracting of piece-work, he believed, could be slowly and judiciously extended in scale, thus laying the 'foundations of thousands of middling, and of very many large fortunes'.[43] This, he triumphantly proclaimed, was 'the broadest, the easiest, and the safest of the various channels by which diligent, sagacious, and frugal individuals emerge from poverty, and attain to respectability and opulence'.[44]

However naive such a belief may appear, and certainly piece-work could lead to contracting in only a very few trades, McCulloch's short-term perspective of labour is certainly less distant and reified than that of either Ricardo or Malthus. Moreover, unlike Ricardo and Malthus, McCulloch sought to incorporate an appraisal of the effect of combinations into his analysis of wage-rate variations. McCulloch's assessment of combinations that appeared in *A Treatise on the Circumstances which Determine the Rate of Wages* (2nd edition, 1854) was based partly on an analysis of the economic impact of the Combination Laws and partly on a certain political and ideological prescription. In the first instance, he argued that the economic effects of legal restrictions on combinations were nugatory. While laws against combinations may serve to limit wage increases and secure higher profits in a particular sector over the short term, in the long run capital necessarily will be attracted by the prospect of higher profits, based on low labour costs, to those same sectors. As capital flows into these high-profit sectors, demand for labour will increase with the consequent effect of raising wages. Laws against combinations, therefore, have little or no long-term effect on wage rates.[45]

Such an analysis, of course, awkwardly displaces an evaluation of the effect of the Combination Laws on the bargaining power of labour as a whole with an intersectoral analysis of capital flows. McCulloch, therefore, further argued that strikes that sought to raise the price of labour above subsistence level, or the 'natural rate of wages', would ultimately fail as well. Following Smith, McCulloch accepted the fact that masters possessed a greater store of stock and credit, both of which would enable them to hold out longer than their employees. Moreover, McCulloch assumed that skill differentials between sectors were not so great as to prevent the substitution of 'blacklegs' or replacement workers for strikers. Finally, he accepted the common notion that strikes were frequently the impetus for the invention and adoption of machinery as a substitute for manual labour. Taken together, the effect of all these factors would be to keep wage rates at or near their 'natural' rate despite the appearance of trade unions or strikes.[46]

Underlying these judgements on the inefficacy of laws against combinations and strikes is the premise that only the unfettered functioning of the labour market can assess the proper rate of wages. And here McCulloch's faith in the market finally undermined his analysis of it. For while he effectively brought the functioning of the labour market back into the study of the movement and variations of wages, McCulloch failed to analyse how the asymmetries of the labour market influenced the form taken by industrial relations. If only in terms of contemporary analytical tools, he ignored the existence of masters' combinations and therefore could not assess their effects. Moreover, he neglected to evaluate the contractual aspect of the working of the labour market and thus failed to follow up Smith's bargaining theory of wages. In the end, therefore, McCulloch was left to wring his hands while declaring his opposition to state interference in matters properly settled between masters and men. Combinations of either workers or masters, he concluded, would inevitably cure themselves and government involvement only served to engender hatred between the two orders of society.[47]

A quite similar reluctance to assess the functioning of wage bargaining while at the same time relying upon the efficacy of the market to settle wages is apparent in Robert Torrens's *On Wages and Combination*, published in 1834. What is indeed remarkable about this work is that it implicitly recognized the presence of masters' combinations in the labour market and included one of the few serious attempts to analyse their effect on wages. Torrens initially posited the theoretical existence of a combination of farmers who seek to reduce agricultural wages in a single parish. Without doubt, as long as the masters' union held together, it would have little difficulty in enforcing wage reductions and consequently increasing profits. The fate of these profits, however, ultimately determined the fate of agricultural wage rates. If, for example, these profits were ploughed back into production, the effect would merely be to advance the demand for labour and hence drive up wages. On the other hand, if these excess profits were withheld from production and expended on unproductive luxuries, then the unintended effect would be to raise the demand for labour, and hence wages, in the manufacturing towns, but not in the countryside. However, seeing rising wages in the towns, agricultural labourers would desert the farms, leaving the countryside with a declining supply of labour. Facing such a threat that may force them to reduce the area under cultivation, farmers would then be compelled to abandon their combination and 'consent to an advance of wages'.[48]

Torrens proceeded to inquire into the effects of the extension of an employers' combination from agriculture into manufacturing. In such a case, when both rural and urban employers have agreed to uniformly reduce wages, profits would rise dramatically.[49] But this would not be the case in the long term. Supposing that the combination could be maintained,[50] a macabre Malthusianism would ensue. The lower wages of labour would necessitate the purchase of lower-quality and less nutritious foods. As a result, working-class families would be 'thinned by death; the delicate and infirm would sink prematurely to the grave; and while more died, fewer would be born'.[51] In the meantime, the 'cautious and prudent' would abstain from marriage, hoping to maintain their previous standards of comforts. After a generation, the labour market would be poised to experience a tremendous 'recoil of wages' as the supply of labour fell below demand.[52] As a result, any combination to reduce the wages of labour, Torrens argued, 'would speedily perish by self-destruction; and its evil influence, after having for a time afflicted the labouring classes, would recoil upon the insane conspirators, lowering, instead of raising, the rate of profit, and elevating, instead of depressing, wages'.[53]

While Torrens should be given credit for broaching a topic that had been ignored by other political economists, the inadequacies of his analysis, especially when compared to Smith, are obvious. His reference, for example, to a situation in which employers might consent to an advance of wages, leaves unresolved the circumstances surrounding the establishment of that consent. If Torrens was seeking to incorporate a bargaining theory into his analysis of combinations, then he failed to explain both the form and content of that bargain. More significantly, however, the logical categories adopted by Torrens could not be sustained analytically. A combination of farmers within a single parish bears only a superficial resemblance to a combination of manufacturers in a single town. A manufacturers' combination, as Torrens conceived it, would need to cover an extraordinary range of industrial and handicraft sectors in order to function in a manner similar to a farmers' combination. Of course, such a manufacturing employers' organization was not likely to occur and even less likely to survive. By defining combinations in this way, Torrens failed to recognize the frequency with which employers' organizations in individual sectors or even portions of individual sectors occurred. Unlike Smith, who acknowledged their existence, and went so far as to chide law-makers for facilitating such combinations,[54] Torrens's analysis misconstrued the activities of such organizations in the market. Rather than emphasizing their tacit and often *ad hoc* nature, as well as their appearance in individual sectors, Torrens's type of employers' organization would never be detected in industrializing Britain. Torrens therefore failed not only to understand the effects that the asymmetric distribution of power in the market had on the wage bargain, but also to recognize the various forms and levels that were taken by wage bargaining.

None of the political economists saw fit to explain fully why their wage theories forsook the short-term analysis of the functioning of the wage bargain in the labour market in favour of a long-term description of the determinants of labour's demand. It is true that they were working within the context of a subsistence model that was both centuries old and shared by many intellectuals of both Britain and Europe.[55] It also is evident that most political economists based their arguments upon an analysis of the functioning of the agricultural labour market, where wages were much stickier and combinations less frequent, rather than the urban manufacturing and industrial labour markets. This labour market certainly appeared to lack many active wage bargaining characteristics, although even in this regard Smith had appeared to be pointing the way to the further analysis of hiring fairs and the like. Yet in some further instances it appears to be the case that the political economists' inability to recognize the way in which labour markets were operating was based at least in part on their unwillingness to accept the political ramifications of such an observation.

G. Poulett Scrope was one such political economist. He was a great and sometimes eloquent defender of the efficacy of the Poor Laws, but nonetheless implied that government interference was preventing the free functioning of labour in the market. In his *Principles of Political Economy*, published in 1833, he directed attention to the 'faulty arrangement of political institutions' in order to explain low wages.[56] Poulett Scrope argued that wealth and abundance could only be secured in a social and political system that both protected the freedom of labour and allowed labour to freely exchange its products for wages.[57] In such a system, labour would be free to make the best bargain it could to gain its fair share of the nation's wealth. That is, it was only through the free and voluntary settlement of such bargains that the relative rewards of land, labour and capital could be properly distributed.

At the same time as he endorsed such a 'voluntary' system of industrial relations, as it would later come to be called, Poulett Scrope wanted to acknowledge that such a system of free exchanges was not present in contemporary Britain. Laws that attempted to set the minimum or maximum of wages, or other factors of production, he noted, violated the principle of free exchange, destroyed any just settlement of the distribution of wealth, and substituted the ignorant and arbitrary power of the state for the free exchange of property and services.[58] Like many others of the time, he condemned in particular the Speenhamland system as 'equally unjustifiable in principle and in law', as well as the settlement provisions of the Poor Laws as a restriction upon the circulation of labour.[59] Yet these observations were only a small portion of a much larger attack upon the impropriety of artificial restraints upon agriculture, trade and commerce that ballooned into a diatribe against a panoply of government institutions ranging from the Corn Laws to the Factory Laws to the Bank of England.[60] As such, Poulett Scrope's radical attack upon government interference ultimately obscured both the recognition of the functioning of the labour market and an adequate analysis of its inequities. Like the Chartists analysed in Gareth

Stedman Jones's famous essay, the strength of radicalism's attack upon the state and political corruption was also its greatest weakness.[61]

Similarly, in Nassau Senior's *Three Lectures on the Rate of Wages*, delivered at Oxford in 1830, an analysis of the way in which labour markets worked was ultimately displaced by a radical critique of the principles of legislative interference. Surprisingly, Senior seems to have acknowledged the functioning of a labour market, but only in certain regions of Britain and the world. In particular, he mentioned its operation in 'the most advanced districts of the continent', lowland Scotland, and throughout the British Empire. The labour market, however, was restricted to only the 'best educated of those classes who derive their chief subsistence from their exertions', by whom he meant professionals, artisans, shopkeepers and domestic servants.[62] These people, Senior wrote, were free labourers because they could refuse employment if they chose, ask any price for their labour that they thought fit, and follow their employment wherever and however long they desired. Yet unlike slave labour, they had no right either to be maintained or to be provided with food, clothing or medical care.[63] Under these circumstances, free labourers were forced to offer their services for sale in the same manner that capitalists were required to attract labourers by offering them wages. Capitalists and labourers meet in the market; they strike a bargain. 'And the bargain', Senior claimed, 'is settled, like all other free bargains, by the respective market values of the things exchanged.'[64] This 'free and open bargain; when the labourer obtains, and knows that he is to obtain just what his services are worth' is 'the natural state of the relation' between capital and labour.[65]

Like Poulett Scrope, however, Senior's discussion of the labour market ended not with an analysis of the exchange of a worker's effort for wages or the respective power of workers and employers in the market, as one might hope, but with an attack upon the administration of the Speenhamland system. He argued that the Poor Laws in southern England sought to unite two irreconcilable forms of labour: free and servile. By providing for the poor, the magistrates separated the necessity to labour from the independence of a free labourer. This meant that the labourer was no longer forced to be diligent, provident or prudent, all of which were the beneficial results of the functioning of a free labour market. Instead, Senior noted using some remarkably modern language, under the Speenhamland system 'the labourer is to be a free agent, but without the hazards of free agency; to be free from the coercion but to enjoy the assured subsistence of the slave'.[66]

Interestingly enough, Senior resolved that the breakdown of the social fabric that he thought was evident in the burning of corn-ricks and the riots of labourers in the early 1830s was the consequence of the collapse of free pay bargaining. Under conditions of wage bargaining, Senior reasoned, labourers learned the value of their services. While they may complain at times that a fall in the price of their labour was a great social evil, they also

understood that it was not a social injustice. During such times, free labourers had recourse not only to 'greater exertion and severer economy' to make
ends meet, but also to the benevolence and generosity of their employers.
This social compact was a product of the 'voluntary association' of labourers
and employers in which both parties were conscious of their mutual depend-
ence. And the nexus of this voluntary association was the free wage bargain
arrived at in the free market. Consequently, Senior heaped great scorn on
measures, however well-meaning, that disturbed the freedom of wage bargaining. The greatest fault of the Speenhamland system, Senior concluded,
was to supplant the free wage bargain with an absolute right to a certain
level of wages. He complained that 'the instant wages cease to be a bargain –
the instant the labourer is paid, not according to his *value*, but his *wants*, he
ceases to be a freeman. He acquires the indolence, the improvidence, the
rapacity, and the malignity, but not the subordination of a slave.'[67]

It must be admitted, however, that these observations comprised only a
small portion of the Preface of Senior's *Three Lectures on Wages*. The *Lectures* themselves do not contain any discussion of the wage bargain but instead are elaborations of the theory of the wage fund. Nor did Senior pay
any greater attention to the wage bargain in his larger work, *An Outline of
the Science of Political Economy*, although he did presume to define all
labour as voluntary.[68] Generally, therefore, Senior's social prescription was
not supported by any further analysis of the labour market or the labour
contract, and like most of his fellow political economists he failed to recognize the asymmetry of them both.[69]

Wage bargaining, socialism and equitable exchanges

Although Senior's elision of wage bargaining, moral values and political
freedoms proved to be a rather awkward one, such a line of reasoning in fact
was quite common among many of the critics of orthodox political
economy. Contrary to the political economists, the notion of wage bargaining was quite central to their analysis of the economy because it was one of
the principal ways in which labour experienced competition. Moreover, for
early British socialists such as Robert Owen and William Thompson as well
as anti-capitalists like Thomas Hodgskin, analysis of the systems of exchange was much more significant than analysis of systems that governed
the creation of wealth. Therefore, the exchanges of labour for effort that
took place in the labour market were more closely scrutinized by these writers than by their more orthodox contemporaries. Surprisingly perhaps, their
most significant contribution in this regard was to revise and extend the
analysis of the asymmetry of the labour market that had begun with the
Physiocrats and Smith. Yet like the political economists, they never sought to
analyse the wage bargain itself or the contemporary forms in which that
bargain was worked out.

Even though the problem of equitable exchanges had gained the attention of many writers in the West from Aristotle onwards, the primacy of exchange analysis among many anti-capitalist writers is without doubt due to the work of Robert Owen.[70] His *Report to the County of Lanark*, published in 1820, highlighted the inequities of 'an artificial system of wages', based on false standards of money, that failed to apportion justly the newly created wealth of early industrial Britain.[71] As is well known, Owen recommended instead the substitution of labour as the standard of exchange values, a substitution that would abolish the practice of making the support of human life 'an article of commerce'.[72] By adopting labour as the standard of value, not only could markets be freed from all artificial restrictions, but domestic demand for products would increase and pauperism would speedily disappear. Of equal importance was the fact that Owen believed that when labour was accepted as the standard of value, the labour market would be reshaped. 'The present demoralising system of bargaining between individuals', Owen wrote, would become both unnecessary and useless. 'No practice', he continued, 'perhaps tends more than this to deteriorate and degrade the human character.'[73] The adoption of labour values, therefore, would lead to the disappearance of wage bargaining. And this remarkable transformation of the labour market would therefore constitute an essential step toward the creation of the new moral world in which competitive individualism would be supplanted by harmonious communitarianism.

Owen's involvement in both the cooperative movement and labour exchanges was obviously a means toward this end.[74] Yet, despite the apparent centrality of wage bargaining to Owen's social project, his own work at this time focused less upon the moral and economic consequences of wage bargaining in particular than upon the moral bankruptcy of competition generally, as well as the distinction between productive and unproductive labour.[75] The social, political and moral problems of unequal exchange, however, were treated quite fully by one of Owen's followers, the Irish landowner William Thompson. His *An Inquiry into the Principles of the Distribution of Wealth Most Conducive to Human Happiness*, published in 1824, is based loosely upon the extension of the Benthamite principle of ensuring the greatest happiness for the greatest number.[76] To do this, Thompson argued, wealth must be created in order 'to afford the means of more extensive pleasures of the senses'; that is, the pleasures of the intellect.[77] Yet the productive powers of society could not be fully unleashed until the limitations placed upon production were removed. According to Thompson, the principal impediment to the creation of wealth had been the manner in which labour acted under the impetus of fear, want or compulsion. Such 'forced labour' was both inefficient and unproductive. Therefore, Thompson wrote, 'the strongest stimulus to production that the nature of things will permit, is *security* in the *entire use* of the products of labor to those who produce them' (emphasis in original).[78]

Still, a society of small, independent producers would not be a happy one because no single person can produce all the articles necessary for his or her own well-being. Instead the division of labour supplemented by a system of voluntary, not forced, exchanges was required to create the wealth needed for human happiness. Thompson clearly believed that such voluntary exchanges in a free market were the foundation not only of economic growth and human happiness, based upon freedom from exploitation, but of the moral perfection of society as well. 'Individual labor without exchanges', he said, 'would be a school of vice.'[79] Isolated, envious and suspicious, the autonomous producer could never learn those benevolent feelings of trust and cooperation upon which happiness depended. But set in motion the wheels of the market and, if based upon voluntary exchanges, the school of vice will become 'a nursery of social virtue'. In freely exchanging the products of their labour, labourers will gain a mutual sense of satisfaction, a mutual sense of sympathy, and the knowledge that one's own self-interest is not necessarily opposed to the self-interest of others. In short, 'the more of these mutually convenient exchanges that take place, the more man becomes dependent on man, the more his feelings become sympathetic, the more social he becomes, the more benevolent'.[80]

The echoes here of eighteenth-century commercial ideology, such as those expressed by the London compositors that will be discussed in the following chapter, are unmistakable.[81] More importantly, however, Thompson's analysis of unequal exchanges led him to confront directly the unequal distribution of power that characterized both the wage bargain and the labour market. He unequivocally condemned low wages not as the unintended effect of population or price movements, but as the result of the collusion of capitalists and the idle rich to keep prices low, the iniquitous operation of laws against labourers, and the competition for employment among labourers generated by forced exchanges and insecurity.[82] In this sense, therefore, Thompson's work marks an important point in the history of the analysis of the labour market. He revived many of Smith's earlier observations concerning the asymmetry of the labour market and embedded these insights within a general theory of unequal exchanges. Moreover, Thompson extended some of Smith's assertions by emphasizing that labour, unlike capital, entered the market by necessity not choice. 'The indirect compulsion of want', he wrote, extorted 'a species of voluntary acquiescence' in a market that extracted labour through both fraud and force.[83] These contributions notwithstanding, Thompson's analysis of unequal exchanges did not lead him to examine the nature of the wage bargain or the labour contract, despite the fact that such an examination was implicit in his project. To him, the absence of voluntary exchanges indicated that wages were fixed in the market by the forces of law, custom and power.[84] Thompson thus did not recognize the extent to which forms of bargaining and negotiation had already penetrated the industrial relations system or perhaps chose to ignore them.

He concentrated instead on heaping attacks upon the obstacles to free and voluntary exchanges, an approach that ironically coincided with those who actively opposed those hoary old demons of free trade, apprenticeship and wage regulations.

This analytical shift was most marked in Thompson's later work *Labor Rewarded: The Claims of Labor and Capital Conciliated* (1827), in which he excoriated the entire notion that the market, without perfectly free labour and voluntary exchanges, could ever satisfactorily distribute profits and wages. Thompson wrote *Labor Rewarded* in response to Thomas Hodgskin's famous tract *Labour Defended against the Claims of Capital*, which had been published in 1825. As we will see in the next chapter, Hodgskin's work gained a great deal of notoriety at the time, largely due to his novel view that capital was not a distinct factor of production but the sum of co-existing and previously accumulated labour.[85] However, while Hodgskin accepted the principle that 'the whole produce of labour ought to belong to the labourer', he faltered when trying to decide how to distribute that produce among 'different individuals who concur in production'.[86] If labour were perfectly free, Hodgskin argued, then relative wages could be settled by Smith's 'higgling of the market'. But this was not the case: labour was not free. Moreover, social prejudices tended to accord greater rewards to mental rather than physical labour, a distinction that Hodgskin rejected.[87] Yet, in the end, Hodgskin's conclusion did not take him very far beyond Smith's 'higgling of the market' distributional strategy. The just apportioning of the rewards of production, he argued, should be left to labour and 'while each labourer claims his own reward, let him cheerfully allow the just claims of every other labourer'.[88]

Such a formulation appeared to Thompson to replace the market that operated between employers and labourers with a market that operated among labourers themselves. Thompson was adamant that such a relocation of market mechanisms was insufficient to attain the goals of freedom and equality. He attacked Hodgskin for failing to recognize that competitive markets, of whatever kind, were incapable of either appropriately or accurately distributing rewards, especially among individual workers whose labour is minutely divided.[89] Moreover, the obstacles to the construction of objectively free and competitive markets were enormous. Their creation would require nothing less than a fundamental restructuring of all political and economic relationships. For exchanges to take place without force or fraud, privilege would have to be abolished, equal education secured, and an equal share of capital assured to all labourers.[90] Even then, a perfectly free competitive system ultimately could not secure human happiness. That could only be obtained, Thompson argued, through the supersession of individual competition by mutual cooperation.[91]

The appearance of Hodgskin's essay and the prominence given in it to the 'higgling of the market' did nonetheless lead Thompson to attempt to identify more satisfactorily some of the mechanisms of wage bargaining. Surprisingly, he omitted any discussion of the impact of employers' organizations or the law on wages and directed his attention instead to actions of labour itself. He rejected, for example, the Smithian notion that differences in pay could be ascribed to differentials of utility, skill or exertion. Instead, Thompson suggested that the unequal distribution of rewards to labour was caused by variations in local labour markets. In particular, he argued that pay differentials were due to the degree to which local markets were controlled or influenced by labour organizations as well as by the local supply of labour in relationship to its demand.[92] There were, he wrote, two ways in which labour sought to control market forces and restrict competition. First, labour acted to control the market 'in a covert way' through the enforcement of apprenticeship restrictions. Thompson could not support such actions, however noble in principle, because they violated 'the grand principle of the freedom of exchanges'. On the other hand, labour also acted in a voluntary and free manner to limit the evils of individual competition through the formation of unions and combinations. These actions, achieved without force or fraud, were laudable and worthy of support. By acting to root out individual competition through 'the gentle means of mutual agreement', trade unions, Thompson believed, could ultimately contribute to the physical, moral and intellectual improvement of the working class.[93]

Both unions and corporate restrictions therefore limited competition among workers, but Thompson reluctantly recognized that neither of these forms of limitation extended to the more general competition between labour and capital. Ironically, Thompson's description of that aspect of market relations was little different from that of Thomas Hodgskin. While labour may act to restrict competition among themselves, Thompson wrote, 'the competition between the capitalists and the industrious, employers and employed, or as it is variously called between masters and men, it leaves to work out its own cure, to find, by the "higgling of the market" amongst large masses, its level'.[94] Such a recognition of the scope of trade unionism is itself notable and, of course, presages many radical diagnoses of reformism later in the century. However, like the other political economists and early socialists, Thompson failed to cross the threshold of the workplace and to identify how wage bargains were worked out on the shopfloor. While the whole force of Thompson's writings was to lay bare the asymmetry of the labour market, the nature of the labour contract and the social and economic factors that determined the exchange of effort for wages, the so-called effort bargain, remained obscure to him.

On the shopfloor: Karl Marx and J.S. Mill

This discussion of analyses of the labour market, wage bargaining and the labour contract in the economic thought of this period may be suitably concluded by examining two of the towering works of mid-century by Karl Marx and John Stuart Mill. In *Capital* (1867), Marx often pointed the way for the study of these aspects of the employment relationship but never fully took the path himself. Nonetheless, Marx's theory of surplus value generally and his distinction between labour and labour-power in particular were important elements of this new direction. Mill similarly began to clear away some of the obstructions that had previously obscured both the recognition and the significance of wage negotiations and effort bargaining, but it was left to later generations of practitioners to penetrate the haze that remained nonetheless.

One of Marx's critical insights in *Capital* was to assert that surplus value could be created only through the application of labour to a commodity, that is, through the labour process, and not during the process of exchange or circulation. In order to add value to a commodity, therefore, the capitalist had to purchase the special value-producing quality of labour, what Marx called labour-power, in the market.[95] Once purchased, however, the capitalist could command the total value capable of being created by labour during a given period specified in the labour contract. This sum of value-creating labour, Marx argued, inevitably was in excess of the value necessary to purchase the labourer's means of subsistence. As a result, the value created by labour-power was also more than the capitalist paid for it. This is the 'trick', to use Marx's term, whereby the laws that governed exchange were not violated but the capitalist nonetheless was able to extract surplus labour, and hence value, from the workforce.[96] Consequently, in Marx's own view, his analysis forsook the noisy and open sphere of the labour market for the 'hidden abode of production'.[97]

Marx's theory of surplus value and the distinction between 'necessary' and 'surplus' labour time led to the grand historical chapters in *Capital* on the working day and large-scale industry that have had the great value at least of directing attention toward the nature of the production process. Moreover, such a perspective entailed a different approach from the definition and analysis of wages. Marx argued that since the political economists had failed to produce an adequate theory of value, they had also failed to define wages accurately. He extracted from Thomas Hodgskin and others the notion that labour, while it was the standard measure of value, was not itself a commodity and thus did not have value.[98] 'It is not labour which directly confronts the possessor of money on the commodity-market', Marx wrote, 'but rather the worker.'[99] To speak of the value or price of labour, as did the classical political economists, was to mistake the incidental market-price of the labourer's subsistence for the unique value-relation between labour-power and commodities.

Wages, therefore, did not denote a certain price or value of labour. Instead they had a much more sinister role to play. The essential 'mystery of wages' was that they extinguished 'every trace of the division of the working day into necessary and surplus labour, into paid and unpaid labour'. That is, labourers were paid by the hour or day and appeared to receive the full value for their labour-power. Yet, according to the theory of surplus value, in the capitalist mode of production they obviously did not. 'The money-relation', Marx wrote, 'conceals the uncompensated labour of the wage-labourer.' Thus, for Marx, the wage form lay at the core of the mystification of capitalism. By making all labour appear as paid labour, wages sustained the workers' illusion of freedom and justice under capitalism and obscured the source of their exploitation.[100]

Marx condemned 'the ordinary economic treatises' that ignored different forms taken by wages, although, as we have seen, he was not the first to discuss the importance of the wage form.[101] He thought it necessary at least to describe both time-wages and piece-wages, which he considered the two fundamental forms taken by wages. By his own admission, Marx's discussion of time-wages was cursory and limited principally to the ways in which variations in working hours affected the price of labour-power.[102] However, the analysis of piece-wages was altogether more incisive. In a well-known formulation, Marx considered the piece-wage to be 'the form of wage most appropriate to the capitalist mode of production' because it transferred management's responsibility to supervise both the quality and intensity of labour to the labourers themselves.[103] The piece-wage, moreover, encouraged competition between workers because individuals possessed of above-average skills, strength or staying-power could earn above-average wages. Yet overall, this same competition, he observed, lowered the general rate of wages. Finally, the piece-wage embodied an ideological element that was equally important for the capitalist mode of production. By restricting direct managerial control, piece-rates fostered in the worker a sense of autonomy and independence that in turn further concealed the competition between workers as well as the extraction of surplus value.[104]

Ultimately, Marx's formulae obscured as much as they revealed of the nature of the wage bargain. Marx's theory of surplus value was inextricably linked to what he called 'the immanent laws of the exchange of commodities' that denoted the exchange of equivalents in a free market.[105] For the trick of surplus value to be turned, the capitalist had to purchase labour-power for its equivalent value of the means of subsistence.[106] A well-functioning labour market, therefore, was a prerequisite for the extraction of surplus labour. As such, although Marx certainly recognized the inequities of the labour market, particularly as it was realized by the 'industrial reserve army' of surplus labour, he apparently felt it unnecessary to assess the impact of employers' organizations and avoided any detailed analysis or description of the fundamental asymmetries of the market created by monopsony.[107] More importantly, however, Marx strictly separated commodity exchange, including the purchase of labour-power, from its consumption. He claimed that the former was a market relationship while the latter was not. 'The consumption of labour-power', Marx wrote, 'is completed, as in the case of every other commodity, outside the market or the sphere of circulation.'[108] In this sense, Marx could also observe the dichotomy whereby within the orbit of the market labour appeared both free and legally equal to capital while within the production process labour was subordinated and exploited.[109] Yet Marx clearly had not penetrated the 'hidden abode of production' deeply enough to recognize the indeterminancy of the labour contract. Given the nature of technology, the continued reliance of British business on labour's skill at the point of production, and the expansion of piece-work during this period, few if any employers exercised the degree of 'real control' over the shopfloor and the labour process envisioned by Marx.[110] Instead, as we shall see, the shopfloor in most trades operated as perhaps the principal 'bargaining zone' of any enterprise where exchanges of effort for pay were frequently renegotiated either openly or furtively.[111] The production process, as a result, while not precisely a market process, certainly exhibited many more of the fundamental features of an exchange process than Marx realized.

In comparison to Marx, the later editions of John Stuart Mill's *Principles of Political Economy*, first published in 1848, show evidence of the author's attempts to understand the vagaries of the labour market. Even before he formally jettisoned the wage-fund theory, Mill's analysis of the role of trade unions had begun to lead him back to Adam Smith's 'bargaining theory' of wages. The 1862 edition of Mill's *Principles* implicitly criticized orthodox political economists who had reified the supply-and-demand relationship embodied in the labour contract.[112] Mill emphasized instead the importance of human agency and maintained that 'the market rate [of wages] is not fixed ... by some self-acting instrument, but is the result of bargaining between human beings'.[113] This did not mean for Mill that wages could ultimately contravene the laws of the market, but it did indicate his recognition that some form of bargaining was essential for the proper functioning of the market. 'Those who do not "higgle"', Mill continued, 'will long continue to pay, even over a counter, more than the market price for their purchases.'[114]

For Mill, the bargaining that was essential for the functioning of a free labour market had been obstructed not only by inequalities of wealth, but also by the asymmetric distribution of information. The great value of trade unions was that they redressed the imbalance of power in the labour market by allowing for both mutual consultation and concerted action. In fact, Mill noted in a well-known phrase that 'far from being a hindrance to a free market for labour, [trade unions] are the necessary instrumentality of that free market'.[115] Moreover, the symmetric distribution of information perhaps held the key to 'any radical improvement in the social and economical relations between labour and capital'. By learning the movement of prices and profits, labourers will also learn to strike only at times when their trades are prosperous and profits buoyant. It is at these same times that employers are most willing to concede advances in wages. As a result, labourers will learn to participate regularly in profits derived from their own labour.[116]

While Mill's work marked a point at which orthodox economic theory once again began to recognize the wage bargain, it nonetheless exhibits many of those same weaknesses of the other writers of this period.[117] Mill's recognition of the importance of monopsony for the articulation of the labour contract was cursory and certainly displayed less interest in the phenomenon than did Adam Smith. His remarks on the asymmetric distribution of power in the labour market were perfunctory and failed to analyse satisfactorily its impact on either the labour contract or wage bargaining. Moreover, even though the first edition of the *Principles* predated Marx's *Capital* by some two decades, none of the later editions sought to go beyond prescriptions for the labour market and to assess the conditions of the exchange of effort for pay on the shopfloor or the nature of collective bargaining. As such, Mill – like the great interpretive frameworks of the early nineteenth century: political economy, socialism and Marxism – only recognized industrial relations 'through a glass, darkly'.

Conclusions

Given the predilections of these political economists and socialists, therefore, their writings are very unreliable guides to any evaluation of the nature of labour relations during the early industrial period. It is perhaps unfortunate that in this respect they have served to provide some of the master narratives around which our understanding of the period have been constructed. Among all of them we can see an aversion of or an analytical retreat before the complexity of the wage bargain and the shopfloor. This is perhaps least true of Marx, who after all pointed the way across the 'threshold [where] there hangs the notice "No admittance except on business"'.[118] Still, perhaps the greatest irony lies in the fact that it may well have been Frederick W. Taylor who first accepted Marx's invitation. His personal vendetta against shopfloor output restriction and the consequent creation of time–motion studies spawned a strain of research and analysis that has been carried through scientific management, schools of human relations, industrial sociology, industrial relations, and many others fields.[119] Such individual or work group shopfloor bargaining that is inscribed in the work process is only one such bargain that the classical economists overlooked. Equally important were the collective bargains waiting to be discovered, identified and named by Sidney and Beatrice Webb. Although the operation and function of collective bargaining had been implicitly accepted by Adam Smith, and before him by the French Physiocrats, these too later became subsumed by the Ricardian vice of aggregation and reification, especially as expressed in the form of the theory of the wage fund. Of course, the fact that intellectuals and academics refused to recognize the presence, legitimacy and efficacy of collective and shopfloor bargaining did not mean that they were not there. Instead the paradigms and discourses upon which they based their understanding of society, industry and industrial relations served to ignore and marginalize such concerns. Such discourses were first breached by the Webbs, who were awkwardly perched on the shoulders of both socialist and neo-classical economic theory, but the effects of their dominance over the historical analysis of the era in which they were born have yet to be fully amended. While the purpose of later chapters will be to initiate this process of recognition and amendment, the following chapter will first turn to a discussion of artisanal and working-class expressions of industrial relations in order to see whether we can learn anything more from those sources.

Notes

1   Graham Wallas, *The Life of Francis Place, 1771–1854*, 4th edn (1898; London: George Allen & Unwin, 1925), pp. 223–37.
2   *Report from the Select Committee on Combination Laws*, Parliamentary Papers, vol. iv (1825), pp. 33–4.
3   Place Papers, British Library Additional Manuscript (hereafter BL Add. Ms.) 27799, f. 138.
4   British Library, Place Collection, Set 51, ff. 219–21.
5   On the building trades generally during this period, see R.W. Postgate, *The Builders' History* (London: National Federation of Building Trade Operatives, 1923); Richard Price, *Masters, Unions and Men: Work Control in Building and the Rise of Labour, 1830–1914* (Cambridge: Cambridge University Press, 1980).
6   Modern Records Centre, University of Warwick Library, Union of Construction, Allied Trades and Technicians: Friendly Society of Operative Stone Masons (hereafter MRC, OSM), Ms. 78/OS/4/1/1, *Fortnightly Returns*, 9 and 23 June 1837.
7   E.J. Hobsbawm, 'Custom, Wages, and Work-load in Nineteenth-Century Industry', in Asa Briggs and John Saville, eds, *Essays in Labour History* (London: Macmillan, 1960), pp. 113–39.
8   Robert Gray, *The Factory Question and Industrial England, 1830–1860* (Cambridge: Cambridge University Press, 1996), especially ch. 5.
9   Antonella Stirati, *The Theory of Wages in Classical Economics: A Study of Adam Smith, David Ricardo and their Contemporaries*, trans. Joan Hall (Aldershot: Edward Elgar, 1994), pp. 35–9, 45–8.
10 P.S. Atiyah comes to the same conclusion, although he attributes political economy's failure to address the issues of wage bargaining to their faith in competition and their lack of concern with questions of distribution. See P.S. Atiyah, *The Rise and Fall of Freedom of Contract* (Oxford: Clarendon Press, 1979), p. 339.
11 An excellent survey of the classical economists' obsession with wage-fund theory appears in Sidney and Beatrice Webb, *Industrial Democracy*, new edn (London: Longman, Green and Co., 1902), pp. 603–53.
12 D.P. O'Brien, *The Classical Economists* (Oxford: Clarendon Press, 1975), pp. 111–13.

13 W.H. Hutt, *The Theory of Collective Bargaining, 1930–1975* (London: Institute of Economic Affairs, 1975), pp. 3–10. Hutt's contention that the Webbs also accepted this notion is unsustainable.

14 V.L. Allen, *The Sociology of Industrial Relations: Studies in Method* (London: Longman Group, 1971), p. 66. A similar opinion is expressed in H.A. Clegg, Alan Fox and A.F. Thompson, *A History of British Trade Unions since 1889, Volume I, 1889–1910* (Oxford: Clarendon Press, 1964), pp. 5–6.

15 Price, *Masters, Unions and Men*, pp. 73–9.

16 Clegg, Fox and Thompson, *History of British Trade Unions*, p. 5.

17 E.H. Phelps Brown, 'The Labour Market', in Thomas Wilson and A.S. Skinner, eds, *The Market and the State: Essays in Honour of Adam Smith* (Oxford: Clarendon Press, 1976), pp. 246–7.

18 Adam Smith, *An Inquiry into the Nature and Causes of the Wealth of Nations*, ed. Edwin Cannan (1776; Chicago: University of Chicago Press, 1976), bk i, ch. viii, p. 74.

19 Smith, *Wealth of Nations*, bk i, ch. viii, pp. 92–4. Smith also attributed an important role to the expectations of both labourers and masters in this context. Low prices encouraged both labourers to strike out on their own and masters to hire more servants thus pushing wages up. High prices, on the other hand, disposed masters to reduce the size of their households at the same time as workmen found it difficult to sustain their independence.

20 Smith, *Wealth of Nations*, bk i, ch. viii, p. 93.

21 Mark Blaug, *Economic Theory in Retrospect*, 3rd edn (Cambridge: Cambridge University Press, 1978), p. 47.

22 It is, I believe, significant that Smith's discussion of masters' combinations is immediately preceded by his definition of the wage contract. See *Wealth of Nations*, bk i, ch. viii, p. 74.

23 Smith, *Wealth of Nations*, bk i, ch. viii, p. 75.

24 Smith, *Wealth of Nations*, bk i, ch. viii, pp. 74–6.

25 David Ricardo, *On the Principles of Political Economy and Taxation*, ed. Piero Sraffa (Cambridge: Cambridge University Press, 1962), pp. 93–4.

26 Smith, *Wealth of Nations*, bk i, ch. vii.

27 Ricardo, *Principles of Political Economy*, pp. 94–5.

28 Ricardo, *Principles of Political Economy*, pp. 101–2.

29 Ricardo, *Principles of Political Economy*, pp. 102–4.

30 Ricardo, *Principles of Political Economy*, p. 11. Schumpeter calls this 'the practical spearhead of his theory value'. Joseph A. Schumpeter, *History of Economic Analysis*, ed. Elizabeth Boody Schumpeter (New York: Oxford University Press, 1954), p. 595.

31 Schumpeter, *History of Economic Analysis*, p. 590.

32 Schumpeter, *History of Economic Analysis*, p. 592.

33 Ricardo, *Principles of Political Economy*, p. 105.

34 Schumpeter, *History of Economic Analysis*, p. 668.

35 Thomas R. Malthus, *Principles of Political Economy*, pt 1, 2nd edn, ed. E.A. Wrigley and David Souden (1836; London: William Pickering, 1986), pp. 177–81.

36 Malthus, *Principles*, pp. 179–80; Smith's five circumstances affecting wage differentials were the agreeableness of employment; the ease of learning the

trade; the constancy of employment; the trust reposed in the employee; and the probability of success. Smith, *Wealth of Nations*, bk i, ch. x, pt i, pp. 112–32.

37   Malthus, *Principles*, pp. 181–5.

38   Malthus, *Principles*, p. 190.

39   Malthus, *Principles*, p. 194.

40   Schumpeter, *History of Economic Analysis*, pp. 476–7, 669.

41   J.R. McCulloch, *A Treatise on the Circumstances which Determine the Rate of Wages and the Condition of the Labouring Classes*, 2nd edn (London, 1854), p. 70.

42   See above, p. 18.

43   McCulloch, *Treatise*, p. 71.

44   McCulloch, *Treatise*, p. 71.

45   McCulloch, *Treatise*, pp. 78–81.

46   McCulloch, *Treatise*, pp. 81–4.

47   McCulloch, *Treatise*, pp. 89–91.

48   Robert Torrens, *On Wages and Combination* (London, 1834), pp. 45–7.

49   According to Torrens, profits would rise in the form of a ratio between the proportion of wages of the total cost of production and the percentage change in total value of wages. Torrens, *On Wages and Combination*, pp. 48–9.

50   This would require a uniform agreement not to expand production, to expend all incomes unproductively or hoard all savings, and to prevent the importation of foreign capital. Torrens, *On Wages and Combination*, pp. 50–3.

51   Torrens, *On Wages and Combination*, p. 54.

52   Torrens, *On Wages and Combination*, p. 55.

53   Torrens, *On Wages and Combination*, p. 56.

54   Smith, *Wealth of Nations*, bk i, ch. x, pt ii, pp. 144–5.

55   Michael Theodore Wermel, *The Evolution of Classical Wage Theory* (New York: Columbia University Press, 1939).

56   G. Poulett Scrope, *Principles of Political Economy* (London, 1833), pp. 94–5.

57   Poulett Scrope, *Principles*, pp. 49–51, 70–2, 85–7.

58   Poulett Scrope, *Principles*, pp. 227–9.

59   Poulett Scrope, *Principles*, pp. 94, 310–14, 426–30.

60   Poulett Scrope, *Principles*, chs xiv–xviii.

61   Gareth Stedman Jones, 'Rethinking Chartism', in *Languages of Class: Studies in English Working Class History, 1832–1982* (Cambridge: Cambridge University Press, 1983), pp. 90–178.

62   Nassau Senior, *Three Lectures on the Rate of Wages* (1831; New York: A.M. Kelley, 1959), pp. vii–ix.

63   Senior, *Three Lectures*, p. vi.

64   Senior, *Three Lectures*, p. viii.

65   Senior, *Three Lectures*, pp. ix–x.

66   Senior, *Three Lectures*, p. ix.

67   Senior, *Three Lectures*, p. x.

68   Nassau Senior, *An Outline of the Science of Political Economy* (1836; New York: A.M. Kelley, 1965), pp. 57–8.

69   This is all the more surprising since in the *Outline of the Science of Political Economy* Senior paid much greater attention to the asymmetries of the market for commodities than his contemporaries. Senior, *Outline*, pp. 102–11.

70 See the useful survey by Gregory Claeys, *Machinery, Money and the Millennium: From Moral Economy to Socialism, 1815–1860* (Princeton: Princeton University Press, 1987), pp. 1–33, as well as the same author's *Citizens and Saints: Politics and Anti-Politics in Early British Socialism* (Cambridge: Cambridge University Press, 1989), pp. 148–50.

71 Robert Owen, *Selected Works of Robert Owen*, ed. Gregory Claeys, 4 vols (London: Willliam Pickering, 1993), vol. i, pp. 290–2; Claeys, *Machinery, Money and the Millennium*, pp. 43–5.

72 Owen, *Selected Works*, vol. i, p. 292.

73 Owen, *Selected Works*, vol. i, p. 293.

74 J.F.C. Harrison, *Robert Owen and the Owenites in Britain and America: The Quest for the New Moral World* (London: Routledge and Kegan Paul, 1969), pp. 195–216; W.H. Oliver, 'The Labour Exchange Phase of the Cooperative Movement', *Oxford Economic Papers*, new ser., vol. 10 (1958), pp. 354–67.

75 Claeys, *Citizens and Saints*, pp. 174–83; Gregory Claeys, 'The Reaction to Political Radicalism and the Popularisation of Political Economy in Early Nineteenth-Century Britain: The Case of "Productive" and "Unproductive" Labour', in Terry Shinn and Richard Whitley, eds, *Expository Science: Forms and Functions of Popularisation* (Boston: Hingham, 1985), pp. 119–36.

76 Claeys, *Machinery, Money and the Millennium*, pp. 107–9; E.K. Hunt, 'Utilitarianism and the Labor Theory of Value: A Critique of the Ideas of William Thompson', *History of Political Economy*, vol. 11 (1979), pp. 545–71.

77 William Thompson, *An Inquiry into the Principles of the Distribution of Wealth Most Conducive to Human Happiness* (1824; New York: A.M. Kelley, 1963), pp. 24–8.

78 Thompson, *Inquiry*, pp. 17–45. See Claeys, *Machinery, Money and the Millennium*, pp. 90–109 for a general assessment of Thompson.

79 Thompson, *Inquiry*, p. 49; see also pp. 369–75.

80 Thompson, *Inquiry*, pp. 49–50.

81 See below, Chapter 2.

82 Thompson, *Inquiry*, pp. 246–9, 258–9, 523–4.

83 Thompson, *Inquiry*, pp. 165, 500–1.

84 Thompson, *Inquiry*, p. 501.

85 See below, Chapter 2 ; E.K. Hunt, 'Value Theory in the Writings of the Classical Economists, Thomas Hodgskin, and Karl Marx', *History of Political Economy*, vol. 9: no. 3 (1977), pp. 322–45; Samuel Hollander, 'The Post-Ricardian Dissension: A Case Study of Economics and Ideology', *Oxford Economic Papers*, vol. 32: no. 3 (November 1980), pp. 370–410.

86 Thomas Hodgskin, *Labour Defended Against the Claims of Capital* (1825; London: Labour Publishing, 1922), p. 83.

87 Hodgskin, *Labour Defended*, pp. 88–90.

88 Hodgskin, *Labour Defended*, p. 90.

89 [William Thompson], *Labor Rewarded: The Claims of Labor and Capital Conciliated* (1827; New York: A.M. Kelley, 1969), pp. 97–8.

90 Thompson, *Labor Rewarded*, pp. 12–15, 51–3.

91 Thompson, *Labor Rewarded*, pp. 95–108.

92 Thompson, *Labor Rewarded*, p. 22.

93 Thompson, *Labor Rewarded*, pp. 77–88. Thompson, an Owenite, did argue

further that the beneficent impact of unions was ultimately limited by the continued existence of private property. While unions could raise wages and encourage education, they would also give rise to new forms of competition between unions themselves. This, he felt, could be resolved by the introduction of a national trade union of labourers. However, even a national union could never fully overcome the evils inherent in 'the exclusive possession of capital by one set of persons and of labor by the rest'. Only by purchasing property and employing labourers could unions end this final struggle. Thus Thompson saw unions, in Claeys's words, 'as a potential vehicle for introducing co-operation'. See Claeys, *Machinery, Money and the Millennium*, pp. 101–2.

94   Thompson, *Labor Rewarded*, p. 76.
95   Karl Marx, *Capital: A Critique of Political Economy*, vol. i (1867; New York: Vintage Books, 1977), ch. 6.
96   Marx, *Capital*, vol. i, especially chs 7 and 9.
97   Marx, *Capital*, vol. i, pp. 279–80.
98   Marx, *Capital*, vol. i, pp. 676–7.
99   Marx, *Capital*, vol. i, p. 677.
100 Marx, *Capital*, vol. i, pp. 680–2.
101 Marx, *Capital*, vol. i, pp. 683.
102 Marx, *Capital*, vol. i, ch. 20.
103 Marx, *Capital*, vol. i, pp. 694–8.
104 The appropriateness of these observations in the case of the early nineteenth-century coal industry have been examined in my *The Struggle for Market Power: Industrial Relations in the British Coal Industry, 1800–1840* (Cambridge: Cambridge University Press, 1991).
105 Marx, *Capital*, vol. i, pp. 268–9.
106 Marx, *Capital*, vol. i, pp. 274–5. Marx, however, maintained that the level of subsistence, and hence the value of labour-power, contained 'a historical and moral element' and varied with the level of civilization attained by a particular country.
107 Marx, *Capital*, vol. i, pp. 792–4.
108 Marx, *Capital*, vol. i, p. 279.
109 Marx, *Capital*, vol. i, ch. 7, especially pp. 291–2.
110 Richard Price, *Labour in British Society: An Intrepretative History* (1986; London: Routledge, 1990), pp. 15–28; Clive Behagg, *Politics and Production in the Early Nineteenth Century* (London: Routledge, 1990), pp. 20–70; John Rule, *The Labouring Classes in Early Industrial England, 1750–1850* (London: Longman, 1986), pp. 120–6; Raphael Samuel, 'The Workshop of the World: Steam Power and Hand Technology in Mid-Victorian Britain', *History Workshop Journal*, no. 3 (Spring 1977), pp. 6–72.
111 On 'bargaining zones' in firms, see P. Abell, ed., *Organisations as Bargaining and Influence Systems*, 2 vols (London: Heinemann, 1975, 1978); and on 'furtive' bargains, see Howard F. Gospel and Gill Palmer, *British Industrial Relations*, 2nd edn (London: Routledge, 1993), pp. 181–2.
112 Ironically, Mill's argument here reflects Marx's earlier criticism of James Mill's *Elements of Political Economy*. See Karl Marx, *Early Writings*, ed. Quintin Hoare (New York: Vintage Books, 1975), p. 260.
113 John Stuart Mill, *Principles of Political Economy*, ed. Sir William Ashley

(1848; New Jersey: A.M. Kelley, 1987), p. 937.

114   Mill, *Principles*, p. 937.
115   Mill, *Principles*, p. 937.
116   Mill, *Principles*, pp. 937–8.
117   Later work by Marshall, Edgeworth and others would serve to further elaborate the indeterminacy of the wage contract during the latter half of the nineteenth century. For their contributions, see Webb and Webb, *Industrial Democracy*, pp. 643–53.
118   Marx, *Capital*, vol. i, pp. 279–80.
119   Daniel Nelson, *Frederick W. Taylor and the Rise of Scientific Management* (Madison: University of Wisconsin Press, 1980).

2

A transactional universe: trade unions and the ideology of labour relations during the Industrial Revolution

The mind is rather invigorated than enfeebled by the labour of the hands ...
(Thomas Hodgskin, *Labour Defended Against the Claims of Capital*, 1825)

The language of radicalism and politics has been the subject of an enormous degree of attention during the last few years, almost to the point of crowding out contemporary views of work and industrial relations. Sparked in part, of course, by the seminal contributions of Gareth Stedman Jones on Chartism, Patrick Joyce on class and populism, and Joan Scott on feminism, recent works by Sonya Rose, James Epstein and James Vernon, among many others, each in their own way have adopted degrees of critical and postmodernist theory to explicate the extent to which discourse and meanings were both contested and constitutive during the nineteenth century. An oft-noted effect of the influence of this 'linguistic turn' has been to reassert the primacy of politics, albeit in a manner that stresses the ways in which 'politics defined and imagined people', as Vernon puts it, rather than the more common historical project of tracing the development of political organizations and institutions.[1] Whether one adopts a poststructuralist approach toward the relationship of power, ideology and identity in the manner of Foucault, or its linguistic formulation as narratology and emplotment, or an uneasy mixture of both, there may be a new consensus emerging that nineteenth-century political discourse offered both an increasingly narrow definition of citizenship and a bounded range of political idioms. In particular, it has been argued, radicals, Whigs and Tories alike shared the 'master narrative' of popular constitutionalism, a narrative whose ultimate meanings, while contested, nonetheless were similarly expressed in the historically embedded terms of the rights and liberties of free-born Englishmen, an Anglo-Saxon heritage, the Norman Conquest, Magna Carta, the legacy of 1688, and so forth.[2] Serious rivals to this narrative were few. Painite republicanism, for example, the other dominant political idiom of the period, which emphasized the immanence and anti-historical nature of natural rights, never gained widespread support and languished among a distinct minority of urban radicals and intellectuals, Richard Carlisle and the zetetics being among the most prominent.[3]

If we turn our attention away from the political sphere and toward the shopfloor or domestic workshop, however, then our understanding of popular ideology becomes altogether more ambiguous and is often taken less seriously. Stedman Jones, for example, has powerfully argued that early nineteenth-century radicalism located the source of economic inequality and exploitation in the endemic corruption and monopolization of power within the British state.[4] While such radical ideas may have come to connote forms of protectionism among some British workers, they did not specifically express a uniquely artisanal set of values or assumptions.[5] Thus in this influential formulation radicalism was never the ideology of a specific class. Instead, radicalism's identity sprang from the protests of the 'people' or the 'nation' against the aristocratic monopoly over law-making.[6] The purchase of radicalism's political analysis of the causes of poverty and oppression extended to the trade union movement of the period as well. Rather than offer a class-based, or any other alternative, trade unionism largely mimicked popular radicalism. Most trade union leaders, Stedman Jones argues, were radicals anyway, and their prescriptions for reform often sought to restore a naturally harmonious system of productive relations between masters and men that they believed to have been degraded and disrupted by a corrupt political system.[7]

Patrick Joyce has elaborated upon and extended many of these insights, albeit in ways that are far different from Stedman Jones's original analysis.[8] Joyce's rejection of class as a privileged analytical category is by now well known among historians, as are his calls to pay greater heed to contemporary intellectual theory. Although Joyce has often been criticized for misrepresenting the ways in which class analysis have been deployed by social historians, he seems to see his own historical project as that of uncovering the multiplicity of identities available to people and the subsequent process by which cultural narratives, such as morality and improvement, became the basis for action and self-knowledge in the nineteenth century.[9] Like Stedman Jones, he rejects the notion that early nineteenth-century workers expressed themselves solely in terms of class, and, at least in one work, seeks to uncover the 'plurality of work-derived interpretations of the social order'.[10] Foremost among these social paradigms was the persistent notion of the trade in which fairness, mutuality and reciprocal obligations between masters and men expressed a 'primarily moral and socially inclusive' picture of society.[11] Therefore, rather than expressing a class-bound vision of social and industrial relations, customary notions of the trade in which labour's moral vision of fairness and mutuality were paramount persisted well into the early nineteenth century.[12]

It would be, of course, both unfair and unwise to attribute to early nineteenth-century labour, or even only to the artisanate, a unitary vision or ideological consistency that their late twentieth-century analysts fail to exhibit themselves. Labour spoke in many voices. It is not at all difficult to find many examples of trade unionists who spoke as political radicals just as it is relatively easy to find those who spoke as moral mutualists and even class warriors. It is also true, however, that by the second half of the nineteenth century trade unionism eventually became dominated by the language of fairness and reciprocity, and therefore a more fruitful line of inquiry might be to seek to uncover how and why such a 'moral cosmology' crowded out alternative voices within the labour movement.[13] Several historians have suggested that the answer may lie in the failure of alternative theories of society to construct a convincing explication of the changing world around them. Thus Stedman Jones's essay on Chartist ideology proposes that radicalism and its step-children, trade unionism and popular political economy, emphasized the centrality of the reform of the state to their goals of justice and humanity, an emphasis that lost its powers of explanation in the face of Peel and Gladstone's own reforms during the 1840s and after.[14] At the same time, Noel Thompson suggests that the ultimate failure of the popular political economists, such as Thomas Hodgskin, John Bray and William Thompson, to secure working-class support was the result of their inability to construct a viable explanation of oppression and exploitation under the conditions of economic growth after mid-century.[15]

However, ideologies become coherent and explanatory not only by force of circumstance but also by force of will. Alternative discourses may not be any more or less comprehensive or comprehensible than those that become dominant, but their failure may be attributed, if only in part, to their inability to control, influence or dominate the institutions that reproduce and disseminate those visions or discourses. Thus, as we shall see, in the trade union movement of the early nineteenth century, labour's moral vision was in part the result of conscious political choices and institutional struggles within or among the unions themselves. Yet of equal importance was the fact that this moral vision was far less of a remnant of an older, customary moral code than has heretofore been acknowledged.[16] Instead, trade union discourses of mutuality and reciprocity may very well have drawn upon 'modern' funds of ideas, formulations, expressions and concerns that circulated throughout the world of 'high culture'. Indeed eighteenth-century political and moral philosophy could be readily adapted to the goals of both trade unionists and popular political economists in the early industrial period, and, in many cases, could serve as a satisfactory means by which work and industrial relations could be articulated. Thus within the organized trades – and this is an admittedly important qualifier – 'customary' notions such as reciprocity and mutuality continued to be important influences and they reveal not only the vibrancy of artisanal culture but also its active engagement with the intellectual influences of the era. Understanding these aspects of artisanal ideology will also bring us one step closer to the recovery of industrial relations because the issues dealt with by popular political economists and trade union activists often reflected and gave expression to daily life on the shopfloors of the early nineteenth century.

Eighteenth-century epistemology and labour theories of wealth

Such an interpretation may at first seem surprising, but a closer examination of the intellectual patrimony of Thomas Hodgskin, to whom E.P. Thompson accorded a leading role in the dissemination of an anti-capitalist labour economics, reveals one level on which this connection may have operated.[17] As we have already noted, Hodgskin is most well known for his 1825 pamphlet *Labour Defended Against the Claims of Capital*, in which he argues that labour was the source of all wealth and that capital was merely the accumulation of pre-existing labour.[18] The widespread popularity of this pamphlet, particularly among trade unionists of the period, appears to be indisputable. In part, the tract's popularity was due to its eclectic and inclusive approach. Hodgskin at times suggests, like most radicals of the period, that a corrupt legislature intent upon protecting capital contributed to the unequal distribution of wealth and rewards in society, yet at other times, like the customary moral economists, he exhibits no modern sense of class but distinguishes society's productive labour, which includes both workers and manufacturers, from unproductive stock-jobbers, middlemen and courtiers.[19] However, even such expansive interpretations do not do justice to the sources of Hodgskin's critique of capital, which lay neither in the language of radicalism nor in the discourse of moral economy; they lay instead in seventeenth- and eighteenth-century epistemology and cognitive theory.

These influences can initially be traced in a tract Hodgksin published in 1827 entitled *The Word BELIEF Defined and Explained*. The tract has been largely forgotten and for the history of philosophy perhaps rightly so. However, for historians its significance lay in the light it sheds on the philosophical and discursive foundations of both *Labour Defended* and the influential series of lectures Hodgskin delivered at the London Mechanics' Institution during the same year that *The Word BELIEF* was published.[20] *The Word BELIEF* bears the imprint of Thomas Brown, a philosopher and medical doctor who had gained a significant degree of notoriety during his tenure as Professor of Moral Philosophy at Edinburgh between 1810 and 1820. Brown's *Inquiry into the Relation between Cause and Effect*, first published in 1818, was both an analysis and critique of Hume's theory of causation. For Hume, as David Pears has written, 'all belief is inferential and ... causal inference is the only kind [of belief] that takes us beyond what we immediately perceive'.[21] Brown, on the other hand, basing his analysis at times upon the observation of infantile behaviour, argued that there was an intuitive tendency to view sequences of events as causally related and that custom or experience only refined or corrected that tendency.[22] In *The Word BELIEF*

Defined and Explained, Hodgskin adopted this perspective. In imitation of Brown, he argues that 'belief' is natural and intuitive rather than inferential. Moreover, like Brown, Hodgskin asserted that all ideas, whether derived from belief, memory or perception, evoked immediate sense-impressions that acted to evoke the same feelings, and hence belief, as the original and initial perception. As David Stack has recently argued, such a perspective was a necessary defence against Hume's theory of causation.[23] To claim that all ideas or observations evoked immediate sense-impressions was intended to confound Hume's theory by asserting that there was an 'external impression of necessity' that evoked the natural and intuitive nature of belief. Pears has labelled this type of response to Hume's theory of causation 'naïve empiricism'.[24]

While such an excursion into epistemology may seem to be arcane and perhaps irrelevant, Hodgskin's contact with Brown's work formed one of the pillars of his analyses of capital and political economy. As such, Hodgskin's work indicates the ways in which theories of labour and the economy were subject to a wide variety of intellectual influences in addition to political radicalism and moral economism. Perhaps of even greater immediate influence upon Hodgskin than Brown's work on causality was his *Sketch of a System of the Philosophy of the Human Mind*, which appeared after Brown's death in 1820. Indeed the analytical structure of *Labour Defended Against the Claims of Capital* appears to have been directly drawn from this work on the 'physiology of the mind'. In his *Sketch*, Brown sought to attack the dominant notions of the group of philosophers he labelled the 'nominalists', including Berkeley, Thomas Reid, Shaftesbury and others, who together had sought to explicate the nature of the mind through the elaboration of its so-called natural faculties such as desire, imagination, genius, memory, and the like. Instead, Brown insisted that the mind was 'simple and indivisible', and that what appeared to some to be a complex set of separate mental faculties was actually an illusion. Following on his work on causality, Brown suggested that all sensations, emotions and intellect were simply 'states of mind' whose relationship could be scientifically deduced through the analysis of the interplay between physical causes and mental effects. Such a focus on the 'successive phenomena' of cause and effect could lay bare the laws of the mind that regulate the transition from one state of mind to the other as different physical causes elicit different states of mind.[25] Brown therefore took particular care to examine the causal relationship between the development of the physical senses and the development of consciousness, and one of the principles he put forth to explain that relationship was that of 'association'.[26] According to Brown, all states of mind arise in response to either external stimuli, the mind's 'external affections', or the intellect and emotions, its 'internal affections'.[27] The mind, however, learns to recognize the external world through a complex associative process of the senses. The sense of smell, for example, has very little abstract meaning if it is not associated, or co-exists, with memories evoked by the other senses such as size, shape, colour, texture or the like. Thus Brown wrote that

> By frequent co-existence with the sensations afforded by other organs, that have previously informed us of the existence of matter, our sensations of mere smell and taste seem of themselves, ultimately, to inform us of the presence of things without. A particular sensation of fragrance has arisen, as often as we have seen or handled a particular flower; it recalls, therefore, the sensations that have previously co-existed with it, and we no longer smell only; we smell a rose. In taste, in like manner, by the influence of similar co-existence of sensations, we have no longer a mere pleasurable feeling; we taste a plum, a pear, a peach. The suggestion of things external is as quick in these cases, as in other cases of association; but the knowledge of these corporeal masses is still a suggestion of memory only, not a part of the primary sensations either of smell or of taste.[28]

In a similar manner, Brown sought to explain the phenomenon of thought on the basis of association or, as he also labelled it, simple and relative suggestion.[29] Every suggestion in a train of thought, Brown believed, is reducible either to the influence of the revival of a thought that had previously co-existed with an initial suggestion or to a thought that had been evoked in immediate succession to that suggestion.[30] In a variety of contexts, Brown continually emphasizes the importance of this associative concept of 'co-existence' rather than unique mental faculties to explain the workings of the mind. Brown argued, for example, that while 'immediate succession' may be a distinct analytical category of inquiry, practically 'the rapid sequence, where one feeling has scarcely ceased when the other has begun, may be considered almost like co-existence'.[31] In another case, that of Brown's Laws of Suggestion that sought to explain how initial suggestions are modified by memories, he posited the principle that 'When all other circumstances are the same, one suggestion will take place rather than another, according to the longer or shorter continuance of the original feelings, when they primarily co-existed or succeeded each other'.[32] Similarly, Brown's analysis of the mind's 'feelings of relations' was broken down into Relations of Succession and Relations of Co-existence.[33] Indeed, it would not be too far wrong to argue, as Brown himself implied, that the association of ideas and feelings which were comprehended through co-existence and succession was the root of consciousness.[34]

It also would not be too far wrong to say that Brown's system of co-existence and succession became the structural foundation for Hodgskin's *Labour Defended Against the Claims of Capital* and thus entered into popular political economics. Hodgskin's argument that labour was the source of all wealth was based upon his analysis of the nature of both circulating and fixed capital. Like Brown, Hodgskin was an astute linguistic analyst who argued that the naming of ideas or things was a prescriptive process. As such, the definition of terms such as circulating and fixed capital needed to be demystified and shorn of the assumptions propagated by the political economists.[35] This was the object of this pamphlet. For Hodgskin, the political economists' definition of circulating capital as a previously accumulated stock of goods that assures workers that their labour will be remunerated inaccurately defined both the nature and effect of circulating capital. Significantly, Hodgskin began by emphasizing the cognitive foundation of circulating capital. Both capitalists and workers undertook their efforts because they had the confidence, knowledge and assurance that their labour would be remunerated and their subsistence secured.[36] The source of this confidence and assurance, however, lay not in the actual physical presence of a stock of accumulated goods, which would have been subject to decay and deterioration, but in the knowledge that other workers were constantly at work to provide the necessaries of life.[37] Thus Hodgskin wrote:

> To enable either the master manufacturer or the labourer to devote himself to any particular occupation, it is only necessary that he should possess – not, as political economists say, a stock of commodities, or circulating capital, but a conviction that while he is labouring at his particular occupation the things which he does not produce himself will be provided for him, and that he will be able to procure them and pay for them by the produce of his own labour.

And in a language drawn unquestionably from Brown's work on causality and psychology, Hodgskin went on to write that

> this conviction arises, in the first instance, without any reflection from habit. As we expect that the sun will rise to-morrow, so we also expect that men in all time to come will be actuated by the same motives as they have been in times past. If we push our inquiries still further, all that we learn is, that there are other men in existence who are preparing those things we need, while we are preparing those which they need. The conviction may, perhaps, ultimately be traced then to our knowledge that *other men* exist and labour, but never to any conviction or knowledge that there is a stored up stock of commodities.[38]

Hodgskin therefore explained circulating capital in Brownian fashion. Moreover, the term with which he sought to define circulating capital was drawn from Brown as well: for Hodgskin, circulating capital was nothing less than 'co-existing labour'. It is worth quoting at length Hodgskin's definition and conclusion:

> If we duly consider the number and importance of those wealth-producing operations which are not completed within the year, and the numberless products of daily labour, necessary to subsistence, which are consumed as soon as produced, we shall, I think, be sensible that the success and productive power of every different species of labour is at all times more dependent on the co-existing productive labour of other men than on any accumulation of circulating capital. The labourer, having no stock of commodities, undertakes to bring up his children, and teach them a useful art, always relying on his own labour; and various classes of persons undertake tasks the produce of which is not

completed for a long period, relying on the labour of other men to procure them, in the meantime, what they require for subsistence. All classes of men carry on their daily toils in the full confidence that while each is engaged in his particular occupation some others will prepare whatever he requires, both for his immediate and future consumption and use. I have already explained that this confidence arises from that law of our nature by which we securely expect the sun will rise to-morrow, and that our fellow men will labour on the morrow and during the next year as they have laboured during the year and the day which have passed. I hope I have also satisfied the reader that there is no knowledge of any produce of previous labour stored up for use, [but] that the effects usually attributed to a stock of commodities are caused by co-existing labour ...[39]

In a similar manner, Hodgskin's analysis of fixed capital reflects Brown's notion of 'succession'. Fixed capital, according to Hodgskin, was actually the composite of the knowledge, skill and labour that produced the tools, machines and buildings that many called fixed capital. Social conventions and political practices, particularly the institution of private property, have reified these products and obscured their origin.[40] For Hodgskin, however, fixed capital was created by labour and skill, is useful only when combined with labour and skill, and is preserved by labour and skill. Only the initial, successive and continuous application of labour and skill to tools and machines constitutes fixed capital.[41]

In constructing the history of the voices of the trades and trade unionism, such influences have tended to be obscured by the emphasis placed upon the customary aspects of labour's moral economy and the predominance of the language of political radicalism. However, the discourse of eighteenth-century moral philosophy as well as metaphysics and epistemology was not lost upon either working-class autodidacts or those, like Hodgskin, who sought out the likes of Brown, J.R. McCulloch or Jeremy Bentham.[42] Contact with these men and their ideas contributed to Hodgskin's understanding of society in which the principal social division was not between the working class and bourgeoisie but between the productive and unproductive classes. Without doubt Stedman Jones was correct to select Hodgskin as a 'limit case' of the extent to which the so-called Ricardian socialists shared the radical analysis of exploitation as arising out of the political domination of the exchange process rather than through production.[43] In *Labour Defended*, Hodgskin certainly did caution against the general 'disposition to restrict the term labour to the operation of the hand' and asserted that 'the knowledge and skill of the master manufacturer, or of the man who plans and arranges a productive operation, who knows the state of the markets and the qualities of the different materials, and who has some tact in buying and selling, are just as necessary for the complete success of any complicated operation as the skill of the workmen whose hands actually alter the shape and fashion of these materials'.[44] Moreover, the opprobrium of 'capitalist' was directed against unproductive middlemen who profited through the operation of inequitable exchanges.[45]

In one sense, therefore, Hodgskin can be placed squarely within the radical tradition. Such a shared discursive heritage, however, should not obscure the ways in which other strands of eighteenth-century thought, in this case epistemology and cognitive theory, contributed to Hodgskin's recognition that the fundamental social chasm lay between those who worked and those who did not, and not between those who were employers and those who laboured.[46] Hodgskin's arguments were founded on the notions that labour was a cognitive process and that the division of labour was premised not on a certain propensity to truck, barter and exchange, as Smith would have it, but on the assurance and confidence that the work of other labourers would provide for their individual needs. This perspective privileged an epistemological analysis of productive and unproductive labour. Hodgskin's 'radical' attacks against corrupt systems of exchange and political institutions need to be located within this Brownian analysis of the cognitive foundations of labour. In a radical manner, he wrote that oppressive middlemen and inequitable social regulations prevented labourers from comprehending the 'natural laws' of society. However, he understood these laws to be predicated on the link in which 'mouths are united with hands and with intelligence', a link that was fundamentally cognitive in nature and not political or economic. Justice will prevail, he believed, and the false claims of capital to profits and interest will be rejected, only when this cognitive unity is re-established by reuniting labour with the whole of its products.[47] Hodgskin's demand that labour possess all that it produces, therefore, was in part a radical claim but it was an ontological one as well.

Commercial ideologies and trade union discourse

While such ideological influences exhibited by Hodgskin's work may reveal an unexpected and largely unrecognized intellectual patrimony, it may be argued nonetheless that early trade unionism in general was relatively immune from such sophistries and was dominated instead by either moral or radical discourses. However, trade union discourses were often embedded in a web of assumptions and expectations that reflected in large part both the concerns and the language of eighteenth-century moral and political philosophy. Indeed such a relationship can be traced in the language of the London-based Union of Compositors, whose records from the early nineteenth century are particularly plentiful. Their language of trade unionism was built upon notions of manners and interests, not constitutional rights or moral economy. Indeed such a language was well suited to the world of early nineteenth-century industrial relations in which the ideal of the trade still flourished, the workshop model still held purchase, and passions still needed to be tamed. More importantly, these trade unionists can be shown to have consciously entertained and rejected alternative idioms until nearly the middle of the century, preferring to hold fast to a transactional view of their universe shaped by the language of civic humanism and commercial ideology. Such voices have largely been lost, but they constitute another important element of trade union discourse that gave shape to their social vision and objectives.

The roots of these trade union idioms lay in the paradigmatic shift in political thought that took place during the eighteenth century toward the recognition of commerce as an important civilizing agent in the modern world. Such a role was perhaps most influentially asserted by Montesquieu and later Hume, but, as Albert Hirschman argues, this line of thought is located within a broad context of post-Machiavellian political arguments on how best to restrain the destructive passions of men, particularly the lust for power and glory.[48] J.G.A. Pocock as well stresses the extent to which the eighteenth century was engrossed with the problem of classical forms of virtue and the impact of commerce. While Pocock's assessment of the eighteenth-century view of the ultimate civilizing power of commerce is much less sanguine and his emphasis upon the dialectical relationship between virtue and commerce is significantly different from that of Hirschman, he nonetheless reveals the extent to which some contemporaries, such as Addison, recognized the importance of commerce for its contributions to the shaping of personal morality and identity.[49] 'Commerce', Pocock writes, 'was the parent of politeness.'[50]

The civilizing mission of commerce was expressed in a number of ways, but of particular importance was the way in which commerce was meant to restrain the passions, elicit the interests, and evoke manners and sociability. 'Commerce tends to wear off those prejudices which maintain distinctions and animosities between nations', the Scottish historian William Robertson wrote in 1769. 'It softens and polishes the manners of men.'[51] While the passions were potentially destructive, they could be controlled and modified by the expansion of commerce and exchange which multiplied the individual's social interactions with others and thereby refined those passions into manners and interests.[52] The refining process generated by commerce, therefore, was not a function of its ability to create wealth but of its epistemological effects; increasing interactions with other people, places and things had the effect of modifying and reforming the personality. It was thus the recognition of the increasingly transactional nature of the universe that required new standards of conduct and discourse.[53]

This would seem to take us a long way from the world of nineteenth-century trade unionism, but it would be odd indeed if this discursive tradition had left no impression on the British working class, even though a group of workers such as the London compositors can hardly be considered representative. Compositors certainly ranked among the traditional labour aristocracy. Since the vast majority of compositors worked according to a complicated piece-rate system, it is notoriously difficult to establish their actual earnings during this period. In the 1830s, however, some could take home as much as 85s in a week, although this was clearly unusual. By 1865, the London Society of Compositors estimated that average workers earned a base pay of about 33s in a 63-hour working week.[54] They could then add significantly more to their pay packages when extra charges for overtime, corrections, composing from manuscript, adding footnotes or sidenotes, working in foreign languages, and a whole host of others 'extras' were added.

London compositors, as we shall see, were also well organized and skilled in the arts of negotiation and arbitration. They had been able to secure a standardized price list for their piece-rates in 1785 and, unlike many other trades, had been able to retain that list, with many additions and amendments, throughout the nineteenth century. The acceptance of these price lists by both employers and journeymen helped to strengthen the compositors' trade organizations and to promote the establishment of an accepted framework for collective bargaining.[55] It is within this framework of regular, albeit not always peaceful, contact between masters and journeymen that the language of rights and constitutional privileges was often eschewed and that of manners and interests was adopted and elaborated.

Of course, the language of interest was not new to the nineteenth century and in fact had enjoyed a 'remarkable vogue' in the late seventeenth century. J.A.W. Gunn suggests that the term was popularized in England by the Duke of Rohan after 1640 and that by the time of the Protectorate it had become *de rigueur* in most 'statesmanlike pronouncements'. However, the meaning of interest in political discourse changed over time. Originally defined in terms of foreign policy, Hirschman argues, by the eighteenth century the meaning of interest had been significantly narrowed to indicate the individual pursuit of material or economic gain.[56] In other instances, one would be suspicious of such linearity, and we would be right to be so here, too. The trade union leaders of the compositors of the nineteenth century often expressed a significantly different understanding of 'interest' from that of individual economic gain. While 'interest' continued to refer to material rewards, the compositors rarely used it to connote the pursuit of individual self-interest. Instead they commonly gave interest a collective definition. In the most frequent formulation among the compositors' records, 'interests' were employed to express the collective material advantages to be gained through unionization, such as when the compositors attacked those journeymen who in the 1820s remained 'wilfully blind to the scale, the rules, and the privileges of the profession, and the interest of the body at large'.[57] Similarly, in the middle of the 1830s, the union explained that 'they consider the compositors employed in London as forming but one body, having but one interest; and, consequently, should be regulated by one code of laws'.[58] As late as the 1870s, the compositors identified questions concerning the regulation of apprenticeships as affecting the 'vital interests' of the union and argued that 'it is of the highest consequence that remedial measures should be adopted in order to avoid a still further extension of the complaint which would un- questionably affect the interests of the whole body'.[59] Perhaps this notion was most clearly stated in 1834 upon completion of a set of negotiations that merged two rival compositors' unions. The so-called Union Committee rejoiced not only at its success, but also about the message that the new union sent to the employers. That message was that the compositors 'do not cherish the bigoted and degrading feelings of prejudice and party, but that they are willing to make another sacrifice (in addition to the many they have already made) in order to advance the general interests of the profession'.[60]

Such a collective identity of interests among nineteenth-century artisans can easily be interpreted as an indication of an emerging craft consciousness, or from a different political angle, as an expression of sectional, trade union consciousness. However, the repeated use of the term 'interests' was not lim- ited to this manner. Among the compositors, the idiom of interests was used just as often to identify and define the collective material advantages poten- tially available to both masters and men in the publishing trade. This com- pounded interest was often articulated in a manner that emphasized the shared or common interests in the success of the trade, yet there are also instances in which the interests of employers and compositors are assumed to be interrelated albeit essentially separate. The compositors do not seem to have adopted the Smithian assumption that the interests of employees were inimical to and incompatible with those of their employers.[61] An argument typical of their construction of interests as mutual or held-in-common was expressed in an early report of the executive committee of the London Gen- eral Trade Society of Compositors. They explained to their members that the executive committee was 'appointed to labour *for the trade in general*, [and] they take the opportunity to declare that they consider all as friends who strive to advance the *interests* of the business' (emphasis in original).[62] Sev- eral years later, the union congratulated a master printer, i.e. an employer, for speedily resolving a dispute with his compositors. At a quarterly meeting in February 1832, the union prefaced its announcement with the sentiment that the mode of resolving this dispute did 'equal honour to the firmness of the members of this Society, and to that conscientious regard to the interests of the business' exhibited by the employer.[63]

By this time, that is, the 1830s and 1840s, however, it also was becoming more common for the compositors to express the notion that the collective interests of employers and employees were reciprocal rather than identical. Thus the compositors wrote of their 'hope that employers will be convinced of their true interests, and in future co-operate with us in maintaining a uniform and regular standard for defining the wages of labour. They are as much interested in this as we are; their profits are regulated by ours; and they should make common cause with us against those who would seek to obtain their work done in such a way, and at such a price, as would rob the respectable master of his fair profits, and the journeyman of his just hire.'[64] Similarly the compositors' union once explained that the purpose of the union was to act fairly and in the 'true Spirit of Justice' because 'the interest of the employed is so strongly identified with the employer'.[65] As late as 1890, the compositors petitioned employers for an increase in wage rates, explaining that since 'the existing Scale for Bookwork was framed so far back as 1810, no apology can be necessary for an attempt being made ... to bring this 80-year-old document up to date, in the interest both of employers and workmen'.[66]

The sources for such a notion of interest are difficult to disentangle. It should be clear by now that the development and use of the term does not precisely reflect Hirschman's account of the 'semantic drift' of the definition of interest from that of the prince or state to that of particular groups in society and then to that of individual economic gain.[67] It may well be that the term was simply grafted onto customary notions of the well-being of the trade and thereafter was allowed to flourish under the peculiar circumstances of the long-term survival of a mutually acceptable scale of wage rates. Similarly, the use of a collective definition of interests may have reflected the competing notions of public and private interests that were also common in seventeenth- and eighteenth-century social and political thought.[68] There are even strong echoes here of natural law doctrines that, according to Gregory Claeys, posited the elementary role of 'reciprocal interest' in the formation of human society.[69]

However, the context of the compositors' notion of interest seems to be especially comprehensible when viewed in the light of the eighteenth-century attempts to formulate a 'commercial humanism' in contrast to the classical civic or republican ideal. As we have seen, the evocation and recognition of interest in this sense was an aspect of the civilizing mission of commerce that served to restrain destructive passions at the same time as it posited a new definition of virtue.[70] The identification of interests was therefore part of the redefinition of personality that simultaneously asserted the importance of manners and politeness. Indeed such an emphasis upon controlling the passions and exercising manners is a further recurring theme in the compositors' records. As early as 1810, the compositors' trade union leaders responded to their employers' refusal to negotiate during a trade dispute by suggesting that their opponents sought 'to inflame the passions and impel to rash measures'. Yet in contrast to the master printers, the trade unionists insisted that they had 'endeavoured to suppress our own feelings' and to cultivate a 'cool and calm temper' because such an attitude and manner is the 'most likely to be advantageous to the interest of our profession'. The path that lay before the union was arduous, the union argued; in order to succeed, the compositors needed not only unanimity but also those qualities that tamed the passions, namely prudence and perseverance. 'We entreat you', the compositors' leaders warned their fellow unionists, 'to guard your minds from the influence of our feelings.'[71]

Similar arguments in similar terms can be traced throughout much of this period. In 1835, for example, the trade union leaders insisted in their annual report to the rank-and-file that 'we will not appeal to your passions, but [to] your reason'.[72] When a break-away union was created in the late 1820s, one of its first quarterly reports to the rank-and-file implicitly recognized the way in which manners were evoked in a 'transactional universe'.[73] 'Your Committee have endeavoured to keep the noiseless tenour of their way', the union official announced,

> avoiding direct controversy, which, is not only useless, but has a tendency to produce unpleasant consequences; and we are conscious, that, as your institution is yet only in an infant state, *one false step* might produce disgrace and immediate ruin; and your Committee in their proceedings, have always endeavoured so to conduct themselves, that, though the society may not be praised its members shall be respected. One great, substantial, and vital object of your committee (and they recommend the same to all members of the Society,) is to endeavour to create in the minds of the masters, a feeling of respect and interest for the Society.[74]

Several years later, the link between manners and the recognition of interests was even more clearly laid out in a series of proposals placed before the rank-and-file on payment practices. This report concluded:

> They [the governing Trade Council], therefore, trust that the propositions will be fairly discussed, and they cannot neglect this opportunity of stating their hope that no unbecoming marks of derision – which are disgraceful only to those who employ them, and not to the object derided – will be bestowed on any person who from a sense of duty may address the meeting. The hint is almost unnecessary, for we are all well aware that, as the sweetest nut oft lies beneath the roughest shell, so also is much sound sense and practical knowledge often conveyed in a rambling and desultory speech. If, therefore, you have any respect for yourselves, for the Chairman, and for the interests of the Union, which can never be promoted by cabal and clamour, we invoke you not to judge hastily, but by patient attention and mature deliberation endeavour to arrive at such conclusions as shall advance your best interests, and impart stability to our yet infant Union, whose very existence now and at all times must depend on the moderation, the firmness and the unanimity of its Members.[75]

Taken together, these quotes are surprisingly similar to Nicholas Phillipson's description of the origins of Scottish 'practical morality' in Addison's principles of voluntarism. 'By cultivating the arts of conversation and friendship', Phillipson writes, '[men from different walks of life] would learn to value tolerance, detachment, moderation and a respect for the value of consensus as a means of maintaining the bonds of society.'[76] Certainly, the avoidance of unrest, of unleashing the passions, was a staple of much trade

union rhetoric, as were elaborate codes of conduct that were regularly fea-
tured in trade union rule books. However, these characteristics of nineteenth-century trade unionism, particularly from early in the century, are
routinely described as attempts 'to adopt at least a public face of "respectability"', as one historian has put it.[77] And such 'plebeian respectability' is
often ascribed to the influences of evangelical religion, the emulatory desire
to keep up appearances, or even the calculative function of working-class
role-playing.[78] It would obviously be unwise to deny these influences altogether. Without doubt the compositors' trade unions of the early Victorian
period were just as interested in fashioning a new identity for their members
as they were in defending their pay packets. Yet the roots of working-class
respectability may lie in sources that are often deemed to be part of 'high
culture'. Indeed Pocock's 'commercial humanism' may accurately identify an
important strand of working-class ideology. Thus the compositors' emphasis
upon manners and politeness was part of an approach to industrial and class
relations that linked the refinement of the passions to the recognition of their
interests. These interests, moreover, were elicited during the transactional
operation of the commercial world where personalities were shaped and
altered: prejudice yielded to tolerance; clamour to consideration; party to
polity. Therefore, the moderation of the compositors' passions was integral
to the recognition of their collective interests, but also essential to the extent
to which those interests were shared with their employers.

Interestingly enough, the adoption of these idioms was part of a conscious
rhetorical effort to avoid the politically contentious implications of asserting
the compositors' rights. In 1809, after having reviewed earlier efforts to
secure rate increases from their employers, the compositors found 'them
written in a bolder style than any the master printers have received from us
during the the present application. In those documents, the words right,
claim &c. occur not infrequently. This language we have avoided.' They
continued:

> In making this remark it is necessary to guard against misapprehension. We
> are far from wishing to inculcate that what we have been asking is not a right:
> we are fully convinced, that it is a claim not only supported, but even dictated,
> by justice. – But, in order to take the most likely course to conduct you with
> safety into the port of justice, we deemed it allowable, that we might steer
> clear of the shoals of pride, to use the language of request.[79]

Yet what the compositors might have meant if they had invoked their 'rights'
is not at all clear from this. Indeed it appears from later usage of the term
that they did not mean to call upon immanent, individualist rights. At times,
'rights' appeared as a synonym for economic interests. Thus, in 1828 the
union executives suggested that 'it is not by cavilling about trifles that we
expected to render *you* a Service; – we carefully avoid the field of useless
debate; but, should your privileges be attacked, or your interests endangered

– your Committee would no longer pause, but with alacrity and dauntless-ness, would maintain their own authority and defend your rights'.[80] How-ever, even more often the compositors' concept of 'rights' was used to define the spheres of legitimate authority accorded to employees and employers that have been sanctioned by custom and usage. For the compositors, these 'rights' appear to have encompassed a satisfactory level of income as well as a significant degree of control over the shopfloor and the labour process. Thus, in 1845, the serving of a legal apprenticeship was recognized as having established a 'right to the trade'.[81] In 1832, trade union officers rebuked an employer for infringing upon 'the rights of the business' when he settled a dispute with workers in his printing office without reference to union regula-tions.[82] Two years later, in 1834, the union of two compositors' trade groups was extolled by its supporters as 'an enlarged and improved system for maintaining the rights of the trade', a term that seems to have been equiva-lent to the maintenance of 'present prices and privileges'.[83]

Compositors' rights were frequently invoked during disputes over proper payments for their work. One union announcement declared that it was the 'the right of the Compositor to be paid for making-up his matter into pages, when that matter had been previously put by him into a shape for pulling, had invariably been admitted in the best and largest [printing] houses; and that any departure from a practice so universally recognized, would be a departure from an equitable and long-established regulation, and a great injury to the Compositor'.[84] Another asserted 'the right of the Compositor to claim the leads put into his matter at the time of making up'.[85] A final exam-ple was the common union complaint during the 1830s against employers who attempted to 'deny the right of the compositor to [be paid for] wrappers and advertising sheets'.[86] It is in this sense that the compositors later spoke of the importance of their 'vested rights'.[87]

What is most striking about this use of the term 'rights' is the way in which it reflects or mimics the usage of rights in natural law theory. In the natural jurisprudential tradition, exclusive property rights were the result of the application of labour. This, of course, is a fundamental element of Locke's *Second Treatise*; similarly, Pufendorf maintains that 'it was im-proper that a man who had contributed no labour should have a right to things equal to his by whose industry a thing had been raised or rendered fit for service'.[88] Indeed such a labour theory of property rights was not uncom-mon among artisans of the period. John Rule, for example, has shown from a slightly different perspective how artisanal skill was defined as a form of property during the early nineteenth century and thus came to be defended through the language of rights.[89] However, artisans did not deploy 'rights' according to a Painite definition, as even Paine himself recognized.[90] Instead not only were 'rights' specific to a trade and governed work and wages, but employers' reciprocal property rights in the trade had to be recognized as well. Therefore, the rather awkward claim that the compositors made in

1837 that it was 'an undeniable principle that the employed has an equal right with the employer to fix or adjust the price of labour' reflects an attempt to accommodate competing claims to rights as they were defined in natural jurisprudential thought.[91]

In his discussion of radical political thought, Gregory Claeys has noted that contemporary opinions were drawn from a spectrum of ideas, some of which at first sight might appear to be antithetical, and 'paradigmatic purity' was not an overwhelming concern.[92] Such a caution might be equally applicable to an understanding of trade union ideas. The compositors, for example, seem to have broadly adopted a voice that was derived from the commercial ideology of the eighteenth century. This dominant commercial idiom itself had been drawn from a stream of political language that had developed in response to civic humanist, or republican, ideologies. Yet rather than expressing an exclusively or even primarily political ideology, the compositors tended to express a set of social ideals that were civil rather than civic in nature.[93] The conscious adoption of this rhetorical position served to articulate both the reciprocal and joint interests that tied employers and employees, masters and journeymen, together. It may be quite possible that the language of political radicalism or popular constitutionalism was closed to them because their actions as trade unionists were perceived of as illegal under the common law. Nevertheless, the idiom of manners, interests and property entailed the assumption that all those who performed labour and exchange shared a similar function and therefore position in society.

The struggle for labour's voice

As we have seen, the dominance of discourses of mutuality and reciprocity in trade union ideology was due in part to the conscious adoption of eighteenth-century intellectual paradigms. In the case of Thomas Hodgskin, his contact with Thomas Brown's theories of cognition proved to have played an enormously influential role in his articulation of a 'labourist' vision of society. In the case of the London compositors, the language of the commercial ideologists crowded out alternative forms of expression and formed the basis for their understanding of civil society. Yet it is equally true that the idioms and vision of social reciprocity and mutuality were secured in some unions only as a result of struggles for control over its language, policies and purpose. Such struggles were often both exacerbated and accentuated by the exigencies of strikes and industrial disputes, which themselves brought into question the purpose and function of trade unions.

The early records of the Society of Operative Stone Masons provide the opportunity to see just how such internal struggles developed and were resolved. Numerous instances are recorded in the union's *Fortnightly Returns* of conflicts over the use of strikes and the control of informal job actions. In these circumstances, the masons' union leadership often cautioned its local lodges to act reciprocally and to refrain from striking in order to protect union funds, union membership and union influence. Thus in October 1837, for example, the Coventry, Weeden and Rhoad lodges wrote to the union's secretary, James Rennie, requesting permission and support for a strike against a local railway contractor. Rennie's response to the lodges' strike request reveals not only a pragmatic recognition of its likely fate but also a fundamental concern that the delicate reciprocal relationship that balanced trade union influence and employers' recognition was clearly at stake:

> In my opinion, [the strike request] is a very injudicious one; the season of the year alone ought to have prevented you from striking for an advance of wages; had it been the spring you would have something worth contending for, but now, should your employers (being pushed for their work) be compelled to accede to your request, and in a few weeks take advantage of you and reduce you again, you must be aware that our society would not assist you in resisting a reduction to 5s. And what would be the consequence? [Y]ou would either be compelled to submit, or go in quest of employment at a season of the year when probably it will not be so easily obtained as at the present period. In Mr. Peto's employment in Birmingham, were the men so inconsistent as to strike for 5s. 6d. per day, I have no doubt but he would soon be compelled to give it, being pushed with his work; still, they are aware it would take advantage of him, and only cause him and all other employers to take every advantage of us in their power. Such conduct would have a great tendency to bring our whole society into contempt.[94]

Such a perspective was perhaps understandable considering the recent collapse and failure of the grand Builders' Union in 1834.[95] However, conflicts between local lodges and the national executives over the necessity and efficacy of strikes seem to have constantly put such ideas to the test. The London lodge in particular appears to have found itself at odds with the union executive over its strike policy. In 1836, for example, it pushed the union to support strikes that had been undertaken contrary to the union's rule of soliciting a strike grant from its central offices before initiating industrial action. In response, the union secretary, Rennie, was forced to remind the lodge that 'it is our undeniable right to prevent Masons from persisting in conduct which ruins the Masons' trade. Experience has shewn, that there are Masons who will not act as they ought unless compelled; and further, that compulsion has the effect of causing their adherence to their duty, even when persuasion and reason will not, for the state of the Union where it flourishes is mainly attributable to the strict enforcement of its rules and penalties.'[96] Then, in 1837, masons at work on Blackfriars Bridge successfully staged an unoffical strike against the introduction of piece-work and a rate reduction while their application for a grant to strike was still being decided by the union.[97] But when related issues led to another unofficial strike among masons working on the Greenwich railway the following February, the union secretary once again weighed in against the local lodge:

That these strikes are legal according to rule there is no doubt, but, we consider, at this inclement season, (seeing the depressed state of our funds) it would
have been more prudent and politic to have submitted to a little infringement,
and refrained from striking untill [*sic*] there was a better opportunity of re-
dressing the grievances; as it must be evident to every observer, we have not the
means of supporting those who have been combating their oppressors all winter, and which have cost our society such a sum to maintain; therefore, by
engaging in conflicts under such circumstances, is placing us in eminent danger
of injuring the most vital interests of our society.[98]

Conflicts between the great London contractors and local masons continued to sour industrial relations in the building trades as work proceeded on
the Parliament buildings and the embankment. The well-known strike
against Grissell and Peto, the contractors for building of Parliament, apparently enforced a degree of unanimity upon the lodge and the union, but by
1844 the union once again could be found resisting the strike weapon. The
union's *Fortnightly Returns* asked:

When will our caution against Strikes have the desired effect? Will our members never be convinced of their destructive tendency, and abandon the thought,
or will they continue to cut off every sprout of prosperity as it makes it[s]
appearance amongst us? Did we not know from whence the evil came, we
might imagine that there were 'snakes in the grass,' that vile wretches were
sent amongst us to sow the seeds of discontent as soon as a few were gathered
together, which, like an 'invisible shell,' explodes and destroys us; but, alas!
such is not the case, it is the hydra much worse to contend with, that has so
long delayed our progress. We may rail against the oppression, – declaim against
tyrants, – and denounce the grasping avarice of our taskmasters, but none of
them are half so great a bar to our progress as our own avaricious and over-
bearing dispositions, our want of fellow-feeling, and brotherly regard for each
other, and finally, our preference of what we miscall our rights, to that which
is more just and expedient.[99]

These appeals to morality, reciprocity, generosity and fraternity are not
solely an artefact of an ancient moral economy or abstract political radicalism. More importantly, they are indicative of a contested terrain of images
and symbols in which a shared discourse was open to conflicting interpretations. Local lodges often found such counsel difficult to comprehend
because union definitions of reciprocity and reasonableness were so far different from their own. Thus when the union executive advised moderating
the demands of the Coventry, Weeden and Rhoad lodges in 1837, noted
previously, they responded:

Now this same secretary of ours ... had the audacity to write ... to Coventry,
deprecating the brothers for what he calls inconsistency, in taking an advantage of our employer in our unreasonable demand. Good God, is it inconsist-
ent in working men to better their condition? Men who are the real producers
of wealth; men who, after toiling and bleeding to keep a set of lazy and indo-

lent plunderers in luxury, are very frequently doomed to pass their declining years in some accursed bastile [*sic*], or in obscurity, starvation and wretchedness! Ah! worthy brothers, we have hitherto been used worse than brutes, let us now strive to be men.[100]

In a similar manner, the London masons defended their negotiations with a group of master builders from the executive's disapproval by resolving, perhaps with a bit of irony, that 'a reciprocal and good understanding should exist between ourselves and our employers'.[101]

The struggle over labour's voice among the masons, however, was perhaps most pronounced over the issue of subcontracting. During the early nineteenth century, the building trades had been racked by the problems caused by the rise of general contracting. As Richard Price has shown, general contracting not only threatened the traditional stability and hierarchies of the building trades, but also encouraged building on speculation, competitive underbidding, and increased exploitation.[102] Subcontracting became a particular source of friction between the building masters and workers because it was often associated with poorer working conditions, lower wages, speed-ups and piece-work. To some building workers, however, subcontracting appeared to offer the opportunity of becoming small masters. The masons' union executive seems to have been particularly interested in maintaining this 'avenue of social mobility'.[103] Yet not all masons agreed, and the dispute within the union over subcontracting revealed an even deeper conflict within the union over the nature and function of trade unionism.

When Thomas Shortt replaced Rennie as secretary of the union in 1838 he was almost immediately faced with this issue. Several Bristol masons at work on the Great Western Railway had solicited the union for a grant to strike against subcontracting on the line. Within days of receiving this request, Shortt received a second letter from another group of masons complaining that a strike would be unproductive not only because 'these subcontractors gave the best wages on Line' but also because it would be likely to lead to the introduction of non-union labour.[104] Shortt's response defended subcontracting at the same time as it rejected the plea to strike:

We must confess, that the conduct of the brothers of Bristol reflects but little credit on their judgment or love of justice, in attempting to coerce the very men who have been instrumental in raising their wages. The season of the year itself should have prevented them making such an application, even had there been any cause – but we see no cause, quite the reverse. We consider any member of our society has a right to sub-contract, and any law to prevent them would be completely despotic and unjust; the principle we should have in view is the wages and hours, and earnestly request our members to pause before they grant a strike on such grounds, particularly at this season of the year ...[105]

This appears to have settled the issue for the moment, but several months later a group of lodges floated the suggestion that the union's *Fortnightly Returns* publish a list of names of all subcontractors. Once again, Shortt was moved to defend subcontracting as a mason's right.[106] This time, however, Shortt's decision elicited a number of angry responses. The Manchester lodge, for example, refused to accept his judgement. They claimed that piece-work and subcontracting were 'the evils that most oppressed them' and that they had 'spared neither money nor labour to put an end to both'.[107] Even more strikingly, however, the Newcastle upon Tyne lodge responded in a manner that revealed that the issues at stake were not merely those of a mason's 'right' to subcontract but concerned the fundamental purpose and objectives of trade unionism. Initially, the lodge argued against the increased exploitation that resulted from subcontracting. 'Subcontracting', they wrote, 'is the means of causing a most unnatural practice of competition amongst the producers of wealth, which competition is always the means of keeping down the price of labour, inasmuch as the sub-contractor puts that into his pocket which ought to go into the pockets of the labourers, while at the same time it encourages a competitive system in the working department, which is injurious to the health and intellect of our members.' However, Shortt's claim that subcontracting was a mason's right evoked an even more expansive attack on the practice as well as the claim that the purpose of trade unionism was not to promote the social advancement of the workers but to redistribute society's wealth. 'As to the "question of right"', the Newcastle lodge protested,

> We conceive that no man has a right to accumulate a fortune out of the labour of another, and as our society is founded on equal rights to all its members, we are at a loss to know how it comes that one of its members is to be the slave of another; for no sooner do we find one of our class raised above us in the scale of society, than we almost uniformly find that man our greatest enemy. Our only object ought to be to get all out of the capitalist we can and keep it to ourselves as a community, and there is no method better calculated to effect this than a reduction in the hours of labour.[108]

Redolent as these statements are of Owenism, the Newcastle lodge continued to promote its cause through the remainder of the year and into the next.[109] During that time, the union formally declared its goal to secure shorter working hours for masons even if this meant smaller wage packets.[110] 'To permanently maintain or enhance the value of labour', the executive later explained, 'we must prevent a surplus supply of labourers from being in the market; this can only be done by decreasing the number of hours we at present toil.'[111] The adoption of a more explicit language of political economy appears to have only exasperated the Newcastle lodge. In August 1840, they proposed stopping union support for strikes altogether and applying the funds to undertake general contracting themselves. Their proposal was buttressed by an appeal to labour theories of value: 'IT IS BY LABOUR, AND LABOUR ALONE, THAT ALL WEALTH IS PRO-DUCED. The wealth by us so produced, by being accumulated in the hands of the idles, has become the only barrier between us and our attaining the honest reward of our industry.' Their proposal even included a plan to raise nearly £12,000, 'a capital sufficient to commence contracting upon no very small scale'.[112]

Such plans, however, elicited complaints from Manchester, one of the largest and most powerful lodges in the union. The Manchester lodge pro-tested against placing 'such wild and visionary schemes as that from New-castle-upon-Tyne' in the *Returns*, especially when there are more immediate issues that needed to be debated such as whether to merge the strike funds and sick funds.[113] Perhaps not surprisingly, the discussion of such 'schemes' was silenced thereafter. Whether other issues effectively displaced this debate cannot be determined, but its disappearance is striking nonetheless.[114] In-deed it is likely that the business of trade unionism superseded its utopian aspirations.

Conclusion

For our purposes, both the practicality of the Newcastle lodge's scheme and the extent of its support within the union is less significant than the fact that the influence of one of the largest lodges with the implicit backing of the union executive was able to short-circuit such a debate. It is not even neces-sary to argue in a romantic strain that trade unionism was thereby impover-ished by the silencing of such utopian voices. The path to a labourist vision of society was often indirect and sometimes tortuously so. Its intellectual contributors were numerous and not limited to political radicalism, moral economism or religious sentimentalism. Many working-class autodidacts were either directly or indirectly familiar with the language, discourse and theory of eighteenth-century 'elite culture', a term which now obviously needs to be re-examined. Moreover, labour's vision of society was not imma-nent in such sets of ideas. As the case of the Operative Stone Masons hope-fully shows, such a vision was a result of struggles within the union to define its purpose as well as its language. The fact that such languages of reciproc-ity and morality still held purchase was perhaps not because they were bear-ers of the dead hand of custom but because they still had the power to make sense of an otherwise incomprehensible world. Why this might be so and what this world was like are the subjects of the remainder of this book.

Notes

1 James Vernon, *Politics and the People: A Study in English Political Culture, c. 1815–1867* (Cambridge: Cambridge University Press, 1993), p. 6; David

Mayfield and Susan Thorne, 'Social History and its Discontents: Gareth Stedman Jones and the Politics of Language', *Social History*, vol. 17: no. 2 (May 1992), pp. 165–9.

2 James Epstein, *Radical Expression: Political Language, Ritual and Symbol in England, 1790–1850* (New York: Oxford University Press, 1994), pp. 3–28; Vernon, *Politics and the People*, pp. 295–33.

3 Epstein, *Radical Expression*, pp. 100–46.

4 Gareth Stedman Jones, 'Rethinking Chartism', in *Languages of Class: Studies in English Working Class History, 1832–1982* (Cambridge: Cambridge University Press, 1983), pp. 90–178.

5 John Belchem, *Popular Radicalism in Nineteenth-Century Britain* (New York: St Martin's Press, 1996), p. 36; Stedman Jones, *Languages of Class*, pp. 18–19.

6 Stedman Jones, 'Rethinking Chartism', pp. 102–10.

7 Stedman Jones, 'Rethinking Chartism', pp. 112–44.

8 For a brief account of the perceived areas of divergence between the two, see Jon Lawrence and Miles Taylor, 'The Poverty of Protest: Gareth Stedman Jones and the Politics of Language: A Reply', *Social History*, vol. 18: no. 1 (January 1993), pp. 7–8. However, Joyce's own response, 'The Imaginary Discontents of Social History: A Note of Response to Mayfield and Thorne, and Lawrence and Taylor', is printed in the same issue of *Social History* at pp. 81–5.

9 Patrick Joyce, *Democratic Subjects: The Self and the Social in Nineteenth-Century England* (Cambridge: Cambridge University Press, 1994); see also Joyce's brief description of his contribution to the debate about class in Joyce, ed., *Class* (Oxford: Oxford University Press, 1995), pp. 127–30.

10 Patrick Joyce, *Visions of the People: Industrial England and the Question of Class, 1840–1914* (Cambridge: Cambridge University Press, 1991), p. 113.

11 Joyce, *Visions of the People*, pp. 87–113.

12 Joyce, *Visions of the People*, pp. 88–91, 99–102.

13 Keith McClelland, 'Time to Work, Time to Live: Some Aspects of Work and the Re-Formation of Class in Britain, 1850–1880', in Patrick Joyce, ed., *The Historical Meanings of Work* (Cambridge: Cambridge University Press, 1987), p. 196.

14 Stedman Jones, 'Rethinking Chartism', pp. 175–8.

15 Noel W. Thompson, *The People's Science: The Popular Political Economy of Exploitation and Crisis, 1816–34* (Cambridge: Cambridge University Press, 1984), pp. 219–28.

16 Such a notion is expressed by Joyce, *Visions of the People*, pp. 101–2, and is perhaps reflective of William H. Sewell Jr's influential book, *Work and Revolution in France: The Language of Labor from the Old Regime to 1848* (Cambridge: Cambridge University Press, 1980).

17 E.P. Thompson, *The Making of the English Working Class* (New York: Vintage Books, 1963), pp. 778–9.

18 Thomas Hodgskin, *Labour Defended Against the Claims of Capital* (1825; London: Labour Publishing, 1922). See also E.K. Hunt, 'Value Theory in the Writings of the Classical Economists, Thomas Hodgskin, and Karl Marx', *History of Political Economy*, vol. 9: no. 3 (1977), pp. 322–45, and Samuel Hollander, 'The Post-Ricardian Dissension: A Case Study of Economics and

Ideology', *Oxford Economic Papers*, vol. 32: no. 3 (November 1980), pp. 370–410. Some of this material has previously appeared in my 'The Origins of Thomas Hodgskin's Critique of Political Economy', *History of Political Economy*, vol. 27: no. 3 (1995), pp. 493–515, where further references to the secondary literature may be found. Many of the propositions that first appeared there have now been more thoroughly addressed in David Stack, *Nature and Artifice: The Life and Thought of Thomas Hodgskin (1787–1869)* (Woodbridge, Suffolk: Boydell Press, 1998).

19 Hodgskin, *Labour Defended*, pp. 21–8, 71–2, 103–4.
20 These lectures were published under the title *Popular Political Economy*. Hodgskin went on to publish *The Natural and Artificial Right of Property Contrasted* in 1832. As argued in my 'Origins of Thomas Hodgskin's Critique of Political Economy', these works, as well as Hodgskin's other early publications, exhibit the pre-eminent place cognitive and epistemological theory held in his analysis of contemporary society.
21 David Pears, *Hume's System: An Examination of the First Book of his TREATISE* (Oxford: Oxford University Press, 1990), p. 63.
22 See Bernard Rollin's introduction to Thomas Brown, *Inquiry into the Relation of Cause and Effect*, 4th edn (1835; Delmar, N.Y.: Scholar's Facsimiles and Reprints, 1977), pp. v–xvii.
23 Thomas Hodgskin, *The Word BELIEF Defined and Explained* (London, 1827), p. 18; Stack, *Nature and Artifice*, pp. 92–3.
24 Pears, *Hume's System*, pp. 65–6, 75.
25 Thomas Brown, *Sketch of a System of the Philosophy of the Human Mind*, ed. Daniel Robinson (1820; Washington, D.C.: University Publications of America, 1977), pp. xi–xiii.
26 The principle of association was similarly important to Hume. See Pears, *Hume's System*, pp. 67–74.
27 Brown, *Sketch of a System*, pp. 42–4.
28 Brown, *Sketch of a System*, p. 70.
29 Brown, *Sketch of a System*, pp. 183–4.
30 Brown, *Sketch of a System*, pp. 192–5.
31 Brown, *Sketch of a System*, p. 192.
32 Brown, *Sketch of a System*, p. 199.
33 Brown, *Sketch of a System*, p. 260.
34 Brown, *Sketch of a System*, p. 228.
35 Jaffe, 'Origins', pp. 498–9; Hollander, 'Post-Ricardian Dissension', pp. 381–2; see also the comments of Daniel Robinson in his introduction to Brown's *Sketch of a System*, p. xxxiii.
36 Hodgskin, *Labour Defended*, pp. 36–7; Jaffe, 'Origins', p. 499.
37 Hodgskin, *Labour Defended*, pp. 38–44.
38 Hodgskin, *Labour Defended*, pp. 45–6.
39 Hodgskin, *Labour Defended*, pp. 51–2.
40 Hodgskin, *Labour Defended*, pp, 66–7.
41 Hodgskin, *Labour Defended*, pp. 52–66.
42 Hodgskin had secured an introduction to Francis Place in 1815, who subsequently introduced him to the circle of utilitarians, including James Mill and Jeremy Bentham. They encouraged Hodgskin to undertake a trip to Germany

and Mill actually drew up a research plan for him. Upon his return, Hodgskin resided in Edinburgh, where he was frequently in contact with J.R. McCulloch. By 1819 and 1820, however, he had become increasingly dissatisfied with many of the tenets of political economy, especially the theories of Malthus and Ricardo, and by 1821–22 he had completed a manuscript article on Brown but twice had failed to get it published. That manuscript apparently has not survived, except as it may have been incorporated into *The Word BELIEF*. On Hodgskin's references to this article, see Place Papers, British Library Additional Manuscript 35153, ff. 200–3, 215–16. On Hodgskin's life, see Elie Halévy, *Thomas Hodgskin*, ed. and trans. A.J. Taylor (London: Ernest Benn Ltd, 1956) and Stark, *Nature and Artifice*, pp. 34–88.

43   Stedman Jones, 'Rethinking Chartism', pp. 134–7; see also Stark, *Nature and Artifice*, *passim*. The term 'Ricardian socialism' is of little value, as most authors now agree. However, whether some other generic term can be employed to tie together the anti-capitalist writings of Hodgskin, William Thompson, J.F. Bray, Piercy Ravenstone and John Gray is less certain. It has recently become popular to label Hodgskin a 'Smithian socialist', a notion first propounded in Noel Thompson's *The People's Science*, p. 98. This has since been repeated by several authors, including John Saville, *1848: The British State and the Chartist Movement* (Cambridge: Cambridge University Press, 1987), p. 214, and William Stafford, *Socialism, Radicalism and Nostalgia: Social Criticism in Britain, 1775–1830* (Cambridge: Cambridge University Press, 1987), p. 239. However, Hodgskin clearly envisioned his work as a direct assault on several essential elements of Smith's work, particularly the origins of the division of labour and the specialization of labour: see Jaffe, 'Origins', pp. 504–7. More recently, Stark has elaborated Stedman Jones's contention that Hodgskin was essentially within the mainstream of popular political radicalism.

44   Hodgskin, *Labour Defended*, pp. 86, 88.

45   Hodgskin, *Labour Defended*, pp. 71–2; Steadman Jones, 'Rethinking Chartism', pp. 134–5; Jaffe, 'Origins', pp. 500–1.

46   William Sewell's recent analysis of the Abbé Sieyes offers a French perspective on the significance of this social concept. See William H. Sewell Jr, *A Rhetoric of Bourgeois Revolution: The Abbé Sieyes and What is the Third Estate?* (Durham, N.C.: Duke University Press, 1994), pp. 75–108.

47   Hodgskin, *Labour Defended*, pp. 108–9.

48   Albert O. Hirschman, *The Passions and the Interests: Political Arguments for Capitalism before its Triumph* (Princeton: Princeton University Press, 1977).

49   J.G.A. Pocock, *The Machiavellian Moment: Florentine Political Thought and the Atlantic Republican Tradition* (Princeton: Princeton University Press, 1975), pp. 423–505.

50   J.G.A. Pocock, 'Cambridge Paradigms and Scotch Philosophers: A Study of the Relations between the Civic Humanist and the Civil Jurisprudential Interpretation of Eighteenth-century Social Thought', in I. Hont and M. Ignatieff, eds, *Wealth and Virtue: The Shaping of Political Economy in the Scottish Enlightenment* (Cambridge: Cambridge University Press, 1983), p. 241.

51   W. Robertson, *History of the Reign of the Emperor Charles V*, ed. Felix Gilbert (Chicago: University of Chicago Press, 1972), p. 67, cited in Hirschman,

Passions and the Interests, p. 61.

52 J.G.A. Pocock, *Virtue, Commerce, and History* (Cambridge: Cambridge University Press, 1985), pp. 48–9, 113–21.

53 Pocock, *Virtue, Commerce, and History*, pp. 48–9.

54 Ellic Howe, ed., *The London Compositor: Documents Relating to Wages, Working Conditions and Customs of the London Printing Trade, 1785–1900* (London: Oxford University Press, 1947), pp. 202, 268–9.

55 See below, Chapter 6; see also Howe, ed., *London Compositor*, *passim*; L.D. Schwarz, *London in the Age of Industrialisation* (Cambridge: Cambridge University Press, 1992), pp. 169–75; Iorwerth Prothero, *Artisans and Politics in Early Nineteenth-Century London: John Gast and His Times* (1979; London: Methuen and Co., 1981), pp. 40–3.

56 J.A.W. Gunn, *Politics and the Public Interest in the Seventeenth Century* (London: Routledge, 1969), pp. 3–4, 41; Hirschman, *Passions and the Interests*, pp. 36–8.

57 Modern Records Centre, University of Warwick Library, National Graphical Association, London Region: London Society of Compositors (hereafter MRC, NGA), Mss. 28/CO/1/1/1, Minute Books of the London General Trade Society of Compositors (hereafter LGTSC Minute Books), 1827–29.

58 *Address of the General Trade Committee* (1834) quoted in Howe, ed., *London Compositor*, p. 207.

59 *Report of the Special Committee on the Apprenticeship Question* (1877) quoted in Howe, ed., *London Compositor*, pp. 309, 313.

60 *Report of the General Trade Committee of the Compositors of London* (1834) quoted in Howe, ed., *London Compositor*, p. 211.

61 Adam Smith, *An Inquiry into the Nature and Causes of the Wealth of Nations*, ed. E. Cannan (1776; Chicago: University of Chicago Press, 1976), bk i, ch. viii, p. 74.

62 MRC, NGA, Mss. 28/CO/1/1/1, LGTSC Minute Books, 5 February 1828.

63 MRC, NGA, Mss. 28/CO/1/1/2, LGTSC Minute Books, 13 February 1832.

64 *Annual Report* (1836), London Union of Compositors, quoted in Howe, ed., *London Compositor*, p. 236.

65 MRC, NGA, Mss. 28/CO/1/1/2, LGTSC Minute Books, 5 May 1829.

66 *To the Employers in the Printing Trade of the Metropolis*, 24 November 1890, reprinted in Howe, ed., *London Compositor*, p. 318.

67 Hirschman, *Passions and the Interests*, pp. 31–48.

68 Gunn, *Politics and the Public Interest*, *passim*.

69 The term 'reciprocal interest' is taken from Gregory Claeys, *Thomas Paine: Social and Political Thought* (Boston: Unwin Hyman, 1989), p. 94.

70 Pocock, *Virtue, Commerce, and History*, pp. 48–50, 110–15.

71 Howe, ed., *London Compositor*, pp. 155–6.

72 Howe, ed., *London Compositor*, p. 220.

73 The term is Pocock's. See *Virtue, Commerce, and History*, p. 48, and 'Cambridge Paradigms and Scotch Philosophers', pp. 242–3.

74 MRC, NGA, Mss. 28/CO/1/1/1, LGTSC Minute Books, 5 February 1828.

75 Howe, ed., *London Compositor*, p. 232.

76 N. Phillipson, 'Adam Smith as Civic Moralist', in Hont and Ignatieff, eds, *Wealth and Virtue*, p. 189.

77   John Rule, 'The Formative Years of British Trade Unionism: An Overview', in Rule, ed., *British Trade Unionism, 1750–1850: The Formative Years* (London: Longman, 1988), p. 15.

78   See, for example, P. Bailey, '"Will the Real Bill Banks Please Stand Up": Towards a Role Analysis of Mid-Victorian Respectability', *Journal of Social History*, vol. 12: no. 3 (Spring 1979), pp. 336–53; Anna Clark, *The Struggle for the Breeches: Gender and the Making of the British Working Class* (Berkeley: University of California Press, 1995).

79   Howe, ed., *London Compositor*, p. 152.

80   MRC, NGA, Mss. 28/CO/1/1/1, LGTSC Minute Books, 5 February 1828.

81   Howe, ed., *London Compositor*, p. 261.

82   MRC, NGA, Mss. 28/CO/1/1/2, LGTSC Minute Books, 13 February 1832.

83   Howe, ed., *London Compositor*, pp. 207–8.

84   *Report of the Proceedings respecting Periodical Publications* (London, 1834) reprinted in Howe, ed., *London Compositor*, p. 198.

85   MRC, NGA, Mss. 28/CO/1/1/3, Union Committee Minute Books, 10 October 1833.

86   MRC, NGA, Mss. 28/CO/4/1/1/10, *Annual Report of the Trade Council to the Members of the London Union Committee* (London, 1839).

87   Howe, ed., *London Compositor*, p. 217.

88   Quoted in I. Hont and M. Ignatieff, 'Needs and Justice in the *Wealth of Nations*: An Introductory Essay', in Hont and Ignatieff, eds, *Wealth and Virtue*, p. 33; see also I. Hont, 'The Language of Sociability and Commerce: Samuel Pufendorf and the Theoretical Foundations of the "Four-Stages Theory"', in A. Pagden, ed., *The Languages of Political Theory in Early-Modern Europe* (Cambridge: Cambridge University Press, 1987), pp. 253–76.

89   J. Rule, 'The Property of Skill in the Period of Manufacture', in Joyce, ed., *Historical Meanings of Work*, pp. 99–118.

90   Rule, 'Property of Skill', p. 110.

91   MRC, NGA, Mss. 28/CO/1/1/6, Trade Council Minute Books, 27 December 1837.

92   Claeys, *Thomas Paine*, pp. 5, 9, 16–18.

93   Pocock, 'Cambridge Paradigms and Scotch Philosphers', p. 240.

94   MRC, Union of Construction, Allied Trades and Technicians: Friendly Society of Operative Stone Masons (hereafter MRC, OSM), Mss. 78/OS/4/1/1, *Fortnightly Returns*, 13 October 1837.

95   On the Builders' Union, see Sidney and Beatrice Webb, *The History of Trade Unionism*, new edn (1894; London: Longman, 1920), pp. 124–32, 150–1.

96   MRC, OSM, Mss. 78/OS/4/1/1, *Fortnightly Returns*, 2 September 1836.

97   MRC, OSM, Mss. 78/OS/4/1/1, *Fortnightly Returns*, 4 August, 1 September, 15 September 1837.

98   MRC, OSM, Mss. 78/OS/4/1/1, *Fortnightly Returns*, 16 February 1838.

99   MRC, OSM, Mss. 78/OS/4/1/6, *Fortnightly Returns*, 5 September 1844.

100 MRC, OSM, Mss. 78/OS/4/1/1, *Fortnightly Returns*, 13 October 1837.

101 MRC, OSM, Mss. 78/OS/4/1/1, *Fortnightly Returns*, 17 January 1839.

102 On the building trades generally, see Richard Price, *Masters, Unions and Men: Work Control in Building and the Rise of Labour, 1830–1914* (Cambridge: Cambridge University Press, 1980), especially pp. 19–39 for this period.

103 Price, *Masters, Unions and Men*, pp. 29–31.
104 MRC, OSM, Mss. 78/OS/4/1/1, *Fortnightly Returns*, 11 October 1838.
105 MRC, OSM, Mss. 78/OS/4/1/1, *Fortnightly Returns*, 11 October 1838.
106 MRC, OSM, Mss. 78/OS/4/1/1, *Fortnightly Returns*, 9 May 1839; Shortt's response is quoted in Price, *Masters, Unions and Men*, pp. 29–30.
107 MRC, OSM, Mss. 78/OS/4/1/1, *Fortnightly Returns*, 6 June 1839.
108 MRC, OSM, Mss. 78/OS/4/1/1, *Fortnightly Returns*, 6 June 1839.
109 See, for example, MRC, OSM, Mss. 78/OS/4/1/1, *Fortnightly Returns*, 1 August 1839.
110 MRC, OSM, Mss. 78/OS/4/1/1, *Fortnightly Returns*, 13 February 1840.
111 MRC, OSM, Mss. 78/OS/4/1/1, *Fortnightly Returns*, 9 April 1840.
112 MRC, OSM, Mss. 78/OS/4/1/1, *Fortnightly Returns*, 13 August 1840.
113 MRC, OSM, Mss. 78/OS/4/1/1, *Fortnightly Returns*, 27 August 1840.
114 Vigorous disputes erupted within the union over alleged improprieties by the executive committee which were then followed by the Parliament strike in 1841.

3

Workplace bargaining during the Industrial Revolution

> ... about 90 percent of interactions with management is developing relations. The other 10 percent is you need to be able to squeeze them when the time comes. (Tom Balanoff, Service Employees' International Union, 1999[1])

Bargaining and historians

It is commonly assumed that before the middle of the nineteenth century workers and their employers rarely bargained over wages. While social and economic historians have laboured for decades to uncover a wealth of information on the different types and forms of wages and payments to workers during the early industrial period, on the political struggles of the early nineteenth century that focused on such important developments as the Combination Acts or the repeal of the apprenticeship clauses of the Elizabethan Statute of Artificers, and on the characteristics of early trade union organization, there is still surprisingly little research on how wages were set, whether wage rates were negotiated, and what forms these negotiations may have taken.[2] Most historians would probably still accept as accurate this description of early nineteenth-century industrial relations which was written nearly three decades ago:

> In so far as there was a pattern of industrial action up till 1860, it took this shape. The action had some marked characteristics. Notice of intended or desired changes was sometimes given in writing. Employers posted notices in their works, workers put notices in the press or submitted them by letter. Usually, date lines were given after which strikes or lockouts were enforced. In some cases workers gave notice of their intentions by striking. Wherever resistance to a demand was met there would be an immediate strike or lockout action.[3]

Industrial relations, by this account, were fractured, communications between the parties were cryptic, and the terms were unconditional. Notably, this description does not provide for the possibility that negotiations could occur or that compromise was possible. It is a description that satisfies a certain romantic notion of nineteenth-century industrial relations as well as an economistic one, even though it might run counter to our intuitive understanding of how shopfloor relations are, at least in part, mutually constructed.

Still it is perhaps not unfair to say that this portrait of industrial relations, drawn here by V.L. Allen, is the one that continues to dominate the perceptions of both professionals and non-professionals alike. Its persistence can be explained by a number reasons, one of which is the role it plays in the 'master narratives' of British social and economic history during the early industrial period. Such a master narrative may read roughly as follows: industrialization and its handmaiden political economy engendered a dramatic confrontation between customary and modern forms of work and employment relationships. Neither the inclination nor the institutional machinery existed to negotiate this crisis. The early nineteenth century was therefore characterized by similarly dramatic forms of confrontation, which some prefer to call class conflict, including popular political activism, the rise of socialism, and a wave of strikes and lock-outs.[4] The evident defeat of these movements, and the apparent victory of both industrialization and the principles of political economy by 1850, led workers to recognize that their future could be secured only through accommodation. Since labour could not resist capitalism, it instead had to learn 'the rules of the game'.[5] Modifications in political economic theory, especially the abandonment of the wage-fund theory, also reflected this new economic era.[6] The second half of the nineteenth century, therefore, was characterized by the rise of forms of industrial relations that were more appropriate for this new age. Trade unions retrenched themselves and moderated their goals, while businesses sought social peace and industrial stability; collective bargaining regimes became the characteristic expression of this *rapprochement* between capital and labour.

Of course, despite its staying power, ongoing research has significantly revised and amended this thesis. The old chronology of industrialization that formed the background to this social crisis and implied the widespread and rapid transformation of Britain's economy by 1830 or 1840 has been replaced by a much slower and more uneven Industrial Revolution.[7] The acceptance of political economy and capitalism that seemed to characterize the post-1850 trade union leaders has been questioned by those who seek to assert the persistence of popular radicalism among trade unionists.[8] The success of the doctrines of political economy, *laissez-faire* ideology, Free Trade and individualism can now be viewed in a Christian and evangelical light.[9] The dominance of class in nineteenth-century social thought, as we have seen, is now hotly contested.[10] Yet such insights and revisions seem to have had relatively little effect on those deeper romantic narratives that either avoid the workplace altogether or have replaced the drama of the shopfloor with Victorian melodrama. Put simply, how people lived on the job is still a relatively unknown terrain.

In many important respects, our images of life on the job are both the creation and the legacy of the industrial literature of the mid-nineteenth century. There is often surprisingly little that separates the 'serious' analysis of industrial relations before 1850 from the scenarios constructed by Dickens or Gaskell. However, this convergence should serve to make historians more circumspect of their assumptions and not less so, particularly after the 'linguistic turn'. As Robert Gray has pointed out, mid-nineteenth-century discussions of employment relations in both the journalistic accounts of workplaces and the industrial novels of the period are located within the contexts of rather specific literary forms and social debates. Generally, this literature studiously avoids discussion of the workplace experience, and contemporary accounts of the social relations between employers and workers are usually deployed to serve didactic purposes. Thus the investigative literature of the period almost inevitably shifts the focus of its inquiry from the people on the shopfloor to the machines in the factory. The industrial novel, on the other hand, locates employment and class relations largely within the context of contemporary debates over the most appropriate models of paternalism, gender relations, sympathy, and the like. In both, the workplace experience itself remains enigmatic.[11] One important effect of the dominance of these literary forms may have been the failure to create a language with which to discuss forms of industrial relations that were not cast either in the form of melodramatic confrontations or in the form of benign paternalism. Consequently, historians have been left the difficult task of reconstructing the characteristics of early nineteenth-century industrial relations from accounts that either ignored the workplace altogether or were made to suit specific ideological purposes.

However, the romantic discourse to which Dickens, Gaskell, Trollope and others contributed was only one of several narrative traditions that created the image of early nineteenth-century industrial relations as convulsive, atavistic and atomistic. Of at least equal importance, as we have seen, was the discourse of political economy, a discipline that emphasized the assumptions that there was an irreconcilable conflict of interests inherent in the employment relationship and that there were theoretical restraints placed upon the efficacy of negotiation and compromise by the 'iron law of wages' and the wage-fund theory.[12] The contemporary and subsequent influence of political economy's discourse was, of course, commanding; its constructs and categories were eventually adopted at least in part both in law and public policy. Even among the early socialists, there was a general failure on the part of social and economic theorists to construct models of either industrial relations or the wider labour market that incorporated a role for wage bargaining and shopfloor negotiations.[13] That failure was of the imagination as much as discourse. Therefore, it is not surprising to find that evidence of these forms of industrial relations was ignored by contemporaries because, as in the industrial novel, there were no categories or languages to comprehend them.

It would seem likely that the generation of professionals who fashioned themselves as labour historians, including this author, would have been well-placed to rectify these omissions – that is, supposing for the moment that there have been omissions. However, significantly different ideological influences and narrative traditions ironically reproduced similar obstacles to comprehension. Obviously, many labour historians who came of age in the 1960s and 1970s, when the field itself was established, were groomed upon Marxist and *marxisant* ideas or found them very appealing. Thus the research agenda was often dominated by attempts to find examples of class consciousness, class struggle or class hegemony. Negotiation and compromise found little space here, except as they may have served to have exemplify certain accommodationist elements within the working class. In a related way, Sidney and Beatrice Webb's landmark examinations of British trade unionism, *The History of Trade Unionism* and *Industrial Democracy*, provided not only a storyline for nineteenth-century trade union development but also a set of institutional yardsticks by which to measure labour's progress. Although the Webbs clearly recognized the existence of workplace and district-wide collective bargaining in the nineteenth century, they nonetheless focused instead on the development of labour's national and institutional apparatus.[14] One does not have to go to the extent of dismissing class entirely as an analytical concept, as Patrick Joyce has done, to recognize that the embeddedness of these tropes or themes in the narrative of industrialization may have led labour historians to dismiss or at best marginalize evidence that did not fit the plot.

Perhaps surprisingly, these narratives also continue to hold sway among industrial relations specialists where the intense study of collective bargaining institutions is staple fare. According to one prominent industrial relations textbook, there may be some early evidence of collective bargaining, but 'major and sustained development did not take place until the middle of the nineteenth century'.[15] Richard Hyman similarly locates the origins of collective bargaining in the second half of the nineteenth century, when a series of legislative enactments carved out a collection of unique legal 'immunities' that served to protect collective bargaining from prosecution under the common law.[16] Keith Sisson marks 1898 as a key date, for it was then that engineering employers constructed a set of model collective bargaining agreements with their workers.[17] Alan Fox recognized, as the Webbs did, that the repeal of the Combination Acts in 1825 technically established the legal foundation for collective bargaining. And, like the Webbs again, he understood that with or without the Combination Laws some employers found it to their advantage to meet and negotiate with unions or workers' representatives.[18] Nevertheless, even while rejecting a 'Whig version of industrial relations history', Fox saw the second half of the century as the period during which collective bargaining became one of the 'preferred strategies' among trade unions because 'it was simply the best means available for self-defence against superior power and arbitrary rule'. At the same time, middle-class employers, basking in the glow of mid-Victorian prosperity, leaned confidently toward a more conciliatory set of social relations with their employees. The Victorian state, Fox concludes, made a virtue out of necessity and recognized that the establishment of 'procedural equality' through the passage of new laws governing collective bargaining was preferable to the potential harm of outright trade union suppression.[19]

Collective bargaining and workplace organization

But given the traditional tools of interpretation employed by historians and industrial relations specialists, how is one to interpret the following events? In 1831, Thomas Hepburn led a union movement among the Durham and Northumberland coal-miners that sought specifically to alter nine terms of their annual hiring contracts.[20] On 29 April, seven delegates of the pitmen's union met with seven mining 'viewers', or colliery managers, representing nearly forty firms in the region. Their meeting was convened at the Turk's Head Inn in Newcastle upon Tyne. After some discussion, provisional agreements were reached that day on three issues: on two, management conceded to labour's terms, while on a third labour accepted management's counter-offer. Both parties, however, agreed to meet for a second round of bargaining on 3 May at noon. At this session, management requested an amendment to one item already agreed upon at the previous meeting, which labour accepted. A further item of contention was agreed upon after management acknowledged their willingness to revise the language of the contracts. Significant progress was made toward the resolution of an additional issue. By the day's end, therefore, four major issues remained to be resolved and an agreement was close at hand on a fifth.

The following day, however, management's position hardened and its representatives were instructed to refuse to negotiate on the remaining terms in dispute. The union subsequently staged a large rally on the next day, at the conclusion of which the union leader, Hepburn, informally discussed the status of the negotiations with the Marquess of Londonderry, the head of one of the largest collieries in the region, who had been observing the rally at the head of a brigade of dragoons. Hepburn intimated that the parties were close to an agreement and that the union was eager to resolve the impasse. Upon Londonderry's report of this discussion, management's negotiating committee was instructed to re-open negotiations. In the ensuing days, however, management's unanimity broke down, individual firms began to broker their own bargains with their employees, and labour's goals were achieved, if only for this contract period.[21]

Such a series of events seem highly unlikely in the context of our current understanding of industrial relations in Britain before 1850. Many of the characteristics of 'modern' collective bargaining appear to be present here. If, for argument's sake, we use some of the Webbs' standards to define collective bargaining, this example reveals the presence of a collective, not individual, agreement of regional or district-wide influence, as well as the negotiation of contracts through representatives.[22] Moreover, an apparently civil discussion of the issues was entered into personally by Hepburn and Londonderry, which itself might appear extraordinary to our sensibilities, particularly considering Londonderry's later reputation as a vicious and vindictive strike-breaker. Admittedly, several other aspects of 'advanced' collective bargaining institutions are not present. For example, there are no salaried, professional negotiators, although management's viewers may well qualify in this regard, and, while there was a rudimentary system of dispute resolution that could be applied to individual cases,[23] there was no permanent machinery to resolve disputes over the district contract. Finally, the union itself was not a permanent institution. This, as has often been remarked, was one of the most important characteristics the Webbs used to define a modern trade union.[24]

Of course, it has also been noticed that the Webbs' standards of judgement were based upon a notion that might be called institutional teleology, as well as upon a particular set of moral and political values. While they scrupulously noted variations in trade union and collective bargaining forms, the Webbs nonetheless implied that industrial relations in Britain had developed *from* individual or shop bargains *to* collective bargains administered by permanent, professional, salaried officials. Similarly, they believed that trade union institutions had evolved *from* local 'primitive' democratic forms *to* 'advanced' forms of national representation. In their opinion, the complex agreements covering the Lancashire cotton operatives most closely approached the ideal of collective bargaining because 'the whole machinery appears admirably contrived to bring about the maximum deliberation, security, stability, and promptitude of application'.[25] Subsequent developments during the first half of the twentieth century seemed to confirm this trajectory as union officials became professionalized, national amalgamations emerged, and state policy promoted the 'tradition of voluntarism'.[26]

However well this model may have characterized the historical trends of British industrial relations between 1850 and 1950, it can be made to apply to either end of this long nineteenth century only with great difficulty. At the latter end of this period, the report of the Donovan Commission of the mid-1960s revealed that there were indeed two systems of industrial relations in Britain, not one. The first corresponded roughly to the Webbs' description of industry-wide, professionalized bargaining institutions, but the second was characterized by a multiplicity of autonomous shopfloor bargains negotiated by powerful shop stewards.[27] A distinction, in fact, was drawn between the negotiating functions and authority of these 'workshop democracies' and the more distant constitutional institutions of the trade union proper.[28]

The former was often described as an 'informal' system of industrial relations, while the latter was more 'formal'. The Webbs' narrative also became less convincing in the years after 1979 when the Conservative governments' legislative programmes unequivocally rejected the voluntarist tradition of industrial relations in order to weaken trade union power generally, remove the unions' most significant immunities from civil and criminal liabilities, prop up employer authority, and generally subject labour (but not necessarily employers) to a free, competitive market.[29] Therefore, the contours of both trade union history and the history of industrial relations are now much less distinct than they may have been before 1950, and the suitability of the Webbs' standards of analysis are much less convincing.

Indeed, considering these new perspectives, one could easily stand the Webbs on their heads and assert that the 'permanent' institutions of British industrial relations are not the constitutional organizations of trade unionism that the Webbs recognized, and that have waxed and waned according to state policy and legal opinion, but those 'workshop democracies' described in detail by the Donovan Commission.[30] These organizations, however primitive the Webbs may have thought they were, constituted the foundation of much collective action not only in the post-Second World War period but also in the late eighteenth and the early nineteenth centuries, the other end of the long nineteenth century. Indeed, as Clive Behagg notes, before 1850 the incidences of formal trade unionism are exceedingly rare compared to the continuous process of workplace organization and the 'network of tacit agreements' that mediated relations among workers and, it might be added, between workers and their employers.[31] These late eighteenth- and early nineteenth-century workplace organizations had much in common with the 'workshop democracies' that appeared to spring up after the 1950s, but which Richard Price has shown were already characteristic of the late nineteenth-century building trades.[32]

As in the case of those twentieth-century shop stewards, the earlier shopfloor organizations tended to arise in circumstances where bargaining opportunities presented themselves.[33] Thus industries that relied on piece-rates, such as mining, printing and textiles, often bore witness to active workplace organizations, although the term 'workplace' should be defined as broadly as possible. In many trades where outworking was common – the woollen or silk trades, for example – the locus of piece-rate bargaining often shifted out of the household and into the wider community.[34] 'Workplace' organizations could arise not only among workers who shared the same shopfloor, but also out of the collective action of numerous households who had similar arrangements with merchants or factors. Moreover, beyond the piece-rate itself, extensive bargaining opportunities were also opened by the wide variety of special payments and allowances that modified the wage packet. In mining, for example, the north-east pitmen received different piece-rates if the seam of coal was above or below a certain width, while

London compositors received higher rates for working in candlelight during the winter or setting type in a foreign language. The presence of perquisites, such as the well-known cases of 'chips' in the royal dockyards or 'thrums' among woollen-weavers, could easily become a bargaining issue.[35] In a similar manner, the large number of deductions often imposed on workers' wages frequently became the subject of shopfloor bargaining efforts. In addition to deductions for rent, tools or candles, some workers, such as stone masons, regularly suffered reduced rates of pay during the winter, the extent or timing of which could become the subject of bargaining efforts.[36]

Typically, the workplace organizations that arose to respond to these bargaining opportunities were both democratic and decentralized, two characteristics that were also common to the modern shop steward movement.[37] To the Webbs' credit, they described the democratic nature of early unions in detail, although they consistently applied pejorative qualifiers such as 'primitive', 'rudimentary', 'childlike' and 'infant' to them.[38] Yet, as in the shop steward movement, the democratic structure of early workplace organizations was often able to accurately give voice to workplace concerns as well as to provide an acceptable means by which workplace disputes could be mutually resolved. It is interesting to note in this regard that the antipathy most employers expressed toward workers' organizations during the late eighteenth and early nineteenth centuries was commonly directed against formal, constitutional trade union structures and not necessarily shopfloor organizations. Many employers may have agreed with Lord Londonderry, who, in the circumstances described above, professed a willingness to bargain and negotiate with his own employees but vehemently protested against the 'interference' of a wider union.[39] Similarly, the Preston cotton master Samuel Robinson 'dismissed as invalid any form of association beyond a mill committee'.[40] As late as the 1860s, the general secretary of the Amalgamated Society of Engineers, William Allan, testified before a parliamentary commission that 'as a rule the employers are prepared to meet a deputation from their own workmen'.[41] Of course, this did not make other employers any less hesitant to rely upon military or legal force to prevent or dissolve organizing efforts they viewed as a threat to their authority. Indeed, as Anthony Howe suggests, despite the fact that most masters accepted the proposition that supply-and-demand forces necessitated wage bargaining, such issues 'were often inextricably confused in the mind of the entrepreneur' with those of authority and 'mastery'.[42] Nonetheless, as in the case of the Coventry ribbon-weavers discussed in the following chapter, even 'unfair' employers could sometimes be found at the bargaining table when workshop organizations and 'fair' masters combined to try to negotiate a local or regional settlement.[43]

Like the shop stewards of the late twentieth century, the strengths of these workplace organizations were complemented by what modern industrial relations specialists have perhaps unfairly described as 'weaknesses' or 'inadequacies'.[44] Foremost among these was the extreme decentralization of authority and the consequent conflict between the shop steward's authority and that of the 'formal' union, if and when there was one. Although formal unionization efforts in the early period were obviously not as common as they were to become later, identical conflicts and issues often arose nonetheless. Among the London compositors, for example, a famous union boycott of one printing firm, which lasted over seventy-five years, was precipitated by one shopfloor group's refusal to adhere to union working rules.[45] The break-up of the Durham and Northumberland coal-owners' committee in 1831, referred to earlier, was in fact prompted by the miners' acceptance of management's offer at one or two collieries despite the union's official rejection.[46]

These jurisdictional conflicts between shopfloor and union organizations were, as Michael Terry notes for the modern case, 'intimately related to steward ideology'.[47] Modern shop stewards as well as early nineteenth-century workplace organizations tended to give priority to bargaining over pay rather than to 'bigger' issues. In fact, they often prided themselves on both their autonomy from 'formal' trade union structures and the primacy they gave to satisfactorily resolving immediate shopfloor problems. Consequently, shop stewards' interests, and those of their earlier counterparts, have sometimes been characterized as 'narrow', 'sectional' or 'short-term', and their understanding of society as limited to 'trade union consciousness', 'reformism', 'economism' or 'factory consciousness'. Implicit in this judgement is the assumption that shop stewards, or early workplace organizations, should have known better; they should have addressed the broader issues of class, capitalism or social revolution. However, perhaps a more appropriate means of interpreting such ideas has been suggested by the work of James Scott, who argues that resistance to declining incomes, poor working conditions or other social and economic problems begins 'close to the ground [and is] rooted firmly in the homely but meaningful realities of daily experience'. Enemies are personalized; the values being defended are commonplace ones; the goals are modest; and the means of resistance are prudent and realistic.[48] The historian need not revere or demonize such actions – nor need they segregate experience from discourse – to recognize that such a pattern of resistance and compromise was also typical of most early nineteenth-century workplace organizations. Most workplace groups and unions fought against 'unfair' or 'dishonourable' masters. They defended commonplace values such as 'fairness', 'honour' and 'rights'. Their goals were 'fair play', 'justice', 'reciprocity' or 'common humanity'. Their methods included petitioning, deputations, output restriction, bargaining or the strike, while they simultaneously sought recourse at times to appeals to law, mediation and arbitration.

Such attempts to 'civilize capital', as Patrick Joyce calls this working-class perspective, were nonetheless located within a set of social and economic relationships that were distinctly unequal. A common discourse, as Scott's study suggests, does not elide such differences.[49] Nor should the presence of various bargaining regimes in the late eighteenth and early nineteenth centuries – workplace bargaining, collective bargaining, mediation or arbitration – be allowed to obscure these fundamental differences. To borrow a portion of William Reddy's term – a term now *de rigueur* among economists – the relationship between workers and their employers was 'asymmetrical'.[50] Put simply and obviously (but not in the sense that economists necessarily deploy the term), this means that employers wielded greater political and legal authority, controlled greater economic resources, and maintained a wider sphere of social influence than their employees.[51] This gave employers enormous advantages both in the labour market and on the shop floor. However, where Reddy sees this asymmetry solely in terms of how it was used to discipline and control workers, what he terms the 'exchange asymmetry' inherent in the employment relationship might be better understood as an association that was characterized by unequal power relations as well as reciprocal needs. Not only did the worker need a job, but the employer needed workers. Indeed many employers probably preferred to sustain long-term attachments with workers if for no other reason than it reduced the costs of retraining and supervision. This ambivalence between power and needs is what gave meaning and a measure of influence to working-class demands for justice and fairness.

Theories of collective bargaining

One prominent way in which this relationship came to be institutionalized in Britain was through the elaboration of a variety of collective bargaining regimes. Certainly, such developments have garnered much less attention from historians than strikes for a variety of reasons, several of which already have been discussed. Yet added to these must be the unavailability of suitable and adequate historical sources. Negotiations were far less 'newsworthy' than strikes and therefore probably attracted far less attention, as continues to be the case today.[52] This makes the recovery of these events extraordinarily difficult; it also leaves open the question of whether or not the events that will be discussed below are representative of common practices. While it would be enormously difficult to calculate the incidence of collective bargaining during the late eighteenth and early nineteenth centuries, a largely descriptive account of their types, scope and functions is feasible here. Later chapters will attempt to analyse in detail the terms, process and character of these bargaining relationships.[53]

The Webbs' importance for any discussion of these issues cannot be overestimated, as has already been intimated. After all, they coined the term 'collective bargaining', which they understood not only as a practice that functioned in the same manner as individual bargains struck between employers and employees, but also as one of the three methods by which trade unions enforced rules designed to assist and protect their members.[54] The Webbs identified several different stages in the development of collective bargaining institutions, each of which was determined by the extent of a trade union's influence over the labour market. In the first, 'shop club' bargains were collectively negotiated between individual workshop committees or representatives and their employers or foremen. In the second stage, local masters and union representatives of the same trade met to negotiate and settle wage rates and working rules for a particular town or district. And in the third stage, national collective agreements superseded and governed both 'shop club' bargains and district-wide bargains. The influence of classical economic theory here is obvious. Not only does the 'higgling of the market' retain its significance in these observations, but the relationship between specialization and the extent of the market is wholly applied to trade union development. Indeed the Webbs concluded that 'the development of a definite and differentiated machinery for collective bargaining in the trade union world coincides, as might be expected, with its enlargement from the workshop to the whole town, and from the town to the whole industry'.[55]

The Webbs' work, however, receives as many plaudits for its pioneering observations as condemnations for its 'institutionalist' perspective. In fact, many years ago the Webbs' description and definition of collective bargaining became the focus of a rather heated academic exchange among industrial relations specialists.[56] The debate was initiated by Allan Flanders, who lamented the use of the term 'collective bargaining' because it was inaccurate and misleading.[57] For Flanders, while collective bargaining may have been collective it was not an economic bargain. Parties to collective bargaining, he argued, did not stand in the same relation to each other as did buyers and sellers in the market. Instead, collective bargaining was a political relationship between organizations. As in politics, diplomatic tools of persuasion and compromise were more characteristic of collective bargaining sessions than marketplace buying and selling. More importantly, however, Flanders argued that far from being a market activity, collective bargaining was a form of 'job regulation', that is, a process that establishes rules to govern the employment relationship.[58] Further, he noted, and most industrial relations specialists would still agree, that different types of job regulation were primarily distinguished by the authorship of the employment and work rules, that is, who wrote the rules.[59] On this basis, Flanders concluded that collective bargaining was a misnomer because the process actually involved two parties sitting down together and, through the deployment of various means of diplomatic persuasion, jointly creating a set of working rules that both sides could accept. Far from being a market activity, therefore, Flanders construed collective bargaining as a form of 'joint regulation'. As such, collective bargaining was not principally about pay claims or other economic matters. Since joint regulation was a rule-making process, collective bargaining was actually an activity that established laws and 'rights'. Therefore, Flanders asserted, the principal success of a trade union 'lies less in its economic achievements than in its capacity to protect [its members'] dignity'.[60]

The Webbs' 'classical view', as Flanders called it, was not left undefended. However, as in many such debates, a satisfactory definition of collective bargaining lay somewhere in the middle. It is clear, as Alan Fox wrote in his response to Flanders, that the attempt to sever collective bargaining and trade unionism from its economic functions was misguided.[61] To dismiss 'the intensity of conviction, effort, and feeling which many trade unionists appear to invest in pay claims' was ill-conceived, as was the more general denial of the economic elements of collective bargaining.[62] Conversely, the extra-economic elements of collective bargaining are clearly of great importance as well. Collective bargaining is a rule-making activity that often governs more than pay claims. Even in the late eighteenth and early nineteenth centuries, 'joint regulation' in many trades covered a wide spectrum of issues, including dispute resolution, working conditions, hours, manning or apprenticeship, and quality or craftsmanship. The results of such collective bargains often became translated into custom and thereby established 'rights'. Moreover, collective bargains, even if ostensibly about pay alone, were intimately connected with non- or semi-economic criteria such as status, reputation, honour, dignity and fairness. Therefore, collective bargaining combines the functions of settling pay claims and wage disputes as well as establishing working rules and other forms of joint regulation.

There have been a bewildering variety of attempts to classify types of collective bargaining according to the levels at which bargaining is conducted, the scope of the bargaining agreements, the nature of the rule-making process, the origins and authorship of working rules, and doubtless many more. However, in the introduction to a standard textbook on British industrial relations first published in 1979, Hugh Clegg was probably right to note that there was no logical starting point for a discussion of the subject. Nonetheless, he began his book with an analysis of workplace bargaining because it was 'uniquely important in contemporary Britain compared with the past'.[63] While I would vigorously dispute workplace bargaining's historical uniqueness, this study follows Clegg in assigning it primacy of place. Even in the most well-organized trades of this period, such as the London compositors, there were several areas of pay bargaining that were reserved for negotiation at the workplace. In areas governed by price lists, various additions or reductions from the standard rates were bargained over at the workshop, pit or factory level. Workplace bargaining therefore was not a result of the particular economic conditions of post-Second World War Britain, as Clegg argued, but it was instead characteristic of British industrial relations from its inception.

The law, the state, and collective bargaining

Before entering into a discussion of these aspects of collective bargaining, however, it is important to say something briefly about the role of the state and the legal context of employment relations generally in the late eighteenth and early nineteenth centuries. Of course, there was no such thing as employment or labour law during this period. Instead, laws covering employment relations variously originated in common and statute law, torts and criminal law. Moreover, contracts played only a very small role in the eighteenth and nineteenth centuries, as Otto Kahn-Freund observed. Much of what he called 'the atrophy of the contract of employment in nineteenth century England' was due to jurists, Blackstone in particular, who viewed employment as a status relationship rather than a contractual one.[64] As a result, employees could enforce at law few if any 'rights' granted to them by contract, but often had to rely instead on legislative remedies – and legislative penalties – to secure legal standing.[65]

Foremost among these were the laws governing masters and servants as well as combination and conspiracy. The law of master and servant was derived largely from the Elizabethan Statute of Artificers (1562) and, as Douglas Hay has written, 'obliged the servant to work faithfully, diligently, and obediently; the master to maintain the servant in sickness and pay wages when due; and either to give a quarter's notice before terminating the relationship'.[66] Subsequent case law and legislation during the seventeenth and eighteenth centuries increasingly provided for magistrates' summary jurisdiction over employment-related disputes such as the failure to pay wages, leaving work unfinished, absenteeism, and the like. However, for the late eighteenth and early nineteenth centuries, the overall effect of magisterial intervention is not at all clear. Hay suggests that rural magistrates may have employed a much harsher form of disciplinary 'paternalism' than justices in urban manufacturing areas. In the larger towns and cities, magistrates often served to mediate informally in disputes between masters and servants, a point that Norman McCord also has emphasized.[67] When magistrates did make an order, they ruled in favour of the servant's complaint about as often as they ruled in favour of the master.[68] Moreover, magistrates in industrial areas could often be found encouraging workers to select representatives to meet a like number of employers over the bargaining table. Evidence for this type of activity can be found in areas as distinct as Macclesfield, Newcastle upon Tyne or London, as will be discussed later in this chapter.

There may have been several reasons why magistrates in manufacturing areas appear to have acted more equitably in master and servant disputes than their rural counterparts. Hay suggests that in many urban areas it was still uncommon during this period for justices to be industrial employers. Therefore, they could afford to be paternal. Yet even in places where magistrates were interested parties, the threat of unions, organized resistance or rioting by large groups of workers may have weighed heavily on their minds.[69] Magistrates may also have been motivated by a desire to avert the difficulties of unemployment that inevitably added to the burden of the local rates. Nevertheless, Hay reminds us that for whatever reasons and however well-disposed magistrates may have been toward hearing employment cases fairly, there were still two sets of penalties for breaking the law. For servants, remedies were limited to fines upon the master; the master, however, could seek both fines and penal sanctions, including imprisonment, hard labour and whipping. In master and servant cases, therefore, charges were brought and settlements often made 'in the shadow of the prison'.[70]

The laws of master and servant, however, contained no provisions for groups of workers who sought collectively to alter the terms of their employment. In these circumstances, common laws against conspiracy and statute laws against combination could be brought to bear. The connection between combination and conspiracy dates at least to the 1720s, and the large number of statutes against combination in particular trades after that date would appear to be indicative not only of the growth of trade unions but also of the increasing importance of collective bargaining.[71] Indeed, as James Moher points out, several of the eighteenth-century combination acts included some form of wage regulation or wage-fixing machinery.[72] Of course, between 1799 and 1825 combinations were outlawed altogether, but the precise impact of the Combination Laws is difficult to measure. Moher is convinced that masters often preferred to avoid recourse to the Combination Laws and that workers were rather adept at evading it.[73] While there is no evidence of a nationwide crackdown on trade unions, the very least that may be said is that the relatively few prosecutions for combination during this period must have had a chilling effect on trade unions generally. Indeed the great burst of union activity in 1825–26 would seem to testify to this.

Still, the legislative intent of the Combination Laws is in marked contrast to the observed actions of the urban magistracy. As will be discussed below, local officials and magistrates often responded to the growth of trade unions not by prosecuting them, but by attempting to consolidate and regularize collective bargaining. Masters' and workers' representatives were urged to resolve their disputes peacefully, sometimes at a local inn or pub. An urban paternalism, a fear of rising rates, and the desire to avoid disorder and riot all may have contributed to this tendency to encourage a voluntary system of resolving industrial disputes. Another factor may have been their often evident lack of experience or expertise necessary to make informed decisions on disputes that arose within the mysteries of a trade. For these reasons, urban magistrates could frequently be found acting without regard to the Combination Laws through their mediation of industrial disputes. In the end, what Parliament seemingly had taken away from the sphere of industrial relations with one hand, the local magistracy may have given back with the other.

Finally, workers and their employers could frequently find themselves before the law on cases that arose out of actions for debt. Rather than proceed through the summary jurisdiction of a magistrate under the master and servant laws, workers often had recourse to courts of requests to resolve wage disputes. Although this aspect of the legal context of industrial relations is relatively under-studied and is much less known than either the Combination Laws or the master and servant laws, one legal historian has suggested that these courts were 'the most ubiquitous institutions of civil justice in the first half of the nineteenth century'.[74] The origins of these courts lay in an Act of Common Council that first created the London Court of Requests in 1518. The act provided for the appointment of two aldermen and four commoners by the Court of Aldermen to meet twice weekly at the Guildhall and hear cases for the recovery of small debts not exceeding 40s. In 1606, the jurisdiction of the court was confirmed by an act of Parliament, which also limited appeals to the superior courts at Westminster and thus avoided costly litigation.[75]

During the late seventeenth century, similar courts of requests were established by local acts of Parliament in Bristol and Newcastle upon Tyne. After the middle of the eighteenth century, courts of requests began to be established even more widely throughout the country. An estimated fifty such local acts were passed before 1800, and by 1846, when the jurisdiction of the courts was effectively transferred to the new county courts, there were about 400 courts nationwide. Nationally, the courts of requests heard as many as 200,000 claims in 1830, a figure that had doubled to about 400,000 by 1840.[76]

The popularity of these courts was principally based on their economy, accessibility and expeditiousness.[77] Although the particular authority of each court varied slightly according to the terms of the original act, proceedings and judgments in all courts of requests were supposed to be swift and conclusive. Generally, courts of requests prohibited or severely restricted the participation of barristers or attorneys. Summonses were produced and served for only a nominal fee.[78] The courts sat year round and hearings were usually scheduled within two or three days of the initial summons. Both plaintiffs and defendants presented their own testimonies, even though such testimonies would have been inadmissible in the common law courts. No juries were employed and decisions were issued summarily by the lay judges, called commissioners, who were unpaid and accepted no fees except perhaps for a monthly dinner. The principal duty of a commissioner, as stated in most acts, was to decide cases in 'equity and good conscience', not law or precedent. Attempts to appeal the court's decisions were rarely successful and strict limits on appeals were imposed by statute in the early seventeenth century.[79]

The caseloads of many of these courts was substantial. In 1830 alone, the Tower Hamlets Court of Requests handled over 28,000 claims, while the City of London court heard nearly 10,000. Roughly comparable numbers were heard before courts of requests in the major provincial cities such as Manchester (over 10,000), Sheffield (over 11,000) and Birmingham (nearly 8,000).[80] Unfortunately, for the historian, these were not courts of record and therefore the remaining archival material is surprisingly meagre. Information on the occupations or social status of defendants and plaintiffs was rarely recorded, although it does survive for a very few jurisdictions. In a sample of cases heard between 1830 and 1840, for example, Arthurs found that as much as 10 or 11 per cent of all claims before the Bristol and Sheffield courts involved wages or claims for unpaid work and materials.[81] Margot Finn's analysis of the Bath court similarly reveals the frequency with which artisans, labourers and servants sued for back wages or unpaid bills.[82]

Indeed it is apparent that the regulation of the employment relationship was considered by many courts to be one of their more important functions. In 1774, for example, an inquiry into corruption and other irregularities among the London court beadles, those officials who were responsible for processing warrants and executing attachments, found that their abuses were a particular 'Inconvenience to the several Plaintiffs, applying to recover small Debts, many of whom being Women-Servants, Journeymen, Handicrafts-Men or Labourers, to recover Wages, and others, whose Time is of first Consequence to themselves or Families'.[83] Similarly, William Hutton, who was a commissioner on the Birmingham Court of Requests and author of one of the few extant treatises on the procedures and judgments of these courts, noted that the 'fluctuation of wages is a constant source of wrangling between master and man' because 'new work, or new methods of working, demand new prices'. In deciding such cases, Hutton claimed that the commissioners often relied solely on common sense and the 'going rate' for wages in the trade.[84]

Like the master and servant laws, however, these courts primarily dealt with cases between individual employers and employees, but there is some evidence from London that trade unions regularly referred their members to them in order to recover back wages. The Minute Books of the London compositors' union from the 1820s and 1830s contain accounts of several instances in which union members were encouraged to pursue their claim against a master printer through the Court of Requests.[85] Moreover, some employers evidently felt that the courts favoured working-class plaintiffs. The famous radical reformer Henry Hetherington was hauled before the Court of Requests for failure to pay for the printing of a broadside on parliamentary reform. He lost and complained loudly about the decision.[86] Alexander Galloway, owner of one of London's largest engineering firms, testified before Parliament that the Court of Requests 'invariably give verdicts against the employers' and 'they have always allowed the men to be judges of their own value, if there was no special agreement to the contrary'.[87]

The legal context of employment relations and collective bargaining was therefore quite complex and its impact not at all clear. Urban magistrates may have acted to mitigate the disadvantages that workers suffered under the master and servant laws and even encouraged collective bargaining. Nevertheless, recognizing the asymmetry of those laws is necessary to understanding the context of their application. Similarly, the Combination Laws may have been frequently evaded by workers and avoided by employers, but their potential for harm regularly affected how disputes were resolved and how workers organized. Finally, the courts of requests may have provided a measure of relief for working-class plaintiffs in employment disputes. However, without a great deal more research and the recovery of more archival materials, the full extent of that relief is still a matter of conjecture.

Workplace bargaining

Despite the renewed emphasis upon the role of the state and law in society, there remains good reason to suspect that not only do people know very little about the substantive rules of the law, but also that they construct a set of rules for their relationships that are beyond (or beneath) it.[88] Often these rules are derived from social norms or ethics and are enforced by forms of 'self help', such as gossip, ostracism, retaliation, or even personal violence. It should not be surprising, therefore, to find that groups of workers in a shop would seek to establish a set of working rules with their employer or manager that both regulated their relationship and adhered to a set of jointly held ethical standards. The interpretation of precisely how these ethical standards applied to certain situations need not be identical for both groups. Indeed many if not most shopfloor conflicts grew out of divergent interpretations of a shared discourse of values of what was 'fair', 'honourable' or 'manly'. However, this did not necessarily prevent the construction of collective bargains. Forms of collective bargaining grew up beyond the limits set by the law and constituted a method of self-made rule-making that is not uncommon even in the most highly regulated legal regimes.

The manner in which workers and employers sought to establish their own 'order without law' was often sensible and expedient.[89] Obviously, most workers were not members of formal trade unions, but, as is still the case today, this did not prevent them from entering into collective bargaining agreements with their employers.[90] Still, it is perhaps understandable that much of the surviving evidence of workplace bargaining comes from or is related to unionization efforts of the period because, as with periodicals, this was when the event became 'newsworthy'. Many workplace bargaining systems were already accepted as customary in the beginning of the nineteenth century. Particularly in piece-work industries, piece-rates were often collectively negotiated according to custom.[91] Perhaps the clearest example of this comes from the Durham and Northumberland coal industry. Although there are many instances of this that will continue to reappear throughout this book, certainly the clearest case can be built from the survival of a set of petitions and bargaining notes saved by John Watson, colliery engineer, or 'viewer', at Cowpen Colliery, Northumberland, in the early 1830s.

The workplace bargaining at this colliery began with the submission of a 'petetion' on 12 March 1831.[92] The five points of the petition are cryptic, seemingly arcane and nearly unintelligible to those not conversant with early nineteenth-century mining terms:

  1st We wish the Shilling's Corves to be abolish'd and at their Primitave state
  2[d] The Double Working 8[d] per Score
  3[d] The Wet Working 4[d] D°
  4th The 3[d] per yd advance for Narrow Work
  5th The Candle Money

While petitions were common during this period, and their connection to political petitioning important, this list of demands was not an ultimatum, as some historians would have it. Watson apparently understood this as the presentation of a bargaining position and he had his clerk draw up a copy of the petition with his responses.[93] He rejected the first and fifth demands but offered a negotiated response to the second, third and fourth. In the case of 'double working', for example, when two men work together in a single underground stall, Watson was willing to accept the increase of 8d per score of filled coal baskets, or 'corves', but only if the stalls were 4 yards wide or more. The 3d per yard increase for digging out walls or cutting doors – the 'narrow work' – was accepted because 'the old men have hitherto paid it to the young ones for doing this description of work'. And the higher rates for 'wet working', when the work had to be done in standing water, was accepted on the condition that it would be paid only when the water was coming in from the roof but apparently not if it was seeping up through the floor.

Three days later, on 15 March, Watson received a second petition. This one contained an additional five demands, three of which had been adopted from the general proposals put forth by the nascent union movement led by Tommy Hepburn.[94] The form of collective bargaining had thus shifted from a workplace bargain to 'multi-tiered' collective bargaining in which district-wide negotiations were complemented by agreements reached in individual workplaces.[95] The relationship between workplace bargaining and trade unions will be discussed in greater detail below. However, two new workplace demands were also added, illustrating the continuing process of negotiation. These new workplace demands concerned payments to younger pit workers involved in the movement of coal from the face, where the coal was dug, to the bottom of the mine shaft, where it was hauled above ground. Again, the terminology is obscure, but the bargaining process is apparent. The colliers demanded that the 'putters', who manually dragged the filled coal baskets from the face to the underground tramway, receive 1s 4d for each score of baskets they hauled up to 60 yards. They also asked that the day-rate of 'rolley drivers', who guided horse-drawn tubs full of coal along the main underground tramways, be increased to 1s 4d.

As in the first petition, the colliery clerk drew up a list of the petition's demands and included Watson's response.[96] For the putters, Watson offered 1s 2d for an initial distance of 80 yards or less; for the rolley drivers, he offered 1s 2d per day and reminded the colliers that the owners already provided an additional daily allowance for candles to the drivers. It is not quite clear how the negotiations continued from this point in part because Watson subsequently began serving as one of the employers' principal representatives to the district-wide negotiating sessions in Newcastle mentioned earlier. However, an undated note appears to indicate that bargaining continued and that meetings were planned between labour and management at the workplace level. This particular memorandum bears the heading 'General Grievances stated to exist by the Pitmen which is to be discussed' and includes a list of the principal issues in dispute as well as several notes that appear to be discussion points for a forthcoming meeting.[97]

Such workplace bargaining, or pit bargaining, was quite common throughout the northern coalfield at this time and remained so well into the twentieth century.[98] Further evidence of such bargaining can be culled from the newspapers of the period. While some have argued that the resort to the publication of demands by miners for rate changes was evidence of the lack of any system of collective bargaining during this period, in fact the opposite is the case.[99] For example, John Buddle, the region's most respected mining engineer, sought to resolve a dispute at Wallsend Colliery, Northumberland, by publishing an account of the colliers' demands and the owners' offers. The handbill, if read out of context, seems to portray the absence of bargaining. Buddle, of course, sought to represent the miners' demands as unreasonable and the handbill largely reads as if the miners' demands were rejected outright. However, the fortuitous survival of Buddle's own copy of the handbill reveals a different story altogether.[100] In the margin, Buddle has noted that for each offer he made, the pitmen responded with a second counter-offer that subsequently led to an agreement. Again, we have to make our way through the complex terminology of nineteenth-century coal-mining practices. Some demands, such as an increase of 6d for each score of corves worked in areas of the mine that required Davy lamps, were simply 'given up by the men'. However, others were not. Whereas the published language of the handbill unequivocally rejects the men's demands for an advance of 6d per score of baskets of thin 'rammel' coal that has been separated from large 'round' coal, Buddle's marginal note reads: 'Have agreed to take 4'. And where the text rejects the men's demand to reduce by half the fines for mixing stone with coal from 3d per quart, Buddle writes in the margin: 'Have agreed to pay 3^d for 3 quarts and 6^d for 4 quarts'. Thus, rather than reveal evidence of the absence of workplace bargaining, the publication of these details was itself a tool of negotiation employed to mobilize public support.

Workplace bargaining was not limited to the pits of the northern coalfield, but is evident as well in the workshops of the London printing masters and journeymen compositors. There the compositors' workplace organizations, called 'chapels', can be traced as far back as the seventeenth century and, as the Webbs noted, were possibly as old as printing itself.[101] The federation of these chapels into unions dates back to at least 1785 when a trade price list was first negotiated. Even as the compositors' unions became more prominent in the nineteenth century, a process that will be discussed in greater detail below, the function of the chapel to negotiate certain items of work continued to be important. In fact, the 1810 London Scale of Prices, which regulated many piece-rates throughout most of the century, specifically set aside several items 'to be paid by agreement between the employer and the journeymen'.[102] (Among these items, particular reference was made to the setting of footnotes in historical works 'if attended with more than ordinary trouble'.)

Workplace bargaining in the London printing houses could be undertaken amicably, but it could also easily become a test of wills as threats from both sides established a cycle of retribution. This was the case, for example, during a dispute at Gilbert & Rivington's printing house when three compositors were summarily dismissed after they had demanded payment for setting the type for the paper mailing wrappers of a tract. This issue was, in fact, a matter of great dispute during this period as periodicals became an increasingly important part of the printing trade.[103] Upon the advice of the compositors' union, the chapel was advised to insist on payment for the wrappers, and if refused, to demand a fortnight's notice before the men's dismissal, as required by the master and servant laws.[104] The chapel, amounting to forty journeymen compositors, refused to report to work the next morning and instead 'adjourned themselves ... to a neighbouring house' until the three dismissed men had met with the employer. The employer refused to yield on the matter of paying for the wrappers and, amidst complaints about union interference, gave the men their notice. The rest of the chapel returned to work after dinner apparently cowed by their master's authority.

However, these appearances masked only a temporary retreat in the process of workplace bargaining. At three o'clock that same afternoon, the manager, or overseer, of the shop appointed three other compositors to continue the same job. They refused. Upon hearing this, Gilbert himself, the master printer, assigned the job to another three compositors who 'went into the counting house, and informed the employers that they would not do the job without [payment for] the wrapper'. Recognizing the extent of this shopfloor unity, Gilbert wavered and began to negotiate directly with the compositors. During a lengthy conversation with the men, he asked them to do the work and to trust that no advantage would be taken of them. This was not sufficient for the chapel, which, in a second meeting, resolved to appoint a deputation to ask for 'an express promise' that all wrappers would be paid for, that all of the men would be reinstated, and that the three original compositors would be assigned to that job. This time the overseer met with the deputation. He encouraged them to forget about the dispute, go back to work, and again to trust him to 'do all in his power to obtain [payment for] the wrappers' for them. Still not satisfied, however, the chapel refused to work any more that day. A meeting was called for ten o'clock the next morning and a penalty of 2s 6d was levied on anyone who tried to work before then.

This action had the desired effect. The next morning, the overseer met again with the deputation from the chapel. He finally promised to pay the compositors for all wrappers, but asked that the men accept an exception for wrappers of tracts, the original subject of the dispute, which were printed on only half-sheets of paper. Moreover, he indicated that such work would be rare in the future and he would try to give the work to 'persons on the piece', who were roughly equivalent to part-time employees.[105] He concluded by assuring the chapel that they 'might rely on his carefully abstaining from coming in collision with them on disputed points; but if any of the works now disputed were given to the journeymen they were to go with them without asking any questions, as the required price would be paid'.

Obviously, not all workplace bargains were concluded on such favourable terms for the workers. The central office of the Operative Stone Masons often received reports of wage disputes in which workplace bargaining either failed to secure a negotiated settlement or was undertaken in only the most perfunctory manner. In 1836, for example, a contractor in Exeter sought to reduce the prices paid for building steps from 1s 2d to 10d per linear foot. When the masons offered to meet him half way and accept a reduction to 1s per foot, he 'haughtily refused' and the masons were forced out on strike.[106] However, even among the stone masons, whose *Fortnightly Returns* are a catalogue of strikes and lock-outs, evidence of more extensive workplace bargaining survives. The case of several Plymouth masons is perhaps not atypical. 'We have to inform you that we cannot settle matters with our masters', the secretary of the Plymouth lodge wrote to the Central Committee of the union, 'we have done everything in our power to come to a fair arrangement with them. We have offered to give up the breakfast-time, and have the hour to dinner, but they will not hear of it. When we wrote last, we did not think that any other master would attempt it, but Mr. Mitchell has got two more with him, where our members were working ...'.[107] Subsequently, a large meeting of union and non-union stone masons was held that apparently encouraged the employers to yield slightly. One of them eventually accepted the masons' offer, while Mr Mitchell would only agree to re-employ two of the union members and no more. The conclusion of this dispute was never reported to the union, but the final report indicates that five masons continued on strike and were being supported by strike funds.[108]

Indeed a great many strikes reported to the union were accompanied by some form of workplace bargaining. At Swindon, the building workers employed to erect a new station house in 1841 were involved in repeated conflicts over the introduction of piece-work, attempted wage reductions and extended working hours. An initial strike finally resulted in a written agreement that was produced only after 'several interviews with ... petty authorities'. The agreement read as follows:

REGULATIONS AS TO TIME UPON THE WORKS AT
SWINDON STATION
From 7 to 6 on Mondays
_____ 6 to 6 on Tuesdays, Wednesdays, Thursdays, & Fridays
_____ 6 to 4 on Saturdays
Taking ½ hour for Breakfast
_____ 1 ditto – Dinner
_____ ½ ditto – Watering each day.
Signed for Messrs. Rigby, GEO. LEWIS.

However, when the contractor arrived several days later he refused to ratify the agreement and this initiated another round of strike action.[109] In another instance at Birmingham, the masons refused to work with a non-union labourer. The next day discussions were held with the foreman, but when those failed to resolve the dispute a second round of negotiations was held with the contractor. The union reported:

After a deal of quibbling [the contractor] consented to re-employ those [union] men, but objected to pay what he had stopped in time and money from them, on their last and only pay on that job. He was however led to understand that he must do so before they would resume their employment. A little reflection had the desired effect, his foreman being again commissioned to inform our secretary the he would agree to *our* stipulation, and the men returned to work on the Tuesday morning.[110]

The actions of the Hebden Bridge lodge of masons may also serve to illustrate the tactical rather than antithetical relationship between strikes and workplace bargaining. There, the masons had reached an agreement with the contractors to reduce wages by 6d per day for the six weeks before and after Christmas. After the expiration of the final six weeks, the contractors refused to restore the 6d and consequently the masons went on strike. However, they also immediately contacted their foreman, who attended the union's meeting the following day. That meeting appears to have been quite perfunctory and yielded little more than the lodge's promise to poll the members of the neighbouring Todmorden lodge, who had also been covered by the Christmas agreement. However, during the course of the meeting the foreman awkwardly threatened to pay the higher rates but only to those masons that he favoured. Moreover, the masons insisted that they be reimbursed for any time lost. When the Todmorden masons later expressed their support for the Hebden Bridge lodge, the masons called out all of the other skilled trades on the site and initiated a 'general strike' the following day. The same morning that the strike began, the masons sent a letter to their foreman warning that 'if he did not come to an agreement he would have to pay all the men for their lost time for that day and after as long as he kept them out'. This seems to have had some effect. The foreman returned to the lodge at eleven o'clock that morning and acceded to the demand that all the masons' wages be restored uniformly but refused to pay for time lost because of the dispute. The masons steadfastly refused and the foreman was left to seek a meeting with the contractors on this final issue. At one o'clock that afternoon, he returned to the masons' lodge and agreed 'to pay every man for that day on the contract, which amounted to the sum of £20 5s. 6d. being only one day's wages for every man that he had prevented from working'.[111]

The apparent ready recourse to strikes exhibited by the compositors or stone masons, therefore, may not necessarily be indicative of the absence or failure of workplace bargaining. Unfortunately, this has often been the conclusion drawn from the admittedly fragmentary and often partial sources that survive, but it is also an assumption that is derived from a stadial interpretation of class relations under industrial capitalism. In fact, the purpose of strikes might have been precisely the opposite of that implied by this interpretation. Indeed a Liverpool architect in the 1830s suggested that building workers generally used strikes as a tool to initiate bargaining rather than to resolve a bargaining impasse. He noted a distinct contrast between this older 'tactical' use of the strike and a more confrontational form adopted by the newer broad-based but short-lived Builders' Union in 1833. When asked whether he had experienced any strikes before the formation of the Builders' Union, the architect responded:

> We have had strikes, but they assumed a different feature altogether; they have had strikes to get an advance of 1s. or 2s., then they have generally come with a deputation in a day or two and endeavoured to get us to agree to their terms; but on this occasion, although those men have been off nearly a fortnight, there has never been a man near the place ...[112]

While it may be too rash to argue that something as ephemeral and enigmatic as workplace bargaining was more important or more pervasive than the better-known established trade societies, the evidence from other regions and other trades suggests at least that a history of such 'informal' unionism needs to be more thoroughly integrated into the histories of both 'formal' trade unions and British industrial relations in the early nineteenth century, as Clive Behagg notes.[113] Workplace bargaining was probably a common and increasingly important aspect of working life in the early nineteenth century. In the case of Birmingham's small workshops, Behagg emphasizes the recurrent but transitory nature of workplace organization, its democratic form and its 'essentially opportunist' methods. 'Most trade-based action', he argues, 'was the work, not of formal trade societies but rather of groups of workers acting together to deal with a specific problem in their shop or in their trade.'[114] In the same town, T.J. Wilkinson, secretary of the Flint Glass Makers' Society, testified in 1868 that 'the great bulk of labour differences that come before the men in the trade are settled by the men and the employer in their own factory. I may say that 19 cases out of the 20 are settled by the men and the employers amongst themselves, and we [the union officials] do not know anything about it'.[115]

Mines and workshops were not the only locations where workplace bargaining thrived. The factories of the Lancashire cotton industry were the scenes of similar developments, although they have often been over-shadowed in the literature by the seemingly more dramatic accounts of district trade unionism. Fortunately, the work of H.A. Turner, an industrial relations specialist, illuminated the connections between modern trade unionism among cotton workers and their early nineteenth-century ancestors. Most importantly, he emphasized that the vitality and persistence of cotton workers' unions was based above all on 'informal' workplace organizations. It is perhaps worth quoting at length Turner's account of these organizations:

> In many ways, in fact, the early cotton unions resembled the 'unofficial movements' which have so frequently embarrassed official British union leaderships in modern times. There is the same basis in the workplace group, which may have informal 'friendly' functions as well as trade ones. There is the same federal super-structure – the shop stewards ('head shopmen' or 'box-stewards') forming the local committee, the representatives of local committees forming the 'movement'.... The modern 'unofficial movements', like the early unions, show an apparently flickering activity. They come alive – often formidably so – in times that the workers they influence consider critical, and subside when these crises have passed.[116]

'Head shopmen' not only acted as representatives to the wider unions, but at least among the Manchester spinners they also were 'individually responsible for bargaining at their own mills'.[117] Michael Huberman has done a great deal of work to uncover the nature and extent of the effort bargain between work and wages in the early nineteenth-century Lancashire cotton industry.[118] Such effort bargains were likely to have followed the general trends that Huberman lays out, but they were also subject to innumerable short-term shopfloor bargains that were negotiated between the 'head shopmen' and the cotton masters. Perhaps surprisingly, these bargains were sometimes initiated by masters who sought changes in working practices or prices. W.R. Greg, an avowed opponent of trade unions, admitted in 1833 that 'when I first went to short [time] work I did so in connexion [*sic*] with five other mills surrounding'. However, when the neighbouring mills broke the compact, several of Greg's workers planned to leave his mill. 'I called them together', he recalled, 'and stated my view of the case, and that I would either stop half of the mill or divide the work among them all; and they all said they would rather divide the work, and that they were willing to stay with me. I have generally found them sensible when matters were explained to them.'[119]

The existence of plant bargaining early in the nineteenth century almost certainly underlay the local and district-wide attempts by early cotton-spinners' unions to equalize wages. Indeed without its ubiquity the 'rolling strike' tactic, which was deployed as early as 1822, could hardly have been possible.[120] Perhaps the first 'rolling strike' and its relations to plant bargaining were described by William Bolling, a Bolton cotton master and later member of Parliament. In 1822, Bolton cotton masters had introduced new mules with about one hundred more spindles than the older models. In an attempt to recapture some of the higher piece-rate earnings that may have been ceded to the spinners through greater productivity, Bolling introduced steep 'discounts' for working on these 'larger wheels'. 'Our intention', Bolling admitted, 'in fixing the discount was to make the earnings equal, in the same time, on the different sized wheels.' The spinners resisted and eventually went out on strike. The dispute ended after a fortnight, but only after 'we had in the interval several conversations with the men, and it was at length agreed, that we should give them, I think it was, one-half of what they asked'.[121]

The success of the spinners at Bolling's mill encouraged other head shopmen to negotiate similar advances at two or three other mills in Bolton. In December 1822, the head shopmen at John Jones's Tydesley mill approached him seeking a comparable settlement. Jones reported:

> We stated that we could not advance your wages; and we supposed they had no cause to ask for an advance, because our numbers were fine, and they had very superior work to any mill in the neighbourhood, and therefore we hoped, they would be satisfied with what they got; they stated, that they had done their duty in asking, and would report our answer to the rest of the men. A week after this, some other men came down, and asked us if we had re-considered what they had asked for the week before; we said we had considered it, and we concluded that we would not advance; they then told us, that if we did not comply with their request, the shop would certainly strike.[122]

On 4 January 1823, the thirty-nine spinners at Jones's mill gave notice that they would strike in a fortnight's time, which they did. Jones claimed that over the next few weeks he repeatedly met with and tried to negotiate a resolution to the dispute. However, his failure to do so eventually led him to organize the Bolton cotton masters to produce a price list of their own, lock out the operative spinners, and prosecute several upon charges of both combination and criminal assault. As a result of this coordinated counter-attack, the Bolton 'rolling strike' collapsed and the spinners were forced to accept the masters' price list.[123]

The prevalence and spontaneity of shopfloor bargaining in textile factories is illustrated in particular detail for a slightly later date by the diaries of John O'Neil, a powerloom-weaver at Thomas Garnett & Sons in Low Moor near Clitheroe, Lancashire. In January 1860, the weavers there became alarmed by the volume of dust that was being produced by a new dressing mixture. 'There is more dust now in one day', O'Neil wrote in his diary, 'than we used to have in a week formerly.'[124] On 19 January, 'the weavers went as a body to the Master but he would give them no satisfaction'. The following day, there was a second meeting of the weavers who apparently stayed off work and selected a deputation of shopmen to meet the master, Thomas Garnett, again. This second meeting again failed to produce any result: 'When we went in we laid our complaint down, but he said he would not believe us, the stuff would injure no one, and if anybody had left through it they were sickly delicate people who were always badly. We tried to reason with him but he said he would not be dictated to by any weaver or body of weavers, and he would do just as he pleased, and if they did not like it they were at liberty to leave the place'. Upon reporting the results of their meeting to the rest of the weavers, it was decided to hold another shopfloor meeting the following Monday.

On Monday, O'Neil was elected chairman of a new group of weavers who were deputed to meet Garnett for a third time. Remaining off work, this meeting achieved more satisfactory results. Garnett agreed to reduce dust levels in the factory and upon that promise the men agreed to go back to work the following morning. The next morning, the weavers had not been at work for more than an hour when one of them was 'sent home' for 'making bad work'.[125] They 'all struck work again', held a shopfloor meeting, and agreed to send still another deputation to their employer. At this point, Garnett refused to meet again with the shopmen. Instead, it appears that he called upon Abraham Pinder, secretary of the East Lancashire Amalgamation of Power Loom Weavers' Associations, to intervene. Garnett later explained in his diary that 'we have put an end to the strike at Low Moor by having Mr. Pinder, the weavers' secretary at the mill. He is much better to do business with than the hands because he can calculate.'[126]

Nevertheless, Pinder's intervention reshaped the nature of the dispute. He encouraged the Low Moor weavers to organize public subscriptions for their support and to expand their demands to include broader rate increases. However, the district union's intervention did not subsume the importance of the shopfloor negotiations. As the weavers were canvassing the neighbourhood, they heard rumours that Garnett had complained that 'none of the weavers had been near him to see what he would do'. The weavers' deputation, therefore, was assembled once more and sent to meet him. This meeting produced an agreement to invite Pinder along with 'some of the weavers who could go into calculations' to a meeting the next morning. The meeting, O'Neil recalled, lasted three hours and was 'very courteous, very civil'. Moreover, it finally produced an agreement to raise most piece-rates and was widely approved by the weavers themselves.

As Turner rightly noted, these shopfloor organizations appear to have been ephemeral. They came alive in times of crisis and then subsided when they had passed. However, the ephemeral nature of these shopfloor organizations did not denote a lack of continuity. Often the same shop stewards, or 'shopmen', were repeatedly called upon to resolve disputes whenever they arose. This certainly seems to have been the case for O'Neil, who noted at least three further shop meetings on different issues over the following month and another interview with Garnett.[127] Moreover, while this particular dispute was ultimately transformed into a piece-rate issue, which was perhaps the most common source of workplace bargaining, its origin actually lay in a series of conflicts over workplace hazards and employment.

The opportunities that existed to elaborate workplace bargaining systems in the early nineteenth century were extremely varied. Along with piecework, closed shops and workplace hazards, the presence in several sectors of forms of subcontracting, many of which incorporated piece-work as well, was equally important. In some London shipyards, for example, the shipwrights subcontracted from a shipbuilder to build an entire ship by bargaining over the total cost of the job. Clifford Wigram, who owned a substantial shipbuilding firm on the Thames, indicated in testimony before Parliament that at least from mid-century, and probably dating back to 1825, some shipyards bargained with a representative of the shipwrights in their yard to undertake the construction of a new ship for an agreed price. The shipwrights then hired their own labourers in order to complete the task. P.J. Robson, the president of the Shipwrights' Provident Union, confirmed the fact that the men's representative was chosen from among the working shipwrights because 'between him and his mates he is considered to have better judgment'. A group of six or eight shipwrights representing the men's 'company', or gang, would then sign a contract with the employer to build the ship or a part of it.[128] When asked whether he felt confident that the men would carry out the bargain, he responded: 'With the men we know we do [have confidence]. The great difficulty always is to define what work is to be done. If more work has to be done than was understood at the time of making the bargain, we generally have to pay for it.'[129] While such work-group collective bargaining was not the custom of every shipyard, Wigram concluded that 'job work is the custom of the trade' and another shipbuilder confirmed the prevalence of the practice because 'it works considerably better than day work'.[130]

In shipbuilding, the shipwrights often appear to have been insulated from what we would today term 'cost overruns'. In fact, a secretary at the Thames Shipbuilding Company testified that if the shipwrights' work came in under cost the men kept the difference between the negotiated bid and the final cost. On the other hand, if the bargain underestimated the ship's final cost the shipbuilders continued to pay the workers until the ship was finished.[131]

However, similar work-group bargains in other manufacturing and extractive sectors were less secure. The bargaining system in the Cornish mining industry, in which the 'tributers' bargained to work portions of the tin or copper mine based on their assessment of the likelihood of a good return, presented the great risk to the miners of promising a significant reward but returning only a pittance.[132] A similar system among the lead-miners of the northern Pennines led the employers there to reform the bargaining system during the early nineteenth century in order to reduce the potential discrepancies in earnings between work groups.[133]

Such workplace bargaining practices as have been discussed here were likely to have been common features of the manufacturing and early industrial shopfloor. This admittedly descriptive and largely anecdotal account, however, does not fully illuminate either the range of bargaining regimes in early industrial Britain or the structural dynamics of bargaining and negotiating itself. Therefore, both a more expansive view and a more intensive analysis of industrial bargaining during this era need to be undertaken. The chapters that follow will attempt to do just that.

Conclusion

Richard Price, the author of an extraordinary work on the building trades after 1850, has noted that 'to anyone who has examined mid-Victorian industrial relations, the idea that individual bargaining was the major, or sole, determinant of working conditions must be patently absurd'.[134] One might do well to apply Professor Price's observation to a much wider swath of British industrial relations, especially to the period before the so-called 'mid-Victorian compromise'. Work groups and shop stewards were extremely important during this earlier period, and while the law may not have recognized the collective contract, workplace bargaining based upon such work groups was a common feature. Such bargaining through the work group most often arose through the opportunities presented by forms of piece-rate payment, but they were as likely to arise over changes in working conditions and threats to the closed shop, as well as through processes of subcontracting. Workplace bargaining could be incorporated into a 'bifurcated' system of industrial relations in which shopfloor bargains were negotiated separately from district or regional bargains, such as happened among the London compositors or Clitheroe powerloom-weavers, but it was also as likely to take place on the shopfloor and autonomously.

For Professor Price, however, the dominance of 'informal' systems of industrial relations and the relative weakness of 'formal' systems, such as later became embodied in collective bargaining agreements between trade unions and employers' organizations, largely precluded the likelihood of the development of forms of mutual negotiation between work groups and employers. Industrial relations specialists have asserted that unlike formal systems of industrial relations, which often create procedural rules in order to define the process of resolving a dispute, 'informal' systems create substantive rules on how work should be done, rates of pay, overtime and other aspects of work itself. [135] Therefore, Professor Price surmises that without the elaboration of those dispute resolution procedures that were characteristic of formal systems, the informal systems of the mid-nineteenth century must have been less likely to seek compromise and more likely to attempt to impose 'autonomous regulation', that is, rules promulgated by either one side or the other. Negotiation and compromise, Price suggests, only occurred 'when the tactics of confrontation had been stalemated by the inability of either side to force an undisputed victory'. Otherwise, both workers and masters believed in the primacy of autonomous regulation. [136]

Yet such conclusions are not necessarily supported by a wider range of evidence. There were, of course, always winners and losers in bargaining situations, and failures to negotiate the resolution of a dispute could often lead to cycles of intimidation, retribution and violence. However, this did not seem to dampen workers' desire to negotiate with their employers or the employers' evident desire to avoid the disruption of production. As we shall see, with or without a set of laws or rules to structure and promote it, the prevalence of workplace bargaining in part reflected a belief that undertaking such actions was a form of 'self-help' and a sign of independence. [137] Negotiations were often understood as 'manly' meetings to resolve differences based on notions of 'fairness' and 'honour'. More importantly, as is the case in the twentieth century, the prevalence of 'informal' and 'autonomous' industrial relations practices does not at all indicate the absence of bargaining, but only the resolution of disputes outside of the purview of any formal arrangements between trade unions and employers' organizations. Indeed perhaps the most salient characteristic of modern 'informal' industrial relations has been the proliferation of shopfloor bargains that proceed under the auspices of shop stewards. When Allan Flanders testified before the Donovan Commission in the mid-1960s, he described workplace bargaining as 'largely informal, largely fragmented and largely autonomous'. [138] To a great extent, that was the context within which many trade groups operated in the early nineteenth century and it was likely to have been the substratum of trade unionism throughout the modern period.

Notes

1   *New York Times*, 27 February 1999, p. A10.
2   Sidney and Beatrice Webb's *The History of Trade Unionism*, new edn (1894; London: Longman, 1920) remains unsurpassed, as does E.P. Thompson's, *The Making of the English Working Class* (New York: Vintage, 1963) and J.L. and Barbara Hammond, *The Skilled Labourer*, new edn (1919; London: Longman, 1979), but several important recent surveys include John Rule, *The Labouring*

Classes in Early Industrial England, 1750–1850 (London: Longman, 1986); John Belchem, *Industrialization and the Working Class: The English Experience, 1750–1900* (Aldershot: Scolar Press, 1990); and Richard Price, *Labour in British Society: An Interpretative History* (1986; London: Routledge, 1990). The relative paucity of more recent surveys is a significant statement on the state of this sub-discipline.

3   V.L. Allen, *The Sociology of Industrial Relations: Studies in Method* (London: Longman, 1971), p. 66. A roughly similar formulation can be found in H.A. Clegg, Alan Fox and A.F. Thompson, *A History of British Trade Unions since 1889, Volume I, 1889–1910* (Oxford: Clarendon Press, 1964), pp. 4–5, where the authors note that 'widespread conflict and collective bargaining with organized employers were both untypical' and that 'the enforcement of craft rules usually involved contacts with the individual employer through letters, memorials, or deputations, and occasionally strikes ...'. In a recent history of industrial relations in British coal-mining, the authors also rely on Allen and submit that for the period before 1914 'workers would resist changes by submitting a letter or putting a notice in the press. Usually a deadline would be attached and strike, lock-out or restriction would follow. Where discussions took place they usually started after, rather than before, the action.' Roy Church and Quentin Outram, *Strikes and Solidarity: Coalfield Conflict in Britain, 1889–1966* (Cambridge: Cambridge University Press, 1998), p. 39.

4   Undoubtedly, the *locus classicus* of this view is E.P. Thompson's *The Making of the English Working Class*, which itself owes a good deal to the Webbs' description of this era as a 'revolutionary period' as well as J.L. and Barbara Hammond's works such as *The Skilled Labourer*, first published in 1919.

5   E.J. Hobsbawm, 'Custom, Wages, and Work-load in Nineteenth-Century Industry', in Asa Briggs and John Saville, eds, *Essays in Labour History* (London: Macmillan, 1960), pp. 113–39.

6   Interestingly enough, W.H. Hutt, whose work was published by the Thatcherite Institute of Economic Affairs, agreed with the Webbs that collective bargaining proliferated only after the wage-fund theory had been debunked by John Stuart Mill among others in the mid-nineteenth century. In his view, of course, this was a lamentable development. See W.H. Hutt, *The Theory of Collective Bargaining, 1930–1975* (London: Institute of Economic Affairs, 1975), pp. 3–10.

7   The literature here is enormous, of course, but excellent (and sceptical) guides to the debates can be found in Pat Hudson, *The Industrial Revolution* (London: Edward Arnold, 1992) and the Editor's Introduction to Joel Mokyr, ed., *The British Industrial Revolution: An Economic Perspective* (Boulder, Colo.: Westview Press, 1993).

8   Eugenio Biagini and Alastair Reid, eds, *Currents of Radicalism: Popular Radicalism, Organised Labour and Party Politics, 1850–1914* (Cambridge: Cambridge University Press, 1991).

9   Boyd Hilton, *The Age of Atonement: The Influence of Evangelicalism on Social and Economic Thought, 1785–1865* (Oxford: Clarendon Press, 1988).

10   See above, Introduction.

11   Robert Gray, *The Factory Question and Industrial England, 1830–1860* (Cambridge: Cambridge University Press, 1996), pp. 142–59.

12   Related assumptions among modern economists about 'free' market condi-
     tions during the early nineteenth century are examined in Michael Huberman,
     Escape from the Market: Negotiating Work in Lancashire (Cambridge: Cam-
     bridge University Press, 1996), pp. 1–13.
13   See above, Chapters 1 and 2.
14   Sidney and Beatrice Webb, *Industrial Democracy*, new edn (London:
     Longman, Green and Co., 1902), pp. 145–278.
15   Michael P. Jackson, *An Introduction to Industrial Relations* (London:
     Routledge, 1991), p. 142.
16   Richard Hyman, 'The Historical Evolution of British Industrial Relations', in
     Paul Edwards, ed., *Industrial Relations: Theory and Practice in Britain* (Ox-
     ford: Blackwell, 1995), pp. 28–9.
17   Keith Sisson, *The Management of Collective Bargaining: An Interactive Com-
     parison* (Oxford: Blackwell, 1987), pp. 11, 162–9.
18   Alan Fox, *History and Heritage: The Social Origins of the British Industrial
     Relations System* (London: George Allen & Unwin, 1985), pp. 89, 118.
19   Fox, *History and Heritage*, pp. 131–4, 167–73.
20   The following is drawn from the reports of the negotiating sessions recorded in
     Northumberland Record Office (hereafter NRO), Minutes of the General
     Meetings of the Coal Owners of the Rivers Tyne and Wear, 25, 29 and 30
     April, 3, 4 and 6 May 1831, pp. 92–101.
21   Fuller accounts of the 1831 and 1832 strikes and lock-outs can be found in
     Robert Colls, *The Pitmen of the Northern Coalfield: Work, Culture and Pro-
     test, 1790–1850* (Manchester: Manchester University Press, 1987) and James
     Jaffe, *The Struggle for Market Power: Industrial Relations in the British Coal
     Industry, 1800–1840* (Cambridge: Cambridge University Press, 1991).
22   Webb and Webb, *Industrial Democracy*, pp. 173–221.
23   See below, Chapter 3.
24   Criticisms of the Webbs' work often rests heavily on this criterion. See John
     Rule, 'The Formative Years of British Trade Unionism: An Overview', in Rule,
     ed., *British Trade Unionism, 1750–1850: The Formative Years* (London:
     Longman, 1988), pp. 1–2.
25   Webb and Webb, *Industrial Democracy*, p. 203.
26   Hyman, 'Historical Evolution', pp. 28–32.
27   Hyman, 'Historical Evolution', pp. 43–5.
28   See W.E.J. McCarthy, *The Role of Shop Stewards in British Industrial Rela-
     tions*, Research Paper No. 1: Royal Commission on Trade Unions and Em-
     ployers' Associations (London: HMSO, 1967).
29   Linda Dickens and Mark Hall, 'The State: Labour Law and Industrial Rela-
     tions', in Edwards, ed., *Industrial Relations*, pp. 255–303.
30   Keith Sisson sees the process beginning much later. He argues that the origins
     of this system were largely the result of the 1897–98 engineering dispute that
     'set a seal of legitimacy on workplace bargaining and guaranteed that it would
     be largely autonomous of the trade unions and employers' organization'. See
     The Management of Collective Bargaining, p. 166, quoted in Dave Lyddon,
     'Industrial-Relations Theory and Labor History', *International Labor and
     Working-Class History*, no. 46 (Fall 1994), p. 136. Since 1979, however, the
     role of workplace organization has also been significantly curtailed in some

areas. See Michael Terry, 'Trade Unions: Shop Stewards and the Workplace', in Edwards, ed., *Industrial Relations*, pp. 203–28.

31 Clive Behagg, 'The Democracy of Work, 1820–1850', in Rule, ed., *British Trade Unionism*, pp. 163–9, 173–4.

32 Richard Price, *Masters, Unions and Men: Work Control in Building and the Rise of Labour, 1830–1914* (Cambridge: Cambridge University Press, 1980).

33 McCarthy, *Role of Shop Stewards*, pp. 10–11.

34 See, for example, the account of the woollen trades in Adrian Randall, *Before the Luddites: Custom, Community and Machinery in the English Woollen Industry, 1776–1809* (Cambridge: Cambridge University Press, 1991).

35 Rule, *Labouring Classes*, pp. 111–17.

36 Rule, *Labouring Classes*, pp. 112–15; Modern Records Centre, University of Warwick Library, Union of Construction, Allied Trades and Technicians: Friendly Society of Operative Stone Masons (hereafter MRC, OSM), Mss. 78/OS/4/1/1, *Fortnightly Returns*, 14 November 1834.

37 Terry, 'Trade Unions', pp. 205–8.

38 Webbs, *Industrial Democracy*, ch. 1.

39 *Newcastle Chronicle*, 11 June 1831.

40 Anthony Howe, *The Cotton Masters, 1830–1860* (Oxford: Clarendon Press, 1984), p. 170.

41 Quoted in Lyddon, 'Industrial-Relations Theory and Labor History', p. 135.

42 Howe, *Cotton Masters*, pp. 165–6.

43 On the distinction between 'fair' and 'unfair' employers, see Patrick Joyce, *Visions of the People: Industrial England and the Question of Class, 1840–1914* (Cambridge: Cambridge University Press, 1991), pp. 87–113; Gray, *The Factory Question*, pp. 48–50, 121–9, 219–29.

44 See Terry, 'Trade Unions', pp. 208–10.

45 See below, Chapter 3, and James A. Jaffe, 'Authority and Job Regulation: Rule-Making by the London Compositors during the Early Nineteenth Century', *Historical Studies in Industrial Relations*, no. 3 (March 1997), pp. 22–5.

46 Durham County Record Office (hereafter DCRO), Londonderry Papers, D/Lo/C 142 (702), John Buddle to Lord Londonderry, 9 May 1831; Jaffe, *Struggle for Market Power*, pp. 173–5.

47 Terry, 'Trade Unions', p. 209.

48 James C. Scott, *Weapons of the Weak: Everyday Forms of Peasant Resistance* (New Haven: Yale University Press, 1985), pp. 348–9.

49 Scott, *Weapons of the Weak*, ch. 6.

50 One common consequence of the recognition of this asymmetry has been the inference that wages were set solely by market mechanisms. This was because, the often unstated argument goes, employers could rely upon a vast pool of unemployed or underemployed workers of both sexes to force wages down to near subsistence levels. There has therefore been an unfortunate elision of the recognition of the labour market's asymmetry with the assumption that bargaining, in the modern sense of the term, rarely took place. Michael Huberman notes related consequences of these arguments for the examination of wages and the labour market in nineteenth-century Lancashire in *Escape from the Market*, pp. 1–13.

51 William M. Reddy, *Money and Liberty in Modern Europe: A Critique of*

Historical Understanding (Cambridge: Cambridge University Press, 1987).

52   Howard F. Gospel and Gill Palmer, *British Industrial Relations*, 2nd edn (London: Routledge, 1993), p. 1, notes the modern partiality of news reporting to covering strikes rather than negotiations. This is likely to have been the case during the previous century as well. Additionally, P.K. Edwards notes that according to recent data from the North America only about one in seven negotiations involved a strike. See his 'Industrial Conflict: Themes and Issues in Recent Research', *British Journal of Industrial Relations*, vol. 30: no. 3 (September 1992), p. 369. Similar proportions may not have applied to the nineteenth century, but it is suggestive of the relationship between the two.

53   See below, Chapters 3 and 4.

54   The other two methods were 'mutual insurance' and 'legal enactment'. See Webb and Webb, *Industrial Democracy*, pp. 145–51.

55   Webb and Webb, *Industrial Democracy*, pp. 173–9.

56   A survey of the debate can be found in Jackson, *Introduction to Industrial Relations*, ch. 6.

57   Allan Flanders, 'Collective Bargaining: A Theoretical Analysis', reprinted in *Management and Unions: The Theory and Reform of Industrial Relations* (London: Faber and Faber, 1970), pp. 213–40.

58   The study of the rule-making process continues to be understood as a defining characteristic of industrial relations research. See Paul Edwards, 'The Employment Relationship', in Edwards, ed., *Industrial Relations*, p. 5.

59   Flanders, and later Hugh Clegg, argued that there were two principal types of rules: 'substantive rules' determine rates of pay, hours of work, and the like, while 'procedural rules' govern how substantive rules should be made and how disputes over substantive issues should be settled. The emphasis upon such distinctions is less in evidence today than it may have been thirty years ago. Edwards, for example, suggests that rule-making should be conceived as broadly as possible by taking into account the influences of employment's legal, political, economic, social and historical context. See Edwards, 'Employment Relationship', p. 5. For a classic statement of the typologies of rule-making, see H.A. Clegg, *The Changing System of Industrial Relations in Great Britain* (Oxford: Blackwell, 1979), pp. 1–5.

60   Flanders, 'Collective Bargaining', p. 239.

61   See Alan Fox, 'Collective Bargaining, Flanders, and the Webbs', *British Journal of Industrial Relations*, vol. 8: no. 2 (1975), pp. 151–74.

62   Fox, 'Collective Bargaining, Flanders, and the Webbs', pp. 153–6, 170.

63   Clegg, *Changing System of Industrial Relations*, p. 7.

64   Otto Kahn-Freund, 'Blackstone's Neglected Child: The Contract of Employment', *Law Quarterly Review*, vol. 93 (October 1977), pp. 508–28.

65   During the nineteenth century, statutory changes were excluded from the general law of contract. By a 'semantic trick', if statutory enactments, such as the Factory Acts, affected employment relations then they were no longer matters of contract. See P.S. Atiyah, *The Rise and Fall of the Freedom of Contract* (Oxford: Clarendon Press, 1979), pp. 404–5.

66   Douglas Hay, 'Patronage, Paternalism, and Welfare: Masters, Workers, and Magistrates in Eighteenth-Century England', *International Labor and Working-Class History*, no. 53 (Spring 1998), p. 28.

67   Hay, 'Patronage, Paternalism, and Welfare', p. 37; Norman McCord, 'The Government of Tyneside, 1800–1850', *Transactions of the Royal Historical Society*, 5th ser., vol. 20 (1970), pp. 5–30. Significant work on the mediative actions of the clerical magistrates in local labour disputes is currently being conducted by W.B. Maynard.

68   Hay, 'Patronage, Paternalism, and Welfare', pp. 36–8.

69   This appears to have been the motivation behind the efforts of Northumberland magistrates to mediate mining disputes in the north-east. See Jaffe, *Struggle for Market Power*, pp. 165–6.

70   Hay, 'Patronage, Paternalism, and Welfare', pp. 28–9, 38.

71   John V. Orth, *Combination and Conspiracy: A Legal History of Trade Unionism, 1721–1906* (Oxford: Clarendon Press, 1991), pp. 5–42; James Moher, 'From Suppression to Containment: Roots of Trade Union Law to 1825', in Rule, ed., *British Trade Unionism*, pp. 74–97.

72   Moher, 'From Suppression to Containment', pp. 77–80.

73   Moher, 'From Suppression to Containment', pp. 84–90.

74   H.W. Arthurs, '"Without the Law": Courts of Local and Special Jurisdiction in Nineteenth Century England', in A. Kiralfy, M. Slatter and R. Virgoe, eds, *Customs, Courts and Counsel: Selected Papers from the Sixth British Legal History Conference, Norwich 1983* (London: Frank Cass and Co., 1985), p. 130; see also H.W. Arthurs, *'Without the Law': Administrative Justice and Legal Pluralism in Nineteenth-Century England* (Toronto: University of Toronto Press, 1985), pp. 25–34.

75   Corporation of London Record Office (hereafter CLRO), Misc. Mss. 135.5, 'Historical Notes on the Court of Requests'; W.H.D. Winder, 'The Courts of Request', *Law Quarterly Review*, vol. 52 (July 1936), pp. 370–7.

76   Winder, 'Courts of Requests', pp. 377–84; Arthurs, '"Without the Law"', pp. 131–2; Margot Finn, 'Debt and Credit in Bath's Court of Requests, 1829–39', *Urban History*, vol. 21: pt 2 (October 1994), pp. 213–14; C.W. Brooks, 'Interpersonal Conflict and Social Tension: Civil Litigation in England, 1640–1830', in A.L. Beier, D. Cannadine and J. Rosenheim, eds, *The First Modern Society: Essays in English History in Honour of Lawrence Stone* (Cambridge: Cambridge University Press, 1989), pp. 357–99.

77   The term 'popularity' is used here advisedly. In some jurisdictions, the courts were corrupt and inept, as was alleged by Joseph Parkes in the charges against the Birmingham Court of Requests contained in *The State of the Court of Requests and the Public Office of Birmingham* (Birmingham, 1828). The degree of opposition to these courts is also highlighted by Brooks, 'Interpersonal Conflict and Social Tension', pp. 375–6.

78   In the City of London's Court of Requests, for example, the fee was 1s 6d.

79   In addition to the works cited above, on the courts generally, see William Hutton, *The Courts of Requests: Their Utility and Powers* (1787; Edinburgh, 1840); Samuel Miller, *Small Debts: Three Letters ... showing the Manifold Advantages of Enlarging the Powers of the Court of Requests* (London, 1830); *Report from the Select Committee on the Recovery of Small Debts in England and Wales*, Parliamentary Papers (hereafter PP), vol. iv (1823); *Fourth Report of the Royal Commission on the Practice and Proceedings of the Courts of Common Law*, PP, vol. xxv (1831–32); *Returns of the Number of Causes,*

Officers, Jurisdictions and Committals of the Courts of Requests, PP, vol. xliii (1839).

80   Arthurs, '"Without the Law"', p. 132, Table 1.

81   Arthurs, '"Without the Law"', p. 133, Table 3.

82   Finn, 'Debt and Credit', pp. 217, 220–1, 224–7.

83   CLRO, PD 114.21, Court of Requests: *Report of Committee to enquire into the Practice and Fees of the Court of Requests*, 23 June 1774.

84   Hutton, *Court of Requests*, p. 52.

85   See below, Chapter 6.

86   MRC, National Graphical Association, London Region: London Society of Compositors (hereafter NGA), Mss. 28/CO/1/1/2, Minute Books of the London General Trade Society of Compositors, 19 April, 3 May 1830. See below, pp. 192–3.

87   *First Report from the Select Committee on Artizans and Machinery*, PP, vol. v (1824), p. 28.

88   Robert C. Ellickson, *Order without Law: How Neighbors Settle Disputes* (Cambridge, Mass.: Harvard University Press, 1991), especially ch. 8. The importance of the law for the construction of identities in society has been suggested by Patrick Joyce, 'Refabricating Labour History; or, From Labour History to the History of Labour', *Labour History Review*, vol. 62: no. 2 (Summer 1997), pp. 150–1, and is based in part on the work of Christopher Tomlins. I would like to thank Dr Tomlins for providing me with a copy of his paper 'Waiting for Industrialism: Work, Law Culture and the Rediscovery in [*sic*] Early America', American Bar Foundation Working Paper 9613.

89   The term comes from the title of Ellickson's book, *Order without Law*.

90   Thus in 1984 the Workplace Industrial Relations Survey estimated that 71 per cent of all employees in Britain were covered by collective bargaining agreements, but at the same time only about 45 per cent of the labour force was unionized. See Jackson, *Industrial Relations*, pp. 146–7, and Jeremy Waddington and Colin Whitson, 'Trade Unions: Growth, Structure and Policy', in Edwards, ed., *Industrial Relations*, p. 156, Table 6.1.

91   For the modern case, see William Brown, 'A Consideration of "Custom and Practice"', *British Journal of Industrial Relations*, vol. 11 (March 1972), pp. 42–61. As Brown indicates, many customs were probably not the autonomous creation of labour. Employers knowingly (and unknowingly) connived at the creation of customs.

92   Watson Mss., NRO 3410/Wat/1/5/91.

93   Watson Mss., NRO 3410/Wat/1/5/92.

94   Watson Mss., NRO 3410/Wat/1/5/91.

95   On multi-tiered bargaining, see Sisson, *Management of Collective Bargaining*, p. 3.

96   Watson Mss., NRO 3410/Wat/1/5/92.

97   Watson Mss., NRO 3410/Wat/1/5/93.

98   J.W.F. Rowe, *Wages in the Coal Industry* (London: P.S. King & Son, 1923), pp. 49–51.

99   Church and Outram, *Strikes and Solidarity*, p. 39. See above, n. 3.

100 DCRO, Londonderry Papers, D/Lo/C 142 (736). See also, Jaffe, *Struggle for Market Power*, pp. 63–4.

101 Webb and Webb, *History of Trade Unionism*, p. 27; Ellic Howe, ed., *The London Compositor: Documents Relating to Wages, Working Conditions and Customs of the London Printing Trade, 1785–1900* (London: Oxford University Press, 1947), pp. 22–32.
102 Howe, ed., *London Compositor*, pp. 339, 344, 345, 349, 350, 351, 352, reprints portions of the scale that include workplace bargains for such things as footnotes, sidenotes, mathematical equations, musical notation, and the like. Further provisions for workplace bargaining were added throughout the century as well.
103 Howe, ed., *London Compositor*, pp. 222–5.
104 The following account is based on MRC, NGA, Mss. 28/CO/1/1/5, Trade Council Minutes, 17 June and 19 June 1834.
105 The context does not seem to indicate the more common distinction in the trade between 'establishment' workers who were paid weekly and 'piece hands' who were paid piece-rates. Here, the reference appears to be to compositors who were not regularly employed by the printing house.
106 MRC, OSM, Mss. 78/OS/4/1/1, *Fortnightly Returns*, 11 November 1836.
107 MRC, OSM, Mss. 78/OS/4/1/6, *Fortnightly Returns*, 28 November 1844.
108 MRC, OSM, Mss. 78/OS/4/1/6, *Fortnightly Returns*, 12 December 1844.
109 MRC, OSM, Mss. 78/OS/4/1/4, *Fortnightly Returns*, 17 June 1841.
110 MRC, OSM, Mss. 78/OS/4/1/4, *Fortnightly Returns*, 17 June 1841.
111 MRC, OSM, Mss. 78/OS/4/1/1, *Fortnightly Returns*, 26 March 1840.
112 *Report from the Select Committee on Manufactures, Commerce, and Shipping*, PP, vol. vi (1833), Q. 4869, p. 292; on the Builders' Union, see Webb and Webb, *History of Trade Unionism*, pp. 124–32.
113 Clive Behagg, *Politics and Production in the Early Nineteenth Century* (London: Routledge, 1990), p. 122. The debate between the so-called 'rank-and-filists' and 'institutionalists' that briefly flared up several years go missed this point, I believe. See, for example, Jonathan Zeitlin, 'From Labour History to the History of Industrial Relations', *Economic History Review*, 2nd ser., vol. 11: no. 2 (May 1987), pp. 159–84, or Price, *Labour in British Society*, especially ch. 4.
114 Behagg, *Politics and Production*, pp. 120–1.
115 *Tenth Report of the Commissioners appointed to inquire into the Organization and Rules of Trades Unions and other Associations*, PP, vol. xxxii (1867–69), p. 32, quoted in Behagg, *Politics and Production*, p. 121. Unfortunately, Takao Matsumura's *The Labour Aristocracy Revisited: The Victorian Flint Glass Makers, 1850–80* (Manchester: Manchester University Press, 1983) does not deal with the subject.
116 H.A. Turner, *Trade Union Growth, Structure and Policy: A Comparative Study of the Cotton Unions* (London: George Allen & Unwin, 1962), p. 85.
117 Turner, *Trade Union Growth, Structure and Policy*, p. 81; see also Alan Fowler and Terry Wyke, eds, *The Barefoot Aristocrats: A History of the Amalgamated Association of Operative Cotton Spinners* (Littleborough, Lancs.: George Kelsall, 1987), pp. 15–16.
118 Huberman, *Escape from the Market, passim.*
119 *Report from the Select Committee on Manufactures, Commerce, and Shipping*, pp. 684–5; on W.R. Greg, see Mary B. Rose, *The Gregs of Quarry Bank*

Mill: The Rise and Decline of a Family Firm, 1750–1914 (Cambridge: Cambridge University Press, 1986), pp. 127–8, 136–7.

120   On the 'rolling strike', see Turner, *Trade Union Growth, Structure and Policy*, pp. 57–8, and R.G. Kirby and A.E. Musson, *The Voice of the People: John Doherty, 1798–1854, Trade Unionist, Radical and Factory Reformer* (Manchester: Manchester University Press, 1975), pp. 28–9.

121   *Fifth Report from the Select Committee on Artizans and Machinery*, PP, vol. v (1824), pp. 556–7. This account of the nature of the 1822 Bolton dispute differs slightly from the description provided by Kirby and Musson, *Voice of the People*, p. 28.

122   *Fifth Report from the Select Committee on Artizans and Machinery*, pp. 557.

123   *Fifth Report from the Select Committee on Artizans and Machinery*, pp. 558–61; Kirby and Musson, *Voice of the People*, 28–9; and Fowler and Wyke, *Barefoot Aristocrats*, pp. 23–4, whose conclusion that the strike ended in a negotiated settlement apparently contradicts Bolling's testimony that the new price list was not only below his 1822 prices, but they were 'also below the old rate we had been paying them before'.

124   The following account is taken from John O'Neill, *The Journals of a Lancashire Weaver: 1856–60, 1860–64, 1872–75*, ed. Mary Brigg (n.p.: Record Society of Lancashire and Cheshire, 1982), pp. 92–6.

125   Garnett Diary quoted in O'Neill, *Journals of a Lancashire Weaver*, p. 190.

126   Garnett Diary quoted in O'Neill, *Journals of a Lancashire Weaver*, p. 190.

127   O'Neill, *Journals of a Lancashire Weaver*, pp. 95–6.

128   *Ninth Report of the Commissioners appointed to inquire into the Organization and Rules of Trades Unions and other Associations*, PP, vol. xxxii (1867–69), pp. 48–9.

129   *Ninth Report of the Commissioners appointed to inquire into the Organization and Rules of Trades Unions and other Associations*, pp. 7–9.

130   *Ninth Report of the Commissioners appointed to inquire into the Organization and Rules of Trades Unions and other Associations*, pp. 10, 28–9.

131   *Ninth Report of the Commissioners appointed to inquire into the Organization and Rules of Trades Unions and other Associations*, p. 29.

132   John Rule, *The Experience of Labour in Eighteenth-Century English Industry* (New York: St Martin's Press, 1981), pp. 66–7.

133   C.J. Hunt, 'The Lead Miners of the Northern Pennines', *North East Group for the Study of Labour History*, Bulletin no. 1 (October 1967), pp. 10–12.

134   Price, *Masters, Unions and Men*, p. 58.

135   This distinction is, of course, standard in industrial relations literature. See Clegg, *Changing System of Industrial Relations*, pp. 1–2; Price, *Masters, Unions and Men*, pp. 73–9.

136   Price, *Masters, Unions and Men*, p. 74.

137   On forms of 'self-help enforcement' without law, see Ellickson, *Order without Law*, pp. 143–7, 207–19.

138   *Report of the Royal Commission on Trade Unions and Employers' Associations, 1965–1968* (London: HMSO, 1968), p. 18. Flanders used 'autonomous' to mean independent of nationally negotiated agreements between unions and employers' organizations, not unilaterally imposed job rules, as Price suggests.

4

Employers' organizations, trade unions and collective bargaining

I hate ambiguity; my motto is, 'Reciprocal rights'. (John Gast, *Mechanics'* *Magazine*, 9 July 1825)

Collective bargaining is commonly understood as a system of industrial relations in which representatives of a group or groups of workers organized in a trade union negotiate questions of pay, working conditions, and the like with a single employer or a group of employers who themselves are often organized within an employers' association. This was the focus of the Webbs' analysis of the collective bargaining process and the term is still regularly defined in this manner.[1] As has already been noted, the phenomenon of collective as opposed to individual bargaining often operates at several levels, the most prevalent of which in the early nineteenth century was workplace bargaining. In its more organized and more readily recognizable form, however, collective bargaining between employers and trade unions is only rarely deemed to have been a prominent feature of British industrial relations before 1860. As in the case of workplace bargaining, the narratives of industrialization, the doctrines of political economy, and the perceived antipathy of the nineteenth-century state all militate against the recognition of collective bargaining before that date. A closer look at the history of industrial relations in the half-century before 1865, however, reveals that wide areas of the manufacturing economy exhibited repeated examples of collective bargaining, many of which were encouraged by the local magistracy. And, as in the case of workplace bargaining, while many of these instances of collective bargaining appear to have been ephemeral, there are nonetheless important continuities of forms, objectives and individuals. Indeed the protest that is most often lodged against the Webbs' definition of trade unions – that their insistence on permanency was misplaced – can similarly be applied to historians of collective bargaining and industrial relations.

By 1865, collective bargaining already possessed a rather long history in Britain. Certainly, by that time, the employers and employees in many trades had been acting collectively for many decades. Historians now readily accept the notion that trade unions were widespread throughout much of the British manufacturing sector during the eighteenth and early nineteenth centuries. It has been shown not only that journeymen and other wage-earners readily organized numerous strikes throughout this period, but also that their purposive and determined attempts to construct trade unions and undertake collective negotiation stretched as far back as the late fifteenth century. Moreover, while such union or guild actions were once seen as largely defensive efforts to protect customary privileges, there is an increasing awareness that these early shop-clubs, fraternal associations and trade unions were more calculative, more organized and altogether more 'modern' than has previously been acknowledged.[2]

While collective bargaining does not require the presence of employers' associations, these may have been just as common as trade unions during this period. Unfortunately, the history of employers' organizations during this period has received much less attention than that of trade unions. They appear to have been numerous, but it is difficult to say just how numerous. They appear to have been 'ephemeral', but they were probably ephemeral in the same manner as were trade unions.[3] Much of our 'serious' knowledge of employers' associations goes little beyond recounting Adam Smith's famous observation that 'whoever imagines ... that masters rarely combine, is as ignorant of the world as of the subject. Masters are always and every where in a sort of tacit, but constant and uniform combination, not to raise wages above their actual rate.'[4] Elsewhere, Smith acknowledged that employers' organizations owed their origins to a variety of causes.[5] Some of them, he wrote, undoubtedly began as conspiracies to lower wages, but others began as efforts to restrict competition and control product markets. Still others owed their origins to the necessity of lobbying Parliament or as responses to trade union efforts to encourage collective bargaining. Yet Smith's insistence on their ubiquity was probably not a great exaggeration. Both Sir John Clapham and T.S. Ashton vigorously asserted the importance of employers' associations during the late eighteenth and early nineteenth centuries and urged others to undertake a systematic study of them.[6] There is indeed a great deal of truth to Ashton's observation in reference to employers that 'the strangest of all legends by which the story of the industrial revolution has been obscured' is the one that posits a rapid revolutionary transformation of British society and culture from one based upon the club, coffee house and association in the eighteenth century to a self-centred, anti-social and individualistic culture in the early nineteenth century.[7]

As we shall see, when workers and employers bargained collectively during the early nineteenth century they often followed a customary format: representatives from among the masters of a town or region were selected to meet a similar number of representatives of trade unionists. The authority of these delegates to conclude bargains varied, but both employers' groups and trade unions tended to rely upon the 'democratic' affirmation of the bargains reached by their representatives. Significantly, the 'system of voluntarism' in which employers and employees bargained autonomously beyond the reach of the state, and which is often claimed to be a unique aspect of British industrial relations, was less in evidence during this period than perhaps might have become the case later.[8] Magistrates and other local officials were often found either acting as mediators or being encouraged to intercede in such bargaining sessions. As we have noted previously, while the national-state may have sought to eliminate the collective aspect of bargaining in industry, local officials often acted to sanction it.[9]

Charles Sabel and Jonathan Zeitlin have suggested that in continental Europe similar institutions of bargaining were often characteristic of the industrial zones of flexible regional economies. They have argued that institutions such as collective bargaining, *Conseils de Prud'hommes*, and price lists or *tarifs* are illustrative of the ways in which flexible economies constructed a regulatory mechanism that tried to cope with 'the temptations of opportunism and free-riding'.[10] While the historical significance of the theory of flexibility may still be in contention, such a perspective is in fact quite helpful to an understanding of the function of collective bargaining during the late eighteenth and early nineteenth centuries. Many collective bargains, as we shall see, were the result of attempts to restrict or rein in competitive rate-cutting, which was seen as injurious to both capital and labour. In some remarkable instances, workers even helped to supervise and enforce trade regulations that had been mutually constructed. However, such tendencies and attributes need not be restricted to modes of flexible production, at least not in the way flexibility has been defined in opposition to mass production. As several authors have recently shown, price lists were an integral part of the Lancashire cotton industry's attempt to regulate 'flexibly' the effort-for-pay bargain under rapidly changing conditions perhaps from as early as 1813.[11]

Indeed the last two decades of the eighteenth century and the first third of the nineteenth century seem to have been a particularly propitious moment for collective bargaining in Britain. This was likely to have been the result of the confluence of a variety of events. Certainly, one reason many workers were eager to negotiate collective bargains at this time was that they were extremely sensitive to rising prices and the threat this posed to their standard of living.[12] The adverse effect of rising food prices and rents to workers' incomes was perhaps the most common argument used at this time to initiate negotiations with employers. Secondly, the disruptions within the British economy caused by the Revolutionary Wars and their aftermath made the regulation of industrial relations more palatable to many employers. In particular, price lists or other bargains were often adopted or attempted where and when they promised to restrain competition based on price, equalize labour costs or promote labour peace. Thirdly, as already noted, in trades affected by technological change, such as cotton, collective bargains were one of the methods whereby work practices and pay could be regulated or readily renegotiated. Finally, industrial regulation through collective bargains was often understood as a way to avoid civil unrest and protect property. Magistrates and other local officials, therefore, could frequently be found not only promoting meetings of masters and men but actively mediating between the parties as well.

A current textbook on British industrial relations argues that because employers wield not only more power but a greater variety of forms of industrial power they historically 'have played the major part in shaping the British system of industrial relations'.[13] This is a salutary reminder that, contrary to the Webbs' contention, collective bargaining did not arise solely as a method of trade union regulation.[14] However, it is possible to overstate the case. In the history of late eighteenth- and early nineteenth-century collective bargaining, employers were important, of course, and they can often be seen actively innovating new systems of industrial relations. Yet collective bargaining practices were not adopted solely upon their insistence or recommendation. Equally important were the numerous attempts of trade union activists, local magistrates and other local notables to establish new means of resolving industrial disputes. It was often the case that some form of community pressure – the intervention of local justices or rate-payers' fears of the effect of a prolonged strike or lock-out – was a necessary prerequisite to the advent of collective bargaining during this period. The origins of collective bargaining in Britain, therefore, owe as much to the nation's political culture as they do to capitalists and workers.

Nevertheless, the economic, social and political conditions of the early nineteenth century appear to have made employers more willing, or less afraid, to act collectively and in full view of the public. A count of the earliest mention of nearly fifty employers' organizations, with no claims to being exhaustive, reveals a marked upswing in their appearance, or at least the reporting of their appearance, after 1790. There are notable peaks in the appearance of employers' organizations in the decade after the beginning of the French Revolution and then again in the decade after the fall of Napoleon. (See Figure 1 and the list of employers' organizations in the Appendix to this chapter.) Of course, the 'appearance' of these organizations may be a function of the creation and survival of new forms of evidence, particularly newspapers and parliamentary reports. As Adam Smith noted, masters frequently met informally to settle industrial matters. However, the fact that these organizations became the subject of more intense public and political interest, and that they appear to have begun to adopt more formal institutional structures, may be a reflection of the more prominent role they had begun to play. Indeed the heightened awareness of employers' organizations expressed in the 1824 parliamentary investigations that led to the repeal of the Combination Laws is indicative of their growing notoriety.[15]

Forms and processes

In principle, there were two broad forms of collective bargaining during this period. The first may be conveniently labelled 'multi-level collective bargaining', adopting the modern term for the practice whereby general rules of employment are negotiated at the level of the trade union and employers' organization while particular working practices and pay-levels are negotiated at the level of the individual plant or firm. Multi-tiered bargaining was relatively uncommon during this period, appearing most prominently in the northern coal industry, although it would become the model most widely followed in Britain in the late nineteenth and twentieth centuries. More commonly, however, were collective negotiations over price lists that sought to standardize the exchange of pay for effort both between firms, across a range of different products and within a single town or district. For lack of a better term, I refer to this form as 'standardized collective bargaining'. As in modern collective bargaining, these two different levels of bargaining on the shopfloor or across the trade were not mutually exclusive and indeed exerted an important influence upon one another. However, the distinction made here between attempts to standardize wages and those to negotiate pay separately from other terms of employment at the very least may serve to highlight how collective bargaining practices developed in several different trades.

The origins of standardized collective bargaining practices and many price lists are obscure, but it is likely that those who advocated them often drew upon models of earlier practices of wage regulation incorporated into the Elizabethan Statute of Artificers.[16] As has already been noted, trade price lists might be adopted for several reasons. Price lists could serve to restrict competition, especially competition sparked by price-cutting, but they could also help control the 'free-rider' problem whereby one firm's investment in costly skills or information were appropriated by competing firms. Workers, on the other hand, often sought the implementation of price lists in order to standardize piece-rates in the face of their employers' competitive price-cutting, but they could also be used to ensure some proportionality between effort, output and pay. The historian John Rule has rightly noted that the elaboration and publication of price lists was a common concern of unions during this period.[17]

Given the fact that price lists appeared to contemporaries to have both customary and statutory legitimacy, and that they could help to solve especially difficult problems of industrial policy in a manner mutually satisfactory to both employers and employees, it is understandable that, as the Webbs wrote, 'in many cases we find employers apparently accepting or conniving at their men's combinations' even in the face of the Combination Laws.[18] In 1824, for example, a master printer testified before Parliament that 'there have been a good many conferences between the masters and the men, to equalize the prices of work, which have been very beneficial to the trade, and we have been much more at peace since that was done'. During these conferences, he added, 'we of course waived the availing ourselves of the Combination Laws ... [because] if we stood on the law, we never could approach each other'.[19] However, the customary role of the state in setting price lists continued to have an effect on industrial relations during this period. Not only did many workers look to the state for protection, but, of equal importance, local officials frequently facilitated and encouraged the resolution of industrial disputes through collective bargaining.

This connection between the state and collective bargaining is especially clear in the case of the Spitalfields silk-weavers. At first sight, it may appear that Spitalfields is perhaps the least likely venue for collective bargaining given the fact that the well-known Spitalfields Act of 1773 empowered the London, Middlesex and Westminster magistrates to fix piece-rates for the weavers there.[20] However, the magistrates there expected that silk manufacturers and the silk-weavers would first resolve their disputes through collective bargaining before passing their agreements on to the local quarter sessions for confirmation and publication. Given the glaring lack of expertise in the silk trade on the part of most justices and the enormous number of variations in silk production, the magistrates' inability or unwillingness to decide and impose prices is understandable. By the first decade of the nineteenth century, there were several distinct branches of the trade, including Engine-weaving, Strong Plain, Foot-figured, and Flowered branches, and price lists could cover more than forty different variations.[21] Thomas Gibbons, a Spitalfields silk manufacturer, noted that 'the magistrates are entirely ignorant of those terms used in weaving, by which an estimate is to be formed of the quantity of skill and labour required'.[22]

Under such circumstances, the representatives of masters and weavers undertook the collective negotiation of price lists prior to their presentation to the magistrates. Indeed, as Clapham noted, collective bargaining to produce a book of prices probably predated the 1773 Act itself and continued into the early nineteenth century.[23] The Assistant Handloom Weavers Commissioner for the Midlands, Joseph Fletcher, who investigated the operation of the Spitalfields Act in order to judge its possible application to textile trades elsewhere, concluded that 'practically, the Magistrates did not regulate the wages, but left the masters and men to make their own bargain *collectively*, and these terms they enforced, under the penalties stated in the Act, upon all *individually*'.[24] One silk manufacturer noted that 'whenever an appeal has been made to them [the magistrates], they invariably, I believe, have referred it to the employers and employed to decide; and when the decision has been agreed, they have merely recorded such agreement as a law, which shall in future govern this kind of work'.[25] Similarly, William Hale, a prominent defender of the Spitalfields Act and London silk manufacturer, claimed that one of the act's greatest assets was that it enables the master manufacturer, and the journeymen weavers of the silk trade, to settle *between themselves* what shall be a fair remuneration for the operative labour in every department of their weaving. When after the requisite and mutual consideration they have agreed as to the price of making any particular article, they take their agreement to the magistrates, who ratify it in pursuance of the powers vested in the them by the Act. The price thus fixed becomes by law the regular wages of the journeymen, until it be altered by any subsequent *mutual agreement*.[26]

The precise form of bargaining in the Spitalfields silk trade appears to have varied considerably. A petition to the London quarter sessions from several specialized groups of silk-weavers dating from the mid-1820s indicates that the journeymen's representatives 'applied by Public Advertizement as well as individually to several of the Master Weavers' before drawing up a revised price list. They then circulated this list in the form of a petition and gained the signatures of 'many of the Masters and Journeymen in the Narrow Ribbon, Velvet and Trimming Weaving Branch'. Only after this type of 'mature consideration' was the price list 'respectfully submitted for the Sanction of the Court of Sessions'.[27] At the same time, however, another group of silk-weavers conducted much more formal collective bargaining sessions. An account of one such bargaining session in 1824 is preserved in Francis Place's papers:

The Manufacturers and Committee of Journeymen Engine Weavers met again at the King's Head Tavern, in the Poultry on Monday night, for the purpose of endeavouring to effect an amicable adjustment of prices. A letter sent by John Thorp, Esq. to the Secretary of the Committee, naturally induced an expectation of accomplishing the desired arrangement, and which, we are happy to say, bids fair to be speedily attained. The greatest difference existed in the prices named by the two parties for the manufacture of galloons, doubles, and bands; on these much discussion took place, Mr. Thorp having been previously called to the Chair. – They were considered *seriatim*, and in each case, after great but fair contention on either side, both parties reduced from their original terms and at length compromised at about half-way of the differences of price asked and offered.[28]

Local magistrates appear to have rarely intervened in these collective negotiations unless bargaining reached an impasse. The Assistant Handloom Weavers Commissioner wrote:

The main operative principle of the Act was, to enforce upon individuals by a penal law, the varying contracts for labour made by the masters and the men in mass; such contracts being liable to readjustment at the wish of either party, *with an appeal, in case of difference, to the Magistrates in Quarter-Sessions,* who, to the nearest of their judgment, *without any commercial considerations whatever,* fixed the prices, so as to afford the journeyman, *if he could get full work,* the income of other low-skilled handicraftsmen, calculating by the price of bread.[29]

Similarly, Stephen Wilson, a Spitalfields silk manufacturer, recalled that in 1807 a list of working prices had been given to the magistrates only after direct bargaining talks had reached an impasse. At that time, he said, 'a list of twenty folio pages was given in at the sessions [by the journeymen weavers], for the magistrates to settle the prices; *the masters and the men had had several meetings, they could not agree, and when they applied to the sessions, one of the folios contained between thirty and forty articles*'.[30]

The Spitalfields Act, therefore, served less as a method of government wage regulation than as a means to institutionalize both collective bargaining practices and the resolution of disputes through mediation. In this, the London magistrates' actions were not exceptional. Indeed such activities may have been more common than heretofore acknowledged. For example, a handbill from the Sheffield journeymen spring-knife cutlers noted in 1824 that 'our Employers agreed in 1810, and also a few weeks ago, that the statement we took at that time was a fair remunerating price for labour, and that statement was agreed to by Masters and Men, and was ratified by the Magistrates'.[31] Moreover, magistrates' efforts to mediate industrial disputes, as C.R. Dobson has shown, had become quite common by the end of the eighteenth century.[32] Norman McCord has also emphasized the mediative function of the local magistracy in the north-east during the nineteenth century, and the recent work of Peter King has confirmed this observation in the case of Essex and other parts of the south.[33] However, it is less often appreciated that such mediative efforts served to foster habits of collective bargaining and sanctioned the development of a system of industrial relations that later writers mistakenly believed had evolved outside the state's influence. On the contrary, the state was closely involved in the evolution of collective bargaining even though such activities may have escaped the notice of its legislators.

A particularly striking example of a local official's efforts to facilitate collective bargaining is provided by the actions of the mayor of Macclesfield during a silk-spinners' dispute in 1824.[34] The strike had been precipitated by the employers, who had pasted notices on the walls of the local factories declaring that working hours were going to be lengthened from eleven to twelve hours per day without any commensurate increase in wages. Understandably, a handbill was subsequently drafted and circulated among the spinners calling for a general meeting on 3 April. According to one spinner, when the rally was held that day the mayor 'came amongst them, and requested that a deputation of two from each factory would meet him on the 5th of April, the day those new regulations were to commence'.[35] Fourteen spinners were chosen from among the operatives to meet the mayor, which they did two days later. At that meeting, for which there is a particularly full account, the mayor asked the spinners' deputies why they refused to work the additional hour and they told him simply that the extra hour's work constituted a reduction in wages. In addition, the spinners considered it particularly harmful to extend their children's working day another full hour. The mayor tried to get the spinners to agree to accept the extra hour's work, but when they refused he told them that he would then meet immediately with the masters.

By the evening of that day, the mayor had met with the master spinners and had set up a meeting between the masters and the spinners at six o'clock. A poster put up by the masters outside the Macclesfield Hotel called for one man from each factory to meet in turn with the masters. The spinners refused to bargain in this form and instead insisted that the masters meet the spinners' representatives as a group. This delayed the opening of the bargaining session. After two hours, however, the masters agreed to meet with the spinners 'as a body'. Although it is unclear from the surviving accounts whether the mayor himself was in attendance, it is clear that the session did not go well. The masters insisted that they needed the extra hour's work in order to compete with the products of neighbouring towns, and the workers had responded that the spinners in neighbouring towns had privileges that compensated for their lower rates. Thus, the spinners' deputies pointed out that other spinners paid lower taxes, bought provisions at lower prices, paid lower rents, and were given the opportunity to leave the factory during the course of the day. The meeting then broke up without having reached a settlement, the parties agreeing only to meet again at nine o'clock the next morning.

Meanwhile, the mayor worked hard to gain a settlement. He first met with the masters and succeeded in obtaining from them an agreement to offer the spinners an advance in wages proportionate to the additional hour's work. He then met with the spinners but with less satisfactory results. The spinners refused to work the extra hour under any circumstances. When the next bargaining session opened, the mayor was once again much in evidence. He showed up at the Macclesfield Hotel where the meetings were held, although it is again unclear as to whether he actually participated in the discussions. One of the spinners' representatives recalled that the 'forty [representatives] waited that morning a long time at the hotel; the mayor came, and he said that the masters requested six should go up, and they told them that the men were determined not to work the extra hour to the day'. In fact, the spinners had begun to prepare for a strike by calling for a general subscription to be raised for a strike fund. As it became apparent that the workers were determined not to yield on this point, the masters withdrew their demand for the extra hour of work. A particularly colourful account of the end of the strike was reported to Peter Moore, an MP on the Select Committee on Artizans and Machinery, by James Holland, the chairman of the Macclesfield silk-workers' union. According to Holland, the owners' abrupt capitulation was due to the death-bed request of one manufacturer, who demanded that his partner (and brother) 'must again call in his hands at the usual wages, and for the usual time of working; and, in short, that he would not die till this was done'.[36]

Whether this death-bed request ultimately broke the owners' resolve is unclear, but the mayor of Macclesfield's actions were quite typical of the way in which some local officials intervened in industrial disputes. They can often be found offering their services as mediators or serving as intermediaries between masters and employees. What motivated these officials is still not entirely clear, but it is likely that several factors combined to encourage such actions. Some of them certainly acted out of a sense of paternalism and a belief in 'a coherent society linked by ties of mutual responsibilities and respect', as Professor McCord describes the world-view of one Durham magistrate.[37] Others obviously acted out of self-interest; they were after all protecting their own property in the event that the dispute became violent.[38] Moreover, it is often quite difficult to assess the effectiveness of this sort of intervention on the national scale. Not all such efforts resolved disputes amicably. On Tyneside, for example, the intervention of the mayor of Newcastle and several Northumberland magistrates in a coal-mining dispute in 1831 only hardened the demands of the owners and contributed to the genesis of one of the most famous strikes of the century.[39] Nevertheless, intervention forced the Durham and Northumberland coal-owners to send representatives to negotiate with the miners.[40] Many times deals may ostensibly have been struck under the auspices of a magistrate, but they then were just as readily repudiated. Thus, in 1812, the Stockport weavers asked the local magistrate to assist them in their goal to raise their wages. The magistrate arranged a meeting between the masters and men and appeared to secure a settlement. According to a local weaver, however, 'after the meeting had dispersed, and the manufacturers had returned home and consulted among one another, they never raised the two shillings'.[41] In Leicester, the parish officers intervened in 1817 to help support the framework-knitters' wages by encouraging the weavers to meet with the manufacturers. After the two sides had reached an agreement over a price list, the manufacturers violated the agreement within the following week.[42] Finally, many calls for magisterial intervention probably fell on deaf ears. During the 1829 Manchester spinners' strike, for example, John Doherty failed to convince either the local magistracy or the clergy to mediate that dispute.[43] Still, it remains true that in many cases local officials acted to encourage the resolution of disputes by facilitating collective bargaining, and this is an important albeit often neglected element of the heritage of British industrial relations.

Not all forms of collective bargaining, however, took place under the aegis of a magistrate or other local official. Some took place autonomously between employers and employees, and are more typical of what later came to be recognized as Britain's 'voluntary' system of industrial relations. Perhaps the clearest evidence of such developments comes from the surviving evidence of negotiations between the London journeymen compositors and printing masters over their price list in the late eighteenth and early nineteenth centuries. A trade price list for compositors' wage rates had first been produced there as early as 1785, although there is little evidence of any direct negotiations at that time. It appears that at that time the journeymen compositors submitted a list of eight proposals to the master printers embodying a mixture of piece-rate advances and standardization of rates for different types of work across the trade. The masters subsequently met in November 1785, accepted five of the proposals, rejected three, and unilaterally resolved to appoint a committee to enforce the new rates.[44] According to the handbook of the London Union of Compositors published in 1836, which included a brief history of the union's industrial relations, 'the compositors, do not appear to have been present when these propositions were discussed, or to have been permitted to offer any arguments in their favour; but the masters assumed the right to set a price upon the labour of others'.[45]

Eight years later, the journeymen compositors sought to revise the price list in the face of rapid inflation and by this time the form of the industrial relations between master printers and compositors had changed noticeably. In 1793, a representative committee of five master printers was chosen to hold a joint conference with deputies from the compositors. The impetus to adopt this form of direct collective bargaining almost certainly came from the masters. The compositors' request for a rate change, which still survives, makes no mention of such a meeting. However, the masters' motivation is unclear. It may very well have been an *ad hoc* response to a new situation. A committee of masters' representatives had already been named after the first dispute in 1785 to oversee the imposition of those regulations.[46] Perhaps a joint bargaining session by representatives of both sides was viewed as a logical way to decide the issues at hand and to avoid a strike. On the other hand, since the 1793 petition requested rate changes principally because the price of provisions had risen dramatically, perhaps the masters saw more room for negotiation. Whichever may have been the case, this format of collective negotiation did not firmly take hold for more than another decade. Subsequent demands for rate changes that were put forth in 1795 and then again in 1800–1 were treated much as they had been in the 1780s, that is, by fiat of the master printers.

Collective bargaining was revived again in 1805 and, interestingly enough, the compositors later tried to take credit for it. According to the compositors' history, the establishment of a trade society in 1801 had changed the landscape of industrial relations in the printing trade. That union, it was claimed, formed a committee in 1805 that was responsible for meeting with an equal number of representatives of master printers in order to negotiate an acceptable list of prices.[47] This was done with a 'purity of ... intentions' so that an end might be brought to 'the many disagreeable differences that occur on the introduction of almost every new work'.[48] Unfortunately, the available documentary evidence does not support this claim. While the compositors probably did take the initiative to draw up a price scale for the twenty-seven most common operations in the trade in February 1805, the first proposal for a collective bargaining session appears in the master printers' response to that scale of prices. At a general meeting of the master printers, a committee of eight was appointed to meet an equal number of representatives of the compositors at the York Hotel on Bridge Street.[49]

Eventually, three collective bargaining sessions were held and a general scale of prices was adopted that met with the general assent of both the masters and journeymen. Ellic Howe, the compositors' historian, suggests that the sessions were free of rancour largely because the negotiations concerned the 'clarification of existing customs and charges rather than an advance in prices'.[50] Certainly, both the masters and their journeymen were proud of their accomplishment. The masters' committee reported that 'on first examining this Business, it was thought a labyrinth and sea intricate and unfathomable: but, in the free conference which followed with the Deputation from the Compositors, after three successive meetings and labourious discussions, your Committee are pleased in having it in their power to state, that much was done to compose the differences and variations alleged in their [the compositors'] Address'.[51] On their part, two decades later the compositors still recalled that

> [a] committee, consisting of an equal number of masters and journeymen ... were duly authorised by their respective bodies to frame regulations for the future payment of labour. This committee, who had only the preceding meagre scale as the basis of their labours, toiled diligently to remedy the various evils they had felt, and finally succeeded in producing a scale composed of twenty-seven articles, calculated, in their opinion, to meet every emergency; and, whatever may be said of its present inadequacy, every impartial person must admit that it reflects honour on its framers, and is, indeed, a rare example of diligence, talent, and knowledge, which it is not likely will ever be equalled, or, in aptitude and general clearness, ever surpassed.[52]

With a basic price list in place, formal face-to-face collective bargaining receded to the background for nearly half of a century, only to be revived again in the guise of an Arbitration Committee in 1847.[53] However, collective negotiations continued throughout this period, although it was now done by petition and at arm's length. The most famous and long-lived price scale, the compositors' 1810 scale of prices, which governed the trade into the 1890s, was negotiated in this manner, as were several subsequent important amendments.[54] While such 'formal' collective bargaining events became uncommon during the remainder of this period, 'informal' workplace bargaining remained vibrant. Indeed, as discussed in Chapter 3 above, certain working practices were left to be priced by negotiations on the shopfloor. Moreover, as will be shown in a subsequent chapter, during the 1820s and 1830s the compositors' union was able to establish its authority over the interpretation and application of the scale. As we shall see, the collective origin of the 1805 and 1810 price lists was later understood as an essential element of their continuing legitimacy through the remainder of the century.

A similar attempt to construct a price list through collective bargaining occurred in the Coventry ribbon trade. The earliest price list here probably dates to 1796 or 1797 and a variety of forms of joint regulation preceded the more formal collective bargaining agreement that evolved after 1818. In one early case, the Coventry silk-weavers acted to mediate a bout of competitive price-cutting that had erupted over the production of handkerchiefs in 1809 and 1810. According to the manager of one silk factory, 'the body of operative weavers, foreseeing the consequences that must accrue by this inequality of prices, met and submitted a list to the masters, to which they in the end, I think within six or seven days of consideration, agreed, by which those who paid the lowest prices stated in the book made in 1797, were brought a little higher, and those who paid a very high rate, more than what they actually ought to have done, were reduced as much lower as three shillings a dozen'.[55] In another case, after the weavers demanded to meet directly with the manufacturers to help stop the collapse of wages and prices that had set in after 1815, the manufacturers responded by calling upon the trade's 'undertakers' to revise the list of prices. The undertakers in the ribbon trade were a group of petty capitalists who often combined the functions of independent weaver, small-scale employer, and factor. They were particularly responsible for the collection and return of silk to the master manufacturers, but their responsibilities also extended to the setting up of weavers' patterns, the maintenance of looms, and the like. For all this, they received a commission of about a third of the wage bill.[56] In 1816, a collective agreement between representatives of each group successfully negotiated a price list, which was subsequently enrolled as a deed in Chancery.[57]

This price list, however, failed to rein in undercutting manufacturers both within Coventry and from the neighbouring weaving villages. Between 1816 and 1818, enormous community pressure began to be exerted upon the master manufacturers in the silk ribbon trade to stop the precipitous fall in piece-rate prices. Community action on this issue was in part motivated by the dramatic jump in the poor rates.[58] In at least one Warwickshire weaving parish, the poor rates rose from 3s in the pound in 1814 to 7s in 1816 to 9s in the pound in 1818. Poor law expenditures in the parish more than doubled during the same period.[59] Once again in 1818 the weavers asked to meet with the manufacturers to negotiate a price list and once again they were refused. This time, however, the weavers met to frame their own price list and, as was common in the Spitalfields trade, submitted it to the local magistrates for their approval. Surprisingly, the magistrates approved the list, although they seem to have done so principally in order to bring the masters to the bargaining table. William Webb, a local weaver, recalled that after the magistrates had ordered the implementation of the weavers' price list, 'some of the masters complained, that it was too high, and we then met the masters to arrange [a new list]'.[60]

The next year, 1819, witnessed an even more dramatic change in the form and function of the collective bargaining process. Two brief strikes rocked Coventry that year, the second of which encouraged the manufacturers, led by Jonathan Hale, to put industrial relations on a new footing. A meeting of the manufacturers held at the Castle Inn on 17 August brought forth a series of resolutions, including the appointment of a committee of nine manufacturers to 'receive the report of the Weavers' Committee', a representative body of the weavers first formed to organize support for the extension of the Spitalfields Act, and an expression of desire to work for the mutual acceptance of a trade price list. An agreed price list was subsequently adopted in the first week of September, although again details of the bargaining sessions are not available. As a result, however, the weavers agreed to select two representatives from each ward of the city to form an 'Aggregate Committee' whose function was to protect the price list by ensuring that weavers did not accept employment at rates lower than those stipulated in the book of prices. Towards this end, the weavers and manufacturers established a joint fund to support those who refused to accept rates below the price list. A retired manufacturer, Charles Lilly, was treasurer of the fund and by April 1820 it was claimed that the fund contained over £1,600.[61]

The history of the weaving community in Coventry and its surrounding parishes over the next few decades reveals not only repeated attempts to break through the price lists but also determined attempts collectively to resurrect them. Within the space of a decade, the price list was broken through in 1822, 1824, 1826, 1829 and 1831. After each disruption, community pressure helped to bring the parties back to the bargaining table and a new settlement was reached, often but not always at a lower level. The historian John Prest describes the trade during the 1830s as one in which 'wages were still paid according to an agreed "list of prices" which, if it was not legally enforceable, was nevertheless imposed by public opinion on both masters and men. The ideas behind the list were that surplus labour should not be the means of lowering wages, and that the weaver in work should receive a living wage.'[62] Throughout this period, the weavers and manufacturers met or communicated regularly. In 1822, it was reported that the weavers' committee had been reformed after a 'general strike', which had succeeded in gaining the support of shopkeepers, townspeople and even many manufacturers. From that time on, the committee met weekly and held quarterly ward elections.[63] By 1831, the social interests of the two groups had become so intertwined that several weavers' representatives were sworn in as special constables to assist in the suppression of a riot that had been sparked by widespread undercutting of the price list.[64]

In fact, this last incident, in which one factory was set on fire, led to a set of collective bargaining sessions for which we have some first-hand testimony, thanks to the diligent work of an Assistant Handloom Weavers

Commissioner whose report was published in 1840. After interviewing three members of the weavers' committee, this account of industrial relations after the riot emerged:

> The night [after the riot] passed without any further disturbance, and the next day (Tuesday, November 8th) the manufacturers met at the Castle Inn. There was still considerable commotion in the minds of the people, of whom great numbers had left their work, and assembled in the Cross Cheaping [Inn] and other places. As circumstances transpired they [the weavers] were informed by their Committeemen of the favourable position in which matters were towards a settlement. There were no further acts of violence, nor so much as an insult (to the knowledge of these witnesses) to a single one, even of the under-paying manufacturers, in coming to the inn. The manufacturers set earnestly to work to prepare a list of prices, more full, perhaps, than had ever previously existed, or at least since that of 1819. The course they pursued was to invite deputies from each branch of the trade, from the plain weavers and figure weavers of Coventry, who may be said to have represented the engine-trade, and from the single-hand weavers of the country districts. Those delegates were all invited to their meeting, and the lists which had been broken in upon were produced. Each article was discussed by the whole body of manufacturers here assembled, with the delegates of the weavers; the old lists were made the groundwork of the new; a few trifling reductions were proposed on some articles by the manufacturers, and discussed with the weavers, who acceded readily to some, and put in a plea against others; but all was amicably settled; and advances were volunteered by the masters on the article of loves, and obtained also on one or two others.[65]

This collective bargaining agreement introduced specialized subcommittees to negotiate price lists separately for the Coventry engine trade and the single-hand trade from the surrounding villages of Nuneaton, Bedworth, Bulkington, Foleshill and elsewhere.[66] Along with the more elaborate institutional structure, a more reliable monitoring system was adopted to ensure adherence to the price list. One of the weavers' committeemen noted that after these reforms the weavers' committees 'met as often as occasion required, and communicated monthly with the committee of masters, the whole of the delegates waiting upon the manufacturers.... The object of the monthly meeting was to report whether the list were faithfully maintained, and to write to the manufacturers to remonstrate with the parties who violated it.'[67] However, the power of these new committees was still strictly limited to the arts of persuasion and the politics of reputation. In the event that a manufacturer refused to follow the price, the weavers' representative recalled that

> certain individuals of each committee, of the masters or operatives, would wait upon the parties, and the subject was amicably explained. Sometimes it was merely a misunderstanding, – a false report, – that a lower price was being paid. The manufacturers having all signed the list, any deviation from it was a

breach of honour, which the committee thus undertook to expose. Sometimes a master, who wanted to underpay, would circulate a report against an 'honourable' manufacturer, that he was underpaying, and consequently that his example must be followed; and it became necessary to clear this up, to avoid the consequences. No other intimidation was resorted to, since it would have been illegal. In the case of the men who took out under-price work, the masters did not wait upon the men with the committee of weavers, to reprehend their conduct in taking out under price; but the weavers' committee remonstrated with him, and endeavoured to explain to him the injury he was inflicting on his fellow-operatives, by reducing the price of their labour in offering his own for less, since all manufacturers must follow the example of one.[68]

Within a year and a half, this elaborate system of collective regulation and monitoring began to break down. Manufacturers involved in the single-hand village trade regularly violated the list, and although negotiations were again attempted in 1834, that branch of the trade never restored the price list. On the other hand, the Coventry engine trade maintained its list much longer, perhaps as late as 1840. The longevity of the list in Coventry was perhaps due to its substantial and widespread community support. This accorded the price list not only an important degree of legitimacy, but also a significant measure of the power of enforcement even though it was primarily through shaming and social ostracism.[69]

Surprisingly hybrid forms of standardized collective bargaining can also be found in this period of institutional experimentation. In 1839, for example, several prominent carpet-weaving firms in Yorkshire and Durham aggressively sought simultaneously to stamp out trade unionism and reduce competition by forming an employers' association to regulate and equalize wages throughout the district. While the carpet-weavers were expressly forbidden to join trade unions, the masters promised them protection from wage reductions and ultimately recognized a small measure of collective bargaining. According to one carpet-weaver's testimony before Parliament, about a month before the annual meeting of the employers' organization, the weavers elected delegates from each factory to draw up a list of wage proposals. 'The delegates', he testified, 'go to the same town [as the masters]; the delegates meet in one room and the masters in another. The masters have a chairman and the delegates have a chairman; the chairman of the masters and the chairman of the delegates alone generally debate upon the propriety of the suggestions, and the others put questions if they think anything left out.'[70]

Moreover, many collective negotiations were probably undertaken in an *ad hoc* manner. For example, a Wiltshire shearman's strike in 1802 was marked by a least two collective bargaining sessions. During the first, five deputies from the Brief Institution, the shearman's union, met five clothiers and appeared to resolve the strike issues temporarily. However, when several mills were set on fire a few weeks later, a second bargaining session was convened at the Bradford-upon-Avon home of John Jones, a leading manufacturer. This meeting was attended by seven shearmen's deputies, seven manufacturers, and several other local notables, including Benjamin Hobhouse, the local MP.[71] During the 1818 Bolton weavers' strike, the weavers' deputies and manufacturers met in Manchester on the same day but at separate locations. In an attempt to resolve the strike, two weavers recalled, two manufacturers came to the deputies' meeting at the Bull's Head Inn and offered to raise their rates in instalments.[72] Similarly, after ten weeks on strike in 1822, the Sheffield filesmiths received a letter from manufacturers 'requesting them to appoint a deputation to meet a deputation of theirs, to settle the differences'. After the time, place and size of the deputations had been agreed upon, the representatives met and 'an amicable arrangement was agreed to'.[73]

In the Staffordshire potteries, despite several significant strikes, a variety of negotiating forums were either tried or suggested in the mid-1830s.[74] There is evidence that some form of collective negotiation may have produced the trade's 1833–34 price list, which was adopted after the successful potters' strike of 1834. That year's list was published under the heading 'The Minimum List of Prices as agreed upon between a Deputation of Manufacturers and Operatives'.[75] By 1836, the disputes over the terms of the potters' employment, especially their annual hiring contract, were first discussed in negotiations between delegates from the National Union of Operative Potters and the employers' Chamber of Commerce.[76] G.W. Prideaux, a delegate to the union from Bristol, seems to have been most committed to this course of action. He successfully argued at a public meeting of the union in December 1836 that 'we should not be doing our duty to those who sent us, if we do not make at least an attempt to appeal to the Chamber of Commerce'.[77] An initial meeting did take place on 29 December 1836 when a deputation of seven potters appeared before the Chamber of Commerce. That deputation, according to Prideaux, 'was received in the most gentlemanlike manner, and I rejoiced in it, not because it had the least effect on me individually, but because I thought it was an omen of good to the potters'.[78] The meeting focused not only on the presentation of the potters' demands, but also on the format for a negotiating session. The result was another hybrid bargaining form. The potters and manufacturers agreed to construct a bargaining panel comprised of six manufacturers, six union potters and six non-union potters. In an apparent attempt to avoid controversy, all of the members of the bargaining panel were to meet 'as individuals' rather than as representatives of an association, although the precise meaning of this proviso was hardly clear.[79] This panel, it was agreed, would meet before two local magistrates, who would 'constitute a kind of friendly court for the purpose of discussing the questions at issue' and would serve to mediate rather than arbitrate the matter.[80]

By all accounts, the negotiating session was a failure. The owners objected to the presence of the union delegates, who, they claimed, violated the spirit of the previous day's agreement by yielding their positions as union officials for the day in order to serve on the bargaining committee. They also objected to the presence of Mark Lancaster, the potters' trade union leader, and Mr Mousely, the union secretary, and forced them to leave the session. The potters, for their part, were equally dissatisfied. They claimed that the manufacturers packed the meeting with their supporters and constantly appealed to them. More significantly, the potters complained that the manufacturers were 'shuffling' and 'evasive'. Rather than discuss important matters of principle, the manufacturers blamed the union for the trade's difficulties while asserting their own innocence and good faith. Inevitably, the session broke up amid charges of bad faith on both sides.

The failure of the bargaining session was only a prelude to the failure of the union movement. The potters' strike of 1836–37 eventually led to a negotiated settlement but at the high cost of the union's destruction.[81] Nevertheless, the Union of Operative Potters was unique in its efforts to renegotiate the terms of employment and the 'customs of the trade' rather than wages or piece-rates.[82] In this, it looked forward to the development of multi-level bargaining systems in which the terms of employment are negotiated at the national or district level while wage bargaining takes place on the shopfloor or at the plant level.[83] Such multi-level bargaining, however, did briefly appear in the Durham and Northumberland coal trade and is further testimony of the vigour of collective bargaining during this period.

Like the Staffordshire pottery trades, the northern coal trade had adopted the practice of hiring workers on the basis of annual contracts and this accounts in part for the rise of multi-level bargaining there. Among the northern coal-miners, the institution of the annual 'bond' by individual colliery owners dates back at least to the eighteenth century, but it was only in the nineteenth century that bonds became increasingly standardized, and, then again, only in 1826 that a uniform, printed form was adopted throughout the coalfield. The bonds, which in most years were not subject to negotiation, contained several standard clauses that exclusively concerned the terms of employment and general working practices. However, the enormous variety of underground working conditions also necessitated that they be flexibly adapted to each colliery and sometimes to each pit. Therefore, piece-rates and other elements of the miners' remuneration were subject to pit or colliery-level bargaining. Typically, these negotiations occurred at the annual 'binding time' when workers customarily submitted their petitions, as discussed in the previous chapter. Yet there is a significant amount of evidence that indicates that bargaining could occur at any time when underground conditions changed or working practices were altered. The nature of these bargains will be analysed in the following chapter.

The standard terms of the bonds typically articulated the number of working days the owners promised to provide each fortnight, the calculation of working hours, standards of measurement for production, the amount of payment or work to be provided in the event of a mine being shut down due to an accident, whether housing was provided, and the method for resolving workplace disputes. But each colliery negotiated a unique set of rates for working in different pits, working different coal seams, separating large 'round' coal from 'small' coal or stones, digging out doors or passageways, working singly or in teams, working at the coal face or in the areas already excavated, working with Davy lamps, working in areas where there was leaking water, and many others aspects of underground mining. In addition, each colliery imposed a unique set of fines for a wide variety of unsatisfactory working practices, although most these had become standardized by custom throughout the coalfield.[84]

This bifurcated system of industrial relations was later reflected in the forms of collective bargaining adopted in the north-east coal trade. As we have already seen, by the 1820s and 1830s coalfield union movements had already sought to negotiate with their employers, and, at least in 1831, had done so. However, those negotiations in Newcastle, which were briefly outlined in Chapter 3, were limited to the general terms of bond. One of the employers' representatives to the 29 April 1831 talks listed the pitmen's grievances as follows: the exclusion of housing provisions from the bond, the limitation of working hours, the date of signing the bonds, the number of days' work provided each fortnight, the size of coal baskets used to measure production, standard measurements for payments for transporting coal underground and fining practices.[85] Indeed, the bargaining sessions of late April and early May successfully resolved or narrowed the differences on all of the major issues except the number of working days each fortnight and the level of fines.[86] These negotiations, however, never touched upon the calculation of piece-rates for the dominant work group down the pits, the adult male coal-miners or hewers. Certainly, the coal-owners recognized that a district-wide standardization of piece-rates would serve to limit competition for labour based upon wages and rationalize production costs. In the early nineteenth century, they had tried to do just that. But attempts to regulate hewers' wages had failed each time when confronted by either the workers' resistance or the unpredictability of working conditions and practices. Thus by the 1820s, the major colliery owners in the north-east had admitted that they could not regulate wages.[87] In fact, during Tommy Hepburn's strike in 1831, they had protested that despite the existence of the bond 'with the rate of wages at the respective collieries the Coal-owners do not, as a body, interfere, the prices being entirely governed by local circumstances'.[88]

The obvious appearance of multi-level bargaining in this bifurcated form was unique, however. Yet it is possible, perhaps even likely, that in several other trades the negotiation and adoption of price lists masked similar developments. Alain Cottereau's detailed analysis of the London silk trade under the Spitalfields Act, for example, revealed that bargaining over quality, deadlines, the number of looms employed and the use of apprentices characterized industrial relations there despite the presence of a mutually negotiated price list.[89] Similarly, if later practices are any guide to earlier conventions, pottery workers regularly bargained over and about their price lists. Richard Whipp noted for the first decade of the twentieth century that 'the "trade" or "district" price for an article or pattern became benchmarks for occupational or craft bargaining'.[90] Even among the miners themselves, the establishment of district-wide price lists or sliding scales in the second half of the nineteenth century never eliminated regular and repeated recourse to bargaining at the pit or colliery level.[91] Nevertheless, one should be wary of positing the origins of the system of collective bargaining in the late nineteenth century, as is frequently done. Collective bargaining was quite alive long before then and its ephemerality should not obscure either its innovations or adaptability.

The rhetoric and theatre of collective bargaining

The forms and processes of collective bargaining varied significantly, but its existence, however ephemeral, should by now be quite obvious. As has been noted, collective bargaining was probably most common among the artisanal piece-work trades and frequently manifested itself in the form of the price list or rate book. There were, moreover, several groups who advocated these new forms of industrial relations. In some circumstances, local magistrates or other officials took the lead in bringing masters and workers to the bargaining table. In others, the manufacturers or workers themselves were eager to promote collective bargains. In still others, shopkeepers and rate-payers encouraged and facilitated this type of negotiation and settlement. In sum, there were powerful and variegated social and institutional forces that contributed to the advent of collective bargaining.

Many of these collective bargaining sessions for which records survive appear to have displayed pronounced affinities to British political and legal culture generally. Indeed, Joseph Fletcher, the Assistant Handloom Weavers Commissioner, noted this in his 1840 report to Parliament. 'We see lists of prices made by a council of masters on the petition of the men, in like manner as the Commons of England used to apply to the king in council', he wrote.

> They receive the sanction of the great body of the 'trade,' a little *imperium in imperio*, of which the law of the land has no cognizance. They are enacted by the representatives of the two parties, and ratified by public opinion; but are enforced only by *moral* sanctions, of a character unrecognised by the law, liable to be extended by intimidation, and vested in the hands of masters or men, little skilled in, and little scrupulous about their application, except that they both still bow to the appellate tribunal of *public opinion*. This tribunal we have seen repeatedly convoked to ratify the acts of a trade convention, to give

weight to their revision, and to overawe the disobedient by its disapprobation.[92]

Fletcher himself was obviously struggling to reconcile the prescriptions of the law and the existence of the forms of collective bargains.[93] However, such an analogy to parliamentary institutions is not inapt. Many collective bargaining sessions, like trade unions, benefit societies and employers' organizations, were governed by a sophisticated set of rules of order, including the presence of secretaries, the appointment of chairs, and the moving and seconding of resolutions. In Ashton, for example, the operative spinners who attended a collective bargaining session in January 1831 were at first exasperated by the masters' failure to follow some of these rules of political association. Even before the session had opened, one spinner 'wished that as the masters' secretary was present, their secretary should also be allowed in the room'.[94] After this had been acceded to, the meeting proceeded by the submission of propositions, the moving of resolutions, the seconding of those resolutions, and finally voting. The initial proposition concerned a masters' resolution, which had been previously published in the papers, to adopt a price list based on a 'fair average of the price paid in the immediate surrounding districts', a list that the spinners thought was significantly 'under a true average list'.[95] The merits of the resolution were discussed and a vote quickly followed. The spinners unanimously rejected the masters' list and then moved on to a second masters' proposition to regulate prices by the number of spindles. In the ensuing discussion, the spinners objected to paying all spindles equally since some machines employed large wheels and others small. One spinner suggested that establishing a true average for all spinners was impossible and instead put forward a resolution that both parties submit their proposals for a price list to an independent investigation. This resolution was moved, seconded and passed. Such a resolution, however, apparently surprised the masters and they subsequently withdrew from the negotiations.[96]

Equally common was the adoption of the format and language of petitioning. As is well known, many artisans 'humbly petitioned' their masters for higher wages or piece-rates, yet the sources of this practice have never been fully examined. It may well be that the form of petitioning was a custom derived from the magistracy's former role in setting prices or wage rates, and then given greater currency by the political agitation of late eighteenth and early nineteenth centuries. However, these forms of address and submission were theatrical. Despite the obvious inequities between masters and men, they offered a negotiated language that both journeymen and masters could readily adopt and comfortably deploy. Thus, in 1810, the London compositors concluded an address to the master printers employing many of the most common themes of harmony couched in the language of supplication: 'If sentiments of benevolence, and a regard for our common interests should prompt you, Gentlemen, to any measures designed to restore universal harmony and good-will, whatever you may condescend to propose with that view, will be gratefully received, and met with correspondent dispositions and endeavours, as far as our duty will allow, by Your humble servants, The Compositors'.[97] Employers were similarly quite attuned to the significance of language. In 1834, one master tailor declared that 'the masters had always shown a ready attention to the wishes of the men when couched in proper language'.[98] Thus it appears that the ritualistic process of supplication and response was considered an essential element of successful negotiations.

Such humility and supplication should not be mistaken for evidence of a supplicatory consciousness, however. The London compositors certainly understood that by using these particular forms of address they were adopting a conciliatory approach to negotiations, which, in turn, was meant to elicit a similarly conciliatory gesture from their masters. Yet in the event that this was not forthcoming the compositors were prepared to adopt both a more confrontational approach and a more defiant language. It is worth quoting at length the compositors' explanation of their rhetoric of negotiation in the case of their 1809 and 1810 negotiations with the master printers:

> having perused our addresses and letters, we find that the supplicatory style of the first was rather departed from in those which followed: but this difference of style proceeded naturally from the different circumstances under which they were written: in the first, we endeavoured to make the master printers sensible of our sufferings, and dispose them to afford us that assistance which justice and humanity should prompt them to give; but those which followed, being in consequence of their refusal to comply with what we had requested in our first, had somewhat of an expostulatory air, but certainly contained nothing offensive.
>
> We have also perused some communications, which were addressed to the master printers by the compositors in former times, when they had occasion to make an application for an advance of prices, and we find them written in a bolder style than any master printer have received from us during the present application. In those documents, the words right, claim, &c. occur not unfrequently. This language we have avoided. – In making this remark it is necessary to guard against misapprehension. We are far from wishing to inculcate that what we have been asking is not a right: we are fully convinced, that it is a claim not only supported, but even dictated, by justice. – But, in order to take the most likely course to conduct you with safety into the port of justice, we deemed it allowable, that we might steer clear of the shoals of pride, to use the language of request.[99]

This conscious rhetorical positioning supports Raymond Friedman's observation that negotiations are dramaturgical. Negotiators in collective bargaining situations are only partially influenced by utilitarian objectives; they are equally 'influenced by role expectations and the desire to perform one's role well, create perceptions in the audience, and remind everyone of how society is organized'.[100] Moreover, the negotiator/actors both influence and are influenced by these role expectations. They are able to elicit a particular response from their audiences, but only if their actions largely conform to that audience's expectations. Negotiators can therefore lead their groups to the bargaining arena but they are often expected to act in an adversarial role once there.[101] If a negotiator's actions do not conform to an audience's expectations, their motives and credibility come into question. More broadly, however, negotiator/actors often find their roles already cast for them. That is, they enter into the negotiating process as workers, journeymen, viewers, overseers, merchants or masters. Their public position is already understood even before they undertake the role. Negotiators therefore often find themselves reproducing the roles that are expected of them and thus confirming their social position. Yet the negotiations themselves often implicitly concern the relative social position of the actors: where does an employer's authority begin and end? When does an employer's authority impinge upon a worker's autonomy? In this way, Friedman suggests, negotiators both influence and are influenced by their understanding of society and their place in it.[102]

In the nineteenth-century theatre of industrial relations, the masters assumed the role of fathers or monarchs to their child-subjects. Robert Gray has perceptively noticed how the 'duties of employers were ... constructed by reference to the family on one hand, the state on the other', and this certainly spilled over into the rhetoric of collective bargaining.[103] Thus, employers' organizations often responded to workers' petitions or demands by declaration, announcing the decision of their committees *ex cathedra*. Still, as Gray rightly argues in a slightly different context, 'the language of deference was a language of negotiation'.[104] Despite the apparently arbitrary nature of many employers' organization announcements, some form of negotiation was certainly expected. In the case of the London compositors, the master printers' announcements often avoided mention of the fact that they were continuously meeting and negotiating with their journeymen.[105] Similarly, a meeting of Manchester fustian manufacturers and merchants, which had been convened to regulate competition among firms, admitted a delegation of fustian-cutters, who, upon 'most respectfully solicit[ing] permission to be admitted for the purpose of stating our present and future intentions', were granted a negotiating session on wages.[106]

In the theatre of collective bargaining, masters often drew upon the same fund of moral values and the same vocabulary that their workers used regardless of the rhetorical form in which they were presented. Claims to fairness, justice, mutual understanding and reciprocity were freely appropriated and deployed by both sides. Indeed securing the moral justification for one's claims was essential in most disputes because it mobilized public opinion, whose approbation and support was often critical in industrial disputes. John Doherty's *The Voice of the People* recognized that this was the principal motive behind the Ashton cotton masters' offer to meet with the spinners in 1831. 'They had an object, however, to attain', the paper's leader argued, 'and that object was to appear well with the public. They felt that their attempted reduction was a dirty affair. They knew that, unless they could cheat the public into a belief that they were acting with some degree of fairness, they would be viewed as a set of greedy, unfeeling, and unprincipled fellows, who wished to wring the last farthing, which could possibly be extorted from the incessant toil of their exhausted and unhappy workmen, to add to their already too great gains'.[107] Many employers were acutely aware that public support was gained by establishing their claims to fairness and justice, which explains why many labour disputes were fought simultaneously on the shopfloor and in the press.[108]

The employers' explication and use of the languages of fairness and reciprocity, however, was often distinctly at odds with their workers'. For employers, reciprocity, for example, often connoted deference and respect for authority. Thus, in 1831, the Durham and Northumberland coal-owners issued only a thinly veiled threat when they announced that 'mutual confidence and a good understanding can never be established, and a proper submission to the law maintained, by the coal-owners timidly abandoning their undoubted rights'.[109] Similarly, many masters believed it was grossly 'unfair' for workers to set piece-rates or control entry to the trade. At a meeting of master tailors in 1834, for example, one Cheapside master proclaimed that 'all unions would be but productive of discord if founded on wrong principles, for they were a departure from that great moral rule, to do as you would be done by.... The masters acted on the principle of doing as they would be done by, and it was ridiculous for the men to dictate to them ...'.[110] While many manufacturers, such as the Coventry silk manufacturer John Robinson, were sincere in their efforts to bring about a reconciliation between masters and workers, most industrial disputes necessitated struggles for public opinion in which the interpretations of the shared language of reciprocity and fairness were hotly contested.[111]

The careful attention to such political rituals and theatre, however, did have the effect of imposing order upon collective bargaining meetings as well as according them some legitimacy, as the Ashton meeting of spinners and masters suggests. These same reasons might also explain the similar attention to courtesy and manners that is often discernible. When representatives of the Durham and Northumberland coal-owners first approached the delegates of Tommy Hepburn's union in April 1831,

> they found the Delegates assembled to the amt. of about 200 all seated at tables so contrived as to bring them all into one large room. Hebburn [*sic*] was chairman, and Dixon (of Cowpen [Colliery]) was secretary – pen, ink, and paper was placed at the corners of all the tables. When Hunter and Forster [the owners' representatives] were introduced by a Backworth [Colliery] delegate, Hebburn was on his legs speaking. After repremanding [*sic*] the delegate, for

having introduced 'the Viewers' so unceremoniously without first duly announcing them, and stating the object of their visit – they were asked, what they came there for? They replied, to inquire if they adhered to their proposition of meeting the Viewers on Monday.[112]

Friedman's notion that negotiations possess a dramatic structure – that is, bargainers adopt roles in relation to their audience – is also derived from the observation that bargaining takes place in two venues: frontstage and backstage.[113] Frontstage negotiations, he suggests, are composed of 'rituals of opposition, representation, and control', but backstage negotiations are significantly different. There, negotiators deploy a different set of bargaining tools, including 'discounting' the performance aspect of negotiation rituals or 'signalling' the relative importance of different bargaining issues. More importantly, perhaps, backstage bargaining often occurs in so-called 'sidebar' meetings where negotiators meet privately without an audience. These meetings are not necessarily more productive or successful but they can allow for the presentation of exploratory ideas before publicly committing to them. During the early nineteenth century, such sidebar meetings were perhaps more common than might be expected. There were numerous informal meetings between miners and the owners' agents, for example, during the 1831–32 Durham and Northumberland coal-miners' strike. Lord Londonderry's agent, or viewer, John Buddle, met with Sammy Waddle, the union's secretary, and even offered to make a bet with him on who would win the strike.[114] Fortunately, Waddle did not take the bet. Similarly, Henry Morton, Lord Durham's viewer, 'met the Lambton pitmen this morning in front of Bowes' House – a part of the men and the delegates came forward to me, and the great mass remained at some little distance. We had a long discussion ...'.[115] Certainly, the most surprising 'sidebar' meeting took place between Lord Londonderry and Tommy Hepburn. Acting as Lord Lieutenant, Londonderry had dispersed an allegedly unlawful union rally held on Black Fell, 'conceiving that, with banners and with martial array, such an assemblage was entirely illegal'.[116] As the miners left the fell, Londonderry and Hepburn met and began to talk. Hepburn indicated 'that the differences between them and their Employers was now reduced to a single point, which being settled, the Pitmen would immediately return to their work'.[117] Londonderry reported this conversation to the other coal-owners, and negotiations, which had been broken off for several weeks, were resumed. The new bargaining sessions, however, failed to reach a settlement. Apparently frustrated with the industry's failure to settle the strike and needy of cash, Londonderry thereafter directed his viewers to give in to the miners' demands. He later recalled that 'I hoped to have been able to remove the only two remaining difficulties with the pitmen; but the Hetton delegate, Hepburn, disappointed and misled me'.[118]

The importance of procedures, rituals, and the existence of frontstage and backstage negotiations are all significant aspects of early nineteenth-century collective bargaining, but the authority of the bargaining agents to conclude a settlement was often in question and this frequently complicated the negotiation of agreements. Given the spontaneous and sometimes *ad hoc* nature of some of these collective negotiations, this is understandable. During a strike of journeymen carvers and gilders, for example, four masters and four journeymen met to discuss the issues in dispute. The bargaining session ended with the masters' offer of 34s a week to the journeymen, but the journeymen's negotiators had been instructed to demand 35s. 'To this proposal', it was noted, 'the delegates from the men had not been furnished with the power to accede; their instructions being to insist on 35 shillings.' Therefore, 'the deputation from the men having reported to the committee [of journeymen], the committee called the whole body of workmen together, and the deputies related what had passed at the interview with the masters, when, after some discussion, it was agreed to accept the offer made by the masters, and the men are all at work again as usual'.[119] The London printing masters were perhaps revealing their greater experience with collective bargaining when, in 1810, they offered to negotiate on the condition that the journeymen compositors 'invest your delegates with full powers'.[120]

The question of the authority of the bargaining agents to conclude agreements also exacerbated the very tense negotiating sessions between the Durham and Northumberland coal-owners' representatives and the delegates from Tommy Hepburn's miners' union in April and May 1831. Upon the recommendation of the miners' union, both the miners and the owners sent seven delegates to the Turk's Head Inn, Newcastle, to discuss the disputed issues.[121] According to the report of the one of the owners' delegates, as was described in the preceding chapter, some of the issues were resolved while others required further negotiation.[122] At the end of the session, however, the miners' delegates explained that their authority was only provisional and any agreement had to be ratified by the rank-and-file. 'The Delegates declared', the owners' representatives reported, 'that they were not authorized by the Body of Pitmen to agree finally to the Propositions of the Viewers, and that they could only communicate and consult with the Body upon them.' This may have surprised the owners' representatives. In response, they indicated that under these circumstances their offers were only provisional as well and 'gave them to understand, that this being the case, they could not allow their Propositions to be binding on the Coalowners'.[123] The next day, the owners resolved to hold fast to three of their bargaining positions but at the same time gave their negotiators 'full Powers to settle all the Minor Points'.[124] When the next bargaining session opened on 3 May, the miners' delegates now 'stated that they had full Powers to settle all differences' and this appears to have helped push the negotiations forward.[125]

As in contemporary collective bargaining situations, therefore, in the first half of the nineteenth century collective bargaining was often ritualistic and ceremonial. Both the ritual of supplication and the language of fairness and reciprocity were central to this culture of bargaining and negotiation. Moreover, the bargaining process itself was circumscribed by the limits placed upon negotiators by their constituencies. Collective bargaining therefore involved negotiations not only between labour and management but between labour negotiators and other workers as well as management's negotiators and other masters. The positioning of negotiators and their adoption of particular roles thus made collective bargaining sessions both dramatic and theatrical.

The notion that collective bargaining in the early nineteenth century contained many ritualistic as well as dramaturgical elements is certainly confirmed by the evidence uncovered so far. However, many of the reports of collective bargaining presented here were culled from newspaper reports or public handbills and thus follow their own rhetorical or narrative structures.[126] What historians lack is any detailed account of how negotiators talked to each other. Of course, to collect this information requires a rare entry into the collective bargaining sessions themselves. While there seems to have been little or no desire to lock collective bargaining sessions behind closed doors – collective bargaining was a public ritual, after all – there are few detailed accounts of negotiating sessions themselves that might allow for such a reconstruction. That is, there is no Hansard of collective bargaining debates.

However, at least one remarkable account of such a session does survive in the form of a broadside published in 1825 after a meeting between representatives of the West Riding Fancy Union and the woollen manufacturers in Huddersfield.[127] As a source, it is not untainted. It was published by the union in the hope of garnering public support, yet it purports to be a verbatim account of a collective bargaining session and in this it is unique. Of particular interest is not only the manner in which language performed a negotiative function but also the way in which arguments were framed through the use of narratives or stories. These analytical features of collective bargaining will be discussed further below, but for the moment it is sufficient merely to bring attention to these characteristics of the process.

The meeting was convened after a series of events in which the formation of the union and a strike against one manufacturer had been met by the masters' attempt to adopt the 'document'. The document, which would require their workers to abjure the union, was put forward in the form of a written bond between the masters.[128] One master, G. Senior, seems to have been largely responsible for calling together the two sides in order to avoid a lengthy dispute and 'to have the [weavers'] case properly investigated'. The bargaining session itself opened with a revealing exchange of personal forms of address. The rhetorical and theatrical positioning of the actors began as soon as Senior informally asked the 'lads' to enumerate their complaints and Amos Cowgill, president of the union, responded to the collected 'gentlemen'. Cowgill proceeded in a diffident tone, adopting the humble posture of a supplicant. 'Gentlemen', he began, 'you cannot expect that eloquence in a workman which belongs to an orator, therefore our statements will of course be plain and homely.' The form of this claim obviously belies its content. Cowgill's principal complaints related to falling piece-rate prices on weaving plaid patterns and variations between manufacturers on measurement of the final product. One weavers' representative, John Spivey, put the matter succinctly: 'I have a loom or two of this kind of work, and I have lately been lowered three times in one warp, and have suffered eleven yards by illegal measurement at the same warp'. Cowgill, speaking more plainly, called these practices 'fraud' and 'dead robbery' and thus shifted the intention of his remarks from supplication to accusation.

The ensuing dialogue underscored distinctly different experiences and understandings of the functioning of the local labour market. A wool merchant, Mr Dixon, interjected the question '[W]hy do you not leave such a man and get work some where else?', and the following exchange transpired:

> Cowgill: '[I]t would be of no use, for the precedent being established he would exactly find the same treatment if he removed to another warehouse: for my part, gentlemen, I think this shews the necessity of a Union.'
> Dixon: '[W]hy do you not take such cases to a magistrate?'
> Cowgill: 'Sir, such men would lose their character, and be reported for taking their master before the magistrate, so that the remedy would be worse than the disease.'

Dixon, of course, projected the image of the labourer who was free to sell his labour-power to any employer and whose freedoms were ultimately protected by the state. On the other hand, the forces of circumstance that limited this *de facto* freedom are here rehearsed by the union's president. Significantly, the union did not reject the concept of market relations *per se* but only the notion that the labour market, as it operated in practice, was free. They were subject, it is clear, to that 'dull compulsion of economic relations' that Marx recognized many years later.

Such a disagreement over market relations, and its implicit attack on the owners' comprehension of daily practice, elicited a counter-charge from Beaumont Taylor, a woollen master. Taylor complained that the union planned to equalize wages throughout the district by initiating a series of 'rolling strikes' against one warehouse or manufacturer at a time, if necessary. Thus the dispute over the masters' control of the labour market was dialectically transformed by Taylor into an accusation concerning the union's control of the labour market. This charge appears to have thrown the union representatives onto the defensive. They not only denied that it was true but also tried to explain why they had been seen publicly writing down men's names. This, they weakly suggested, was 'merely to ascertain how many was in and how many out of the union'.

One union speaker tried to break this cycle of recriminations by illuminating the threat that a free labour market posed to the customary values of the community, especially those of order, respect and fair play. He introduced the issue of the masters' opposition to formal apprenticeships, which the speaker contended were essential schools of restraint and deference.

> Only think of a lad being turned into the world at the age of 14 or 15 years and to be told that he is a man: he becomes, as might be expected, presumptuous in his views, defective in his knowledge, and over-bearing in his manners; a plague and burthen to himself, his parents, and to all around him. The columns of the criminal calender [*sic*] are often crowded with the victims of such indiscretion, who, by hardened dispositions and inveterate habits, are in a state of preparation for the scaffold or the gibbet.

Moreover, he asserted, the practices of an unregulated market were inimical to the manufacturers, who were daily threatened by the 'free rider' problem. The language of free trade, he declared, 'is the language used ... by some person who is eager to supplant you by taking your workmen, and your trade, after you have plodded through labyrinths of difficulties, to bring things to perfection'. Indeed a free market jeopardized everyone's livelihood by threatening to reveal the mysteries of the woollen trade: 'Such language [of free trade] might suit a foreigner, who would generally rifle us of our genius, drain us of our treasure, and rob us of our wealth, but ill becomes Mr. Oldfield [a Huddersfield woollen master] who has been so long acquainted with the fancy trade, and knows that secrecy is so requisite in its pursuit'.

The masters attempted to avoid the question of apprenticeship but when John Swift, a union representative, insisted they talk about the issue the bargaining session devolved into a series of personal attacks with an even more pronounced political edge. One master, Mr Sugden, noted that 'we have heard some unpleasant things that were said at a meeting at Skelman Thorpe, by you, Swift', to which Swift responded that it was unlikely he would have said anything 'unpleasant' about the master manufacturers since he had invited them to attend the Skelman Thorpe rally. Sugden, however, ominously announced: 'It was about property'. Swift, apparently surprised by this, acknowledged that he had repeated the biblical maxim concerning the camel and the needle's eye. However, he refused to offer any further comment on Scripture – because the meeting was being held in a public house – except to say that 'our manufacturers' splendid buildings ... have come through the eye of a shuttle', an obvious reference again to the parable of the rich man and the camel.

These growing personal animosities then took a surprising turn when two weavers' representatives, John Heaton and John Rollison, were able to direct the discussions back to the 'bread-and-butter' questions of the measurement and weighing of the finished product. Heaton complained that the weavers were 'losing yards' when their work was measured by the masters, and despite an attempt by Sugden to divert this line of conversation, Rollison confirmed the fact that different masters maintained different standards of measurement. One manufacturer felt compelled to defend the practice. 'Measurement', he explained, 'was divided between law and custom', to which a union delegate rhetorically asked whether '36 inches was not a yard'. To the shock of some in the room, the answer was 'No'. 'Our yard', Mr Norton stated, 'is 37 inches, and always was, and for ever shall be.'

Mr Senior, who had called the meeting together, was nonplussed. For him, 36 inches was a yard and those who practised 'long measure' were in effect cheating him out of several hundred pounds of profit each year. Declaring himself to be 'at a loss for language to express his just indignation', he later went on to state that he would rather have his head cut off than sign an agreement with these other masters. At that moment, Mr Wood of Dalton, one of the manufacturers who had been specifically mentioned as using false measurements, stormed into the meeting room. 'What', he asked, 'what are these men about? Are these manufacturers? Have you a chairman? Who gave orders for them to come here? I never did. What's the subject?' Apparently apprised of the issues under discussion, Wood claimed that 'I will not allow another manufacturer's workmen to examine the customs of my warehouse; when I measure a piece, if it be 2 or 3 inches over a yard, I do not call that a yard; and this was the custom in my father's days, and I will not change'.

For some time, the manufacturers wrangled among themselves over the practice of 'long measure' and the rift between them became so pronounced that those who defended the practice were at one point asked to leave. When the meeting settled back down, the weavers were asked to withdraw while the masters discussed the signing of their anti-union bond. Given the split among them, it is not surprising that the bond was 'committed to the flames' and Mr Senior, who had apparently been holding £10 surety for the bond, threw the money on the table. Another master told him to put the note back in his pocket, but he responded, 'No, never; it shall not go into my pocket again. I have done with this business forever.'

The weavers were then called in again and negotiations over wages and the strike resumed. The masters asked that the strike against one of them be called off but the delegates argued that they did not have the authority to do so. Swift, the weaver's delegate, appears to have sensed that the rift among the manufacturers may have made them more amenable to a settlement. His arguments now began to focus on the employers' obligations and responsibilities toward the weaving community. Seeking to promote 'friendship between masters and men', Swift compared the generosity of the Leeds woollen employers, who had recently endowed working-men's libraries and mechanical institutions, to the failure of the Huddersfield masters to do the same. This, he implied, had had an adverse effect on the entire trade because it prevented workmen from gaining the knowledge necessary to invent new production techniques. In one finale riposte, Beaumont Taylor implicitly admitted the central role of workers in the adaptation of technology but at the same time he pointed out the workers' failure in this regard. 'I have seen a great defect in genius these many years', he said, 'the men have produced nothing new.' Swift deftly turned this observation around and claimed that it only proved his point: wages are so low that men only have time to work and sleep.

By this point, the earlier animosities had disappeared and the respective roles of supplicant and master were taken up once again. Swift apologized for the humble talents of himself and the other delegates; Taylor accepted their complaints and sought to hammer out the final agreement. He asked if the weavers were satisfied with the higher rates given by some of the warehouses. The union responded that they were but wanted all the warehouses' rates in the district to be raised to the same level. This formed the basis of the final accord. The manufacturers agreed to equalize piece-rates throughout Huddersfield 'as soon as trade will permit'. Interestingly enough, the question of measurement was forgotten. Nonetheless, the weavers accepted the manufacturers' offer averring that their union was not an unreasonable institution. A voice from the manufacturers cried out, 'Go on, lads!', and this seemed to confirm their actions.

The records of these Huddersfield discussions are rare not only in the sense that they preserve a unique transcription of a collective bargaining session, but also in the way they indicate how such bargaining sessions were likely to have proceeded. Within the context of the supplicant–grantor relationship, negotiation was neither unexpected nor uncommon. Indeed the language of supplication and deference presupposed a negotiated relationship. Furthermore, both sides immediately assumed their respective roles and thus initially confirmed each other's expectations of their relative social position and status. However, once bargaining began, the negotiations themselves were characterized by the process of 'framing'. Framing indicates both that parties to a dispute bring different frames of reference to the bargaining table and the process whereby the objects of negotiation are subject to the effects of 'reframing' as negotiators juxtapose contending positions and amend or revise their original understanding of the issues.[129] There are a variety of theories of how frames of reference are constructed, that of Erving Goffman perhaps being the most well known.[130] However, of particular relevance here is Donald Schon's argument that frames of reference are narrative structures that 'give coherence to the analysis of issues ... often through reliance on a unifying metaphor which enables the frame holder to make a graceful normative leap from is to ought'.[131] Such a method of framing functions diagnostically to identify a problem at the same time as it operates prescriptively to posit its solution. Thus the framing of an issue implicitly limits the range of possible outcomes. Moreover, framing narratives helps to identify heroes from villains, right from wrong, good from evil.[132] In this sense, framing adopts many of the features of melodrama by serving to organize stories of work, pay and labour relations on the basis of sharp moral polarities.[133]

One can clearly see the process of narrative framing in these negotiations. Indeed issues of wages and prices mingled quite freely with broad political and social issues but both were framed through accessible stories replete with lessons and morals. Thus the presumed functioning of the free labour market was counterposed by both the story of the magistracy's ultimate inefficacy and the threat of the 'free rider'; the alleged evils of trade unionism were supported by the story of men's names being recorded and the threats against property; the importance of defending apprenticeship was underlined by the climactic tale of the scaffold. However, if these narratives serve to both anchor and express bargaining positions at the same time as they indicate the path to an intended settlement, then one can see how these melodramatic expressions of experience circulated around a core of moral and ethical values. For example, when a weaver was asked why he did not report masters who gave 'long measure' to the local magistrate, the weaver's response indicated that he would likely lose his 'character'. Thus the nature of market relations was understood not only as a commodity relationship but also as the source of honour and shame.[134] Even more obvious was the manner in which one unknown weaver expressed his opposition to free trade and free labour. In this instance, the continuing support for maintaining apprenticeship regulations was understood as a prerequisite to learning the 'art and mystery of a weaver' as well as a source of good manners, proper behaviour and self-sufficiency. Freedom at the age of fourteen or fifteen, he argued, was inimical to order and thus led nowhere but to the scaffold or the gibbet. 'Proper restraint' was necessary until boys 'arrived at [the] years of discretion'. Notions of the importance of honour and shame are again quite evident here, but it is perhaps even more important that the market is comprehended and expressed, and thus served to constitute the market experience, in terms of moral narratives. Such tales of dissoluteness, disgrace and criminality that eventually concluded with scaffold scenes were among the most popular moral narratives of the early nineteenth century, as V.A.C. Gatrell has so brilliantly shown.[135] Indeed, one weaver's complaint against long measure during the bargaining session was summed up in terms of honourable behaviour: 'I think such conduct, gentlemen, is too bad', he lamented.

Such antithetical framing, or tit-for-tat storytelling, took place nevertheless within some shared patterns of discourse. However, that shared discourse appears to have been revealed only by the disruptive effect of the 'long measure' controversy among the owners, a disruption that also took physical form with the remarkable entrance of Mr Wood of Dalton onto the scene. The resolution of the conflict was marked by the resumption of the roles and language of supplicant and master. It was perhaps only within this context that the negotiative authority of custom and community could be safely asserted. Therefore, in the case of collective bargaining during the early nineteenth century, conflicts over market relations were often expressed and understood in terms other than those of the market itself. Perhaps the conscious identification of a distinct economic sphere had yet to be accepted, and with it labour's identification as a commodity, and thus moral definitions of the market were common.[136] Nevertheless, collective bargaining itself may be said to have expressed several important aspects of British culture. Collective bargaining institutions drew upon political and associational models for their structure. The rhetorical and dramaturgical aspects of collective bargaining drew upon commonly recognized tropes as well as distinctions between actors and their audiences. Finally, the content of such sessions were 'framed' by perspectives and goals that were given expression through culturally significant narratives and story structures. Collective bargaining might therefore be better understood as an expression of British culture and not as an adaptive response of workers or employers to the changing fortunes of nineteenth-century capitalism.

Appendix: Employers' organizations, 1745–1850 (date founded or first recorded)

I. 1745–1775
Association of Salt Proprietors (Dunfermline), 1746[137]
Master Tailors (London), 1764[138]
Durham and Northumberland Coal Owners' Association, 1771–1844[139]
Silver Platers' Trade Association (Sheffield), 1773–84[140]

II. 1776–1800
Yorkshire Worsted Committee, 1777[141]
Midlands Ironmasters, 1777[142]
Nottingham Hosiers' Association, 1777–79[143]
Associated Smelters (Bristol and South Wales), *c.* 1785[144]
London Master Printers, 1785[145]
London Master Bookbinders, 1786[146]
Cornish Copper Producers, 1787[147]
Birmingham Steel Manufacturers, 1790[148]
Yorkshire Ironmasters, *c.* 1790s–1828[149]
London Society of Master Letter-Founders, 1793–1820[150]
Committee of Porter Brewers, 1795[151]
East Midlands Coal Owners' Association, 1798[152]
Association of Weavers (Stockport, Bolton, Manchester), 1799[153]

III. 1801–1825
United Committee of Gloucestershire and Somerset Clothiers, 1802[154]
South Wales Ironmasters, 1802–24[155]

Figure 1 Employers' Organizations, 1745–1850

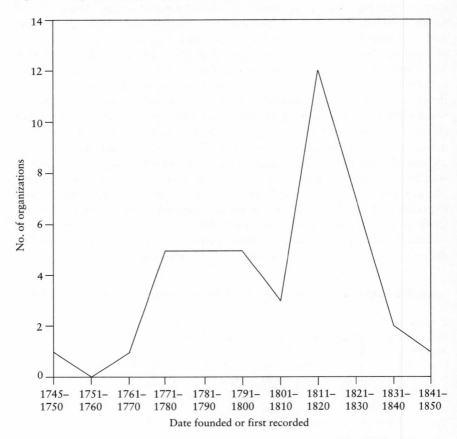

Society of Master Carpenters, London, *c.* 1810[156]
Glasgow Cotton Masters, 1812[157]
Nottingham Silk Manufacturers, 1814[158]
Sheffield Mercantile and Manufacturing Union (Master Cutlers), 1814[159]
Preston Calico Masters, 1815[160]
General Committee of Shipowners (North Shields), 1815[161]
Whitehaven Shipowners, 1816[162]
Coventry Manufacturers' Committee, 1816[163]
Leicester Hosiers, 1817[164]
Cheshire Salt Producers, 1817[165]
Master Hatters (London), 1817[166]
Macclesfield Silk Manufacturers and Throwsters, 1818[167]
Spitalfields Silk Weaving Masters, 1818[168]
Master Shipwrights Association (Liverpool), 1823[169]
London Master Sadlers, *c.* 1824[170]

Staffordshire Ironmasters, 1824[171]
London Master Shoemakers, 1825[172]
Thames Shipbuilders, 1825[173]
Chamber of Commerce (Staffordshire Master Potters), 1825[174]

IV. 1826–1850
Master Cotton Spinners and Power-loom Manufacturers of Manchester, 1829[175]
Leeds Clothier Masters, 1833[176]
Yorkshire and Durham Carpet Manufacturers' Association, 1839[177]
Leeds Flax Spinners, 1842[178]

Notes

1   Sidney and Beatrice Webb, *Industrial Democracy*, new edn (1897; London: Longman, Green and Co., 1902), pp. 173–221; Michael P. Jackson, *An Introduction to Industrial Relations* (London: Routledge, 1991), p. 135; Howard F. Gospel and Gillian Palmer, *British Industrial Relations*, 2nd edn (London: Routledge, 1993), pp. 176–7.

2   Catharina Lis and Hugo Soly, '"An Irresistible Phalanx": Journeymen Associations in Western Europe, 1300–1800', *International Review of Social History*, vol. 39 (1994), supplement no. 2, pp. 11–52; John Rule, 'Proto-Unions?', *Historical Studies in Industrial Relations*, no. 2 (September 1996), pp. 139–52. For Britain, the surest guides to these themes are C.R. Dobson, *Masters and Journeymen: A Prehistory of Industrial Relations, 1717–1800* (London: Croom Helm, 1980); John Rule, *The Experience of Labour in Eighteenth-Century English Industry* (New York: St Martin's Press, 1981); and John Rule, ed., *British Trade Unionism, 1750–1850: The Formative Years* (London: Longman, 1988).

3   H.A. Clegg, *The Changing System of Industrial Relations in Great Britain* (Oxford: Blackwell, 1979), p. 63.

4   Adam Smith, *An Inquiry into the Nature and Causes of the Wealth of Nations*, ed. E. Cannan (1776; Chicago: University of Chicago Press, 1976), bk i, ch. viii, p. 75.

5   Smith, *Wealth of Nations*, bk i, ch. x, pt ii, p. 144: 'People of the same trade seldom meet together, even for merriment and diversion, but the conversation ends in a conspiracy against the public, or in some contrivance to raise prices'.

6   As Ashton noted: 'So numerous and diverse, in fact, were the forms in which the corporate sense of the early industrialists found expression, that justice could be done to them only by a special study, which ... might throw a flood of new light on the economic life of the late eighteenth and early nineteenth centuries'. T.S. Ashton, *Iron and Steel in the Industrial Revolution* (Manchester: Manchester University Press, 1924), p. 185. See also T.S. Ashton, *The Industrial Revolution, 1760–1830* (1948; Oxford: Oxford University Press, 1980), ch. 5; and J.H. Clapham, *An Economic History of Modern Britain: The Early Railway Age, 1820–1850* (Cambridge: Cambridge University Press, 1959), pp. 199–205.

7   Ashton, *Industrial Revolution*, p. 88.

8   The British state's alleged absence from the sphere of industrial relations has
    been recently questioned by K.D. Ewing, 'The State and Industrial Relations:
    "Collective Laissez-Faire" Revisited', *Historical Studies in Industrial Rela-
    tions*, no. 5 (Spring 1998), pp. 1–31.
9   See above, Chapter 3.
10 Charles F. Sabel and Jonathan Zeitlin, 'Stories, Strategies, Structures: Rethink-
    ing Historical Alternatives to Mass Production', in Sabel and Zeitlin, eds,
    *World of Possibilities: Flexibility and Mass Production in Western Industriali-
    zation* (Cambridge: Cambridge University Press, 1997), pp. 20–8.
11 William Lazonick, *Competitive Advantage on the Shop Floor* (Cambridge,
    Mass.: Harvard University Press, 1990), pp. 103–5; Michael Huberman, *Es-
    cape from the Market: Negotiating Work in Lancashire* (Cambridge: Cam-
    bridge University Press, 1996), pp. 132–48.
12 There is no need to rehearse the entire 'standard-of-living debate' here. For a
    useful guide to some of the more recent contributions, see Joel Mokyr, 'Edi-
    tor's Introduction: The New Economic History and the Industrial Revolution',
    in Mokyr, ed., *The British Industrial Revolution: An Economic Perspective*
    (Boulder, Colo.: Westview Press, 1993), pp. 118–30. Many of the original con-
    tributions to the debate are collected in A.J. Taylor, ed., *The Standard of Liv-
    ing in Britain in the Industrial Revolution* (London: Methuen, 1975).
13 Gospel and Palmer, *British Industrial Relations*, p. 35.
14 Webb and Webb, *Industrial Democracy*, pp. 173–221.
15 See the several *Reports from the Select Committee on Artizans and Machinery*,
    Parliamentary Papers (hereafter PP), vol. v (1824), which often investigated
    the activities of employers' organizations as well as trade unions. Francis
    Place, whose influence upon this committee is well known, was convinced that
    trade unions were in part a response to the employers' organizations. See
    Graham Wallas, *The Life of Francis Place, 1771–1854*, 4th edn (1898; Lon-
    don: George Allen & Unwin, 1951), p. 217.
16 For this aspect of the 1563 Act and some of its later effects, see
    W.E. Minchinton, ed., *Wage Regulation in Pre-Industrial England* (Newton
    Abbot: David & Charles, 1972).
17 John Rule, 'Against Innovation?: Custom and Resistance in the Workplace,
    1700–1850', in T. Harris, ed., *Popular Culture in England, c. 1500–1850*
    (New York: St Martin's Press, 1995), pp. 170–9.
18 Sidney and Beatrice Webb, *The History of Trade Unionism*, new edn (1894;
    London: Longman, 1920), p. 74.
19 *Second Report from the Select Committee on Artizans and Machinery*, PP,
    vol. v (1824), pp. 54–5.
20 13 Geo. III, c. 68. Classic accounts include Webb and Webb, *History of Trade
    Unionism*, pp. 54–5; J.H. Clapham, 'The Spitalfields Acts, 1773–1824', *Eco-
    nomic Journal*, vol. 26: no. 104 (December 1916), pp. 459–71; and M.
    Dorothy George, *London Life in the Eighteenth Century* (1925; New York:
    Capricorn Books, 1965), pp. 176–95. More recently, see the work of Marc
    Steinberg, especially '"The Labour of the Country is the Wealth of the
    Country": Class Identity, Consciousness, and the Role of Discourse in the
    Making of the English Working Class', *International Labor and Working-
    Class History*, no. 49 (Spring 1996), pp. 1–25, and '"The Great End of All

Government ...": Working People's Construction of Citizenship Claims in Early Nineteenth-Century England and the Matter of Class', *International Review of Social History*, vol. 40 (1995), supplement no. 3, pp. 19–50. I am grateful to Professor Steinberg for making copies of his articles available to me. Unfortunately, his book *Fighting Words: Working-Class Formation, Collective Action, and Discourse in Early Nineteenth-Century England* (Ithaca: Cornell University Press, 1999) appeared too late for inclusion here. The superb article by Alain Cottereau, 'The Fate of Collective Manufactures in the Industrial World: The Silk Industries of Lyon and London, 1800–1850', in Sabel and Zeitlin, eds, *World of Possibilities*, pp. 75–152, reaches many similar conclusions discussed here.

21 See, for example, the various price lists in the Corporation of London Record Office (hereafter CLRO), Orders of Quarter Sessions and Orders upon Appeals, May 1804–February 1808, vol. 15, 22 April 45 Geo. III; 20 November 46 Geo. III; 29 April 46 Geo. III; and 5 February 48 Geo. III.

22 *Report from the Select Committee on Silk Ribbon Weavers Petition*, PP, vol. ix (1818), p. 142.

23 Clapham, 'The Spitalfields Acts', pp. 460 n. 2, 461.

24 *Reports from Commissioners: Handloom Weavers*, PP, vol. xxiv (1840), Reports from Assistant Handloom Weavers Commissioners, pt iv, p. 204. Emphasis in original.

25 *Report from the Select Committee on Silk Ribbon Weavers Petitions*, p. 142.

26 William Hale, *An Appeal to the Public, in Defense of the Spitalfields Act: with Remarks on the Causes which have led to the Miseries and Moral Deterioration of the Poor* (London, 1822), p. 6. Emphasis in original.

27 CLRO, Orders of Quarter Sessions and Orders upon Appeal, vol. 19, 21 October 3 Geo. IV.

28 Place Papers, British Library Additional Manuscript (hereafter BL Add. Ms.) 27800, f. 49.

29 *Report from Commissioners: Handloom Weavers*, Reports from Assistant Handloom Weavers Commissioners, pt iv, p. 213.

30 *Report from the Select Committee on Silk Ribbon Weavers Petitions*, p. 58.

31 Place Papers, BL Add. Ms. 27801, f. 221.

32 Dobson, *Masters and Journeymen*, pp. 74–92.

33 Norman McCord, 'The Government of Tyneside, 1800–1850', *Transactions of the Royal Historical Society*, 5th ser., vol. 20 (1970), pp. 17–19; Peter King, 'Edward Thompson's Contribution to Eighteenth-Century Studies: The Patrician–Plebeian Model Re-examined', *Social History*, vol. 21: no. 2 (May 1996), pp. 226–8.

34 For a fine introduction and background to industrial relations in Macclesfield during this period, see Gail Malmgreen, *Silk Town: Industry and Culture in Macclesfield, 1750–1835* (Hull: Hull University Press, 1985), ch. 2.

35 The following account is drawn from the Place Papers, BL Add. Ms. 27801, ff. 224–31 and *Fifth Report from the Select Committee on Artizans and Machinery*, PP, vol. v (1824), pp. 582–7.

36 Place Papers, BL Add. Ms. 27801, ff. 225–31.

37 McCord, 'Government of Tyneside', p. 17.

38 James A. Jaffe, *The Struggle for Market Power: Industrial Relations in the*

    British Coal Industry, 1800–1840 (Cambridge: Cambridge University Press, 1991), pp. 165–6.

39 Jaffe, *Struggle for Market Power*, pp. 166–78.

40 These meetings have been outlined above, see Chapter 3.

41 *Fifth Report from the Select Committee on Artizans and Machinery*, p. 417.

42 *Fifth Report from the Select Committee on Artizans and Machinery*, pp. 263–5.

43 R.G. Kirby and A.E. Musson, *The Voice of the People: John Doherty, 1798–1854, Trade Unionist, Radical and Factory Reformer* (Manchester: Manchester University Press, 1975), pp. 72–5.

44 Ellic Howe, ed., *The London Compositor: Documents Relating to Wages, Working Conditions and Customs of the London Printing Trade, 1785–1900* (London: Oxford University Press, 1947), pp. 72–4.

45 Quoted in Howe, ed., *London Compositor*, p. 72.

46 Howe, ed., *London Compositor*, p. 74.

47 London Union of Compositors, *The London Scale of Prices for Compositors' Work: Agreed upon, April 16th, 1810, with Explanatory Notes*, 2nd edn (London, 1837), pp. 17–18.

48 Quoted in Howe, ed., *London Compositor*, p. 84.

49 Howe, ed., *London Compositor*, pp. 87–8.

50 Howe, ed., *London Compositor*, p. 88.

51 Quoted in Howe, ed., *London Compositor*, p. 89.

52 London Union of Compositors, *The London Scale of Prices*, pp. 17–18.

53 Modern Records Centre, University of Warwick Library, National Graphical Association, London Region: London Union of Compositors (hereafter MRC, NGA), Mss. 28/CO/1/10/1.

54 Howe, ed., *London Compositor*, ch. 5.

55 *Report from the Committee on Silk Ribbon Weavers Petitions*, p. 113.

56 *Report from the Committee on Silk Ribbon Weavers Petitions*, p. 8.

57 *Reports from Commissioners: Handloom Weavers*, Reports from Assistant Handloom Weavers Commissioners, pt iv, pp. 199–201.

58 Similar attempts by shopkeepers and manufacturers to bring the Manchester cotton-spinners and their masters to the bargaining table occurred during the 1828–29 cotton-spinners' strike. See Kirby and Musson, *Voice of the People*, p. 74.

59 *Report from the Committee on Silk Ribbon Weavers Petitions*, p. 34.

60 *Reports from Commissioners: Handloom Weavers*, Reports from Assistant Handloom Weavers Commissioners, pt iv, p. 205.

61 *Reports from Commissioners: Handloom Weavers*, Reports from Assistant Handloom Weavers Commissioners, pt iv, pp. 216–18.

62 John Prest, *The Industrial Revolution in Coventry* (Oxford: Oxford University Press, 1960), p. ix.

63 *Reports from Commissioners: Handloom Weavers*, Reports from Assistant Handloom Weavers Commissioners, pt iv, p. 218.

64 *Reports from Commissioners: Handloom Weavers*, Reports from Assistant Handloom Weavers Commissioners, pt iv, p. 221.

65 *Reports from Commissioners: Handloom Weavers*, Reports from Assistant Handloom Weavers Commissioners, pt iv, p. 221.

66 *Reports from Commissioners: Handloom Weavers*, Reports from Assistant Handloom Weavers Commissioners, pt iv, pp. 221–2.

67 *Reports from Commissioners: Handloom Weavers*, Reports from Assistant Handloom Weavers Commissioners, pt iv, pp. 222.

68 *Reports from Commissioners: Handloom Weavers*, Reports from Assistant Handloom Weavers Commissioners, pt iv, pp. 223–4.

69 There are many similarities here with the early history of the formation and maintenance of price lists in the Nottingham hosiery and lace trades. There, a price list had been negotiated in 1787 and maintained for more than two decades thereafter. Efforts to maintain price lists were often characterized by attempts both to raise the prices offered by undercutting manufacturers and to prevent workers from accepting such prices. In this, hosiers and workers frequently worked together. Malcolm Thomis, *Politics and Society in Nottingham, 1785–1835* (Oxford: Blackwell, 1969), pp. 39–41; Norman H. Cuthbert, *The Lace Makers' Society: A Study of Trade Unionism in the British Lace Industry, 1760–1960* (Nottingham: Amalgamated Society of Operative Lace Makers and Auxiliary Workers, 1960), pp. 7–9, 19–20.

70 *Select Committee on Masters and Operatives (Equitable Councils of Conciliation)*, PP, vol. xiii (1856), pp. 100–1.

71 Adrian Randall, *Before the Luddites: Custom, Community and Machinery in the English Woollen Industry, 1776–1809* (Cambridge: Cambridge University Press, 1991), pp. 144–5; J.L. and Barbara Hammond, *The Skilled Labourer*, rev. edn (1919; London: Longman, 1979), pp. 136–9.

72 *Fifth Report from the Select Committee on Artizans and Machinery*, p. 394.

73 *Fifth Report from the Select Committee on Artizans and Machinery*, pp. 405–6. The settlement was later scuttled by the manufacturers' prosecution of the filesmiths' deputies for combination. The prosecution, however, was withdrawn and the matter settled by arbitration.

74 On the potters' strikes, see John Boyle, 'An Account of Strikes in the Potteries, in the Years 1834 and 1836', *Journal of the Royal Statistical Society*, vol. 1 (1839), pp. 37–45; W.H. Warburton, *The History of Trade Union Organisation in the North Staffordshire Potteries* (London: George Allen & Unwin, 1931), pp. 80–101; Robert Fyson, 'Unionism, Class and Community in the 1830s: Aspects of the National Union of Operative Potters', in Rule, ed., *British Trade Unionism*, pp. 200–19.

75 Staffordshire Record Office (hereafter SRO), Samuel Allcock Letterbook, MF/49 Frame 27.

76 British Library of Political and Economic Science, London School of Economics, Webb Trade Union Collection, Section A, XLIV, f. 249. The union had offered to negotiate with the manufacturers as early as October, but the latter refused to meet with a 'secret' union. See Warburton, *History of Trade Union Organisation*, p. 91.

77 SRO, Samuel Allcock Letterbook, MF/49 Frame 15, reprinted in Warburton, *History of Trade Union Organisation*, pp. 264–82.

78 SRO, Samuel Allcock Letterbook, MF/49 Frame 15.

79 Although Warburton emphasizes the fact that the conference was conditional upon the potters' representatives being selected from among those not on the union's Board of Management, the same was true for the manufacturers. Their

representatives had to be 'individuals divested of their characters of the members of the Chamber of Commerce'. See SRO, Samuel Allcock Letterbook, MF/49 Frame 15, and Warburton, *History of Trade Union Organisation*, pp. 94–5.

80   SRO, Samuel Allcock Letterbook, MF/49 Frame15; Warburton, *History of Trade Union Organisation*, p. 96.

81   Warburton, *History of Trade Union Organisation*, pp. 98–9.

82   Multi-level bargaining of this sort did take hold in the trades after mid-century. See Richard Whipp, *Patterns of Labour: Work and Social Change in the Pottery Industry* (London: Routledge, 1990), pp. 58–63, 146–56.

83   This remains one of the most obvious characteristics of contemporary British collective bargaining systems. See William Brown, Paul Marginson and Janet Walsh, 'Management: Pay Determination and Collective Bargaining', in Paul Edwards, ed., *Industrial Relations: Theory and Practice in Britain* (Oxford: Blackwell, 1995), pp. 134–42, and Clegg, *Changing System of Industrial Relations*, pp. 9–19.

84   Michael W. Flinn, *The History of the British Coal Industry, Volume 2, 1700–1830: The Industrial Revolution* (Oxford: Clarendon Press, 1984), pp. 352–3; see also Hylton Scott, 'The Miners' Bond in Northumberland and Durham', pts 1 and 2, *Proceedings of the Antiquaries of Newcastle-upon-Tyne*, 4th ser., vol. 11: nos 2 and 3 (1947), pp. 55–78, 87–98; P.E.H. Hair, 'The Binding of the Pitmen of the North-East, 1800–1809', *Durham University Journal*, new ser., vol. 27: no. 3 (1965), pp. 1–13; Robert Colls, *The Pitmen of the Northern Coalfield: Work, Culture and Protest, 1790–1850* (Manchester: Manchester University Press, 1987), pp. 45–51; Jaffe, *Struggle for Market Power*, pp. 100–5.

85   Northumberland Record Office (hereafter NRO), Watson Mss., NRO 3410/Wat/1/5/97; see also NRO, Minutes of the General Meetings of the Coal Owners of the Rivers Tyne and Wear, 29 April 1831, p. 93. See above, pp. 78–9.

86   NRO, Minutes of the General Meetings of the Coal Owners of the Rivers Tyne and Wear, 3 May 1831, pp. 96–7.

87   Colls, *Pitmen of the Northern Coalfield*, p. 83; Jaffe, *Struggle for Market Power*, p. 111.

88   Bell Collection, NRO 3410/Bell/11/368.

89   Cottereau, 'Silk Industries of Lyons and London', pp. 116–18.

90   Whipp, *Patterns of Labour*, p. 151.

91   J.W.F. Rowe, *Wages in the Coal Industry* (London: P.S. King & Son, 1923), pp. 49–51; Jaffe, *Struggle for Market Power*, pp. 107–8, 112–13.

92   *Reports from Commissioners: Handloom Weavers*, Reports from Assistant Handloom Weavers Commissioners, pt iv, p. 241.

93   He noted not only that these types of proceedings were 'wholly unrecognized by economical science' but also that 'on both sides, the strict letter of the law has been systematically though almost unconsciously violated, in proceedings which the judge would condemn, but which it is incumbent upon the legislator carefully to observe, as indicating the elements which he has to meet, to pacify and to govern'. *Reports from Commissioners: Handloom Weavers*, Reports from Assistant Handloom Weavers Commissioners, pt iv, p. 241.

94   *The Voice of the People*, 22 January 1831, p. 32.

95   The resolution is reprinted in *The Voice of the People*, 29 January 1831, p. 36; the spinners' response in *The Voice of the People*, 22 January 1831, p. 32.

96   *The Voice of the People*, 22 January 1831, p. 32.

97   Quoted in Howe, ed., *London Compositor*, p. 165.

98   British Library, Place Collection, Set 51, f. 247.

99   Quoted in Howe, ed., *London Compositor*, p. 152.

100 Raymond A. Friedman, *Front Stage, Backstage: The Dramatic Structure of Labor Negotiations* (Cambridge, Mass.: MIT Press, 1994), pp. 16–17.

101 Friedman, *Front Stage, Backstage*, pp. 14, 86–90.

102 Friedman, *Front Stage, Backstage*, p. 15.

103 Robert Gray, *The Factory Question and Industrial England, 1830–1860* (Cambridge: Cambridge University Press, 1996), p. 122.

104 Gray, *Factory Question and Industrial England* , p. 226.

105 Howe, ed., *London Compositor*, pp. 169–70.

106 Place Papers, BL Add. Ms. 27803, f. 299.

107 *The Voice of the People*, 29 January 1831, p. 36.

108 The master tailors, for example, desired that 'the greatest publicity be given to their proceedings' in order that the 'Nobility, Gentry, and public' might suspend their orders until the end of their dispute with the journeymen tailors in 1834. See Place Papers, BL Add. Ms. 27803, f. 247.

109 *Newcastle Chronicle*, 17 March 1832.

110 British Library, Place Collection, Set 51, f. 247.

111 On Robinson's efforts, see *Report from the Committee on Silk Ribbon Weavers Petitions*, pp. 34–5.

112 Durham County Record Office (hereafter DCRO), Londonderry Papers, D/Lo/C 142(672), Buddle to Londonderry, 10 April 1831.

113 Friedman, *Front Stage, Backstage*, ch. 5.

114 DCRO, Londonderry Papers, D/Lo/C 142(842), Buddle to Londonderry, no date (*c*. June 1832).

115 Lambton Estate Archive, Lambton Mss., Henry Morton to Lord Durham, 6 April 1831.

116 See Lord Londonderry's address to the coal trade in the *Newcastle Chronicle*, 11 June 1831.

117 NRO, General Meetings of the Coal Owners of the Rivers Tyne and Wear, 6 May 1831, p. 100; see also, Bell Collection, NRO 3410/Bell/11/327; Jaffe, *Struggle for Market Power*, pp. 172–3.

118 *Newcastle Chronicle*, 11 June 1831; Bell Collection, NRO 3410/Bell/11/327.

119 Place Papers, BL Add. Ms. 27803, f. 518v.

120 Howe, ed., *London Compositor*, p. 158.

121 NRO, Minutes of the Committee Meetings of the Coal Owners of the Rivers Tyne and Wear, 23 April 1831, p. 320.

122 See above, pp. 78–9.

123 NRO, Minutes of the General Meetings of the Coal Owners of the Rivers Tyne and Wear, 29 April 1831, pp. 93–4.

124 NRO, Minutes of the General Meetings of the Coal Owners of the Rivers Tyne and Wear, 30 April 1831, p. 95.

125 NRO, Minutes of the General Meetings of the Coal Owners of the Rivers Tyne and Wear, 3 May 1831, pp. 96–7.

126 Gray, *Factory Question and Industrial England*, pp. 135–5.

127 The broadside is preserved among the Place Papers, BL Add. Ms. 27803, f. 369. Subsequent references pertain to this document unless noted otherwise.

128 The union's rules were adopted in 1824 and published as *Articles and Regulations of the West Riding Fancy Union, for the Protection of the Trade of the Fancy Manufacturer* (Huddersfield, 1824). A copy is preserved in Place Papers, BL Add. Ms. 27803, ff. 358–63. The 'document' was a common defence against trade unionism throughout the textile trades. See Kirby and Musson, *Voice of the People*, pp. 10, 21, 31, 59.

129 An excellent introduction to these issues within the context of negotiations is Linda L. Putnam and Majia Holmer, 'Framing, Reframing, and Issue Development', in Linda L. Putnam and Michael Roloff, eds, *Communication and Negotiation* (Newbury Park, Calif.: Sage Publications: 1992), pp. 128–55. I would like to thank Raymond Friedman for suggesting these references.

130 Erving Goffman, *Frame Analysis: An Essay on the Organization of Experience* (New York: Harper & Row, 1974).

131 Donald Schon and Martin Rein, 'Frame-Critical Policy Analysis and Frame-Reflective Policy Practice', *Knowledge and Policy*, vol. 9: no. 1 (Spring 1996), pp. 85–105.

132 Linda L. Putnam, Shirley A. Van Hoeven and Connie Bullis, 'The Role of Rituals and Fantasy in Teachers' Bargaining', *Western Journal of Speech Communication*, vol. 55 (Winter 1991), pp. 85–103.

133 Peter Brooks, *The Melodramatic Imagination: Balzac, Henry James, Melodrama, and the Mode of Excess* (New Haven: Yale University Press, 1976) has been an especially important influence on a variety of historians, including Sarah Maza, *Private Live and Public Affairs: The Causes Célèbres of Prerevolutionary France* (Berkeley: University of California Press, 1993); Lynn Hunt, *The Family Romance of the French Revolution* (Berkeley: University of California Press, 1992); and Anna Clark, *The Struggle for the Breeches: Gender and the Making of the British Working Class* (Berkeley: University of California Press, 1995), pp. 220–32. See also Maza's survey of the uses of narrative in contemporary historical research, 'Stories in History: Cultural Narratives in Recent Works in European History', *American Historical Review*, vol. 101: no. 5 (December 1996), pp. 1493–515.

134 For some useful remarks on the role of honour and shame in nineteenth-century industrial relations, see William Reddy, *Money and Liberty in Modern Europe: A Critique of Historical Understanding* (Cambridge: Cambridge University Press, 1987), pp. 161–5, 219–20.

135 V.A.C. Gatrell, *The Hanging Tree: Execution and English People, 1770–1868* (Oxford: Oxford University Press, 1994), especially chs 4 and 5.

136 The definition of labour as a commodity, however, is itself culturally constructed. See Richard Biernacki, *The Fabrication of Labor: Germany and Britain, 1640–1914* (Berkeley: University of California Press, 1995).

137 Peter Payne, 'Halbeath Colliery and Saltworks', in A. Slaven and D.H. Aldcroft, eds, *Business, Banking and Urban History: Essays in Honour of S.G. Checkland* (Edinburgh: J. Donald, 1982).

138 Dobson, *Masters and Journeyman*, p. 45. Even earlier action could be traced to the 1720 dispute over the tailors' combination act. See also Francis Place's

testimony before the *Select Committee on Artizans and Machinery*, PP, vol. v (1824), p. 45.

139 Jaffe, *Struggle for Market Power*.

140 Sheffield City Library, Minute Books, MD 2086; Ashton, *Iron and Steel in the Industrial Revolution*, p. 184.

141 D.T. Jenkins, *The West Riding Wool Textile Industry, 1770–1835: A Study of Fixed Capital Formation* (Edington, Wilts.: Pasold Research Fund, 1975).

142 Ashton, *Iron and Steel in the Industrial Revolution*, p. 164.

143 Thomis, *Politics and Society in Nottingham*, pp. 41–2.

144 Clapham, *Economic History of Modern Britain*, p. 200.

145 Testimony of Richard Taylor, printer, before *Select Committee on Artizans and Machinery*, pp. 52–6; see also D.H.S. Bewley, *The Federation of Master Printers, How it Began* (London: W. Sessions, 1950); Ellic Howe, *The British Federation of Master Printers, 1900–1950* (London: British Federation of Master Printers, 1950).

146 Andrew H. Yarmie, 'Employers' Associations in Mid-Victorian England', *International Review of Social History*, vol. 25 (1980), p. 211.

147 Ashton, *Iron and Steel in the Industrial Revolution*, p. 184n.

148 Ashton, *Iron and Steel in the Industrial Revolution*, p. 184.

149 Clapham, *Economic History of Modern Britain*, p. 204.

150 A.E. Musson, 'The London Society of Master Letter-Founders, 1793–1820', reprinted in *Trade Union and Social History* (London: Frank Cass, 1974), pp. 137–56.

151 Peter Mathias, *The Brewing Industry in England, 1700–1830* (Cambridge: Cambridge University Press, 1959).

152 A.R. Griffin and C.P. Griffin, 'The Role of Coal Owners' Associations in the East Midlands in the Nineteenth Century', *Renaissance and Modern Studies*, vol. 15 (1973), pp. 95–121.

153 Robert Glen, *Urban Workers in the Early Industrial Revolution* (London: Croom Helm, 1984), p. 147.

154 Randall, *Before the Luddites*, pp. 204–6; Gloucestershire Record Office, Gloucestershire Collection, JF.13.25, Minutes of the Manufacturer's Committee.

155 Clapham, *Economic History of Modern Britain*, p. 204

156 *Report from the Select Committee on Artizans and Machinery*, pp. 165–72, testimony of Thomas Martin.

157 A. Aspinall, *The Early English Trade Unions* (London: Blatchworth Press, 1949), pp. 142–51.

158 Aspinall, *Early English Trade Unions*, pp. 175–7.

159 Webb and Webb, *History of Trade Unionism*, p. 73; Ashton, *Iron and Steel in the Industrial Revolution*, p. 184; *Report from the Select Committee on Artizans and Machinery*, pp. 401–4.

160 Aspinall, *Early English Trade Unions*, pp. 185–6 .

161 Aspinall, *Early English Trade Unions*, p. 185.

162 Aspinall, *Early English Trade Unions*, p. 223.

163 *Reports from Commissioners: Handloom Weavers*, pp. 199, 219–24.

164 Aspinall, *Early English Trade Unions*, pp. 230, 237; *Leicester Chronicle*, 5 July 1817.

165 Edward Hughes, *Studies in Administration and Finance, 1558–1825* (Manchester: Manchester University Press, 1934) cited in Clapham, *Economic History of Modern Britain*, p. 200; *Committee on the Use of Rock Salt in the Fisheries*, PP, vol. iii (1817), p. 22.

166 *Report from the Select Committee on Artizans and Machinery*, pp. 73–4, 91–5.

167 *Report from the Select Committee on Petitions of Ribbon Weavers*, p. 79; *Report from the Select Committee on Artizans and Machinery*, pp. 582–7.

168 *Report from the Select Committee on Petitions of Ribbon Weavers*, p. 191.

169 *Report from the Select Committee on Artizans and Machinery*, pp. 234–5; testimony of John Cain, secretary of Shipwright's Benefit Society.

170 See Francis Place's testimony before the *Select Committee on Artizans and Machinery*, p. 45.

171 Testimony of John Martineau, engineer, *Select Committee on Artizans and Machinery*, p.12; also testimony of Samuel Walker and William Yates, ironmasters of Gospel Oak, Staff., pp. 130–2.

172 *Report from the Select Committee on Artizans and Machinery*, p. 147; *The Times*, 15 November 1825.

173 *Select Committee on Combination Laws*, PP, vol. iv (1825), pp. 404, 166, cited in Clapham, *Economic History of Modern Britain*.

174 Warburton, *History of Trade Union Organization*.

175 Kirby and Musson, *Voice of the People*, p. 59; Alan Fowler and Terry Wyke, eds, *The Barefoot Aristocrats: A History of the Amalgamated Association of Operative Cotton Spinners* (Littleborough, Lancs.: G. Kelsall, 1987), p. 27.

176 Webb and Webb, *History of Trade Unionism*, p. 133; *The Times*, 28 October 1833.

177 Yarmie, 'Employers' Organizations', p. 212.

178 W.G. Rimmer, *Marshalls of Leeds, Flax-Spinners 1788–1886* (Cambridge: Cambridge University Press, 1960).

5

The gift at work?: the effort bargain and shopfloor restriction in the early industrial workplace

The Pitmen are a most singular race, and are really possessed of all the Crafty wiles of the American Indians. (Henry Morton to J.G. Lambton [later Lord Durham], 17 May 1831)

The gift and industrial relations

Industrial relations take place at many levels and appear in many forms. Disputes and grievances that are articulated by one or more parties do not always result in strikes and may instead be discussed and even resolved between individuals or groups of workers and their employers or managers. When this occurs within the workshop, on the shopfloor or at a work site, it should be understood in the context of workplace industrial relations, although such negotiations are distinct from those that occur at the industry-wide level and perhaps concern broader policies or practices. Workplace industrial relations are often quite personal. They can become complicated both by the familiarity that is bred in the workplace and by the understanding that after the dispute ends workers and their bosses need to find a way to work (and live) together again. Consequently, the study of industrial relations need not be limited to either the strike or the record of industry-wide negotiations, although the survival of historical information certainly favours such a perspective.

It is certainly important to understand those conflicts that cause work stoppages, but it is equally important to understand how and why work gets done. Unlike earlier debates on this issue, one need not privilege a historical perspective based upon conflict over one based on consensus, or *vice versa*, in order to comprehend the duality of the workplace.[1] Indeed the study of workplace industrial relations during this period can be employed not only as a method that reveals the cultural and economic issues that generated strikes, but also as a way to comprehend the cultural meanings of the relationship in which, despite legal subordination, work was elicited from workers and authority was ceded to employers.[2]

When the approach to industrial relations centres on strikes or industry-wide conflict, it is logical to adopt a language that best expresses these concerns. Thus much academic work has often been characterized by the language of classical and neoclassical economics in which conflicts are inherent in the antithetical interests of employers and employees. Adam Smith noted this long ago, as did Karl Marx. In later formulations, these antithetical interests have become couched in the language of control that describes the shopfloor as a territorial struggle characterized by a shifting frontier between an employer's authority and the workers' autonomy. This metaphor is largely the legacy of the American economist Carter Goodrich.[3] However, it may well be time to question the prescriptive power of the language of both interests and control. While not denying the importance of these concepts, one might question nevertheless whether either an idealized marketplace metaphor or a metaphor derived in part from the historiography of the American 'Wild West' are sufficient to describe workplace relationships.

Given the extent of wage bargaining in the early industrial British economy, as well as the industrial culture it generated, an equally powerful explanatory tool may be that of the exchange relationship that is generated in a gift economy. This might be especially important for the study of the early industrial workplace because that site was not marked by tangible territorial boundaries, like the frontier, nor was it an impersonal environment where antithetical interests were harmonized by the invisible hand of competition, as in the classical marketplace. Even in large-scale enterprises of the period, the small work group, frequently premised upon family relations, predominated and ties of residential propinquity or employer paternalism might easily weaken or undermine diverging interests. Certainly, such relationships within both workshops and work groups might sometimes be premised on conflict and control, but they may equally be premised on what Avner Offer has recently called 'the economy of regard', that is, the granting of personal recognition in the form of wealth, status, power, attention, friendship and sociability, as well as the acceptance of the obligation to reciprocate this recognition in some form or manner.[4] These forms of reciprocity have been labelled by Marcel Mauss as a 'gift relationship'.[5] Indeed, as was suggested earlier in this book, concepts of reciprocity were among the most important elements of working-class discourse during this period.[6]

Perhaps the greatest impediment to understanding workplace relations as a gift relationship is the language of gifting itself. In contemporary Western culture, the gift has become a sign of benevolence and not exploitation; an expression of positive regard, not contempt. (That this is not wholly true, however, is exemplified by the use of peculiar gifts as evil portents, such as is said to happen among American Mafioso families or Caribbean voodoo cultures.) Moreover, gifting has also become almost solely a relationship of consumption. Gifts are purchased and their value therefore established in part by the market, which is, of course, beyond the bounds of the personal relationship itself. (An exception may be made here as well for handmade or homemade gifts, particularly from children, whose exemption from market values makes them 'priceless'.) The gift relationship, however, has rarely been used to characterize relations of production. Yet there are many reasons why the gift relationship may help outline some neglected aspects of the historical and cultural meanings of work. For example, the gift exchange is premised upon reciprocal relations in which not only goods are transferred between parties but also obligations. As Offer cleverly puts it, gifting 'produces "bads" as well as goods'. In its most direct form, the presentation of a gift initiates an obligation to reciprocate the gesture. This obligation, Offer suggests, may be construed as a type of financial or emotional debt. The reciprocity entailed in the exchange of gifts therefore need not take place between persons of equal social or economic standing, nor need it be premised upon an expression of goodwill. In fact, the asymmetrical relationship between a wealthy or powerful gift-giver and a poorer and less powerful recipient may have the effect of increasing, not decreasing, the emotional and economic burden of debt and thus perpetuating subordination. That such gifting could easily penetrate into the sphere of industrial relations can be seen with reference to nineteenth-century factory paternalism, in which personal obligations, such as loyalty, were readily exchanged for 'gifts' of housing or seaside holidays, thereby sustaining asymmetrical or unequal power relationships.

The potential value of understanding workplace relationships as based at least in part on the exchange of gifts is not only that it emphasizes this asymmetric reciprocity, but also because it can help reveal some otherwise obscure aspects of work in the early industrial period. Gifting often became especially significant in early industrial workplaces because the exchange of wages for work-effort, the effort bargain, involved a significant degree of discretion. An important part of this discretion arose from the artisanal nature of much early industrial work and the extensive degree of autonomy experienced by many so-called 'journeymen'. A further aspect of this discretion also was derived from the unwillingness or inability of employers to manage and monitor production closely. Since supervision was notoriously difficult or lax and the quantity or quality of effort on the shopfloor hard to determine, there was a significant degree of latitude involved in what an employer accepted as a 'fair day's work' and an employee acknowledged as a 'fair wage'. This element of discretion in the wage-effort bargain was often resolved reciprocally.[7] To reach such an agreement involved coming to an understanding, sometimes explicit but more often implicit, of what levels of pay would be exchanged for acceptable levels of effort. The complexity and intricacy of this exchange is often, if not always, beyond the power of even the most detailed contracts to explicate fully.[8] Thus, the exchange of effort for pay often resolved itself into a reciprocal relationship in which there was an understanding and expectation that the relationship would continue only so long as the regard for one another remained mutual – that is, so long as a fair day's work was exchanged for a fair day's pay. In other words, the discretionary aspect of the wage-effort bargain can be construed as a gift relationship.

How workers and employers reach an agreement on the appropriate levels of pay and effort has in fact been the subject of an enormous amount of research by economists, industrial sociologists, and so-called human relations experts. While many researchers in the field were unaware of or ignored the element of gifting in the work relationship, it is not difficult to find it, were one to look for it. The economist George Akerlof, for example, found it in Elton Mayo's famous research on workers' effort at the Hawthorne plant. Mayo had originally argued that individual performance was based not upon managerial directives but upon a standard set by the work group. However, as Akerlof recognized, 'the norm (or "standard" as Mayo termed it) for the proper work effort is quite like the norm that determines the standards of gift giving at Christmas. Such gift giving is a trading relationship – in the sense that if one side of the exchange does not live up to expectations, the other side is likely to curtail its activities.'[9] He went on to construct an enormously influential argument that explained the work relationship as a partial gift exchange based upon norms established by outside references. Market mechanisms, Akerlof suggested, do not fully determine the employment relationship. Indeed a good deal of the behaviour of both workers and employers was noticeably 'non-neoclassical'. Average workers tended to work harder than stipulated by the firm's basic work rules and they received in return a fair, not market, wage. 'Fairness' for both workers and employers was highly relational and based in part on earlier wage rates, perceived levels of unemployment, or wages of other similar workers. However, these employment characteristics do not conform to standard neoclassical models. Instead, employment often appears to be a trading relationship in which part of a worker's effort was disposed of as a gift, while part of the wages paid by the employer was given within the same context.

In a related way, many postwar studies of shopfloor restriction or soldiering reveal not only the extent to which the pay-for-effort bargain was based upon discretion, but also the degree to which shopfloor relations, both between managers and workers and among shopfloor mates, were based upon forms of reciprocity. In some of the most well known studies of shopfloor restriction, Donald Roy emphasized the enormous range of discretionary output practised by workers. By his own estimates and observations, machine shop workers working on piece-rates 'wasted' anywhere from two to four hours each day and could, if necessary, increase output from 33 to 78 per cent. On day-rates, the results were even more striking. There, Roy claimed, workers could have ratcheted up their own output by nearly 200 per cent. Whether and to what extent workers increased their output depended upon a complex web of reciprocity, or what Roy recognized as a 'bimodal pattern' of output. Workers, he argued, tended to increase their output if they felt that they would receive more wages. However, this willingness to respond to incentives was simultaneously constrained by the fear that increased output would entail later piece-rate price-cuts. Under other circumstances, in which increased effort would not appreciably increase take-home pay, workers responded by slowing down or putting out only the minimum work necessary. Roy called the first of these situations 'quota restriction' and the second 'goldbricking'.[10] In both cases, workers maintained a significant degree of control over a discretionary fund of effort and released portions when it was properly appreciated and when it did not entail adverse effects.

These responses, however, were not necessarily the only means by which workers were encouraged to release some of their discretionary labour. Roy suggested that workers often gained satisfaction on the job through their interpretation of work as a game against the clock. This game often led them to increase their output to avoid boredom or fatigue. In addition, workers released effort in order to finish their jobs early and enjoy more free time as well as to receive a measure of prestige from their workmates who valued those who achieved their quotas under difficult circumstances.[11] Under all of these conditions, it might easily be argued that the decisions concerning the amount of additional effort to release from this fund were based upon the understanding that an important element of the workers' effort was a 'gift' that entailed reciprocal obligations from their employers (additional time off or extra pay) or their mates (prestige and approbation). If the gift were properly reciprocated, or there was an expectation of reciprocity, then labour was released; if not, not. It is the element of discretion that is important here and the reciprocity based on discretionary exchange that creates a gift relationship.

The importance of reciprocity on the shopfloor can also be found in the work of the sociologist Michael Burawoy, who pays particular attention to the mechanisms through which workers consent to work as hard as they do. To his own surprise, it appears, Burawoy found himself on the same shopfloor where Roy had undertaken his path-breaking studies some twenty years earlier. Expanding upon several of Roy's earlier observations, Burawoy sought to show in part how the piece-rate method of payment helped to 'manufacture consent' on the shopfloor.[12] Rather than assume a given set of economic interests that workers and management brought to the shopfloor, Burawoy suggests that the specific set of production relations entered into by workers and employers creates the conditions whereby workers consent to both their subordination and exploitation. These conditions take the form of games workers play to relieve the tedium, reduce the strain, and secure certain levels of earnings at work. While Roy had noticed this, of course, Burawoy stresses that the shopfloor game is not an autonomous creation of workers. Instead he emphasizes the observation that this labour process game establishes a set of rules that not only entails management's participation in playing the game but also thereby coordinates the interests of both management and workers.[13]

Such conniving at the labour process game, of course, reiterates the importance of reciprocal relationships on the shopfloor. Managers and foremen actively participated in the games that helped workers to both achieve and limit their quotas in order to maintain a steady flow of production and avoid delays.[14] This is a form of a gift relationship: quota limits are accepted in exchange for the regularity of production. Yet even more revealing is Burawoy's understanding that a worker's sense of 'being screwed' by the bosses was not an expression of exploitation but of what might be termed failed gifting:

> Soon I discovered that such anguish referred to the company's failure to provide the necessary conditions to play the game of making out; for example, drills might have burned up, the blueprint might have disappeared, the machinery might not have been functioning properly, etc. In other words, management was being accused of 'cheating,' of not playing according to the rules of the game; and these accusations served to reassert the legitimacy of the rules and the values of making out. In this way the consensual framework was continually being re-established and reinforced.[15]

While Burawoy may understand 'being screwed' as a failure to follow the rules of the game, it is equally likely that this sense of frustration expressed outrage at the breakdown of a mutually dependent relationship in which the willingness or desire to expend effort is not being adequately reciprocated. Under some circumstances, perhaps such as these, the breakdown of reciprocity can become pathological and lead to feuding or retribution.[16] Gifting, as has been noted, need not be benevolent.

The importance of the gift relationship during the early industrial period can be further understood in a number of ways. Reciprocal gifting, for example, may serve to encourage trust, a relationship that is extremely efficient. Trust, it has been noted, economizes on several significant transaction costs, including supervision, compulsion and coercion.[17] Moreover, when the gift relationship is repeated, as on the shopfloor, it may serve to establish long-term bonds, which reduce replacement and retraining costs. Michael Huberman's striking work on the Lancashire cotton industry may be understood in this way.[18] In Huberman's account, the labour market during the early industrial era evolved away from one based upon a classical 'auction' model of competitive buying and selling of labour toward one that was characterized by fair wages, price lists, firm seniority and relatively low turnover. He aptly labelled this development as an 'escape from the market'. Huberman built his account not only upon the evidence of workers' responses to the piece-rate method of payment that had been revealed by

Roy and others, but also upon a variant of the efficiency-wage model. In this 'fair wage model', repeated bargaining, which was characteristic of much of the early industrial economy, elicited forms of cooperation and commitment from both employers and employees. Such cooperation, as in gifting, was not necessarily altruistic. On the contrary, it often was 'based on the shared knowledge that each can punish the other if either fails to cooperate'. That is, workers can punish their employers by restricting output, while employers, of course, can punish workers through lowering wages, imposing fines, or sacking them. However, once the norms of these reciprocal exchanges are established, they tend to become standardized in the form of guidelines or rules – that is, they become customary. Thus Huberman rightly insists that markets and custom are complementary not antithetical.

To solve this 'effort problem', both sides must agree to commit to help attain the other's goals. Such a commitment may arise under game-like conditions in which a 'tit-for-tat' strategy begins to coordinate the goals of both players.[19] A promise to limit piece-rate cuts, for example, may evoke a promise to produce more. Such mimicking may induce both players to commit to even further cooperation, although the extent of these commitments and the range of possible outcomes is not limitless. Nevertheless, the core of these negotiations often rests upon the exchange of reputations, which is an extremely important notion. Huberman notes that 'firms need to secure a reputation for upholding the wage and abstaining for [*sic*] busting rates; workers need to develop a reputation for not withdrawing effort'. Once again, therefore, the argument can be made that industrial relations is partly an expression of an 'economy of regard' that operates as a gift relationship. Even when expressed in game-theoretic language, the importance of reciprocity inherent in the effort bargain is re-emphasized.

The effort problem

A gift relationship, as Offer sums it up, is characterized by a transfer of goods or services, an expectation of reciprocity, a desire for regard, and a repetitive, self-enforcing bond. Such a personal exchange is reciprocal but not necessarily equitable. As we have noted, the gift exchange often serves to reinforce and express asymmetries rather than obfuscate them. In the workplace, such exchanges are predicated upon the possession of a discretionary fund of labour, wages or other such 'gifts', and repeated workplace bargaining consolidates these exchanges in the guise of custom or fairness. Violations of the rules of gifting do not necessarily end the employment relationship, although they might easily do so. Perhaps more common is the development of a cycle of retribution that includes not only fines and other penalties imposed by the employer, but also the withdrawal of work-effort, often by means of quota restrictions or goldbricking, by workers. Strikes or lock-outs ultimately attempt to break this cycle, but as such they become the last stage on which conflicts over the effort bargain and reciprocity are played out. It is equally possible, however, as we saw in the case of the building workers, that strikes may serve as tactical warning signs that the reciprocal relationship was in need of repair.

The importance, and perhaps prevalence, of reciprocal gifting in the early industrial economy can be observed quite distinctly if one looks in detail at particular employment relationships in individual sectors. In this chapter, the focus will be on the northern coal industry in part because of the unique survival of the relevant documentation and in part because of the historical significance of this sector during the nineteenth and twentieth centuries. Moreover, coal-mining is an especially revealing example of the economy of regard at work because of the vast degree of autonomy miners possessed in the workplace and the unwillingness or inability of owners and managers to supervise production.[20] Even in an industry notorious for poor industrial relations, these circumstances led owners and managers to recognize the degree to which they depended upon the reciprocity generated in the employment relationship. In October 1804, for example, the manager of Lord Delaval's colliery in Northumberland, John Bryers, felt compelled to pay out large signing bonuses to attract workers for the following year. The miners in the north-east were hired on the basis of an annual contract, called the bond, and when conditions were right in either the labour or product market, they could auction off their services at the end of their contract by demanding 'binding money', or signing bonuses. There were, of course, significant risks involved for the workers, particularly that of losing their job altogether, but employers undertook risks as well. Namely, if they did not act quickly enough and bid high enough, their collieries might be undermanned for the coming year, a situation that would severely limit their firm's production. Additionally, they might be forced to hire less skilful workers, which ultimately would have the same effect. In both cases, employers' investments in signing bonuses could be repaid in profits only if workers reciprocated by working harder and producing more. This seems to be what Bryers reckoned when he laid out several hundred pounds extra to sign 121 hewers in 1804. 'The Pitmen's binding money', he wrote to Lord Delaval, 'is an exceeding great sum and is to be paid tomorrow Evening for such as wishes to go to Newcastle the following day.' However, Bryers added the revealing note: 'I hope they will be grateful & make it up in work during the ensuing year, they promise fair, & we will not fail to remind them of their duty if they are not industrious'.[21]

Such a plain pronouncement of the way in which the miners' labour contracts acted as both an exchange of unpredictable levels of effort for pay as well as an exchange of regard is rare. However, as I have argued elsewhere, the industrial relations system of the northern coal industry was based upon a complex pattern of workplace bargaining that served constantly to renegotiate the effort problem.[22] Despite the fact that the northern miners' bond effectively tied them to a single place of employment for a year's time, this contract was as ineffective as most others of its kind in prescribing the amount of effort demanded from workers. The bonds of the second quarter of the nineteenth century were no more specific than to require hewers (that is, miners) to 'do and perform a full day's work on each and every working day, or such quantity as shall be fairly deemed equal to a day's work'.[23] Most workers and employers seemed to agree that this was roughly equivalent to an eight-hour shift, and the several attempts at unionization in the 1820s, 1830s and 1840s were often in response not to a decline in piece-rate payments, but to a reduction in the number of shifts most miners were working. For example, the miners in Tommy Hepburn's union bitterly complained of their inability to secure adequate earnings because they were only allowed down the pits three, four or five days a fortnight – a complaint, incidentally, that was confirmed before a parliamentary select committee by the most prominent colliery engineer in the nation.[24] As we shall see, the bonds themselves came under attack at this time precisely because several of their clauses facilitated the limitation of workers' shifts without technically violating the contract.

The drama of the effort problem, therefore, was played out on a different stage from that of the bond. Workplace bargaining at individual pits or collieries formed the core of the industrial relations system in the northern coalfield. In fact, the general terms of the bond specifically reserved the authority to set piece-rate prices to bargains struck at individual pits and collieries.[25] From a twentieth-century perspective, these workplace bargains, where the evidence survives, appear arcane and in some ways inscrutable. As we have seen, minor variations in the underground environment or mining practices were the subjects of intense interest, and sometimes the cause of significant disturbances. The surviving petition from workers at Cowpen Colliery, Northumberland, in 1831, for example, demands an increase in piece-rates of 4d for every score of baskets of coal sent to the surface from areas of the mine that were affected by drainage problems. (The mine manager responded that 4d was already given, but only when water seeped through the roof.) A similar increase was requested to compensate the miners when two men were forced to work in the same underground stall. (The manager accepted this demand, but only if the stalls were 4 yards wide.[26]) A petition from Wallsend Colliery in the same year asked for a 6d increase per score of baskets for working with Davy lamps and a 3d increase for each new yard the mine was extended.[27] The large number of variations of working conditions and practices at individual collieries, or indeed for working different seams in the same pit, is nowhere more evident than in the well-known pamphlet *A Voice from the Coal Mines*, issued by the United Colliers Association in 1825. While its remarkable prose constitutes an extraordinary expression of working-class *mentalité*, the core of *A Voice from the Coal Mines* is actually a compilation of twelve different petitions listing several grievances and bargaining demands. Many issues in dispute were similar to those at Cow-pen or Wallsend Collieries, but others were as distinct as poor ventilation or the fines imposed for mixing stone in with the coal sent to the surface.[28]

The full practice of effort bargaining is not often revealed, although evidence of its continuing presence throughout the nineteenth century is abundant.[29] An extraordinarily detailed account, however, is recorded in the diary of Matthias Dunn, the viewer of Hetton Colliery in the early 1830s, whose position included responsibility for colliery management, industrial relations and subterranean engineering.[30] In November 1831, Dunn attempted to introduce the practice of separating 'round' from 'small' coal underground. 'Round' coal was distinguishable from 'small' only on the basis of its size. However, this difference also distinguished its markets. Small coal was considered fit only for industrial use or export, whereas round coal was prized by consumers for household heating. The difference in price between the two was significant, and, considering the fact the the cost of production of the two was identical, the volume of sales of round coal often determined a firm's profitability.[31] The practice of separating 'round' from 'small' coal and stowing the latter underground had been a frequent cause of conflict in the industry, particularly because it required more effort to do so. Most firms offered higher piece-rate prices for separation and stowing, but they also imposed stiff fines on the miners who did not adequately perform the extra labour. When Dunn first considered introducing separation, he contemplated offering the miners an allowance of 1½ corves, or baskets of coal, for each score sent to the top of the pit in return for adopting the practice.[32] In other words, he was apparently ready to exchange a premium of some 7.5 per cent in return for the extra effort of separation and stowing.[33]

Within a week, however, he had decided against this allowance and instead offered to the miners at one of the colliery's pits a sizeable advance in piece-rate prices amounting to between 1s and 1s 3d per score depending on the type of coal. This was equivalent to a 20 per cent increase over previous prices. He then conducted a trial separation, apparently to his own satisfaction. This effort bargain was not to be an implicit one, however, for after the trial period, Dunn met with the some of the men to discuss the implementation of his plan. 'Had a meeting', he wrote, 'with four of the Delegates [of the hewers] upon the stowing of Small Coal[;] a great deal of Discussion ensued but a meeting is necessary before any decision can be come to upon the subject.'[34] At another pit, a similar offer was made and the supervisory personnel, or overmen, there were given 'the most positive injunctions' to have the coal stowed away.[35]

The hewers' resistance to the bargain and their unwillingness to expend the extra effort was noticeable, however. Dunn complained repeatedly of the failure of the men to separate and stow the small coal as well as the failure of their supervisors to enforce it. At the Isabella pit, the 'stowing of Small going on very tardily indeed', Dunn wrote. In the George pit, the 'stowing of Small [was] rather doing better here, but far from complete yet', and in the Minor pit there was 'very little progress making in the stowing of Small Coals'. At the Main Coal pit, Dunn was 'severe on [the overman] Geo. Armstrong for paying so little attention to the general orders regarding the stowing of Small Coal and other minor arrangements in his pit'. In fact, both the men and their supervisors eventually came to the colliery office to complain. 'Work rather falling off generally', Dunn lamented.[36]

Faced with such determined resistance, Dunn hit upon the idea of closing down the George pit entirely and setting the hewers and other pit-workers there to work in other pits at the colliery. He seems to have been hoping that by increasing the workforce in the open pits, the savings to be made by reducing expenses, such as those incurred by the employment of additional horses and drivers, would be roughly equivalent to the additional profits to be gained by stowing small coal.[37] By doing this, Dunn also would be avoiding the effort problem since this arrangement would not require him to elicit any additional effort from the men. Nevertheless, he was not free to implement this plan. Dunn had to face not only the organized resistance of the miners themselves, but also the ownership committee of the colliery. When he presented the idea to the owners in the middle of December, they balked at the plan, fearing that it might lead to a strike. 'The Committee decide', he noted in his diary, 'that as the men might object to have such an arrangement carried into Effect, + Stick that therefore it had better be deferred.'[38]

Dunn's attempt to elicit the extra effort necessary for stowing small coal became increasingly punitive after this decision, yet it is questionable whether this had any noticeable effect either. In the Minor West pit, the overman Robert Frazer received a 'very severe talking to' when Dunn found that 'the stowing of Small Coal is also dwindling away very much', while in the Minor East pit he complained of the 'very great laxity of conduct observable here'. 'Neither is the work regulated, Small Cast, nor any thing managed in a Satisfactory way', he wrote.[39] A fortnight later, he visited the Blossom pit only to find 'great looseness observable – the casting of Small, the keeping of Rolley ways etc'.[40] Finally, at the end of January he called all the supervisory overmen into his office 'with a view of getting a Course of better subordination introduced amongst Hewers with regard to Small Casting, etc.' and he 'ordered them to present a few of the worst casters every pay[day]'.[41]

For a week or two he was convinced that this had had some effect, but by the end of February a general meeting of the Hetton colliers had been called to complain 'of the stowing of Small Coals and the Penalties thereon'.[42] Certainly, by the next bi-monthly pay the miners were once again successfully resisting any attempts to expend greater effort. Dunn's only explanation for the men's action was that 'they resist the stowing back of Small Coals under the idea that some ulterior trick is meant to be played [on] them'.[43] Even then he could go no further than to surmise that 'the men see an object in refusing to cast', yet he seemed to have very little clue as to what that object may have been.[44]

At one level, it would appear that their object was to withhold the discretionary fund of labour that was one half of the effort exchange. Dunn's attempt to alter the terms of the effort bargain were perceived as violations of the rules of reciprocal exchange or gifting. In other circumstances, hewers had complained that the fines for bad separation, often a deduction of 6d or 1s, were excessive and unfair. Moreover, conditions that contributed to bad separation were not fully under their control. 'Fines "for bad separation" or too great a quantity of small coals with the round' was one of the grievances listed in a petition included in *A Voice from the Coal Mines*, but 'here the want of light, the lifts, the distance the corf has to travel, and the tenderness of the coals, militate against the most skilful and conscientious workman'.[45] At Hetton Colliery, a cycle of retribution appears to have developed after Dunn sought to enforce the separation and stowing of small coal. The hewers initially resisted by withholding their work-effort, which Dunn was unable to overcome. He then proceeded to impose fines and other penalties, which evoked even greater hostility and resistance.

Such a process of 'negative gifting' was not limited to the shopfloor and indeed subsequently the contest at Hetton became quite personal, a development that highlights the element of regard in the employment relationship. At a meeting of the ownership committee in March 1832, twelve representatives of the miners delivered a petition asking for Dunn to be discharged. The petition drew extraordinary attention throughout the coalfield not only due to its boldness, but also because it came in the midst of Tommy Hepburn's effort to unionize lower-level supervisory personnel, including overmen. The Hetton ownership committee 'received the Petition with suitable disgust', Dunn wrote, 'refusing to see the Deputation but returning a written answer in the most decisive terms'.[46] Moreover, at the next general meeting of the regional coal-owners' association, often known as the Limitation of the Vend, Dunn explained that 'the real grounds of dissatisfaction between the Hetton men' included the stowing of small coal.[47] The coal-owners resolved that their 'approbation ... of Mr. Dunn's conduct, be conveyed to the owners of that Colliery, with a request that they will resist every attempt by their Workmen, to interfere with the appointment of those Gentlemen to whom they may think proper to confide the Management of their Concerns, and that this Meeting will support them against any illegal proceedings on the part of their Men'.[48]

Surprisingly, the effort bargaining still did not break down altogether. By the first week of April, the owners and men had provisionally agreed to fix the amount of small coal to be stowed at 1½ corves per score in the Main Coal seam and 1 corf per score in the Hutton seam.[49] However, the owners at the same time insisted on revising the ninth clause of the bond so that the stowing of small coals became part of the contract.[50] And it is here at last that we come to a full understanding of why the miners were so determined to withhold their effort. Their resistance was not to the principle of separation nor was it solely to the excessive fines, which were undeniably onerous. The principal object of their restriction was to gain a set of working rules that defined how much effort they were to expend on the stowing of small coal. That is, they sought a clearer definition of the terms of their effort bargain. The hewers thought they had reached such an agreement based upon the owners' acceptance of the 1½ and 1 corf standards. However, the owners' subsequent alterations to the bond undermined that achievement. 'This ninth clause', the pitmen wrote, 'the alteration of which is resisted, is the grievance.' They continued:

> It says, 'that each hewer shall cast aside or stow away in the mine the small coals made in the *nicking* and *kirving*, for which he shall be paid by valuation.' On the face of it, this seems fair enough, but like many other parts of the Bond, it is framed only to deceive. There is no quantity of small coals specified in the clause, and when the Viewer examines the quantity cast aside, which he does once a fortnight, if he pleases to think the quantity is not sufficiently large, he orders the Overman or *Keeker* to fine the hewers 2s. 6d. for not stowing away enough, without deigning to examine whether what he considers enough could by any possibility, in fair working, be obtained.[51]

The miners therefore were left once again in a situation that failed both to delineate the limits of their effort and to enjoin any reciprocal responsibilities upon their supervisors.

The case of the Hetton coal-miners serves to highlight not only the significance of the effort bargain in the early industrial workplace but also the importance of elements of reciprocity. The opacity of the workplace, as Clive Behagg calls it, was not only reserved for its customs and rituals.[52] The darkest glass through which employers had to look was the one that obscured the amount of effort that workers would put forth. Try as they might, employers had no way to control a workers' expenditure of effort. Conversely, workers were rarely willing to reveal just how much they could put forth.[53] Consequently, the employment relationship often became based upon an exchange of 'gifts'. An employer's obligation was to recognize what could be fairly expected from a worker and fairly reward it; the worker's reciprocal obligation was to expend the additional effort that comprised a fair day's work. Despite the claims of neoclassical economics, therefore, neither employers nor workers in the coal industry were willing to let the market clear their views. This does not mean that 'fair wages' were egalitarian or that employers and workers were motivated by altruism. It does mean, however, that the nature of industrial relations can be understood in terms other than neoclassical economics, and its cultural dimensions can be better explicated in terms of exchange relationships.

Shopfloor restriction

The miners' withholding of effort in the face of new management practices was only part of an array of tactics that might be deployed to modify the effort bargain. One of the most widely recognized tactics, and the one that has historically been burdened with an immense load of political freight, was the more formal practice of output restriction or 'soldiering'.[54] Surprisingly, output restriction as a distinct phenomenon has rarely received detailed attention from historians of the nineteenth century. Perhaps this is because, as one historian has noted, 'the culture of the workplace remains frustratingly difficult to gain access to at any point that is beyond the chronology of oral history'.[55] However, Michael Huberman's work on the Lancashire cotton industry, mentioned above, is especially important in this regard not only because it uses econometric techniques to address just this issue, but also because it ties the analysis of output restriction to changes in the effort bargain. Yet whether restriction occurred, and the extent to which it did occur, in other sectors has not been adequately addressed. The coal industry again offers an especially important perspective. It would appear that both the geography of production and the consequent autonomy of the underground worker might make coal-mining especially fertile ground for output restriction. Moreover, there is considerable *prima facie* evidence that it did occur during the early nineteenth century. Unlike the Lancashire cotton industry, where Huberman suggests that output restriction operated to balance the effort bargain and resulted in the consolidation of implicit contracts, in the northern coal industry the miners' restrictive efforts were not hidden. Miners' unionization efforts publicly adopted what appear to be restrictive measures and never sought to hide them. Nevertheless, the social, cultural and economic objectives of output restriction are not self-evident. In fact, an analysis of miners' restriction reveals the extraordinary complexity and contingency of the effort bargain during this period.

During the course of the miners' 1831–32 union campaign, a series of explicit restrictive practices were adopted by the hewers throughout the northern coalfield. This movement had been the second regional unionization drive since the repeal of the Combination Acts in 1825. Although piecerates for miners may have fallen slightly since the end of the Napoleonic Wars, the more significant blow to miners' earnings during these years had come from the extensive reduction of working hours. The northern coalowners had widely adopted short-time working in order to limit production and sustain prices on the London market. The cartel that organized and coordinated these actions operated through a pair of regional committees that met regularly in Newcastle. Their most important goal was to establish and distribute quotas to the majority of collieries in the northern coal district, and the cartel itself has come to be known by the term that actually describes it principal function, the Limitation of the Vend.[56]

The quotas distributed to each firm by the Vend were maintained largely by manipulating the terms of the miners' bond. The bond included unique provisions to pay hewers a minimum fortnightly wage because work stoppages due to cave-ins, floods, explosions, and the like were quite common. This remarkable provision was meant to work to the advantage of both parties. In the event that such an accident forced the closure of a mine, the miners and their families would be supported by their minimum wage and the mine-owners would retain their workers until the resumption of production.[57] By 1830, the bonds ostensibly guaranteed the miners the equivalent of nine days' work or 28s each fortnight. However, a clause in the bond further stipulated that in the event of an accident or other such causes, the miners could be laid off work without pay for three consecutive days. On the fourth day, the hewers could then be put to any work in the colliery at a minimum rate of 2s 6d per day. In the event that no work could be found, then the hewers received 1s 6d per day. Proportionally lower rates were also payable to other classifications of workers in the mines.[58] Despite the apparent obligations imposed upon them by such a prominent 'safety net', many coal-owners found these terms to be a convenient way to lower wage bills while at the same time meeting their goal of restricting total production. It was possible, the miners argued, for the coal-owners to reduce earnings of adult male workers to as low as 14s or 18s a fortnight by manipulating the opening and closing of their mines and thereby significantly undercut the 28s minimum wage.[59] Indeed, Lord Durham's own colliery manager estimated hewers' earnings at his extensive collieries to have been only about 17s a fortnight in 1830.[60] Moreover, when a parliamentary commission investigating prices in the London coal market inquired into wages in the northern coal industry, the most prominent colliery engineer in the country responded that piece-rates had held steady since about 1810, but the excess of the supply of coals had meant that hewers' work, and hence earnings, had to be cut back in order to sustain prices. 'The wages would have been quite as good', John Buddle testified, 'if we had employment for the people, but they are at very reduced work'.[61] He told the Select Committee of the House of Lords of the same commission that some collieries did not offer more than three days of work each week.[62]

Despite the apparent elements of a 'fair wage' packet, short-time working in the coal industry appears to have seriously undermined the effort bargain in this period. Unlike the cotton industry, where short-time working was adopted to spread the burden of unemployment and preserve the benefits firms derived from lengthy attachments, the manner in which short-time working operated in the coal industry made it subject to potential abuse.[63] Not only did this short-time working cause serious hardship and distress among the miners, but it was recognized as an abrogation of the commitment that had exchanged a fair day's work for a fair day's pay. This sense of failed reciprocity was expressed by 'A Coal Hewer', whose letters often appeared in the local newspapers, who argued that the men needed to form a union because 'they felt themselves oppressed, and plundered by those who should have protected them and rewarded their industry'.[64]

Under these circumstances, when the union movement began in 1831 the miners' behaviour developed in a way that at first was strikingly at odds with standard effort-bargain theory. Instead of attempting to withdraw effort in the classic forms of quota restriction or goldbricking, the initial demands made upon the owners included the claim to abandon both worker and employer restrictions altogether. The miners were willing to give up what appeared to be a fair wage packet in order to test their earnings potential in a free market: 'We do not agree to be laid idle two days in the fortnight', they petitioned the coal-owners, and 'we take our chance for Employment as it may happen to occur, waiving the 28s. per fortnight'.[65] This extreme demand, however, did not survive long. The owners subsequently took firm steps to back away from the precipice of a free market. At the first bargaining session between the miners' and owners' representatives in Newcastle on 11 April, the owners reported that 'a long discussion ensued, chiefly explanatory of the second and seventh Clauses of the Bond [on minimum working days, guaranteed wages, and temporary pit closures], taken in connection, with which the Pitmen seemed to be satisfied'.[66] At this meeting, the miners appear to have begun to accept the owners' arguments that their 'real intention' was not to exploit the workers but to protect both them and their investments when circumstances made the pit 'unfit for working'.[67] The miners thereafter countered that while they were willing to accept some of the limits placed upon them by the guarantees of employment, in particular they wanted the bond to guarantee them eleven instead of nine days' work each fortnight, they still demanded that both workers and employers allow the market to determine the demand for coal, its price, and ultimately the miners' earnings.[68] As the negotiations proceeded, however, even this aspect of their free market demand was soon dropped and the miners reverted to bargaining over the customary terms of the bond, in particular the number of 'guaranteed' working days each fortnight and minimum earnings. Subsequent miners' requests included those for eleven days' work each fortnight and enough work to earn 33s a fortnight, which then was lowered to ten working days and 30s a fortnight.[69]

As the strike developed, and several owners began to come to terms with their workers, questions of effort and pay began to be resolved in ways that neither the coal-owners nor the union was initially prepared for. On the shopfloor, or, more accurately, at the coal face, hewers began to adopt output restrictions. At Lord Londonderry's collieries, John Buddle reported that the hewers were 'limiting themselves to a limited quantity of Work – no man to work more than 4/. worth for his day's work, as a maximum – so here is *Regulation* for us at once'.[70] At Lord Durham's collieries, Henry Morton, the colliery agent, wrote that there was 'a suspicion that one of the articles of the union enjoins that the men employed shall not earn above a certain turn a day, perhaps 3s/–'.[71] Within a short time, output restriction began to spread throughout the working collieries. A week after Buddle had first recognized it at Lord Londonderry's collieries, he wrote that 'at present we have a *strict regulation* of quantity, and will continue to have, unless something occurs to abate the spirit of domination which the pitmen are exercising. It cannot be denied that they have *entire dominion* over the Trade, at present.'[72]

The union itself, which had never previously announced any policy on output restriction, quickly came to embrace it as one of its fundamental principles.[73] The *Rules and Regulations of the Coal Miners' Friendly Society*, which was established in June 1831 and set union guidelines, contains its first official pronouncement on output restriction.[74] Clause VIII reads:

> That no Members of this Society earn more than 4s. per day, clear of fines and off-takes, while employed as a hewer, for each and every day, if practicable; and in case any Member, being a hewer, earn above 4s. per day, all such sum or sums so earned above 4s. shall be paid into the [union] fund; and in case any Member do not well and truly state to the Committee of this Society the amount of his earnings, or shall either directly or indirectly defraud, or attempt to defraud the Society of his said earnings, or fines or forfeitures, in any or either of the said cases, such Member shall be fined double the sum such Member shall have kept back, or be excluded.

It appears, therefore, that the union had indeed established a restriction on output that limited hewers' earnings to 4s a day, and given eleven days' work a fortnight, which the miners' also demanded, hewers' earnings could reach a maximum of 44s per week.[75]

Yet the union never stated either why output restriction had been adopted or what function it was meant to serve. Many modern observers, such as Roy, would emphasize that some form of individual rational action theory often lay behind output restriction. That is, workers understood their own economic self-interest and operated in ways that tended toward that objective. However, in this case, there appears to be little or no evidence that would support such a contention. The miners did not express any fear of rate cuts if they exceeded their quotas, as might have been the case if they were limiting output under the circumstances Roy labelled 'quota restriction'. Nor did miners restrict their effort because the quotas appeared to be unattainable according to the customary terms of exchanges of effort for pay, what Roy later would call 'goldbricking'.[76]

Along similar lines, perhaps the most common explanation of workers' restriction of output is that it is meant to provide a form of security against future unemployment. The 1967 Donovan Commission's report on restrictive practices in British industry, for example, noted that 'it is a commonplace that a desire by workers for security is a very important motive for imposing restrictions on the use of labour' and that industries with high unemployment appear to have the highest incidence of restrictive labour practices.[77] However, this does not appear to have been precisely the case among the northern coal-miners of a century and a quarter earlier. On the one hand, a 4s limit on earnings was measurably higher than either the coal-owners' earlier offers or the miners' previous demands. At 44s a fortnight, miners had set a limit for themselves that was at least 25 per cent *higher* than any previous offer on the bargaining table and more than 35 per cent higher than the owners' original offer. One may rightly question whether limitations placed at such a high level of production actually merit the term 'output restriction'. On the other hand, the miners themselves recognized the fact that a significant minority of them could not hope to reach the 4s limit regularly. Carbonarius, a pro-union publicist, writing in the *Newcastle Chronicle*, argued that:

> in the whole mine, it takes the *very best men* to work with 'extraordinary exertion' from six to *eight* hours to earn four shillings, and that one-fifth of the hewers cannot do this. The second class of hewers are on an average nine hours a-day in the mine, and there are many who are nearly twelve hours at work; and then have they earned 4s.? I say confidently No! If the 'fortnightly pay-bills' are *your* [the owners'] proofs, the men on *their* part can produce the cheques or notes they receive from the overman, to draw their money by. In my own case, I know I have made about four shillings a-day since May, in eight or nine hours, but I know many collieries where the hewers have not made more than three shillings in eleven and twelve hours.[78]

Indeed at Hetton Colliery, Matthias Dunn observed that the 4s limit was not easily being reached by the hewers: 'the Men are pinched to get as many Coals out as will make their $4 p Day', he noted in his diary.[79] There does not, therefore, appear to be any causal connection being made here between employment security and output restriction. The limits were not set low enough to place them in the range of all workers, a calculation that would have been logically necessary if the miners' goal was either to expand employment immediately or to distribute it more evenly in the future. The 4s limit was not likely to have forced employers to hire more hewers.

Perhaps the likeliest explanation of all may not have anything to do with the effects of output restriction on the individual pay packet or employment situation. Instead, the most significant effect of output restriction may have been felt on the family budget. Hewers were the premier adult, male workers in the mines, but they were also supported by a wide range of ancillary employees. For example, older, superannuated hewers often worked as 'shifters' picking over or screening coal at the surface, or as 'cranesmen' who helped load coal underground.[80] Young boys and teens were also employed on a wide range of tasks underground. Starting at age five or six, the youngest boys were employed as 'trappers' and were responsible for operating the doors in the mine that directed, or 'coursed', the air for ventilation. At thirteen or fourteen, boys could work as 'drivers' guiding the pit ponies and their carts to the shaft where the coal was then lifted to the surface. Some of the most difficult work down the pits was done by 'putters', young teens who manually pushed and dragged carts laden with coals from the coal face. The precise numbers of men and boys in these various groups of workers varied from pit to pit. Older pits often required a greater number of ancillary workers because the distance from the shaft to the face was longer; pits with better natural ventilation obviously required fewer trappers. At Temple Main Colliery, for example, 106 hewers were employed in 1812 along with 165 trappers, putters, drivers and shifters.[81] In 1831, at Lord Londonderry's three main collieries, Rainton, Pensher and Pittington, 502 hewers were complemented by 443 putters, drivers and shifters (the number of trappers was not recorded).[82]

Without doubt, the overwhelming majority of these older men and boys were recruited from the hewers' families. Indeed, in the case of young boys, there were several elements that contributed to their recruitment. Part of the rationale behind hiring the hewers' children was obviously provided by the logic of residential propinquity. Yet there was also a pronounced prejudice among the coal-owners of the north-east for pitmen and children who were brought up in the job. As Flinn notes, a great value was placed on an experienced miner's feel for the coal and sense of impending dangers. Long years of mining experience were expected to culminate in the development of intuitive responses to the underground environment and contributed to the general sentiment that 'pitmen were born and not made'.[83] Therefore, miners' families only occasionally relied solely on the earnings of the male head of household. Like other working-class families of this period, children's earnings were an essential and important part of the family budget.

While it is extremely difficult to quantify the contribution of children to an 'average' mining family's income, and of course this contribution changed over the family life-cycle, some indication may be given by an account drawn up of the earnings of 'six of the best' families at Cowpen Colliery between April 1830 and April 1831 (see Table 1). Admittedly, the colliery agent who drew up this list probably selected examples of families that were at the apex of their earnings potential. Still, the notable information to be drawn from Table 1 is the relatively modest proportion of total family income received by the male head of household. According to this data, those males who appear to be the heads of household (and who are listed first in each family grouping) earned only between 23 per cent and 37 per cent of the total family income. Male children, especially when working as hewers and putters, obviously contributed significantly to the family. It should be noted here as well that girls' and women's earnings in domestic service or farm work have not been included, although these were common enough forms of female employment in the coalfields.

Under these circumstances, miners' had to be cognizant of the impact of their restrictive efforts on the family budget. Especially if output restrictions

Table 1   Earnings of six of the best families at Cowpen Colliery in twelve months
commencing 5 April 1830 and ending 5 April 1831

Name	Employment	Earnings (£, s, d)			Percentage of family earnings
Robert Reed, Sr	Hewer	52	0	0	25.8
Robert Reed, Jr	Hewer	37	18	6	18.8
William Reed	Putter	49	0	0	24.3
John Reed	Putter	47	0	0	23.3
Thomas Reed	Driver	15	12	6	7.8
Robert Dixon, Sr	Hewer	54	17	6	27.7
Thomas Dixon	Putting Hewer[a]	50	0	0	25.3
James Dixon	Putter	46	0	0	23.3
Christopher Dixon	Putter	24	7	6	12.3
Robert Dixon	Putter	22	12	6	11.4
Robert Hunter, Sr	Hewer	43	8	6	25.5
Robert Hunter, Jr	Hewer	46	0	0	27.0
George Hunter	Putter	48	0	0	28.2
William Hunter	Water Leader[b]	22	10	0	13.2
David Hunter	Trapper	10	8	4	6.1
Thomas Heron	Hewer	51	15	0	35.0
Stephen Heron	Putting Hewer	48	11	6	32.8
Henry Heron	Putting Hewer	47	13	6	32.2
James Gilgour	Hewer	52	1	3	36.8
John Gilgour	Putting Hewer	47	18	9	33.8
James Gilgour	Assistant Horsekeeper	26	0	0	18.4
William Gilgour	Driver	15	12	6	11.0
Richard Donkin	Cranesman[c]	31	7	6	23.2
James Donkin	Hewer	40	14	5	30.2
William Donkin	Hewer	47	1	8	34.9
Robert Donkin	Putter	15	16	5	11.7

Source: Northumberland Record Office, Watson Mss., NRO 3410/Wat/1/5/89.

Notes: a Denotes a transitional phase in which aspects of both forms of work
          are undertaken.
          b Helped to transport or direct drainage.
          c Lifted corves into waggons for underground transport. A job often held
          by older or disabled hewers.

were too tight, such limitations might adversely effect family incomes by reducing either the earnings of putters, who were paid piece-rates by the number of loads they hauled and the accumulated length of the distance they travelled, or the earnings of shifters, cranesmen and trappers, who were paid by the day. In order to maintain family income, the miners had to work a large enough quantity of coal to support the putters, while at the same time they had to work enough hours to keep the pits open several days a week so that trappers and shifters could increase their day-wages. Thus one of Lord Durham's colliery agents supposed that the purpose of the miners' restriction was not to limit output, but to ensure 'that employment may be given to a greater number of hands'.[84] More specifically, Lord Londonderry's agent wrote that 'Your Lordship's Men are anxious to work a number of days for the sake of getting the Boys and old men (Shifters) large wages, but the Hewers will not work more than a limited quantity'.[85] This particular form of output restriction, therefore, was not meant to protect the individual hewer's wages, but to ensure that the family wage packet was supported and maintained. In order to do this, the hewer-dominated union movement had to take into account that some members of the miners' families worked by the piece, such as hewers, putters and drivers, while others, particularly the shifters and trappers, worked on a daily wage basis. Four shillings was set as a limit to the hewers' daily earnings, therefore, not because it served to restrict overall output, but principally because it kept the pits open as many days as possible each fortnight. Thus this form of output restriction also served to remedy the miners' most significant grievance, which was too few working days each fortnight.

We may now return to a question raised briefly earlier: did this apparently self-evident example of autonomous output restriction actually seek to limit total output? As Tom Lupton astutely observed, and it is worth quoting at length:

> to support a judgment that a given group of workers was restricting output, one would have to have a neutral measure of a proper day's work. Even if one had such a measure, which is unlikely, one would also require techniques to assess actual against potential output so that those differences entirely due to a deliberate withholding of effort by workers might be isolated. I submit that in most situations there will be neither neutral measures nor effective means of assessment. To speak of restriction of output in such circumstances is merely to express an opinion that workers ought to do more.[86]

Certainly, this appears to be the case for the northern miners. If evidence of output from the period is used, even though about two full months during the peak production period were lost by the majority of collieries (some lost more) during the 1831 strike, total output for the year, as reported by the coal-owners' cartel, fell by only about 5 per cent. In order to explain the miners' shopfloor behaviour, Lupton's description of restrictive behaviour as 'a form of social adjustment to a given job environment' may be of greater explanatory value.[87] As Lupton intimated for the shopfloor workers of the mid-1950s, family concerns played an important role in such behaviour. However, whereas Lupton's workers were interested in maintaining stable earnings because 'they liked to give the same amount each week to their wives', the hewers sought to employ their families more fully and did so by regulating their own production but at a relatively high level.[88]

Interestingly enough, this form of output restriction was finally broken only when the owners were able to turn it against the miners themselves. Before then, most coal-owners and their managers recognized that the miners' levels of output roughly coincided with their own attempts to control production through the cartel. However, the 1832 binding of the pitmen marked a resumption of the owners' effort to break the union, not because of the miners' imposition of output limits, but because the union had effectively secured control of the labour market by regulating the movement of hewers between collieries.[89] The union's response was to tighten the earnings' limit even further to 3s a day. Matthias Dunn understood that this was done 'with a view to rendering Coals scarce' and thus to pressure the owners to negotiate.[90] However, the owners and their managers, the viewers, soon recognized that this restriction, combined with the hewers' regular contributions being made to the union, caused great hardship among the mining families. They therefore decided to keep the miners working only at the minimum levels allowed by the bond.[91] When the union recognized its mistake it offered first to raise the limit back to 4s and then apparently to abolish output limits altogether. John Buddle's letters indicate that the hewers at Lord Londonderry's collieries raised their earnings limit to 4s a day at their own discretion.[92] Towards the end of the strike, however, Dunn reported that the union leader, Tommy Hepburn, was on hand to advise the Hetton Colliery hewers personally when they offered to eliminate the clause altogether from the union rules.[93] Yet by this time the owners still refused to negotiate and with the help of troops and local banks replaced thousands of unionized workers with miners brought in from other parts of the country.

These final events may well serve as a reminder that one of the principal asymmetries of the employment relationship is the worker's inability to control the provision of work. Yet the uniqueness of the effort bargain does not lay solely in this asymmetry. Instead it is the intangibility of effort that makes the effort bargain unique. That is, the effort bargain is not a 'normal' market exchange; it is not an exchange of one tangible or transferrable commodity for another. Instead the effort bargain is the exchange of one commodity, pay, for a range of possible performances. The very inscrutability of effort creates the gifting element in the effort bargain because the quantity of exertion is determined not by objective measurement but by the reciprocity inherent in the exchange. Moreover, the asymmetry of the employment relationship does not abrogate this element of reciprocity in the effort bargain. Indeed it may be more accurate to conclude that the reciprocity of the effort bargain sustains and reproduces the asymmetries of the employment relationship.

Notes

1 Such was nature of the debate, for example, in the mid-1980s between Richard Price and Patrick Joyce in the pages of the journal *Social History*; see R. Price, 'The Labour Process and Labour History', *Social History*, vol. 8: no. 1 (January 1983), pp. 57–75; P. Joyce, 'Labour, Capital and Compromise: A Response to Richard Price', *Social History*, vol. 9: no. 1 (January 1984), pp. 67–76; R. Price, 'Conflict and Co-operation: A Reply to Patrick Joyce', *Social History*, vol. 9: no. 2 (May 1984), pp. 217–24; and P. Joyce, 'Languages of Reciprocity and Conflict: A Further Response to Richard Price', *Social History*, vol. 9: no. 2 (May 1984), pp. 225–31.

2 For the early nineteenth century, there are few studies that seek to explicate such shopfloor relations. The most well known perhaps are Richard Price, *Masters, Unions and Men: Work Control in Building and the Rise of Labour, 1830–1914* (Cambridge: Cambridge University Press, 1980) and Clive Behagg, *Politics and Production in the Early Nineteenth Century* (London: Routledge, 1990). To a lesser extent, sections of Patrick Joyce, *Work, Society and Politics: The Culture of the Factory in Later Victorian England* (Hassocks: Harvester, 1980) and, more recently, Diane Drummond, *Crewe: Railway Town, Company and People, 1840–1914* (Aldershot: Scolar Press, 1995) are also quite important. An interesting review of such literature, but one that focuses on a distinctly later period, is Dave Lyddon, 'Industrial-Relations Theory and Labor History', *International Labor and Working-Class History*, no. 46 (Fall 1994), pp. 122–41. The new journal *Historical Studies in Industrial Relations* published by the Keele University Centre for Industrial Relations seeks to remedy the relative paucity of work in this area.

3 Carter L. Goodrich, *The Frontier of Control: A Study in British Workshop Politics* (1920; London: Pluto Press, 1975).

4 Avner Offer, 'Between the Gift and the Market: The Economy of Regard', *Economic History Review*, vol. 50: no. 3 (1997), pp. 450–76.

5 Marcel Mauss, *The Gift: The Form and Reason for Exchange in Archaic Societies*, trans. W.D. Halls (1950; New York: W.W. Norton & Co., 1990).

6 See Chapter 2, above.

7 Offer, 'Between the Gift and the Market', pp. 462–3; George A. Akerlof, 'Labor Contracts as Partial Gift Exchange', *Quarterly Journal of Economics*, vol. 97: no. 4 (November 1982), pp. 548–51.

8 The importance of the effort bargain was implicitly recognized by several early writers, but it was given its most influential elaboration by Wilhelm Baldamus, who claims that the amount of human effort applied to work is largely unknown, intangible and inaccessible. Discussing the modern shopfloor situation, he argues that the labour market can provide a crude approximation of the relationship of effort to wages, but given the fact that effort is ultimately incalculable, forms of supervision on the shopfloor operate to refine labour

market mechanisms and improve the correlation between effort and pay. They do this through the process of the 'effort bargain', or the continual workplace procedures during which workers and supervisors negotiate the exchange of effort for pay. 'The formal wage contract is never precise in stipulating how much effort is expected for a given wage (and vice versa)', Baldamus wrote. 'The details of the arrangement are left to be worked out through the direct interaction between the partners of the contract. If a worker slackens his effort at one moment, the foreman's job is to remind him, as it were, that he departs from his obligations, and, in certain circumstances, it is quite possible that there may be some haggling between the two as to what is a "fair" degree of effort in relation to the wages paid.' See W. Baldamus, *Efficiency and Effort: An Analysis of Industrial Administration* (London: Tavistock, 1961), pp. 35–6, 46–7.

9 Akerlof, 'Labor Contracts', p. 549.
10 Donald Roy, 'Quota Restriction and Goldbricking in a Machine Shop', *American Journal of Sociology*, vol. 57: no. 5 (March 1952), pp. 427–42.
11 Donald Roy, 'Work Satisfaction and Social Reward in Quota Achievement: An Analysis of Piecework Incentive', *American Sociological Review*, vol. 18: no. 5 (October 1953), pp. 507–14.
12 Michael Burawoy, *Manufacturing Consent: Changes in the Labor Process under Monopoly Capitalism* (Chicago: University of Chicago Press, 1979) and *The Politics of Production: Factory Regimes under Capitalism and Socialism* (London: Verso, 1985).
13 Burawoy, *Manufacturing Consent*, pp. 77–94.
14 Burawoy, *Manufacturing Consent*, pp. 80–1.
15 Burawoy, *Manufacturing Consent*, pp. 82–3.
16 Offer, 'Between the Gift and the Market', p. 455.
17 Offer, 'Between the Gift and the Market', p. 454.
18 Michael Huberman, *Escape from the Market: Negotiating Work in Lancashire* (Cambridge: Cambridge University Press, 1996), see ch. 5.
19 For further discussion of the application of game theory to early industrial bargaining, see below, Chapter 6.
20 James A. Jaffe, *The Struggle for Market Power: Industrial Relations in the British Coal Industry, 1800–1840* (Cambridge: Cambridge University Press, 1991), pp. 61–6, 96–119.
21 Northumberland Record Office (hereafter NRO), Delaval Papers, ZDE 4/26/68, Bryers to Delaval, 25 October 1804.
22 Jaffe, *Struggle for Market Power*, chs 3 and 5.
23 Quoted in Jaffe, *Struggle for Market Power*, p. 117.
24 *Report from the Select Committee on the State of the Coal Trade*, Parliamentary Papers (hereafter PP), vol. viii (1830), p. 315; *Report from the Select Committee of the House of Lords on the State of the Coal Trade*, PP, vol. viii (1830), pp. 66–7, 274.
25 Even after 1826, when the bond was standardized throughout the northern coalfield, the final section delineating working prices was left blank in order that each colliery could fill in its own piece-rates. See Jaffe, *Struggle for Market Power*, pp. 62–3, 111–113; United Colliers Association, *A Candid Appeal to the Coal-owners and the Viewers of the Collieries on the Tyne and Wear*

(Newcastle upon Tyne, 1826), p. 9.

26 Watson Mss., NRO 3410/Wat/1/5/91, 92.

27 'To the Public', Durham County Record Office (hereafter DCRO), London-derry Papers, D/Lo/C 142(736).

28 *A Voice from the Coal Mines; or, A Plain Statement of the Various Grievances of the Pitmen of the Tyne and Wear* (South Shields, 1825).

29 See Jaffe, *Struggle for Market Power*, pp. 61–8, 105–19.

30 The following account is taken from Dunn's diary deposited in the Newcastle upon Tyne Central Library (hereafter NCL).

31 The marketing of coal was complicated by the existence of a wide variety of 'brand names' and types of coal, which is certainly a reflection of its function as an important consumer item. To give but one example, however, between 1838 and 1840 Lord Londonderry's highest grade 'round' coal, the Wallsend brand, sold on average for 11s 6d per ton and earned him gross profits of nearly £80,000 each year. His 'small' coal, on the other hand, on average sold for only 5s 6½d per ton. With working costs varying during these years be-tween 5s and 5s 6½d per ton, small coal was often not even worth the cost of digging it. DCRO, Londonderry Papers, D/Lo/E/514 (7–8). In fact, at North Hetton Colliery, also managed by Dunn, small coal was being burned as waste in November 1832. Dunn estimated that the colliery would save £26 per day by separating and stowing the small coal underground. See NCL, Dunn's Di-ary, 14 November 1832.

32 A corf (pl. corves) was a wicker basket used to carry coal away from the seam. It was therefore a measure of volume, not weight, and its exact size varied at each colliery. Michael Flinn suggests that corves averaged between 16 and 20 pecks, but Matthias Dunn considered a 20-peck corf seriously under measure. He further noted that at North Hetton Colliery in 1832, the miners admitted this to be true. Dunn was eventually able to get the miners there to agree to 21-peck corves, although he suggested that most corves at the surrounding collier-ies contained 21½ pecks and upwards. Indeed the miners at Hetton Colliery came to an agreement with the owners there that corves should contain no more than 22 pecks. See NCL, Dunn's Diary, 21 February, 29 March, 5 April and 23 April 1832. Flinn further notes that a 20-peck corf measured about 26 inches high and 34 inches in diameter. See M.W. Flinn, *The History of the British Coal Industry, Volume 2, 1700–1830: The Industrial Revolution* (Ox-ford: Clarendon Press, 1984), Appendix B, p. 461.

33 NCL, Dunn's Diary, 10 November 1831.

34 NCL, Dunn's Diary, 16 November 1831.

35 NCL, Dunn's Diary, 30 November 1831.

36 NCL, Dunn's Diary, 7, 8 and 15 December 1831.

37 NCL, Dunn's Diary, 14 December 1831.

38 NCL, Dunn's Diary, 15 December 1831.

39 NCL, Dunn's Diary, 4 and 5 January 1832.

40 NCL, Dunn's Diary, 19 January 1832.

41 NCL, Dunn's Diary, 25 January 1832.

42 NCL, Dunn's Diary, 9, 14, 22 and 23 February 1832.

43 NCL, Dunn's Diary, 8 March 1832.

44 NCL, Dunn's Diary, 15 March 1832.

45 *A Voice from the Coal Mines*, pp. 8–9.

46 NCL, Dunn's Diary, 19 March 1832.

47 NCL, Dunn's Diary, 24 March 1832.

48 NRO, Minutes of the General Meetings of the Coal Owners of the Rivers Tyne and Wear, 24 March 1832.

49 NCL, Dunn's Diary, 5 April 1832.

50 Bell Collection, NRO 3410/Bell/11/423.

51 Bell Collection, NRO 3410/Bell/11/405, *Address from the Hetton Pitmen to the Public*, 20 April 1832. 'Nicking' and 'kirving' were techniques used to cut coal from the face. A 'keeker' was one of the ranks of underground supervisory personnel. One petition from *A Voice from the Coal Mines* describes him as 'a petty, contemptible officer, appointed by the masters to watch the men's work and fine them'.

52 Behagg, *Politics and Production*, p. 124.

53 So-called 'hewing matches' that tested masculine prowess in digging coal unwittingly revealed that labour potential was often much greater than expected. On hewing matches and the model of the 'big hewer' in the north-east, see Robert Colls, *The Pitmen of the Northern Coalfield: Work, Culture and Protest, 1790–1850* (Manchester: Manchester University Press, 1987), pp. 32–3.

54 Often better known as 'this damned restriction of output', as Carter Goodrich noted, the causes and significance of output restriction have been the subject of a vast number of studies and interpretations dating at least as far back as Frederick W. Taylor's studies on 'scientific management'. Some of the most prominent studies of it have also included Elton Mayo, *Human Problems of an Industrial Civilization* (New York: Macmillan, 1938); Stanley B. Mathewson, *Restriction of Output among Unorganized Workers* (1931; Carbondale: Southern Illinois University Press, 1969); and T. Lupton, *On the Shop Floor: Two Studies of Workshop Organization and Output* (Oxford: Pergamon Press, 1963). The works mentioned above by Roy and Burawoy belong in this category as well. Whether the actual presence of restrictive practices is quite as prominent as its observers often claim is an important question raised in the modern English context by Nick Tiratsoo and Jim Tomlinson, 'Restrictive Practices on the Shopfloor in Britain, 1945–60: Myth and Reality', *Business History*, vol. 36: no. 2 (1994), pp. 65–84.

55 Clive Behagg, 'Narratives of Control: Informalism and the Workplace in Britain, 1800–1900', in O. Ashton, R. Fyson and S. Roberts, eds, *The Duty of Discontent: Essays for Dorothy Thompson* (London: Mansell Publishing Ltd, 1995), p. 123.

56 There is also an extensive literature on the coal-owners' cartel. For some contributions, see Paul M. Sweezy, *Monopoly and Competition in the English Coal Trade, 1550–1850* (Cambridge, Mass.: Harvard University Press, 1938); Peter Cromar, 'Economic Power and Organisation: The Development of the Coal Industy on Tyneside, 1700–1828' (unpub. Ph.D. dissertation, Cambridge University, 1977); Flinn, *History of the British Coal Industry*, pp. 256–67; Colls, *Pitmen of the Northern Coalfield*, pp. 51–64; and Jaffe, *Struggle for Market Power*, ch. 2.

57 On the miners' bond, see Hylton Scott, 'The Miners' Bond in Northumberland and Durham', pt. 1, *Proceedings of the Society of Antiquaries of Newcastle-*

upon-Tyne, 4th ser., vol. 11: no. 2 (1947), pp. 55–78; Flinn, *History of the British Coal Industry*, pp. 352–8; Colls, *Pitmen of the Northern Coalfield*, pp. 45–51, 64–73; and Jaffe, *Struggle for Market Power*, pp. 98–105.

58 See the exchange of letters between the coal-owners and the miners in the *Newcastle Chronicle*, 16 April 1831.

59 *Newcastle Chronicle*, 9 April 1831.

60 Lambton Estate Archive (hereafter LEA), Lambton Mss., Henry Morton to Lord Durham, 16 March 1831.

61 *Report from the Select Committee on the State of the Coal Trade*, p. 315, quoted in Jaffe, *Struggle for Market Power*, p. 155.

62 *Report from the Select Committee of the House of Lords on the State of the Coal Trade*, pp. 66–7. See also *Report from the Select Committee on the State of the Coal Trade*, pp. 274, 315.

63 Huberman, *Escape from the Market*, pp. 110–25. This does not contradict, however, Huberman's broader contention that aspects of the fair wage developed as a mutually acceptable structure in opposition to market forces, which is an especially appropriate observation relative to these clauses of the miners' bond.

64 *Newcastle Chronicle*, 7 January 1832.

65 NRO, General Meetings of the Coal Owners of the Rivers Tyne and Wear, 13 April 1831.

66 NRO, General Meetings of the Coal Owners of the Rivers Tyne and Wear, 11 April 1831.

67 NRO, General Meetings of the Coal Owners of the Rivers Tyne and Wear, 11 April 1831; *Newcastle Chronicle*, 16 April 1831.

68 Bell Collection, NRO 3410/Bell/11/226.

69 NRO, General Meetings of the Coal Owners of the Rivers Tyne and Wear, 29 April 1831, 6 May 1831, 11 May 1831; LEA, Lambton Mss., Henry Morton to Lord Durham, 6 May 1831, 9 May 1831.

70 DCRO, Londonderry Papers, Buddle to Londonderry, D/Lo/C 142(713), 26 May 1831; see also D/Lo/C 142(715), 29 May 1831.

71 LEA, Lambton Mss., Henry Morton to Lord Durham, 17 May 1831.

72 DCRO, Londonderry Papers, Buddle to Londonderry, D/Lo/C 142(718), 2 June 1831.

73 Interestingly, restriction also appears in the union rules from the United Colliers Association of 1825. Unlike the 1831–32 union, however, the United Colliers never had an opportunity to implement this goal. See §VI, *Rules and Regulations, for the Formation of a Society to be called the United Association of Colliers, on the Rivers Tyne and Wear* (Newcastle upon Tyne, 1825).

74 Bell Collection NRO 3410/Bell/11/312–13.

75 For a detailed account of these developments, see Jaffe, *Struggle for Market Power*, pp. 164–78.

76 Roy, 'Quota Restriction and Goldbricking'.

77 *Royal Commission on Trade Unions and Employers' Organizations*, Research Papers, No. 4:2 (London: HMSO, 1967), p. 50.

78 *Newcastle Chronicle*, 24 March 1832. It should be noted that the reference to working in the 'whole mine' refers to the underground areas not previously excavated. This is opposed to working in the 'broken' areas of the mine that

have already been dug out and contained huge pillars of coal that supported the roof.

79 NCL, Dunn's Diary, 8 March 1832.
80 John Benson, *British Coalminers in the Nineteenth Century: A Social History* (Dublin: Gill and Macmillan, 1980), pp. 28–32, 62–3, who rightly emphasizes our paucity of knowledge of the large number of surface workers in the coal industry.
81 Calculations derived from Flinn, *History of the British Coal Industry*, Table 10.1, p. 332.
82 DCRO, Londonderry Papers, D/Lo/C 142(706), Buddle to Londonderry, 13 May 1831.
83 Flinn, *History of the British Coal Industry*, pp. 339–40.
84 LEA, Lambton Mss., Morton to Lord Durham, 17 May 1831.
85 DCRO, Londonderry Papers, D/Lo/C 142(715), Buddle to Londonderry, 29 May 1831.
86 Lupton, *On the Shop Floor*, p. 182.
87 Lupton, *On the Shop Floor*, pp. 182–3.
88 Lupton, *On the Shop Floor*, p. 181.
89 Jaffe, *Struggle for Market Power*, pp. 179–90.
90 NCL, Dunn's Diary, 29 March 1832.
91 NRO, Minutes of the General Meetings of the Coal Owners of the Rivers Tyne and Wear, 23 June 1832.
92 See DCRO, Londonderry Papers, D/Lo/C142(831), Buddle to Londonderry, 30 May 1832, which relates the fact that one-half of the hewers at Rainton Colliery were working to 4s while the other half remained at 3s.
93 NCL, Dunn's Diary, 9 August 1832.

6

Games at work?: rule-making and reputations

> Most well regulated shops are governed internally by a particular code of laws, for the maintenance of justice and good order among the men ... (T.A., *Mechanics' Magazine*, 20 December 1823)

As the case of the northern coal-miners suggests, the means by which workers and employers resolved the effort problem on the early industrial shopfloor can be fruitfully pursued through the analysis of the ways in which workers and employers sought to codify their relationship. The study of such job regulations and rule-making has long been a prominent aspect of industrial relations research. Indeed the enormously influential text on industrial relations by the late Hugh Clegg defined the discipline as 'the study of the rules governing employment, together with the ways in which the rules are made and changed, interpreted and administered. Put more briefly, it is the study of job regulation.'[1] Even the academic debates between the so-called 'pluralist' and 'radical' writers on British industrial relations in the 1970s, despite their differences, underscored a consensus that the study of industrial relations was principally the task of understanding, interpreting and defining the nature of such processes.[2] These debates did much to clarify the fact that rules and rule-making were tied not only to the distribution of power and authority in industry, but also to the manner in which specific goals were recognized and articulated.[3] They also helped to reveal that working rules are generated at several different levels.[4] Some rules are imposed by the state, some are negotiated or adopted at the institutional level of the trade union or employers' organization, while still others are developed within the workplace.[5] Finally, those earlier debates revealed that the creation of working rules may be founded on a consensual attitude toward industrial relations but they may equally be based upon conflicts over shopfloor or trade union issues.[6]

For many industrial relations specialists, however, the study of rule-making all too often seemed to resolve itself into the construction of antithetical ideal-types: formal *versus* informal rules, procedural *versus* substantive rules, internal *versus* external rules, unilateral *versus* joint regulation.[7] These dichotomies have undoubtedly had great heuristic value. However, here as elsewhere, such dichotomies can sometimes obscure as much as they reveal. This is particularly important for the study of job regulation, since the effort bargain, which constitutes the foundation of the employment relationship, was to an important degree reciprocal. Therefore, an examination of the role of reciprocity in this rule-making process may help to contribute to our understanding of work and employment relationships in the early nineteenth century, as it did that of the effort bargain and output restriction.

One especially important reason why such a perspective on job regulation or rule-making may help to do this is that the classic period of industrialization, if there is any value left in that term, was also an era of extensive rule-making. As John Rule has noted, there was a general trend among craft unions of this era to attempt to regularize workplace practices and customs through the elaboration of price lists and the publication of working rules, a phenomenon that Iorweth Prothero has similarly recognized among the London tailors, carpenters, brush-makers, silk-weavers, and other metropolitan artisanal trades.[8] Michael Huberman's work has also brought renewed attention to the importance of the evolution of such developments in the Lancashire cotton industry.[9] Perhaps typical of this trend was the movement among London compositors after 1780 to establish a price list that also contained a substantial set of working rules, which will be discussed in detail below. Although the compositors almost certainly possessed a level of literacy that exceeded many, if not all, other trades, their working conditions, employment relationships and bargaining positions were not atypical. An examination of their actions, which will be the subject of this chapter, therefore may help to elucidate the forms of gifting and reciprocity that were imbricated in the rule-making processes of this period.

Toward this end, the analysis of rule-making as a reciprocal relationship can itself be deepened by adopting some of the insights and analytical techniques of game theory. Game theory has much to offer the historian of industrial relations, although its limitations need to be specifically acknowledged. Foremost among the latter is the heroic assumption that even though participants in any action may operate under conditions of asymmetric information, they nonetheless possess a common knowledge of the 'rules of the game' and will act rationally in the pursuit of their own best interest.[10] (The famous prisoners' dilemma game, however, illustrates that one's best interest need not be identified either in terms of the individual or the short term.) Whether such a common knowledge existed in the realm of early nineteenth-century industrial relations has been, of course, a subject of significant debate, particularly among labour historians. In *The Making of the English Working Class*, E.P. Thompson, for one, clearly did not believe such a common ground existed. He then saw a distinct dichotomy between the political economy embraced by the bourgeoisie and the moral economy that prevailed among the working class, although he was later to suggest otherwise.[11] More importantly, even if one posits a shared base of common knowledge or rules in order to understand the dynamics of decision-making or consensus-building, which is after all the object of game theory, then how does one analyse the historical construction of the rules themselves? In response, game theorists would probably argue that the 'players' in a rule-making game would select a set of rules that would 'optimize' their strategy as in any other game situation. This seems to be tautological at best and not all that helpful.

Nevertheless, game theory need not be thrown out altogether. As Robert Wilson has suggested, game theory can be especially helpful in understanding the decision-making process in bargaining situations, particularly the role played by personal and institutional reputations. He argues that in many, if not all, bargaining circumstances, decisions are often based upon an understanding that the past behaviour of one party is indicative of their future performance. Such 'reputational effects' are particularly important in situations where labour is difficult or impossible to monitor, supervise or quantify, because under such circumstances decisions concerning the employment relationship often rely upon the exchange of reputations rather than the exchange of goods.[12] While Wilson has applied this perspective to both subcontractors and managers, such insights can be equally applied to shopfloor workers, their employers, the rules they construct to regulate their relationship and, of course, the effort bargain during the early industrial period. The exchange of reputations, I am suggesting here, becomes an important element of the general exchange of effort for pay in situations where labour is not closely monitored, as in the early nineteenth-century workshop, and workers retain a discretionary fund of labour.[13] The creation of working rules attempts to codify this relationship, but the adoption of the work rules themselves depends upon an exchange of promises (that is, reputations) that workers and employers rely on to predict both future pay and future performance. This applies not only to circumstances in which working rules are negotiated, but also to those in which rules are unilaterally imposed by either workers or employees. Regardless of the origin of the rules, the extent to which they appear to be legitimate, and are therefore accepted, is based largely on the reputations that both parties have established to commit to certain acceptable standards of behaviour. Obviously, rules that are not followed not only lose their legitimacy but undermine the reputation of the rule-breaker as well. Rule-making, therefore, was a reciprocal endeavour. Not only were the sources and types of developing working rules of great importance, but the manner in which they were reciprocally elaborated and implemented is of equal significance to an understanding of work relationships during this period.

Reputational effects among the London compositors

The general pattern of work and industrial relations between the journey-men compositors and their master printers shared several characteristics with other artisanal groups. By the end of the eighteenth century, the London printing trades had become specialized into a number of separate occupations, including bookbinding, presswork, papermaking and typesetting. Further specialization had developed among the typesetters themselves, more commonly called compositors, particularly between those who set type for the daily newspapers and those who worked on books and other publications. After 1793, the two branches of this trade negotiated with their own employers and drew up separate price lists.[14] The journeymen who worked on books, journals and broadsides, and who will be the focus of our attention here, worked in small establishments using traditional technologies.[15] Near the end of the first decade of the nineteenth century, there were perhaps 216 printing firms in London, a number that grew to over 300 by 1825.[16] In 1839, the average master printer employed fourteen men and five boys, excluding administrative staff; the largest firm in the country employed only 121 compositors and 55 apprentices.[17] Reliable statistics on the total number of journeymen compositors and apprentices are, of course, difficult to come by. When the working-class activist Francis Place gathered information on trade unionism in England in 1818, an unknown correspondent reported to him that there were 1,882 compositors and 600 apprentices in London.[18] By mid-century, a union secretary estimated that there were 3,000 compositors in London and 1,500 apprentices. Throughout the period, however, it appears that fewer than half of the London compositors were regular members of trade unions.[19]

Within the workshop itself, called the chapel, composition was done exclusively by hand.[20] While steam power had been applied to presses, especially for the daily newspapers after 1825, mechanical composition did not become widespread until the very end of the century.[21] The long-term rise in consumer prices that set in after 1750, and then accelerated during the Revolutionary and Napoleonic periods, engendered the organization of trade societies, the outbreak of strikes and the construction and publication of price lists. The first of these lists was produced in 1785, but subsequent amendments and additions were made in 1793, 1795, 1800, 1805, 1810, 1816 and 1847.[22]

After the first price list had been adopted in 1785, Ellic Howe, one of the foremost historians of the trade, suggests that 'it became an accepted custom for the compositors' committee to approach and negotiate with the employers on wage questions'.[23] While some disputes were amicably settled during this period, not all of them were, and in 1816 the London Trade Society of Compositors (LTSC) was founded after one failed strike. According to one historian and industrial relations expert, the London Trade Society functioned 'mainly as a benefit society providing out-of-work pay and accident compensation'.[24] In this, of course, it was not extraordinary among other trade societies of the period.[25] Ten years later, however, internal policy disputes split this union and in 1826 the London General Trade Society of Compositors (LGTSC) broke off from the main union. While its origins are obscure, this small union ultimately played an extremely important role in the development of the trade's industrial relations.[26]

The new union sought to distinguish itself from the larger parent trade society in two particular areas. First, membership in the LGTSC was open to a much wider pool of workers in the printing trade. While the parent organization limited membership to those who had served and completed a full seven-year apprenticeship, no such limitations were adopted by the LGTSC.[27] Instead, the latter was open to 'every individual ... who wishes to be considered a fair workman and an honourable member of Society'.[28] To facilitate such a policy, the dues and charges assessed to all members were significantly lower than those of the parent society, which, in 1826, had set subscription dues at 3d per week plus an additional quarterly charge of 3d to defray the secretary's salary.[29] The LGTSC, on the other hand, established weekly dues at only 1d, although quarterly charges were slightly higher at 4d.[30] It declared such policies to be 'just and equitable'. Indeed in its early stages, the LGTSC was confident 'that the trade can boast of hundreds of public-spirited men, who will cheerfully contribute their mite to advance the general good; but whose circumstances will not permit them to expend fourteen shillings a year for that purpose'.[31]

The second distinguishing claim of the LGTSC was its desire to improve industrial relations between the printing masters and the compositors. Towards this end, the LGTSC created a committee of eight members to hear and determine disputes between masters and men over piece-work prices, working conditions, and other related matters.[32] The goal of this special committee was to resolve disputes peacefully: 'to keep the noiseless tenour of their way, avoiding direct controversy, which, is not only useless, but has a tendency to produce unpleasant consequences'. Such a policy was meant to establish the union's reputation for fairness and objectivity and, as a result, elicit from the masters a reciprocal commitment to the union's recommendations. 'One great, substantial, and vital object of your committee', the union noted in its Quarterly Report of February 1828, '... is to endeavour to create in the minds of the masters, a feeling of respect and interest for the Society'. This in turn would help 'to ensure a compliance with all fair and reasonable demands'.[33] The ultimate success of this committee's 'reputational effect' was later recognized by the parent union. A Union Committee comprised of delegates from both unions was formed five years later in 1831, serving the same function for the entire trade, and when a new London Union of Compositors was created in 1834 by the merger of the two unions the committee survived and was renamed the Trade Council.[34]

The fact that the LGTSC was attempting unilaterally to enforce and decide working rules, which may seem startling today, was not as significant to the compositors as was the fact that they were trying to evoke a reciprocal commitment from the masters to maintain the price list. Indeed the union's claim to authority over disputes was based on the notion that the mutual agreement upon a standard price list entailed reciprocal obligations upon both parties to commit to its defence. Shortly after the LGTSC was established, the union reminded its members that 'your Committee have kept in view the principal objects of the Society, viz. the decision of disputed points, and the maintenance of the established Rules of the trade'. It went on to warn its new members that 'whenever it is possible, adhere closely to the scale – do not permit a trifling infraction, for it would assuredly lead to a greater violation. It is your sheet anchor – your only hope.'[35] In 1838, the new union's Trade Council defended these activities by arguing that the legitimacy of the scale was based on its origin as a negotiated document: 'The Scale[,] which constitutes the basis of all charges in the printing business was a copact [*sic*] between masters and journeymen'.[36]

These were not the union's sole claims to authority in disputed matters, however. The Union Committee and the Trade Council frequently contended that their actions were justified also by the reciprocal benefits they had for both masters and men.[37] Soon after the formation of the Union Committee in 1831, the LGTSC asserted that 'so long as the business of the society is conducted on its present principles it cannot fail of being beneficial to all parties – employers and workmen'.[38] In 1835, the Trade Council even argued that the compositors' union forced a degree of discipline upon master printers that was necessary to protect the trade from price competition engendered by London booksellers.[39] The Trade Council insisted:

> Does not every man know, who is at all acquainted with the history of the trade for the last twenty years, that there are but a few employers who can meet each other with unblushing countenances – for it were useless to attempt to conceal the fact that masters are more at enmity with each other than with us; and that, in truth, our wages do not so much depend on the master-printers of London, as on the opulent booksellers, who have contrived to throw the apple of discord among our employers, and have made them underwork each other to such an extent, as has excited a degree of hostility among them, which the lapse of many years and the adoption of a different system alone can remove. And may it not be expected that one of the earliest and most beneficial effects of our Union will be, to emancipate the master-printers from a state of slavery so galling and disgraceful.[40]

Such claims to represent the mutual interests of the trade were important aspects of the union's general attempt to initiate an exchange of reputations that would evoke from the master printers a commitment to the scale. In a similar manner, the union constantly portrayed its actions as impartial, fair and just. At its annual meeting in 1828, the LGTSC described the function of the disputes committee as an 'impartial tribunal'. Moreover, it explained to its members that the usefulness of such a tribunal was self-evident. 'Let not the utility and importance of your Society be questioned', the LGTSC declared. 'The usefulness of an institution which arbitrates between two adverse parties, where one is inclined to have, and the other to withhold, must be so apparent to all reasonable men, as to render any observations from your committee wholly unnecessary.'[41]

In its everyday functions, the LGTSC committee was especially concerned to make these claims to impartiality clear to the master printers. Such was the case in 1830 when the master printers Bradbury and Co. contacted the committee in order to track down a union compositor. The compositor, John Dennis, had been loaned 30s by the firm on the understanding that he would gradually work off the debt, but had left off employment while still owing 21s. Over the next six weeks, the committee tried to contact Dennis to force him to pay off the debt. Ultimately, it failed and he was expelled from the union. During the course of this incident, the committee was eager to reassure the masters of its impartiality even in a case against a union member. A copy of the resolution expelling the compositor was sent to the master printer along with a note explaining the committee's hope that 'this will satisfy you of the willingness of the Society to behave in such a manner as will lead our employers to believe, what is really the fact – that we wish to act with impartiality and justice'.[42]

The 'reputational effects' of claims to fairness, justice and impartiality mingled quite readily with affirmations of the reciprocity and mutuality of interests between masters and men. The LGTSC explained at its third annual meeting in 1829 that 'the interest of the employed is so strongly identified with the employer, that your officers have invariably considered themselves as arbitrators – and thereby, acting in the true spirit of Justice'.[43] Yet there were limits. This approach could be defended only so long as the legitimacy of the committee's role and function went largely uncontested. However, the formation of the Association of Master Printers in 1837 and the subsequent creation of a competing masters' disputes committee forced the compositors to articulate their legitimacy in new terms. Notions of justice and reciprocity thereafter began to merge with the defence of the compositors' activities explicated in the more contentious language of rights.[44] Not wishing to lose the perceived advantages of a recognized system of dispute settlement and arbitration, however, the compositors several times advanced proposals to coordinate and integrate the activities of the masters' and union's committees.[45] Nonetheless, the compositors increasingly argued that their participation in the settlement of disputes was based on 'the generally recognised and just principle, that employers and employed have equal rights in the adjustment of the price of labour'.[46]

Rule-making

The regular work of the compositors' disputes committee during this period began when shopfloor conflicts in individual workshops were referred to them for settlement. Indeed LGTSC members were ineligible to make a claim on union funds if they had quit their employment without first presenting their complaint to the committee.[47] In the language of industrial relations specialists, the committee principally functioned as a form of 'external job regulation'. That is, the rules governing work were applied by bodies that were not present at the work site itself. Most cases concerned whether the prices being offered by master printers accorded to the 1810 scale. In the simplest of them, the committee reviewed the disputed material and pronounced a judgement that was accepted by both parties. For example, in 1829 a deputation of compositors from Gilbert's printing house in St John's Square inquired whether the scale reduction of three farthings per thousand ens that normally applied to the casting up of reprinted works also applied to works of one sheet or less.[48] In response, a note was drafted and delivered to the shop's overseer and master printer that read: 'The Committee of the L.G.T.S.C. are of the opinion that the question submitted to them by the delegates from Mr. Gilbert's is answered by Article 20 in the scale of prices agreed to in 1816'.[49] That is, jobs of one sheet or under, with some exceptions, were cast up at 8d per thousand ens with additional charges for foreign languages and smaller typefaces.[50] In another case concerning proper payment for adding chapter headings to a reprint of Hume's *History of England*, the committee sent the master printer a note declaring that 'it is the opinion of the Committee of the London General Trade Society of Compositors, that the first Volume of Hume's History of England, submitted to their consideration by the chapel at Mr. Davison's [printing house], is entitled to 1/– per sheet extra for chapter heads over and above the price paid for bottom notes, as allowed by the scale'.[51]

Many times, however, cases did not fall precisely under the rubrics established by the scale and the committee was forced to create rules for these situations as they arose. Indeed the resolution of these disputes and the formation of new rules to cover these instances was considered to be the most important function of the various disputes committees. When the Union Committee, comprised of representatives of both the LGTSC and the LTSC, was formed in the early 1830s, one of its first reports claimed that the new committee's principal value lay in its efforts to construct a 'Register or Depository' of precedents. The committee noted:

> by carefully preserving the particulars of each individual case, in the course of time a map of information and precedents will be collected which, by a just arrangement, can at all time be easily referred to, and must eventually prove most beneficial to all Compositors by enabling him to obtain, from a reference to these Documents, a knowledge of the law, as well as the customs of the Trade.

Toward this end, the committee urged compositors to forward the rates of payment for any 'peculiar works'. They reasoned that 'by the accumulation of such documents, whose authority would be invaluable in any dispute which rendered law proceedings necessary, and the collection of the existing customs of the various [printing] houses, that the attainment of that desirable object:– the establishment of an invariable rate of payment for Work in all houses, can be accomplished'.[52]

When new working rules or prices were being formulated, however, the compositors' disputes committees acted to mobilize the influence of both the law and reputations to secure the masters' commitment.[53] One of the most surprising methods of settlement was the repeated recourse to the *ad hoc* arbitration of other master printers. For example, when a disagreement over the payment for typesetting a broadside was submitted to the LGTSC disputes committee in 1829, its initial response was to offer a decision on the matter. Yet, apparently unsure of its own position, the committee simultaneously offered to submit the case to 'a reference'. This, as we shall see, is part of the very old language of arbitration.[54] In this case, the father of the chapel brought the original offer to the master printer Mr Taylor, who at first refused to accept the committee's decision, but then agreed to submit the dispute to three master printers and abide by their decision. When one of the referees refused to give an opinion on the matter, the committee appointed a deputation of compositors to call at thirteen leading printing houses to ascertain the opinions of the masters or overseers. In less than a week, twelve printing houses had responded; eight supported the committee's pricing of the job and four opposed it. Mr Taylor did not immediately respond and undertook a series of his own enquiries. It appears that he then referred the case back to the three master printers initially agreed upon. This time, however, the referees were unanimous in their support of the committee's decision, and Taylor finally accepted their verdict. The committee was obviously proud of this achievement and reported to their members that 'the long-disputed broadside was at length settled – on the basis first directed by them, viz. a reference to two or three respectable master printers'.[55]

These negotiations are indicative of the way in which reputations were mobilized to secure commitment to rule-making as well as the manner in which forms of reciprocity were elicited from the compositors' employers. Nor were these actions particularly unique during this period. Similar attempts to mobilize the reputations of 'respectable masters' can be found in many industrial sectors where competitive price-cutting was a significant threat.[56] One important reason why workers developed such a tactic was not only because their pay was threatened, but also because the obscurity of the effort bargain necessitated some supplementary sources of verification. That is, since it was impossible to measure and control work-effort, reputations were marshalled to validate or defend changing standards of the exchange of effort for pay.

In the case of the London compositors, this early form of reciprocity, which relied solely on the reputations of the masters to arbitrate disputes, was replaced in 1834 by a more formal equality in such matters. With the formation of the London Union of Compositors (LUC), the union sought equal standing with the masters on *ad hoc* arbitration councils. Thus Article 7 of the union's *Rules and Regulations* adopted in that year stated:

> to avoid the injustice frequently arising from acting on exparte statements, in all cases of disputes, wherever practicable, the trade-council shall hear the statement of the employer on the subject, either from himself, his overseer, or agent; and whenever desired by masters, the price for disputed works shall be decided by arbitration. The arbitrators to consist of an equal number of masters and members of the trade-council.[57]

Indeed it does appear that the union sought to resolve especially thorny issues in this manner for the next few years at least.[58] For example, the question of 'wrappers', the paper covers of periodicals, generated numerous disputes during the mid-1830s.[59] In one of them at the Penny National Library office, the LUC Trade Council proposed creating a joint arbitration committee of five masters and five Trade Council members. To help ensure the masters' participation, the union even volunteered to return any extra money that the compositors may have earned in the interim if the arbitrators' decision went against them.[60]

The methods and resources that the compositors called upon to enforce working rules were varied and extremely flexible. For example, when a dispute was unlikely to be resolved, the committee often recommended that the journeymen at the particular printing house serve notice to quit in a fortnight's time. This precaution protected employees from prosecution under the master and servant laws, but it also served to protect the union's reputation for avoiding unnecessary confrontation.[61] However, the union was not averse to transgressing that imaginary line that separates external job regulation from so-called internal job regulation, which occurs autonomously by individuals or work groups within the firm.[62] Thus the compositors' unions were often willing to assist members in their efforts to enforce their individual contracts. The unions were well aware that the master and servant laws so often used against workers could also be deployed against employers who themselves failed to fulfil contracts or to give proper notice.[63] The union therefore supported and encouraged their members to pursue such cases before the London Court of Requests, which, during the early nineteenth century, had jurisdiction over the recovery of debts of £10 or less.[64] In 1830, for example, Henry Hetherington, the radical reformer, refused to pay the charges for a broadside, contending that it should have been cast up at a lower rate. The compositor, Mr Coley, summoned Hetherington before the Court of Requests. The commissioners of the court suggested that the dispute should be referred to persons who were familiar with the trade and offered Hetherington the choice of referring the question to either the LTSC or the LGTSC. Hetherington chose the latter. The disputes committee recognized that the rules governing the rates for this type of broadside were ambiguous and they worked to issue a decision 'so as not to injure the employer, and yet secure to the workman his just rights'.[65] Their decision that the broadside should be charged at the higher rate was not accepted by Hetherington. He was then forced to appear again before the court which ordered the master printer to abide by the agreement and to pay Coley at the rate assessed by the union's committee.[66]

This appeal to the courts was the union's most obvious attempt to intervene in the legal relationship between the individual and the employer. However, actions brought before the Court of Requests were not always resolved in as judicious a manner as the Hetherington case. In the case of Mr Fergusson, a compositor working on a broadside for the master printer Bentley, the Trade Council had good reason to suspect that the court commissioners had been unfairly briefed by their adversaries. Fergusson had been dismissed in July 1834 after Bentley had refused to accept his charges for casting up a broadside. The Trade Council recommended that he proceed against Bentley in the Court of Requests and appointed three council members to assist him. At the initial hearing, the chief commissioner was very well disposed towards the compositor until he was informed that a clause in the scale allowed all disputes to be referred to a committee of the masters. This reference certainly does appear in the 1805 scale, but there is no evidence that such a committee had met in the almost two decades prior to this case.[67] Mr Bentley, nevertheless, appears to have made much of it and the court adjourned *sine die*. When the court returned to the case the following week, the chief commissioner was in a different temper. According to the Trade Council minutes, he pulled a large charter out of his pocket and compared it with the broadside in dispute. In the 1810 scale, large charters and broadsides were to be paid at double the rate of common works, with smaller charters and broadsides at a proportionately lower rate. The chief commissioner declared that the broadside and charter he held were clearly not the same. A union official in attendance tried to explain the intricacies of the case but the commissioners decided that the compositor was not entitled to his original charges and dismissed the case. Upon hearing an account of these proceedings, the Trade Council members guessed that the chief commissioner had been approached privately by one or more master printers, and concluded that 'there evidently had been some private communication with the chief commissioner, or else how could he be prepared?'[68]

The historian John Rule's emphasis upon the malleability of custom during this period, and, by extension, the adaptability of craft unions, is quite appropriate.[69] In the case of the compositors, the institutions that characterized craft unionism, such as the benefit society and house of call,[70] were matched by the compositors' unions' use of an array of tactics to both participate in and control the creation of working rules. These tactics included the construction of a rules committee to maintain the industry price list, the adoption of both masters' and joint arbitration, and repeated applications to the courts to help regulate the individual employment relationship. The ideological justification of these actions tended to be drawn from accepted views of general social intercourse such as fairness, usefulness and justice, which were meant to create a 'reputational effect' that might secure a mutual commitment to both the price list and its working rules. The more contentious language of rights was resorted to only at a relatively late date, yet even then it was couched in older notions of fairness.

There were, nonetheless, matters that the union left to be worked out between shopfloor groups in each printing house, and their individual employers. Such 'internal job regulation' was never a simple matter, especially since commitment to the chapel, employer and union were sometimes at odds with one another. At times, the rule-making techniques adopted by the union disputes committees interfered with, and were rejected by, shopfloor workers. This does not mean chapel members rejected the importance of rule-making. They could, however, interpret the principles at stake differently. In such situations, bargaining's reputational effects had the capacity to split the worker's loyalties between the work group's quotidian relationship with foremen, overseers or employers and their relationship with other work groups or the wider union movement.

The potential for such crossed loyalties was a function of the persistence of shopfloor bargaining. As noted earlier, the scale of prices allowed for the negotiation and settlement of some prices at the shopfloor level. For example, side and bottom notes, which became a matter of repeated disputes during this period, were 'to be paid by agreement between the [individual] employer and the journeyman', according to the terms of the 1810 scale.[71] Similarly, the cost of the 'extra trouble' attending the casting up of material in parallel columns was to be determined through workplace bargaining.[72] Although these clauses may appear to relegate such negotiations to bargains struck between the individual worker and the employer, in practice the settlement of such prices was the responsibility of the entire chapel, particularly the 'father of the chapel', who was roughly equivalent to the modern-day shop steward.[73] Throughout this period, the union was willing to recommend appropriate prices, but it scrupulously avoided attempts to establish standard rates for these operations. In 1828, for example, the father of the chapel at Dove's printing house asked the LGTSC disputes committee whether 3s per sheet was adequate compensation for the composition of three oddly spaced columns. The committee's response was 'that three shillings is not an exorbitant charge for the extra trouble of the work, but the Committee of the L.G.T.S. recommend the journeymen to settle with the employer as amicably as possible, it coming only under the head of that *undefined* Article which states *extra trouble* to be settled between the employer and employed'.[74]

Such shopfloor bargaining over rules and practices could at times come into conflict with union attempts to regulate the employment relationship externally. In such cases, it was common for the shopfloor rules to supersede those suggested by the union. The compositors working on *Burke's Peerage* in 1832 were placed in just such a situation. The father of the chapel at Whittingham's printing house submitted to the Union Committee a request to resolve several related questions raised by the reprinting of the work, including charges for mixing different typefaces and the extent to which the work should be charged as being composed from manuscript. The Union Committee appears to have taken the most liberal interpretation of the issues and recommended that the entire work be charged at manuscript rates, with different typefaces charged at the higher rate.[75] When the master printer Whittingham refused at first to accept the committee's decision, the eight compositors at work on the *Peerage* handed him their notices to quit. This action appears to have had some effect because Whittingham responded with an offer to pay for the type-bodies at the higher rate, but to pay for the entire job at only half manuscript and half reprint charges. He even brought in evidence from Burke himself 'that after the letter E, the MS. insertions would be few, and the alterations trifling'. This convinced the chapel members to accept their employer's offer. Although the Union Committee was not pleased with this, it ultimately agreed to sanction the settlement.[76]

Such shopfloor bargaining was clearly not wholly autonomous from the external institutions of trade unionism as the distinction between 'formal' and 'informal' bargaining theory might suggest. Yet the *Burke's Peerage* case clearly violated the union's fundamental goals of standardizing rates of pay and amicably resolving disagreements by vetting conflicts through the disputes committee. In this instance, the rules negotiated by the chapel clearly superseded the union's external efforts to establish standardized working prices. Part of the chapel's authority in these matters appears to have been derived from the moderation exhibited by the compositors themselves, who deemed the settlement offered by the employer to be a fair one. Fairness for both employees and employers, as has been noted, was one of the elemental principles buttressing the union's initiatives to gain commitment to the price list. It was also one of the essential elements of establishing one's bargaining reputation. Yet the union's acceptance of the chapel's authority without doubt further rested on the latter's function as the fundamental unit of shopfloor organization in the printing trades. The legitimacy of this authority was derived in large part from the direct participatory nature of its decision-making process. In circumstances such as this one, chapels decided issues by polling their members or the portion of members working on the disputed work. The decision of the chapel, therefore, was the decision of a shopfloor majority.

Still, it would be unwise to suggest that the apparent unanimity that justified and legitimated the chapel's acceptance of the employer's offer on
Burke's Peerage was always in evidence. At times the chapel might be as
keenly divided against itself as at other times it might appear to be unanimous. An extremely rare insight into how the chapel functioned to regulate
work during this period may be culled from the records of an 1834 dispute
over the casting up of appeal cases printed for the House of Lords. This type
of parliamentary printing was undertaken by a number of specialized firms,
one of the most important of which was owned by Andrew Spottiswoode
and was known through this period variously as Eyre and Strahan,
Spottiswoode and Company, or Eyre and Spottiswoode.[77] Ellic Howe notes
that before the mid-1830s parliamentary printing work had not been covered by any of the earlier scales largely because the special nature of the work
was often paid at a higher rate than that of other printing jobs. Parliamentary printing became a matter of dispute, however, after the Stationery
Office published a set of regulations governing piece-rates to be paid by
government contractors in 1833. Several of these regulations violated practices already established in the 1810 scale, and, immediately after it was
founded in 1834, the London Union of Compositors vigorously sought to
defend the older price list.[78]

In July 1834, George Bacon was called before the LUC Trade Council to
respond to a report that the Spottiswoode chapel was not abiding by union
rates and standards for parliamentary work. As the 'clicker' on an appeal
case job, Bacon coordinated and facilitated the activities of production
teams, called companionships, in the printing office.[79] The dispute concerned two related issues. First, Spottiswoode paid for the casting up of appeal cases by the so-called 'lumping system', that is, payment made by the
sheet rather than by a piece-rate per thousand ens. The union prohibited
lumping throughout the trade because it absorbed the extra charges often
assessed for bottom and side notes and thus had the potential effect of lowering earnings. Second, the lump payment at Spottiswoode usually corresponded to a rate of about 7d per thousand ens. The union parliamentary
scale designated a piece-rate for such work at 8d per thousand ens.[80] Thus
even the lump payments were set below the standard rates. When Bacon, the
union clicker, was called before the union's disputes committee, he told them
that he had charged the job 'in the usual way' and declared that it was his
opinion that Spottiswoode was not subject to the council's decisions. In
response, the council issued directions to the father of the chapel, the *de
facto* shop steward, to call a meeting and to implement the union prices.[81]

The chapel meeting was duly convened the following day. Four of the
chapel members were deputed to express the demands of the union Trade
Council to the overseer, Mr Shaw, who referred the chapel delegates to Mr
Spottiswoode personally. During their interview with Spottiswoode, the
delegates tried to convince him of the validity of their claim apparently by

appealing to the precedents of both earlier practices and the way in which the work was paid at other houses. Spottiswoode was willing to admit that appeal cases might have been paid for differently once, but he defended his current payments by invoking the authority of custom. Spottiswoode insisted that 'as custom had sanctioned another mode of payment, and as his house for the last 50 years had paid a uniform price for cases, he would not consent to have the custom of his house altered, especially as it had originated with a Trade Union'.[82]

The deputies reported Spottiswoode's response to the chapel, where the majority then voted to reject the Trade Council's recommendations and to accept Spottiswoode's 'customary' standards of payment. In addition, the chapel passed a resolution requesting the Trade Council to exempt Spottiswoode from the trade regulations in this matter and to review the union's policy on charges for appeal cases generally. In response, the Trade Council continued to argue that the Spottiswoode chapel should charge appeal cases at the union rate.[83] During the ensuing week, however, an exceedingly rare correspondence was received by the Trade Council. A minority group of thirty journeymen employed at Spottiswoode's lodged a protest against the majority in the chapel, arguing that its decisions had violated the general rules of the union. The language of reciprocity was employed here to assert 'that it is essentially necessary, both for the benefit of Masters and Journeymen, that uniform charges should be made and persevered in'. Yet the protesters insisted on upholding the ultimate authority of the union and its Trade Council: 'We can only acknowledge the Trade, or the Representatives of the Trade, as the proper tribunal to decide disputed charges, – that their decisions should be final, – that no private or General Chapel of this or any other house has the power of departing from such decisions'.[84]

It is unclear from the union's records precisely what happened next. The union certainly deplored the chapel majority for its cowardice and treachery and fined each member of the companionship £1 for refusing to comply with the council's decision.[85] It thereafter probably suspended or expelled some of the members at Spottiswoode since the union records indicate that in August 1835 the Trade Council received an application for readmission to the union from one of the 'seceders at Mr. Spottiswoode's'.[86] A year later, however, the union finally instituted a boycott against the entire printing house, one that would last until 1917.

The dispute at Spottiswoode is significant for the way in which it elucidates the nature of job regulation during this period, as well as the very complex ways in which the authority necessary to create and enforce working rules was mobilized and made to appear legitimate. In this case, the majority of the chapel members ceded the authority to impose rules to management. Earnings, it should be noted, were not a particularly important issue here. The chapel believed that 'they received on the whole the price decided by the [union] Council'.[87] Thus the disagreement between the union and the chapel more clearly concerned the authority to determine working rules on the shopfloor. Management's authority in this instance was confirmed by the chapel's acceptance of the validity of the firm's representation of custom and its apparent reputation for 'fair' wages. The chapel majority was willing to admit 'that the change from the "lumping system" would be desirable', but was unwilling to defend the authority of the union to do it.[88] Moreover, the majority's actions reveal the assumption that in such disputes the internal rules negotiated by the chapel superseded the external rules of the wider union. Obviously, such a notion was not accepted by all chapel members. The general acceptance of management's authority to impose working rules was countered by a minority appeal to the validity of the union scale and the Trade Council's actions. This minority group sought to justify its actions by reiterating the argument that the union's influence was based on utility and reciprocity. These were themes that reflected the union's broader aim to maintain their reputation for committing to the industry scale. This contention, however, was supported by the assertion that the union's authority to enforce working rules was derived ultimately from the compositors in general and not from any single chapel. That is, external job regulation took precedence over internal job regulation. This assertion could not be easily brought into agreement with the chapel's claim to participatory workplace authority.

Conclusion

At the quarterly meeting of the compositors' union in November 1831, the executive committee submitted the following summary of their actions for approval by the rank-and-file:

> Several cases have been submitted and dealt with in the usual fair and impartial manner which has hitherto marked the decisions of your Committees – and they have the satisfaction of stating that generally they have been agreed to with evident satisfaction by our employers – an evidence of some weight to us as a body, as it plainly shows that this Society ranks high in the estimation of those on whom we are dependent for that labour which furnishes a livelihood for ourselves and families – and your Committee have been assured that so long as the business of the society is conducted on its present principles it cannot fail of being beneficial to all parties – employers and workmen ...[89]

In many ways, this summarizes both the intent and policies of trade unionism among the London compositors in the first half of the nineteenth century. Craft unions during the early industrial period clearly exhibited a wide range of goals, purposes and activities. Earlier accounts that stressed their roles as benefit societies, houses of call, and tramping organizations should be, and are being, supplemented by the analysis of how journeymen's institutions operated both in the workplace and in the sphere of industrial relations.[90] The industrial disputes between the London journeymen compositors and master printers, as well as among the compositors themselves, reveal not only that job regulation was an important aspect of craft union activity, but also that such rule-making was a complex and multi-layered process. Rule-making took a variety of forms and operated at a variety of levels emanating from the state, employers, unions and the shopfloor. Job regulation therefore was both an internal and external process. The compositors' unions sought both to stabilize and to standardize working rules by employing a variety of tactics including a form of external control imposed by their disputes committees, joint regulation with the masters through the adoption of arbitration procedures, and the appeals to the local courts. Several areas of potential disputes were also left to be resolved by masters and their journeymen in the workplace. The compositors had perhaps unique success in establishing and maintaining a committee that served to vet disputes that arose between masters and men, but some sort of similar goal was certainly widespread among trade unionists generally. Moreover, as the compositors recognized, the ties that bound masters and men to this form of job regulation were secured by the implicit exchange of reputations. The fairness and impartiality of the union's disputes committee elicited a commitment from the employers to support it; and such reciprocity was perceived be mutually beneficial. Underlying these reputational effects was the effort bargain, the effect of which was to obscure the precise relationship between effort and pay. Under such circumstances, the codification of working rules may help to clarify this relationship, but the efficacy of such rules themselves rely upon the confidence that both parties have in each other's commitment to them. Therefore, the success of the compositors' committee was based to a great extent on the successful exchange of promises, that is, on bargaining's reputational effects.

Notes

1 H.A. Clegg, *The Changing System of Industrial Relations in Great Britain* (Oxford: Blackwell, 1979), p. 1. More recent texts, such as Howard F. Gospel and Gill Palmer, *British Industrial Relations*, 2nd edn (London: Routledge, 1993), p. 174, continue to define the subject in these terms.

2 A. Flanders, 'Industrial Relations: What is Wrong with the System', in *Management and Unions: The Theory and Reform of Industrial Relations* (London: Faber and Faber, 1970) expressed the classic statement of the 'pluralist' approach to rules and rule-making, and R. Hyman's *Industrial Relations: A Marxist Introduction* (London: Macmillan, 1975) expressed the 'radical' critique. In the large body of literature that addressed the subject, some of the more prominent contributions to the debate include the various editions of Clegg, *Changing System of Industrial Relations* and *The System of Industrial Relations in Great Britain* (Oxford: Blackwell, 1970); J.H. Goldthorpe, 'Industrial Relations in Great Britain: A Critique of Reformism', reprinted in

T. Clarke and L. Clements, eds, *Trade Unions under Capitalism* (Atlantic Highlands, N.J.: Humanities Press, 1978); and R. Hyman, 'Pluralism, Procedural Consensus and Collective Bargaining', *British Journal of Industrial Relations*, vol. 16: no. 1 (1978), pp. 16–40. An important summary and application of the literature on job regulation to history is to be found in Dave Lyddon, 'Industrial-Relations Theory and Labor History', *International Labor and Working-Class History*, no. 46 (1994), pp. 121–41.

3	Classic studies include J. Goldthorpe, D. Lockwood, F. Bechofer and J. Platt, *The Affluent Worker: Industrial Attitudes and Behaviour* (Cambridge: Cambridge University Press, 1968) and E. Batstone, I. Boraston and S. Frenkel, *Shop Stewards in Action* (Oxford: Blackwell, 1977). The material is usefully surveyed in Gospel and Palmer, *British Industrial Relations*, ch. 5.

4	This recognition, Hugh Clegg argued, was one of the main contributions of the so-called Oxford school: H. Clegg, 'The Oxford School of Industrial Relations', *Warwick Papers in Industrial Relations*, vol. 31 (1990), pp. 2–3.

5	See, for example, Clegg, *Changing System of Industrial Relations*, ch. 6, and the important essay by W. Brown, 'A Consideration of "Custom and Practice"', *British Journal of Industrial Relations*, vol. 10: no. 1 (1972), pp. 42–61.

6	See P.J. Armstrong, J.F.B. Goodman and J.D. Hyman, *Ideology and Shopfloor Industrial Relations* (London: Croom Helm, 1981), chs 3 and 4.

7	The 'formal–informal' and 'procedural–substantive' models of rule-making are associated particularly with Hugh Clegg and the Oxford School, while the 'internal–external' model was developed by Alan Flanders.

8	J. Rule, 'Against Innovation?: Custom and Resistance in the Workplace, 1700–1850', in T. Harris, ed., *Popular Culture in England, c. 1500–1850* (New York: St Martin's Press, 1995), pp. 170–179; Iorwerth Prothero, *Artisans and Politics in Early Nineteenth-Century London: John Gast and His Times* (1979; London: Methuen, 1981), p. 41. See also L.D. Schwarz, *London in the Age of Industrialisation: Entrepreneurs, Labour Force and Living Conditions, 1700–1850* (Cambridge: Cambridge University Press, 1992), pp. 169–75; and S. and B. Webb, *The History of Trade Unionism*, new edn (London: Longman, 1920), pp. 74–79, and *Industrial Democracy*, new edn (London: Longmans, Green and Co., 1902), chs 2 and 5.

9	Michael Huberman, *Escape from the Market: Negotiating Work in Lancashire* (Cambridge: Cambridge University Press, 1996).

10	Robert Wilson, 'Reputations in Games and Markets', in Alvin E. Roth, ed., *Game-theoretic Models of Bargaining* (Cambridge: Cambridge University Press, 1985), pp. 29–30.

11	E.P. Thompson, *The Making of the English Working Class* (New York: Vintage, 1963), p. 206, and 'The Moral Economy of the English Crowd in the Eighteenth Century', *Past and Present*, no. 50 (1971), pp. 76–136.

12	Wilson, 'Reputations', p. 54.

13	To my knowledge, this type of game-theoretic approach was first applied to a historical situation in Michael Huberman's 'Piece-rates Reconsidered: The Case of Cotton', *Journal of Interdisciplinary History*, vol. 26 (Winter 1996), pp. 393–417; see also Huberman, *Escape from the Market*, pp. 72–6. I would like to thank Professor Huberman for making a copy of his article available to me.

14 On the printing trades generally as well as the compositors, see the classic work by Ellic Howe, ed., *The London Compositor: Documents Relating to Wages, Working Conditions and Customs of the London Printing Trade, 1785–1900* (Oxford: Oxford University Press, 1947); see also E. Howe and H.E. Waite, *The London Society of Compositors: A Centenary History* (London: Cassell and Co., 1948); J. Child, *Industrial Relations in the British Printing Industry: The Quest for Security* (London: George Allen & Unwin, 1967).

15 G. Stedman Jones, *Outcast London: A Study in the Relationship between Classes in Victorian Society* (1971; Harmondsworth: Penguin, 1976), pp. 19–32; Schwarz, *London in the Age of Industrialisation,* pp. 31–42; D.R. Green, *From Artisans to Paupers: Economic Change and Poverty in London, 1790–1870* (Aldershot: Scolar Press, 1995), pp. 26–32; E.J. Hobsbawm, 'The Nineteenth-Century London Labour Market', in *Workers: Worlds of Labor* (New York: Pantheon, 1984), pp. 131–51.

16 Howe, ed., *London Compositor,* p. 53.

17 Howe, ed., *London Compositor,* p. 54.

18 British Library, Additional Manuscript 27799, f. 99; *The Gorgon,* 28 November 1818.

19 Howe, ed., *London Compositor,* p. 54; Howe and Waite, *London Society of Compositors,* pp. 81–3.

20 The chapel was the term given to the compositors' shopfloor organization that, according to Howe, 'enforced the recognized customs of the trade, was a mutual benefit society, and in cases of dispute negotiated with employers'. Written accounts of the chapel go back to at least the seventeenth century. Its principal function, according to Child, was to regulate personal conduct on the shopfloor and promote efficiency. Surviving accounts of chapel rules indicate that by the late eighteenth and early nineteenth centuries most rules concerned such actions as replacing frames, racks or other shared equipment, promptly cleaning forms, using shared fonts and the like. The elected head of each chapel was called the 'father' and he functioned in a capacity quite similar to a shop steward: Howe, ed., *London Compositor,* pp. 22–32; Child, *Industrial Relations in the British Printing Industry,* pp. 35–9. See also A.J.M. Sykes, 'Trade-Union Workshop Organization in the Printing Industry – The Chapel', *Human Relations,* vol. 13 (1960), pp. 49–65, for an account of chapel organization in the early 1950s. However, Sykes's contention that the chapel was subordinate to trade union organizations in the nineteenth century is not supported by evidence given below.

21 Howe and Waite, *London Society of Compositors,* pp. 28–9.

22 Howe and Waite, *London Society of Compositors,* pp. 42 *et seq.*

23 Howe and Waite, *London Society of Compositors,* p. 49.

24 Child, *Industrial Relations in the British Printing Industry,* pp. 74–5.

25 C.R. Dobson, *Masters and Journeymen: A Prehistory of Industrial Relations, 1717–1800* (London: Croom Helm, 1980); K. Laybourn, *A History of British Trade Unionism, c. 1770–1990* (Stroud: Allan Sutton, 1992), pp. 13–14; J. Belchem, *Industrialization and the Working Class: The English Experience, 1750–1900* (Aldershot: Scolar Press, 1990), pp. 62–6; E.H. Hunt, *British Labour History, 1815–1914* (London: Weidenfeld and Nicolson, 1981), pp. 192–7.

26 Neither Howe nor Child fully recognized the significant innovations in indus-
    trial relations that were implemented by the LGTSC. Howe merely notes that
    the LGTSC was founded as a rival union to the London Trade Society, while
    Child indicates that it was 'a militant faction' irked by the latter's conservative
    trade policy. Unfortunately, Child never elaborates the precise ways in which
    LGTSC policy differed from its parent society. See Howe, ed., *London Com-
    positor*, p. 191; Child, *Industrial Relations in the British Printing Industry*,
    pp. 74–5. Relations between the two unions, however, were never absolutely
    severed after their split. The two coordinated their efforts, for example, to
    resist prosecutions for unlawful combination as well as to lobby for the repeal
    of duties on newspapers. Finally, the two unions recombined to form the Lon-
    don Union of Compositors in 1834. See Howe, ed., *London Compositor*,
    pp. 191–2; Howe and Waite, *London Society of Compositors*, pp. 85–6.
27 *Book of Rules of the London Trade Society*, §3–4; sections also reprinted in
    Howe, ed., *London Compositor*, p. 190.
28 Modern Records Centre, University of Warwick Library, National Graphical
    Association, London Region: London Society of Compositors (hereafter
    MRC, NGA), Mss. 28/CO/1/1/1, London General Trade Society of Composi-
    tors Minute Books (hereafter LGTSC Minute Books), Quarterly Report,
    5 February 1828.
29 Howe, ed. , *London Compositor*, p. 190.
30 MRC, NGA, Mss. 28/CO/1/1/1, LGTSC Minute Books, Quarterly Meeting
    and Report, 'Rules and Regulations of the Society', §3, 20–1, 6 November
    1827.
31 MRC, NGA, Mss. 28/CO/1/1/1, LGTSC Minute Books, Quarterly Report,
    5 February 1828.
32 MRC, NGA, Mss. 28/CO/1/1/1, LGTSC Minute Books, Quarterly Meeting
    and Report, 'Rules and Regulations of the Society', §16–17, 6 November
    1827.
33 MRC, NGA, Mss. 28/CO/1/1/1, LGTSC Minute Books, Quarterly Report,
    5 February 1828.
34 MRC, NGA, Mss. 28/CO/1/1/2, LGTSC Minute Books, 3 May 1831. Howe's
    date of 1832 is thus slightly off: *London Compositor*, p. 191. The minutes of
    the Union Committee are catalogued in the MRC as MSS. 28/CO/1/1/3 and
    those of the Trade Council as Mss. 28/CO/1/1/5–6.
35 MRC, NGA, Mss. 28/CO/1/1/1, LGTSC Minute Books, Quarterly Report and
    Meeting, 6 November 1827.
36 MRC, NGA, Mss. 28/CO/1/1/6, LUC Trade Council Minute Books, 17 July
    1838.
37 The fact that masters and journeymen could often become 'natural allies' is
    described by Prothero, *Artisans and Politics*, pp. 37–8. Rule similarly notes
    that artisans often emphasized the importance of mutual respect between the
    two groups: 'The Property of Skill in the Period of Manufacture', in Patrick
    Joyce, ed., *The Historical Meanings of Work* (Cambridge: Cambridge Univer-
    sity Press, 1987), p. 109.
38 MRC, NGA, Mss. 28/CO/1/1/2, LGTSC Minute Books, 14 November 1831.
39 On the intervention of booksellers in the industrial relations of compositors
    and master printers, see Howe and Waite, *London Society of Compositors*,

pp. 48–9, 52–3.

40 MRC, NGA, Mss. 28/CO/4/1/1/3, LUC Trade Reports, 'Annual Report of the Trade Council to the Members of the London Union of Compositors', 1835; portions of this are also quoted in Howe and Waite, *London Society of Compositors*, p. 96.

41 MRC, NGA, Mss. 28/CO/1/1/1, LGTSC Minute Books, 6 May 1828.

42 MRC, NGA, Mss. 28/CO/1/1/2, LGTSC Minute Books, 29 March 1830; see also 8 and 15 March and 19 April 1830.

43 MRC, NGA, Mss. 28/CO/1/1/2, LGTSC Minute Books, 5 May 1829.

44 This was not accidental. The compositors were well aware, as they should have been, of the prescriptive power of language. During the long negotiations over the 1810 scale, the union explained to the master printers that they purposely avoided the language of rights 'in order to take the most likely course to conduct you with safety into the port of justice' and 'to steer clear of the shoals of pride': Howe, ed., *London Compositor*, p. 152. See above, ch. 2.

45 In 1837, for example, the Trade Council first suggested that when the decisions of the two committees were at variance with one another, the dispute should be referred to an arbitration committee composed of an equal number of representatives of the master printers and compositors: MRC, NGA, Mss. 28/CO/1/1/6, LUC Trade Council Minute Books, 3 and 27 December 1837, 20 February and 25 April 1838.

46 MRC, NGA, Mss. 28/CO/1/1/6, LUC Trade Council Minute Books, 3 December 1837.

47 MRC, NGA, Mss. 28/CO/1/1/1, LGTSC Minute Books, Quarterly Meeting and Report, 'Rules and Regulations of the Society', 6 November 1827.

48 An 'en' is a unit of measurement in typesetting and payment per thousand ens was the basic formula for piece-rates. Howe and Child reckon it as roughly equivalent to the width of an individual letter, although the *Oxford English Dictionary* defines it as 'equal to half the body of any size of metal type': Howe, ed., *London Compositor*, p. 59; Child, *Industrial Relations in the British Printing Industry*, pp. 70–1.

49 MRC, NGA, Mss. 28/CO/1/1/1, LGTSC Minute Books, 9 February 1829.

50 Howe, ed., *London Compositor*, reprints the 1810 scale with later amendments. See Article 20, p. 341.

51 MRC, NGA, Mss. 28/CO/1/1/1, LGTSC Minute Books, 19 May 1828.

52 MRC, NGA, Mss. 28/CO/1/1/3, Union Committee Minute Books, 3 January 1832. Unfortunately, this register apparently has not survived.

53 As I have argued elsewhere in another context, these actions could be construed as forms of joint regulation, although the limits of 'joint regulation' are a matter of some dispute. Flanders notes that joint regulation includes not only rule-making by trade unions and employers, but also the recourse to third-party forms of conciliation, arbitration and mediation. In the latter instances, forms of third-party intervention serve as an 'auxiliary aid' to the settlement of the parties' own agreements: 'Industrial Relations: What is Wrong with the System?', p. 94. Lyddon implies that this definition is too narrow since terms of arbitration settlements have sometimes been forced upon employers who had not been party to the negotiations. Thus, rather than being only an aid to collective agreements, some arbitration can be viewed as a form of state

regulation: 'Industrial-Relations Theory and Labor History', p. 130. See also James A. Jaffe, 'Authority and Job Regulation: Rule-Making by the London Compositors during the Early Nineteenth Century', *Historical Studies in Industrial Relations*, no. 3 (March 1997), pp. 1–26.

54   See Chapter 7.

55   MRC, NGA, Mss. 28/CO/1/1/2, LGTSC Minute Books, 8 February 1830; see also 12, 15 and 26 October 1829; 16, 20 and 23 November 1829; 2 February 1830. Such a process also was followed in the resolution of disputes over 'lighting up time', that is, the extra pay compositors expected for working after dark: MRC, NGA, Mss. 28/CO/1/1/3, Union Committee Minute Books, 1 and 15 October 1833.

56   According to R.G. Kirby and A.E. Musson, similar actions occurred during disputes with cotton-spinners in Hyde, Ashton and Stalybridge in 1830, although the masters' resolve was not always long-lived. Indeed John Doherty thought such cooperation was a model of industrial relations. See *The Voice of the People: John Doherty, 1789–1854, Trade Unionist, Radical and Factory Reformer* (Manchester: Manchester University Press, 1975), pp. 103–7. For similar tactics that were brought to bear on undercutting silk-masters in the Coventry ribbon trade, see above, Chapter 4.

57   See *Annual Report of the Trade Council to the Members of the London Union of Compositors … to which are added the Rules & Regulations of the Union, as amended to February 1837* (London, 1837), p. 38.

58   The later history of compositors further bears out this point as well. In 1847, an Arbitration Committee comprised of masters and compositors sought to resolve several points in dispute that were not covered by the 1810 scale. In 1856, it was resurrected. At this time, the Arbitration Committee of three masters and three compositors was chaired by a barrister who was given voting privileges: Howe, ed., *London Compositor*, pp. 262–6; *Proceedings of Arbitration Committee, or Conference of Masters & Journeymen. Freemason's Tavern. Friday, July 9th, 1847*; MRC, NGA, Mss. 28/CO/1/10/1 also includes records of the 1856 arbitration meetings.

59   Howe, ed., *London Compositor*, pp. 222–4, 240–2.

60   See below, pp. 229–32.

61   This was the committee's recommendation to a compositor, Mr Tomlinson, in a dispute over the classification of a list of subscribers in 1831: MRC, NGA, Mss. 28/CO/1/1/2, LGTSC Minute Books, 5, 12 and 19 September 1831. The case became even more complicated when it was discovered that Tomlinson had secretly been at work while he was drawing on union unemployment funds. He was expelled from the union shortly thereafter: MRC, NGA, Mss. 28/CO/1/1/2, LGTSC Minute Books, 10, 17, 24 and 31 October 1831. Similar recommendations to give notice were made during disputes with the printing houses of Bentley's in 1833 and Gilbert and Rivington's in 1834: MRC, NGA, Mss. 28/CO/1/1/3, Union Committee Minute Books, 10 October 1833; Mss. 28/CO/1/1/5, LUC Trade Council Minute Books, 17 June 1834.

62   Flanders, 'Industrial Relations: What is Wrong with the System?', p. 90; Lyddon, 'Industrial-Relations Theory and Labor History', p. 129.

63   Hunt, *British Labour History*, p. 265. Such actions were perhaps not uncommon. David Jones has found that in the Merthyr police district between 1846

and 1864 there were an average of over a hundred prosecutions a year for non-payment of wages: D.J.V. Jones, *Crime in Nineteenth-Century Wales* (Cardiff: University of Wales Press: 1992), p. 160. I owe this reference to Bob Storch.

64 Corporation of London Record Office, Misc. Ms. 135.3, 'Historical Notes on the Court of Requests'.

65 MRC, NGA, Mss. 28/CO/1/1/2, LGTSC Minute Books, 3 May 1830.

66 MRC, NGA, Mss. 28/CO/1/1/2, LGTSC Minute Books, 19 April and 3 May 1830.

67 London Union of Compositors, *The London Scale of Prices for Compositors' Work: Agreed upon, April 16th, 1810, with Explanatory Notes*, 2nd edn (London, 1837). After 1783, it appears that a committee of masters did meet to resolve complaints or violations of trade rates. In 1805, however, the compositors came to recognize the 'evil effects' of this clause and shortly after the ratification of the 1805 agreement they formed their own committee. At that time, the compositors' committee was given the principal responsibility of vetting all disputes before they were submitted to the masters' committee and receiving all communications from them. According to Howe, the masters' union was inactive after 1816. See Howe, ed., *London Compositor*, pp. 203 n. 1, 235–42.

68 MRC, NGA, Mss. 28/CO/1/1/5, LUC Trade Council Minute Books, 23 July and 26 August 1834.

69 Rule, 'Against Innovation?', *passim*; Adrian Randall, *Before the Luddites: Custom, Community and Machinery in the English Woollen Industry, 1776–1809* (Cambridge: Cambridge University Press, 1991) on the flexibility of early union movements.

70 On the institutions of artisan London, see Prothero, *Artisans and Politics*, pp. 28–40; and more generally, Webb and Webb, *History of Trade Unionism*, pp. 25–46.

71 The 1810 scale of prices reprinted in Howe, ed., *London Compositor*, p. 339.

72 The 1810 scale of prices reprinted in Howe, ed., *London Compositor*, p. 344. A number of autonomously negotiated charges were formally added as a result of the 1847 revision of the scale. This may indicate that wage bargaining was increasingly devolving onto the shopfloor during this period. Thus, mathematical fractions, pedigrees, and the extensive use of woodcuts all were to be settled at the workplace level after 1847: *ibid.*, pp. 345, 349.

73 Dave Lyddon identifies this as a form of 'internal bilateral regulation' that occurs in instances when 'groups of workers may bargain with the employer in the absence of a recognized union'. See 'Industrial-Relations Theory and Labor History', p. 129.

74 MRC, NGA, Mss. 28/CO/1/1/1, LGTSC Minute Books, 24 November 1828. Emphasis in original.

75 MRC, NGA, Mss. 28/CO/1/1/2, LGTSC Minute Books, 2 and 9 January 1832. The scale allowed for reprints with numerous manuscript insertions to be charged as if it were being originally cast up from manuscript. See Article 1 of the 1810 scale reprinted in Howe, ed., *London Compositor*, p. 329.

76 MRC, NGA, Mss. 28/CO/1/1/3, Union Committee Minute Books, 17 January 1832.

77 Howe, ed., *London Compositor*, pp. 49, 54, 356–71. The firm was notorious for remaining non-unionized until after the First World War.

78 Howe, ed., *London Compositor*, pp. 360–5.

79 Most printing establishments had a number of companionships that worked to divide the labour and speed up production on certain jobs. Howe notes that the 'function of the clicker was to keep his team supplied with copy, to attend to those phases of production which could not be paid for at piece-rates, such as make-up and imposition, and to act as clerk to his group'. Howe, ed., *London Compositor*, p. 56.

80 Spottiswoode's practices continued for many years. The union found the same violations in 1845 and republished their objections to the house in 1854: Howe, ed., *London Compositor*, pp. 368–71.

81 MRC, NGA, Mss. 28/CO/1/1/5, LUC Trade Council Minute Books, 10 July 1834.

82 MRC, NGA, Mss. 28/CO/1/1/5, LUC Trade Council Minute Books, 17 July 1834. The delegates noted that Spottiswoode's opposition to the union's charges was based largely on his antagonism toward the union itself rather than an objection to the level of the piece-rate.

83 MRC, NGA, Mss. 28/CO/1/1/5, LUC Trade Council Minute Books, 17 July 1834.

84 MRC, NGA, Mss. 28/CO/1/1/5, LUC Trade Council Minute Books, 22 July 1834.

85 MRC, NGA, Mss. 28/CO/1/1/5, LUC Trade Council Minute Books, 31 July 1834.

86 MRC, NGA, Mss. 28/CO/1/1/5, LUC Trade Council Minute Books, 6 August 1835.

87 MRC, NGA, Mss. 28/CO/1/1/5, LUC Trade Council Minute Books, 17 July 1834.

88 MRC, NGA, Mss. 28/CO/1/1/5, LUC Trade Council Minute Books, 17 July 1834.

89 MRC, NGA, Mss. 28/CO/1/1/2, LGTSC Minute Books, 14 November 1831.

90 Prothero, *Artisans and Politics*, pp. 28–37; Hobsbawm, 'Artisans and Labour Aristocrats?', in *Workers*, pp. 258–9; Rule, 'Against Innovation?'; Richard Price, *Masters, Unions and Men: Work Control in Building and the Rise of Labour, 1830–1914* (Cambridge: Cambridge University Press, 1980); Clive Behagg, *Politics and Production in the Early Nineteenth Century* (London: Routledge, 1990), ch. 3.

7

Arbitration and authority

> You can settle any dispute if you keep the lawyers and accountants out of it.
> (Unknown Wisconsin businessperson, c. 1960[1])

In an obscure aside, the well-known English working-class radical Francis Place remarked in his *Autobiography* that even when 'in deepest poverty' he had tried to serve other artisans. Some he had helped to train up as small masters or foremen, while others he aided by working to settle their problems and disputes. 'I had many matters brought to me for adjudication, arbitration or arrangement', he wrote. 'I hardly know the time when for three months together I have been free from this kind of interference.' Most matters it seems had to do with debtors and their creditors, but others appear to have concerned the settlement of estates or even affairs 'related to an association or large body of men'.[2] While he may have been justly proud of his service to the working-class community, Place's comment provides an insight into working-class life that is rarely glimpsed. He did not choose the word arbitration accidentally. By the nineteenth century, life and work in England had been penetrated by forms of dispute resolution that were meant to secure 'order without law'.[3] Indeed the arbitration of disputes by reference to independent individuals, and frequently beyond the interference of the courts, barristers or attorneys, was a well-recognized and common way to resolve contentious issues in many areas of English social life, including business ventures, contracts, property, and employment relations.

During the first half of the nineteenth century, the most vibrant forms of arbitration were largely autonomous of legal oversight and operated independently of most statutory authority. In the language of industrial relations, these forms of arbitration might be deemed 'voluntary'; that is, they had evolved largely without state interference or supervision, thereby avoiding statutory compulsion.[4] Among legal historians and theorists, these same practices might be deemed 'informal', or outside of the formal purview of statutory law.[5] Regardless of the language used to describe them, in an attempt to deal with the apparent social and political unrest of the late eighteenth and early nineteenth centuries, the state increasingly sought to adapt these voluntary and informal systems of arbitration to the resolution of a whole range of civil disputes, most notably to those between employers and employees. In these latter cases, each attempt to 'formalize' the arbitration of industrial disputes failed in the face of resistance from either employers or workers, and sometimes both. Instead, those voluntary systems of arbitration retained their vibrancy and proliferated throughout the first half of the nineteenth century.

Both the adaptation and persistence of these forms of arbitration, voluntary and statutory, raises several intriguing questions for both labour and legal historians. In the first place, parliamentary promotion of arbitration during this period seems to present a striking paradox: at the same time as the 'disciplinary state' was making its presence felt on issues of crime, poverty, social deviance, and even trade unionism, the state also appears to have attempted to construct alternative forms of industrial relations that were largely self-governing and autonomous.[6] Indeed Parliament's repeated attempts to institute arbitration as a means of settling disputes appears to be strikingly at odds with its simultaneous endeavours to criminalize trade unions through the famous Combination Acts. Whether Parliament's repressive attack upon trade unions in 1799 and 1800 therefore is fully indicative of its industrial relations policy may bear further examination. Secondly, despite the repeated failures of parliamentary-sponsored arbitration, the evidence of the persistence of voluntary forms of arbitration may lead us to reconsider the extent to which the law itself imposed a structure upon social relations. Such a possibility has recently been suggested in an attempt to identify the cultural origins of broad social concepts such as 'labour'.[7] However, evidence of the vitality of voluntary systems of dispute resolution serves to emphasize the limits of the law as well as the extent to which social relations are constructed both beneath and beyond the law's grasp.[8] Finally, the persistence of voluntary arbitration apparently contradicts some of the most commonly held assumptions concerning the nature of industrial relations during the early nineteenth century. The labour historiography of this period has been built upon paradigms of struggle, repression and conflict, paradigms that have left very little space for the existence of industrial arbitration or other means of dispute resolution. However, the themes upon which this book has been built, reciprocity and asymmetry, are once again in evidence here and may help to refine our understandings of work relations and indeed class during this period.

To accomplish any of these aims, however, arbitration's claim to equity and fairness must first be distinguished from its effects. Early nineteenth-century arbitration functioned on the premise that fair and impartial observers could decide issues that the participants in a dispute could or would not resolve themselves. Particularly in industrial disputes, arbitration sought to extract disputes from both the labour market and the shopfloor and, by doing so, relocate them to a neutral arena where equitable principles, rather than economic power or the law, might preside. Such claims to equity had a powerful resonance among trade unionists as well as many employers, and continued to attract the attention of business, union and government leaders throughout the century. Yet in practice these pretensions differed significantly from their ultimate effects on the distribution of authority both in the labour market and on the shopfloor. Arbitration, despite its claims to equity, was not neutral. Depending upon the circumstances of its introduction into the industrial relations of employers and workers, many arbitration schemes tended to consolidate asymmetrical power relationships rather than redress them. Thus, workers who already possessed advantages in the labour market could find the implementation of arbitration schemes amenable to the retention of those benefits. Conversely, employer-sponsored schemes rarely shifted significant authority to independent arbitrators except under circumstances that might improve their standing in the labour market or on the shopfloor. Therefore, careful attention must be paid to the circumstances surrounding attempts to institute arbitration as well as to its mechanisms of dispute resolution. However, the full extent of the role of arbitration in British society during this period has yet to be adequately investigated or analysed by historians. Therefore, it is necessary first to lay out the scope of arbitration during the early nineteenth century, after which its role in the industrial setting will be addressed.

Arbitration and British society

The roots of arbitration run deep in British history, although working-class participation in this process is often difficult to measure. The forms and procedures of arbitration were initially developed by canon lawyers in the late twelfth century and appear to have been broadly applied to secular matters after the middle of the fourteenth century. The Church was particularly interested in promoting arbitration, but so too were city and borough courts in their jurisdictions over guilds and corporations. While the most prominent arbitration cases of the medieval period related to feuding magnates and county gentry, medieval practices of arbitration quickly spread to many areas of the law, especially commercial and maritime law as well as contracts.[9] By the Tudor and Stuart periods, a commoner may have had a dispute arbitrated under a great many circumstances. In the cities, masters and merchants might frequently find themselves before arbitrators in matters concerning payment of accounts, the quality of merchandise, or foreign cargoes.[10] Journeymen might also have recourse to arbitrators in disputes with their masters. The City Chamberlain of London often arbitrated such disputes himself or appointed arbitrators from the master's company.[11] In many small towns and villages, disputes over small debts were often arbitrated by neighbours or the local clergy. Ralph Josselin, for example, helped to settle a dispute by laying out 21s of his own money on the promise of repayment.[12] In a similar manner, several 'good friends' tried but failed to settle a dispute between a Hampshire farmer and a Surrey corn factor in 1596.[13] The seventeenth-century order books of the Western Circuit assizes reveal that arbitration was frequently ordered by the civil courts to resolve a vast array of disputes, including those as disparate as conflicts between a local vicar and his parishioners,[14] domestic abuse,[15] the keeping of ale houses,[16] the settlement of paupers,[17] road repairs,[18] wages,[19] the ownership of a gold ring,[20] and even an apparent claim by several of the poor of Jacobstowe, Devon, upon the estate of a deceased woman.[21] In the ecclesiastical courts of the period, arbitration was one of the principal means by which litigants were to be 'positively encouraged to reach an out of court settlement to restore harmony between them as soon as possible'.[22] Arbitration was applied by the church courts to cases involving allegations of defamation and slander, tithe disputes, as well as to resolve conflicts over marriage contracts and the settlement of marriage property.[23]

The forms of arbitration, like the scope of its procedures, varied considerably during this period and seem to attest to its vibrancy and adaptability. Informal arbitration by neighbours was probably quite common, but even when the courts became involved there was no standard form of arbitration. Western Circuit assize records reveal that sometimes the parties themselves were allowed to select their own arbitrators, while at other times arbitrators were appointed by the court, but only after securing the consent of the parties.[24] On most occasions, disputes were referred to local justices of the peace, although even then the procedures were liable to vary. In some cases, one JP was considered sufficient to arbitrate the dispute, more often two or three were appointed, but in still other cases local gentlemen served as arbitrators.[25] In matters concerning the Church, clerics were sometimes called upon to arbitrate disputes, although they could also be found arbitrating disputes between parishioners.[26] In a small number of disputes, a final umpire, or pair of umpires, was provided for in the event that the initial arbitrators could not satisfactorily resolve the controversy.[27]

However, there were few legal methods by which the performance of arbitrators' awards could be enforced and this was repeatedly mentioned as arbitration's principal weakness. Medieval arbitrators had developed the concomitant procedure of entering into mutual bonds to secure the acceptance of the award.[28] The practice was thereby created in which failure to perform an arbitration award could be remedied by a parallel suit in breach of contract. In the seventeenth century, this appears to have happened relatively infrequently, at least from the evidence of the Western Circuit, but further work on early modern contracts may prove otherwise. Most referrals to arbitrators on the Western Circuit occurred without entering into bonds and performance was ensured instead by the threat of imprisonment for contempt of court.[29]

By the end of the Tudor and Stuart period, arbitration was exceptionally popular in the commercial sector, principally in order to avoid the costs and delays engendered by proceedings in the courts of common law and equity. There was, moreover, a growing interest emanating from the Board of Trade to put commercial arbitration on a statutory footing, particularly in order to ensure compliance to arbitrators' awards. John Locke was responsible for drawing up an act to facilitate the resolution of commercial disputes by the use of independent referees and to prevent further appeals to the courts. The result, as noted by Professors Horwitz and Oldham, was largely a confirmation of developing practices. The 1698 Arbitration Act stipulated that arbitration agreements could be enrolled in a court of record and defaulters punished for contempt of court. While the act appears to have had an unsteady initial reception, Lord Mansfield was likely to have been responsible for the more frequent recourse of the Court of King's Bench to court-sponsored arbitration agreements during the late eighteenth century.[30]

The relatively few arbitration agreements registered by the courts (141 in 1785) may indicate a type of sclerosis that such bureaucratization often entails.[31] However, the relative failure of arbitration under rule of court masks the proliferation of arbitration practices that proceeded nonetheless during the eighteenth and nineteenth centuries. Arbitration tended to proliferate beyond the courts' oversight, although not totally beyond its powers of compulsion. Partnership agreements, for example, frequently included provisions pledging the signatories to arbitrate their disputes before seeking satisfaction in the courts.[32] The most respected contemporary guide to late eighteenth- and early nineteenth-century commercial arbitration, Stewart Kyd's *A Treatise on the Law of Awards*, noted that 'it is usual, in articles of copartnership, and not uncommon in other agreements, to insert a provision or covenant, that all disputes arising between the parties relative to their intended transactions, or to any covenant in the articles, shall be referred to arbitration'.[33] Perhaps typical of these arbitration clauses was that included in the partnership agreement between the apothecary to the Duchess of York and a man-midwife in January 1797, who

> did covenant, promise and agree to and with the other of them, his executors and administrators that if at any time during that co-partnership, or at, or after any determination thereof, any variance, dispute, doubt, or question should arise, happen or be moved between the said parties or either of them, their executors or administrators in, for, about or touching the said joint concern or copartnership or an covenant agreement, clause, matter or thing therein contained or in the construction thereof, or in anywise relating thereto, then every such variance, dispute, doubt or question should be referred to and be resolved and determined by two indifferent persons to be elected and chosen by the said partners, that is to say, one by each of them, within twenty days next after such variance, dispute, doubt or question should arise happen or be moved ...[34]

Indeed such covenants to refer disputes to arbitration were also commonly included in insurance policies from at least the second quarter of the eighteenth century, as well as in building contracts before 1830.[35] In the latter case, arbitration regularly resolved disputes between builders, architects and employers, much to the chagrin of the author of a architectural handbook published before mid-century.[36] Henry Horwitz and James Oldham have also found that building contracts for the Grosvenor Estates in Mayfair usually included an arbitration clause that named three referees. In many cases, artisans were among those chosen to act as referees.[37] Arbitration clauses also appear in the rule books of employers' organizations during this period. According to the legal historian A.W.B. Simpson, it was customary practice in the Liverpool Cotton Brokers' Association for disputes arising over the grade or quality of imported cotton to be submitted to arbitrators for resolution. In the early 1860s, this custom was then codified in the form of a standard brokers' contract that included the following provision: 'In case of dispute arising out of this contract the matter to be referred to two respectable brokers for settlement, who shall decide as to quality and the allowance, if any, to be made'. Within the following decade, this arbitration clause was extended from disputes over the quality of cotton to all disputes concerning the brokerage contract. As Professor Simpson notes, 'disputes over the material itself seem always to have been arbitrated; there was no conceivable reason why anyone would go to court over such a dispute. Quite apart from the delay and cost involved, it would have been ridiculous to accept a jury decision from persons not expert in sampling cotton, necessarily based on expert evidence from those who were, instead of accepting the direct decision of a panel of experts.'[38]

Agreements to submit disputes to arbitration need not have been written into a contract nor need they have been ordered by or submitted to any court to be effective. Kyd maintained that a variety of forms of arbitration agreements existed and their promises of performance varied significantly. Oral agreements to seek arbitration, for example, had been recognized in late medieval and early modern contract law and appear to have remained exceedingly common into the early nineteenth century.[39] Some arbitration agreements, both verbal and written, stipulated that disputes would be submitted to arbitration but without any promise to perform the arbitrator's award whatsoever. Other agreements contained promises of performance but omitted any guarantee, customarily the bond, to ensure the performance of an award. Still others included both a promise and some form of security to perform an award.[40] More importantly, however, the courts acquiesced in the extension of the practice of arbitration to cover a wide range of civil and commercial issues. According to Kyd, reference to arbitrators could legally be made in cases of 'debt arising on a simple contract; a demand of rent for use and occupation; a complaint of slander; trespass of every kind, whether personal or on the land of the complainant; and, in general, all kinds of personal wrong, where, by the policy of the state, the injury done to the individual is not considered as merged in the public crime, or where it does not include an offence against the public manners'. Therefore, the matters that were exempt from arbitration were largely those against Church and state, including murder, robbery, adultery, forgery and sacrilege. Disputes concerning the standing of persons in civil law such as bastardy or social status were also exempt, as were most matters of record such as those for the recovery of damages or interest that had been specifically described in a deed or bond.[41]

While the scope of arbitration was therefore quite broad by the end of the eighteenth century, the legal obligation to pursue arbitration was construed relatively narrowly by the courts during this period. An agreement to arbitrate disputes contained in articles of partnership or insurance policies, for example, could not prevent partners and policy-holders from pursuing their cases simultaneously or *in seriatim* in the courts, nor could a party to an arbitration agreement be compelled by the courts to refer a particular dispute to arbitrators.[42] Therefore, if one partner brought suit against another, the defendant could not demand enforcement of the articles of their agreement invoking arbitration.[43] In oral agreements to arbitrate, Kyd notes, merely the recitation of the phrase 'I discharge you from proceeding any further' was sufficient to revoke the authority of the arbitrators to decide the issue.[44] This narrow construction of the power of parties to compel arbitration during this period may have had something to do with the suspicion that some judges maintained of a process that was so obviously beyond their immediate oversight. While some judges such as Lord Kenyon expressed their support for arbitration because 'arbitrators are more competent to the settling of complicated accounts, than the officers of courts of law and equity', others more readily rejected the implication that disputes could be adequately settled without reference to law.[45] In 1802, Lord Chancellor Eldon issued a stinging rebuke to Lord Kenyon's earlier decision, writing that 'it has occurred to me, that in almost every case of this sort the parties have adopted a fancy, that they can make any thing in the contemplation of the Court fit to be considered matter of dispute, upon which they think proper to dispute. That is not so. It must be that, which a Court will say, is fairly and reasonably made matter of dispute.' He went on to remark sarcastically that 'I recollect passages in which courts of justice, however full of eulogia upon these domestic forums, have recollected their own dignity sufficiently to say, they would not be ancillary to these forums'.[46]

Eldon's remarks are evidence, in part, of a jealous guarding of the courts' jurisdiction sometimes masked as legal principle. However, there were also sounder reasons for the courts' contentions as well. As noted above, a particular weakness of arbitration, outside those agreements registered with the courts under the terms of the 1698 Act, was the inability to compel the performance of awards. Thus arbitration did not necessarily settle disputes and indeed some of these disputes inevitably found their way into the courts. In addition, before the middle of the nineteenth century, arbitrators, except under special circumstances, did not have the power to examine people under oath, nor did they have the power to force the submission of papers or other documents on which to base their decisions. Therefore, the extent to which arbitrators could uncover a semblance of the truth was always questionable. Finally, it is also likely that the courts may often have refused to compel arbitration, as opposed to compelling the performance of awards which they did not hesitate to do, largely because the agreement to arbitrate was construed as a wholly voluntary and revocable act that was not subject to a court's power or authority.[47]

The common law and equity courts' reluctance to compel arbitration is interestingly at odds with forms of dispute resolution within the jurisdiction of the courts of admiralty. It has already been noted that many disputes in admiralty had regularly been referred to arbitration since the late medieval period. Disputes over liability for collisions, shipwrecks or loss of cargoes, for example, were often arbitrated by 'expert' sea captains or shipwrights.[48] Similarly, the court arrogated to itself the power to arbitrate disputes concerning seamen's pay and service. Seamen who had been denied all or part of their wages could sue in Admiralty Court where their wages were protected by a lien they held on the ship.[49] By the end of the eighteenth century, such wage disputes were heard by proceedings brought *in rem*, that is, a proceeding brought against the 'the thing', i.e. the ship, rather than *in personam*, against the master or owners.[50] Proceedings *in rem* for wages were initiated by an affidavit that resulted in the issuing of a warrant both to arrest the ship or its cargo and to require the ship's owner or master to appear before the court. If the owner failed to appear, the seaman could file for possession of the ship, although this was largely a legal fiction. Actually, the seaman had to wait a full year before the court would move to appraise the ship and decree its sale. During that period, the owners could appear at any time to enter a defence and halt the proceedings. If they did not do so, however, the ship would be put up for sale, the proceeds deposited to the court's registry and only then distributed to satisfy claims for wages or other debts.

If the owner appeared to answer the affidavit, however, the proceedings took on the character of civil or ecclesiastical arbitration.[51] In some cases, the proceedings were entirely *viva voce*, a practice that appears to have been applied particularly to suits involving small sums, such as wages. In such cases, plaintiffs, defendants and witnesses would all appear before the judge to present their cases, after which the judge would announce his decision. In other cases, however, there was a more complicated procedure that required the filing of allegations, or 'libels', to initiate the suit, the finding of either sureties or recognisances, and the counter-filing of answers or objections. Unless granted extensions, the seaman and owner were then required in the next few days to produce witnesses, draw up a list of questions and submit both to a hearings examiner who deposed the witnesses privately. As in arbitration, the examiners could be nominated by the parties themselves, but by 1800 the examiners were usually officers of the court or a notary public. These testimonies would then be 'published', or referred to a judge who held a further hearing on the suit. In cases of seamen's wages, it was not uncommon for the judge to hold the hearing immediately after the publication of the testimonies, after which the decision was announced.[52]

Certainly, such procedures were analogous to commercial and ecclesiastical arbitration largely because in them the judge acted as arbiter to settle the dispute, followed a distinctly different set of rules of procedure and standards of evidence than in courts of record, did not require attorneys or barristers, avoided the use of juries, and thus avoided the costs and length of proceedings at common law.[53] Interestingly enough, such proceedings were defended by the Admiralty Court not because they were an efficient means of resolving disputes between autonomous parties to a contract, as in civil arbitration, but because seamen were considered childlike and irresponsible, and needed the court's protection from their unscrupulous masters. Lord Stowell, who was most responsible for the significant expansion of Admiralty jurisdiction in the early nineteenth century, treated seaman as virtual wards of the court because he regarded them as thoughtless and ignorant as well as 'apt to be choleric in temper and ... rash and violent in language and conduct'.[54] A modern legal historian has described the Admiralty Court as seeking to act '*in loco parentis* toward the seaman, not only protecting ... but sanctioning chastisement as well'.[55]

The presence of arbitration procedures in other areas of law is also notable. By the middle of the nineteenth century, for example, it was not uncommon for parishes in Scotland to seek to have settlement disputes resolved by an arbiter. In 1858, A. Murray Dunlop arbitrated a dispute between Dundee and Auchtermuchty parishes over the maintenance of Mary Thomson, a pauper who had been committed to the Dundee Lunatic Asylum three years earlier. The dispute concerned whether Mary was chargeable to the parish of her father, who had died before she had been born, or her step-father. Similarly, a dispute between Edinburgh and St Cuthbert parishes over the settlement of a child born outside of the parish of both parents' settlement was resolved through arbitration.[56] Of course, the poor were not direct participants in such arbitration cases, however much their fates may have depended upon the outcome. In these instances, the Scottish poor were the objects of the arbitration process rather than its subject.

Such procedures in admiralty and the Scottish poor laws were also a reflection of significant attempts by legislators of this period to apply arbitration to the resolution of industrial disputes by statute. The so-called Cotton Arbitration Acts of 1800 and 1804 and the second instalment of the Combination Acts in 1800 are perhaps the most well known examples of parliamentary attempts to expand the scope of arbitration. For most of the eighteenth century, Parliament had groped toward an industrial relations policy that combined the criminalization of trade unions with the expansion of the summary jurisdiction of magistrates over wage disputes and working conditions.[57] Part of the source of this policy undoubtedly lay in the famous Elizabethan Statute of Artificers, but the model for much of the eighteenth century's legislation against unions was the act passed in 1720 outlawing combinations among journeymen tailors of London and Westminster. The recourse to legislation at that time was perhaps stimulated by the complaints of the London and Westminster master tailors who had failed to gain convictions of their journeymen for combination under the common law. According to James Moher, the resulting act was neither exceptionally one-sided nor repressive. Instead the act guaranteed certain concessions to the journeymen, including the restriction of working days and the privilege of appealing to magistrates for both the adjustment and enforcement of new wage rates based on the cost of living.[58] Not all of the subsequent Combination Acts, which were aimed at a variety of other trades, followed the same pattern, although the famous Spitalfields Acts of 1773 and 1792 governing the London silk trade notably arrogated to the Lord Mayor the summary jurisdiction over wage.[59]

The Combination Acts of 1799 and 1800 that outlawed trade unions represented an important departure in government policy, although the precise degree of that departure is a matter of some dispute. The acts, of course, effectively outlawed trade unions by making it illegal for workers to enter into contracts or agreements to obtain an advance of wages, alter the hours of work, limit output, or prevent others from working.[60] Yet the criminalization of trade unions or shop clubs either by statute or the common law of conspiracy was certainly nothing new, as historians have frequently noted.[61] Further, contrary to the assumption that the acts represented the final abandonment of traditional policies of wage-regulation, it could be argued with equal legitimacy both that the acts did not eliminate the jurisdiction of magistrates over wage-fixing since a section of them preserved the powers granted to justices of peace by earlier acts of Parliament to settle wage disputes, set wage rates, and monitor working conditions, and that wage-fixing in any case was largely moribund by this time.[62] What then was new in the Combination Acts? The acts significantly expanded the summary jurisdiction of magistrates to prosecute workers who sought to form unions or to deter others from working.[63] It should be noted, however, not only that magistrates could frequently be found mediating industrial disputes during the late eighteenth century, but also that Parliament had found the expansion of JPs' summary authority to be a ready remedy for a variety of ills during the previous century.[64] Moreover, the acts were drafted to be applied to industrial relations generally and not to individual industrial sectors as had been the case with earlier eighteenth-century legislation.[65]

While the purpose of the 1799 act was probably to establish a more speedy and effective remedy to prosecute combinations and not to create any new crime, the petitions of workmen received by the House of Commons after the act's passage uniformly protested against the criminalization of breach of contract.[66] Many petitions appear to have implicitly accepted the criminality of combination; at least none explicitly rejected the notion. Most complained that under the new act employees who refused to work when hired or refused to work with other labourers might become subject to criminal prosecution. Parliamentary reaction to the workers' protests sought both to expand the repressive impact of the law and to blunt the criticism of the criminalization of breach of contract.[66] When the act was reviewed the following year, many amendments either broadened the language of the act or tightened up procedures. For example, the definition of offences was extended significantly from 'direct or indirect actions' to 'wilful and malicious intent'. On the other hand, the summary jurisdiction of one justice in the original act was changed to two.[67] Two further prominent alterations to the 1799 act were the addition of new sections criminalizing masters' combinations and a prohibition against interested masters from serving as justices in combination cases. Yet the most extensive changes by far were the addition of five new sections to the act providing for the resolution of a variety of disputes over wages and work through arbitration.[68] The new act empowered either a master or worker to initiate the arbitration process upon the delivery of a complaint to the other party. As in the admiralty courts, and unlike traditional civil or ecclesiastical practices, arbitration under the 1800 Combination Act seems to have been perceived as both summary and compulsory. No requirements or qualifications were established for arbitrators and, surprisingly, arbitrators were authorized both to issue summonses and to examine witnesses under oath. Persons who refused to enter into arbitration could be fined up to £10 and those who failed to attend an arbitration hearing, refused to give evidence, or failed to perform an award could be imprisoned without bail. If Prime Minister William Pitt and Parliament were intent upon establishing a new industrial relations policy at this time, it may very well have been one based upon something akin to the principle of compulsory arbitration.

Indeed the importance of arbitration for a new industrial relations policy becomes even more apparent when the amended Combination Act of 1800 is viewed alongside the so-called Cotton Arbitration Acts of 1800 and 1804. According to the legal historian John Orth, the committee that revised the Combination Act drew upon the arbitration provisions that were then being drafted for a separate bill governing industrial relations in the cotton trade.[70] The 1800 Cotton Arbitration Act applied solely to the cotton-weaving trade and provided for the appointment of a pair of arbitrators, one each by the worker and master, to resolve disputes concerning wages, deductions, standards of production, and the like.[71] In the event that the arbitrators could not agree on an award, the dispute was to be referred to the nearest justice of the peace for a hearing and summary decision. Justices of the peace were further authorized to imprison or fine those who refused to attend, participate, or abide by the arbitration process. As in the 1800 Combination Act, the arbitrators were accorded the power to summon witnesses and examine them under oath. Also like the Combination Act of the same year, manufacturers (and their workers) were expressly forbidden from acting as magistrates in these cases.[72]

This act proved to be popular among cotton workers, especially for resolving disputes concerning the standards and quality of both raw materials and finished work. James Holcroft, a Bolton warehouseman, was an arbitrator in about 300 cases; Richard Needham, a Bolton weaver, helped arbitrate about 100 other cases during the first two years of the act.[73] However, the act failed to protect the weavers against uniform reductions of piece-rates by manufacturers or to insulate them from the rising cost of living. A particularly clever attempt to adapt the act to these broader goals was made by the weavers of Whitefield, 900 of whom simultaneously submitted their demands for arbitration in response to a general reduction of piece-rates. Significantly, the question of whether the terms of the act could be construed to operate in this way was entertained first by a pair of arbitrators who then agreed to refer the matter to an attorney for an opinion. When the attorney, whose costs were paid jointly by the weavers and manufacturers, returned a judgement favourable to the weavers, the manufacturers sought a further opinion from the irascible Edward Law (soon to be Lord Ellenborough), who wrote a brief more to their liking. Both opinions were referred to the next quarter sessions where the magistrates decided that the weavers' actions were tantamount to an attempt to regulate wages and thus were illegal.[74]

By the beginning of 1802, both the weavers and the manufacturers had reason to be dissatisfied with the act and had begun to organize campaigns either to amend or to abolish it. For the weavers, the act failed to protect them against widespread rate reductions and they therefore sought to revise the act to include mechanisms for the regulation of wages. The manufacturers, on the other hand, sought the act's total repeal. They argued that the act had not only led to a spate of frivolous litigation, but it had also led to the loss of time for both weavers and manufacturers. Moreover, they speciously argued, the litigation engendered by the act had soured the relationship between masters and servants.[75] The new act, passed in 1804, reveals that Parliament's faith in arbitration in many ways had been diminished but not totally extinguished. The most important effect of the new arbitration act was to reduce the discretionary authority of arbitrators.[76] The initial section of the act annulled the legislation of 1800 and specifically repealed an arbitrator's power to administer oaths. Instead, the summary jurisdiction of magistrates became the preferred forum of adjudication on the condition that both parties agreed to submit the dispute to them. Arbitration to settle disputes was retained but only under more significant magisterial regulation, notably including the new power to compel arbitration. In the event that one or more parties rejected the summary adjudication of a dispute, justices were given the authority to force reluctant parties into arbitration and to propose a list of suitable arbitrators. After each of the parties selected an arbitrator from the list, the dispute was to be heard within forty-eight hours and the arbitrators' decision was final. Further discretionary power was given to JPs to appoint arbitrators in the event that the original arbitrator failed to appear or refused to act, as well as to impose a settlement if the arbitrators failed to settle the dispute. The power of the magistrates to imprison those who refused to enter into or abide by arbitration was repealed, but the £10 penalty for non-compliance was retained. Interestingly enough, the prohibition against cotton manufacturers serving as magistrates in weavers' disputes also was repealed.[77]

The gendered nature of arbitration was also recognized by the 1804 Arbitration Act. The standing of married women in arbitration generally was distinctly different under the rules of equity as opposed to the common law.[78] While married women were restricted from submitting their disputes to arbitration according to the common law doctrine of coverture, equity appeared to allow married women a greater degree of autonomy.[79] Since equity courts allowed married women to dispose of their property at will, legal authorities of the period assumed Chancery would also support a married woman's right to submit to arbitration any disputes concerning her own property.[80] One notable example of Chancery's entertainment of a submission to arbitration from a married woman concerned the prominent divorce case between Olivia, Countess of Ross and her second husband, John Bateman.[81] The couple had married in 1770, six years after the death of the Earl of Ross. Upon the earl's death, the countess gained a life interest in an estate in County Tyrone and an annuity of £500 per annum. The marriage settlement with Bateman conveyed the Tyrone property to trustees in return for an additional annuity of a further £500 'by way of pin money'. A house in Dublin owned by Bateman was also put in trust. The countess filed for divorce in 1780 and a year later filed in Chancery against Bateman for his failure both to pay the pin money and to keep up payments on the estate's debts. Bateman answered by alleging that the countess had misrepresented the income of the Tyrone estate and then countersued for an accounting of some clothing and plate that the countess had allegedly taken with her upon their separation. While the suits were still pending, the two agreed to submit their differences to two arbitrators whose award was announced in 1784. Bateman was extremely dissatisfied with the arbitrators' award, which supported the countess's claims and even went so far as to reserve the Dublin house for the sole use of Lady Ross. Over the next few decades he repeatedly attempted to have the award set aside on the grounds that the doctrine of coverture precluded his wife consenting to arbitration, among other things. The case was finally heard before the House of Lords in 1813. In Lord Redesdale's remarks, it was made quite clear that the initial agreement to submit the dispute to arbitration was made with the consent of both parties, a fact that contradicted Bateman's claim to coverture. As such, Lady Ross was regarded by her erstwhile husband as a *feme sole* at the time of the arbitration agreement. The Lords accepted both that standing and the principle that married women could settle disputes through arbitration.

The 1804 Cotton Arbitration Act seems to have tried to split the difference between common law and equity arbitration practices. While the act did not prohibit married women from initiating arbitration altogether, it did permit husbands to enter complaints and proceed to arbitration for their wives. In a similar way, fathers were authorized to act for their children; mothers could not do so, however, unless the father was dead. This policy appears to reflect not only the extent to which the cotton textile trades of Lancashire relied upon women's labour, but also the extent to which women's labour was perceived as complementary, albeit subordinate, to men's.[82]

By all accounts, the new Cotton Arbitration Act was widely disregarded.[83] Indeed it seems to have foundered on the fundamental contradiction inherent in the attempt to apply an individualistic mode of settling disputes to a collective system of industrial relations. Both attempts to reduce wages and attempts to raise them operated uniformly across working groups regardless of the individual nature of the contract. The assumption that individual arbitration could resolve a conflict over a uniform wage reduction was misplaced and likely to fail. As Lord Amulree suggested long ago, industrial arbitration without combination was like 'giving a man a bicycle to make up for the loss of his legs'.[84]

This may have had a chastening affect on the legislature's affinity for arbitration for at least the succeeding two decades. In 1820, however, Parliament revived the application of arbitration to industrial disputes by giving seamen and their masters the opportunity to seek redress through the intervention of arbitrators.[85] In 1824, the effort to expand the application of forms of arbitration was again promoted in conjunction with the repeal of the Combination Act. As in 1800, Parliament sought to encourage arbitration as an 'expedient' remedy to industrial disputes at the same time as it legislated on matters of trade unionism.[86] The 1824 act tried to resuscitate the 1804 legislation and expand its purview by applying arbitration to all employment relations throughout the kingdom. Much of the regulatory power of the magistracy introduced in the 1804 act remained intact, although arbitrators were given new authority to issue summons. Significant authority was also accorded to justices to enforce awards, including the attachment and sale of goods as well as imprisonment without bail.[87] This later led one commentator to remark that by this act 'English judges have been granted powers of compulsory arbitration'.[88] The prohibition against manufacturers acting as justices in industrial disputes was restored and even extended to include their agents. Interestingly enough, Francis Place, who advised the MP Joseph Hume on the repeal of the Combination Acts, suggested that these arbitration clauses were both excessive and restrictive. They were, he wrote, 'unnecessary and making a plain familiar case, complex and difficult. Making in fact the most ordinary occurance [*sic*] of as much importance as one involving thousands of pounds.... People know very well that they may arbitrate without all this cursed Grim-Gribber.'[89] Indeed this act fared no better than its predecessors. A parliamentary committee of the mid-1850s found it difficult to uncover examples of cases that had been arbitrated under its terms and attributed much of the resistance to implementing the act to the unwillingness of workers to bring their cases before the local magistrates. On the one hand, it was noted at the time, such an appearance bore too great a similarity to a criminal proceeding, while on the other hand magistrates in manufacturing districts were not considered to be sufficiently impartial to arbitrate industrial disputes. Francis Place's estimation of the magistracy in this regard was probably not uncommon: 'I never knew an instance of the Magistrates acting towards the men with any thing [*sic*] but insult and injustice'.[90] Other than for some rare exceptions, the 1824 act was practically a dead letter.[91]

In the succeeding years, Parliament's desire to encourage arbitration was noticeable, although equally notable was the fact that these efforts were often directed at institutions whose social composition was largely lower middle or working class. The Savings Banks Act (1828) and the Friendly Societies Act (1829) both bear witness to the legislature's efforts to promote arbitration among the 'lower orders'.[92] Moreover, parliamentary acts in 1833 and after reveal a noticeable trend toward placing arbitration agreements increasingly under the auspices of the courts. Thus, acts of 1833, 1846 and 1854 all expanded judicial oversight of arbitration agreements until the latter act made all arbitration agreements a *de facto* order of the court unless the parties specifically agreed otherwise.[93] The courts may also have been tempted by this trend to impose forms of compulsory arbitration, although this was masked in particularly clever ways. In a landmark liability case of the 1860s, *Rylands* v. *Fletcher*, for example, the judge at the Liverpool Summer Assizes entered a verdict in favour of the plaintiff that was subject to the decision of an arbitrator. According to the legal historian of this case, 'the function of the fictitious verdict was to give the arbitrator's award the status of a court judgment', although the intent clearly was to make the settlement of the case by arbitration compulsory.[94] Nonetheless, as H.W. Arthurs notes, by mid-century, arbitration clauses were routinely appearing in many parliamentary acts, including those as disparate as the Coal Mines Inspection Act of 1855 and most of the public railway acts of the period.[95]

Not surprisingly, a prominent barrister's handbook of the mid-1830s lamented these developments. 'However imperfect and objectionable may be the mode of deciding *facts* by a *jury*', Chitty's *Practice* argued, 'it seems difficult to suggest a more satisfactory tribunal.... [W]e cannot ever anticipate a certain[,] just and correct decision upon any subject, by *one* or *two* individuals ... and hence, men naturally prefer an open trial by jury ... to a private decision by an arbitrator.' Chitty's faith in trial by jury was further supported by the claim that arbitrators frequently lacked knowledge of both the law and rules of evidence, an ignorance that frequently led to errors and faulty judgements. Even when the arbitrators were barristers, Chitty insists, they would probably have little experience because 'those in great practice cannot spare the time to devote several *continuous* hours' and attend the numerous meetings that frequently characterized arbitration proceedings. Chitty concludes:

> It is therefore a natural desire of litigating parties not to trust their case to the decision of a single arbitrator, or even of three; for if *Judges* sometimes will doubt, and sometimes misapprehend the law or the facts, what confidence can be justly reposed in the opinions of men naturally supposed to be of inferior talent. As, therefore, *trial by jury* has long been considered every Englishman's birthright, it is not surprising that hitherto any attempt generally to take away that right, and *force* arbitration, even under the recommendation of a Judge, has been unsuccessful.

Not all members of the legal profession were as hostile to arbitration as this. Country attorneys regularly attempted to resolve disputes through arbitration. M. Miles found that in the second half of the eighteenth century about one of every two disputes referred to the West Riding attorney John Eagle of Bradford was referred to an arbiter.[96] Indeed country barristers often found that their livelihoods depended upon arbitrations. James Losh, a radical London barrister and associate of Tierney, Horne Tooke, Godwin, Wordsworth and others, moved to Newcastle upon Tyne after a nervous breakdown in the 1790s. In 1812, after practising for more than fifteen years in the provinces, he remarked in his diary that in 'some years my profits have been principally derived from Arbitrations', and eight years later he was still reflecting upon the fact that along with bankruptcies arbitrations were among the 'most profitable parts of my profession'.[97] Still Chitty was not too far wrong when he complained that parliamentary developments, particularly after 1820, had the effect not only of sanctioning but of compelling arbitration. Yet even for him, while these recent innovations may have been objectionable, he nonetheless was forced to admit that they were also a form of legislative 'mercy' for 'persons little able to sustain the expense of formal litigation'.[98]

Industrial arbitration and the work group

The statutory expansion of arbitration in the nineteenth century is still not fully indicative of the extent to which this form of dispute resolution influenced working-class Britons during the late eighteenth and early nineteenth centuries. As Francis Place noted, people knew very well that they could settle their disputes through arbitration without recourse to the law. Yet labour and legal historians have often neglected this observation, preferring instead to trace the origins of industrial arbitration to A.J. Mundella's Nottingham Hosiery Board or Sir Rupert Kettle's Midlands schemes of the 1850s and 1860s.[99] Such a view often reflects the assumption of a certain stadial analysis of the maturation of industrialization, a learning of the 'rules of the game', to use Eric Hobsbawm's famous description, whereby the defeat of working-class radicalism and the stabilization of industrial capitalism ushered in an era of pragmatism, reformism and social compromise.[100] Thus the advent of arbitration is frequently understood only as evidence of a mid-Victorian social reconciliation that was ultimately based upon progress and capitalism. However, such a view is seriously misleading. A wide variety of trades, some as distinctive as handloom-weaving, carpentry, printing and coal-mining, elaborated or participated in forms of industrial arbitration before this period, while still others eagerly sought to adopt it. Different formats for collective arbitration developed during the early nineteenth century, either across a trade or among work groups, at the same time that more traditional forms of individual arbitration were still being actively pursued within the context of labour relations. In some instances, individual arbitrations were undertaken as test cases, the results of which were meant to be applied to the trade generally.

Certainly, both employers and workers perceived advantages to be gained from collective arbitration. For workers, several of these advantages are obvious: the avoidance of strikes or lock-outs, the legitimation of their economic demands and their social standing, and the opportunity to receive a 'fair' hearing. There is little reason to doubt that a good many employers, especially small-scale ones, construed the advantages of arbitration in a largely similar manner. A lengthy strike or lock-out might easily threaten the livelihood of a small employer or disrupt production enough to cause significant pecuniary losses. Moreover, employers in highly competitive industries might hope to use arbitrated settlements as an indirect way of controlling competition. Especially when it was applied to large groups of workers, as in the Clitheroe weavers' strike of 1861 or among the London compositors of the 1830s, arbitration had the effect of limiting competitive price-cutting at least to the extent to which these price cuts were based on wage reductions.

Nevertheless, arbitration's appeal to many workers lay fundamentally in the promise of fairness it held out to them. Francis Place suggested that there was widespread acceptance of arbitrators' decisions among the working class. 'I have arbitrated many cases', he wrote, 'always without any written form of submission, always without any [umpire] and never knew the parties refusing to abide by my decision.'[101] In a different context, the London compositors' union justified their maintenance of a price list by explaining that 'your officers have invariably considered themselves as arbitrators – and thereby, acting in the true spirit of Justice'.[102] A Scots handloom-weaver in 1836 lauded the passage of the arbitration acts 'for had it not been for legislative interference in passing [them], the weaver ... would be obliged to submit to the dictation of his employer'.[103] The *Articles and Regulations of the West Riding Fancy Union* in 1824 sought to establish district committees with the power to settle disputes in an amicable way between workers and their employers through arbitration.[104] A poor Leicester framework-knitter pleaded for the creation of an 'impartial body ... to arbitrate between the [masters and workmen], and before whom the merits of the subject in dispute can be fully and frankly debated'.[105]

It is perhaps worth considering for a moment whether the equity promise of arbitration was ever actually fulfilled. The answer, as tends to be the case, is not as simple as it may appear. When applied to industrial relations, arbitration is not solely a benign method to resolve disputes and harmonize divergent interests. It is, more importantly, a method by which working rules are ultimately established and precedents determined. Thus arbitration is a method of job regulation. As noted earlier in this book, an intense debate took place during the 1960s and 1970s among industrial relations experts over the precise focus of the study of job regulation; the so-called 'pluralists' argued that job regulation should comprise the study of both the written and customary rules circumscribing the employment relationship, while the 'radicals' stressed the study of the substantive degree of workers' control of the labour process and labour market.[106] Proponents of both sides of the debate, however, may have agreed that when studying the process of job regulation, the authorship of working rules could be used as an effective cipher for the balance of power within the industrial relations process.[107] That is, the analysis of the procedural and substantive rules themselves is not nearly as revealing of the relative distribution of power in industry or on the shopfloor as the study of who was actually responsible for authoring those rules. The term 'authority', therefore, needs to be understood in two senses: the first referring to the 'authors' of the working rules, and the second to the moral suasion subsequently given to those 'authors' to secure compliance to arbitrated settlements.[108] Thus the question of fairness, while not wholly irrelevant, is often inappropriate. The promise of arbitration was likely to be fulfilled only to those who exercised both the authorship of the pledge to arbitrate and the authority to implement the process. Since both workers and employers could derive benefits from its adoption, the history of the early period of industrial arbitration is most notably marked not by the peaceful resolution of industrial disputes, which nonetheless cannot and should not be ignored, but by the conflicts over the authority to implement and control arbitration schemes.

One of the most extensive and formalized systems of arbitration of the first half of the nineteenth century could be found in the Durham and Northumberland coal industry, an industry certainly not noted for any claims to equity. Coal-miners, it is well known, were among the earliest groups of workers to be employed under the terms of a formal written contract, called 'the bond'. We have seen that by the early nineteenth century, bonds throughout the northern coalfield had become relatively standardized and by 1826 a uniform printed document for all collieries had been produced. The terms of employment commonly included the commitment to work for one full year, a detailed description of wages and allowances, a list of fines and penalties for substandard workmanship, the amount of compensation to be provided in the event of temporary pit closures, the provision of housing, and several other articles.[109] The colliery's viewer, a person who acted as both mining engineer and colliery manager, was responsible for industrial relations at the site and thus negotiated the signing of the bonds on the part of the owner.

As early as 1808, bonds began to include an article providing for the settlement of some disputes by arbitration.[110] The pertinent section from an 1812 bond for the miners at Washington Colliery, Co. Durham, reads as follows:

> AND LASTLY, it is hereby agreed that in case any dispute or difference shall arise between the said hereby contracting parties relative to any matter or thing not hereby provided for, such dispute or difference shall be submitted to the decision of two viewers of collieries, one to be appointed by the said owners, etc. and the other by the said hereby hired parties of the other part, and in case of their disagreement, to the decision of a third person chosen by such two viewers, and the judgment and decision of such two viewers or umpire as the case may happen shall be conclusive between the parties on the matters referred to them ...[111]

Although the bonds referred in a vague way to the use of arbitration to resolve any dispute, it was most common for these provisions to be applied to disputes concerning the piece-work prices offered to miners to work different coal seams under a variety of working conditions. Disputes over these prices could occur quite frequently because conditions at the coal face, where the coal was being dug out, could and did change often.[112] A few bonds, such as the 1830–31 bond from Black Boy Colliery in south Durham, also included arbitration clauses specifically covering disputes over the size of the tubs used to transport coal to the surface, although this does not appear to have been common in the Tyneside area.[113] The important point about the standard piece-work arbitration clause is that, despite the fact that the miners could select a viewer to represent them, it provided for a process that proceeded solely under the auspices of the viewers, who were, of course, interested parties in the dispute itself.

Many miners naturally found this distinctly 'unfair'. An 1826 pamphlet published by the United Association of Colliers suggested that this particular form of arbitration violated an Englishman's right to a jury of his peers and proposed instead to revise the bond so that new arbitration panels would be staffed equally by two viewers appointed by the owners and two miners by workmen.[114] In 1832, a 'grand assemblage' of miners at Hetton Colliery in Durham complained to the owners about a number of the terms of their bond, including apparently the arbitration clause. But the owners 'remained firm to hold them to the terms of their Bond, viz. Reference in case of Dispute', the viewer recorded in his diary, and the miners 'went away completely worsted – and of Course grumbling hugely'.[115]

Without widespread support from the pitmen, the arbitration clauses of the bond may have been only fitfully invoked. Michael Flinn found evidence of one dispute in Lord Durham's collieries that was successfully arbitrated.[116] At Black Boy Colliery, near Bishop Auckland, a dispute over the measurement of tubs was settled by reference to two JPs in June 1831. The JPs found in favour of the miners and ordered the mine's viewer to compensate them accordingly.[117] However, a more informal approach to arbitration procedures is perhaps evident from some incidental testimony given in the 1832 trial of several pitmen for rioting at Waldridge Colliery in Durham. The so-called Waldridge Outrage, when striking miners dumped various gear down the mine shaft, stopped the pumping engines and threatened the lives of several non-union workers at work down the pits, was the culmination of a series of disputes dating back to the opening of the colliery in 1830.[118] In the autumn of 1831, several months after the initially successful strike led by Thomas Hepburn, disputes arose over the piece-work prices being paid there.[119] Whether because the colliery was a relatively new one or the viewer, Anthony Seymour, was unfamiliar with arbitration practice, Seymour at first proposed that the wage dispute be arbitrated by a panel of sixteen men, not necessarily viewers, from eight surrounding collieries. According to Seymour's testimony before the Durham Assizes, the miners were to select one man from each of the neighbouring collieries as arbiters and the colliery masters were to do the same. The miners initially accepted this proposal but it was abandoned for an unknown reason, perhaps because it was so unusual, shortly thereafter.

Subsequently, Seymour adopted the standard form of arbitration and two viewers were chosen, one by the miners and the other by colliery owners, to arbitrate the dispute. The arbitrators met and agreed upon a wage settlement. Although the testimony is somewhat confused on this point, at least some of the miners refused to accept the settlement and left the colliery. Because the prosecution hoped to establish the fact that the colliery owners had undertaken all reasonable attempts to settle the dispute, Seymour was led to insist that despite the initial confusion he had properly adhered to the standard arbitration procedures. 'The wages were settled by 2 men, and not by 16 men', he persistently maintained. 'Two viewers were appointed, one by the men and one by the masters, to arbitrate between them. The arbitrators did not differ. He still has the decision of the viewers in his pocket.' As if to emphasize the miners' responsibility for the failure of arbitration, Seymour concluded that the pitmen even refused to ask for an umpire, which was one of their prerogatives under the terms of arbitration in the bonds.

The northern miners appear to have harboured no great affinity for arbitration, at least so long as the viewers monopolized it. When the Hetton Colliery banksmen, who supervised the unloading of coal at the pit head, demanded an increase in piece-rates, the viewer there first offered to 'leave their Agreement to the decision of any Magistrate or Gentlemen in the neighbourhood'. However, on second thought, he next offered them half of what they originally demanded or the option 'to go to reference', that is, arbitration. The banksmen rejected both offers, went off to try to bargain directly with one of the owners of the colliery, but eventually were forced back to work when the viewer swore out warrants against them for breaking their bonds.[120]

After the failure of the 1844 miners' strike and the introduction of a monthly instead of an annual contract, the arbitration section apparently disappeared from the bonds, although it is not certain whether it disappeared in practice as well.[121] The equity promise of arbitration, however, certainly persisted into the next half of the nineteenth century. In 1871, William Crawford, head of the Durham Miners' Association, revived the process in the form of the so-called Joint Committee, a now formal board of arbitration comprised of both miners' and owners' representatives.[122] Even though the Joint Committee soon came under attack for its failure to protect miners' earnings and was replaced by the sliding scale, which itself was only a type of arbitration based upon reference to the market price of coal, both forms of dispute resolution were introduced under decidedly different terms of authority. Jointly authored (and authorized), the Joint Committee and the sliding scale mark a temporary renegotiation of industrial relations in the industry that gave to these forms of arbitration a much wider aura of legitimacy, if not a great deal of long-term success.

The introduction of a long-term written contract, such as the miners' bond, may have greatly facilitated the adoption of arbitration, if only because commercial contracts regularly included such clauses and local attorneys were familiar with these provisions. The Staffordshire potters of the 1830s provide another example of such a development. This may appear surprising at first since the potters of this era are most well known among historians for their attachment to Owenite socialism.[123] But, like the northern miners, the early existence of contractual forms of individual arbitration provides a link to the more widely recognized adoption and acceptance of the industry's Board of Conciliation and Arbitration in the latter half of the nineteenth century. Indeed, the similarities in the pattern of industrial relations exhibited by the Durham and Northumberland coal-miners and the North Staffordshire potters are too striking to ignore. Both groups operated within the context of an annual contract; both were faced with highly organized combinations of masters; both worked on a complicated piece-rate system; both maintained a tradition of sporadic industry-wide attempts at collective bargaining that overlay a more or less continuous stream of small-scale individual or work group bargaining.[124]

Like the experience of the northern coal industry, arbitration was apparently introduced into the potters' annual contract by the manufacturers at the end of a prolonged rise in wages and a period of intense union activity. Whereas for the miners this coincided with the labour shortages caused by the Napoleonic Wars, potters' wages appear to have been steadily rising for much of the decade following the collapse of their union in 1826.[125] An initial attempt to construct a type of arbitration board occurred in 1833. Composed of an equal number of workmen and manufacturers, this Joint Committee worked to equalize wages throughout the district by elaborating a list of prices for pottery work and then met weekly to resolve further disputes as they arose.[126] However, the apparently 'fair' composition of the committee did not obscure its purpose and effect, for it disbanded shortly thereafter amidst mutual recriminations. Part of the blame for the committee's collapse was attributed to the fact that some branches of the potters' union had become dissatisfied with the agreements reached by arbitration, apparently because they had limited potential wage increases, and refused to sanction the deals entered into by their delegates.[127]

But while the potters were becoming less sanguine about arbitration, it continued to capture the imagination of the pottery manufacturers as a way of controlling rising wages. In 1834, when potters in Burslem and Tunstall went on strike for a wage rise, the manufacturers responded by suggesting the creation of a new arbitration board, this time composed of five manufacturers, three of whom would be appointed by the potters and two others by the manufacturers.[128] When the potters rejected this proposal, the manufacturers then offered to expand the board to twelve members and include six working potters.[129] However, the potters steadfastly refused both offers not only because they believed that their strike demands were just but more importantly because they believed that arbitration had worked against them. Thus they announced that 'having duly considered the resolutions of the manufacturers' meeting ... [the union's executive committee] find that, notwithstanding all its efforts to bring such meeting to acknowledge a fair principle to legislate upon, has hitherto failed in such efforts'.[130] The potters' strike eventually succeeded and gained for the workmen wage increases estimated at between 30 and 35 per cent.

Chastened by their defeat, the manufacturers formed a Chamber of Commerce in 1836 with the intent of turning the terms of the annual contract against the potters. Another strike and corresponding lock-out occurred at the annual hiring time in 1836, and while the results of these actions were initially equivocal, the potters' union subsequently failed under the burden of its strike debts. Under these circumstances, the manufacturers inserted an arbitration clause into the contract that stipulated the resolution of wage or price disputes through arbitration boards composed of three manufacturers and three workmen.[131] The intent of the arbitration clause in the potters' contract, it may be surmised, was to apply a brake to the long-term rise in potters' wages and not to share authority over wage-setting. Despite the plaudits the trade later received for its pioneering efforts in industrial arbitration, workers remained suspicious of it while employers continually sought to reinvigorate it.[132] In 1845, for example, William Evans, editor of the *Potters' Examiner*, spoke out against the creation of regional arbitration boards at the National Conference of Trades.[133] During the next decade, a new arbitration system instituted by the Chamber of Commerce was described by one working potter as a 'proposition of the masters themselves' and 'not so mutual that it might not be improved'.[134] Indeed the establishment of the more well known Board of Arbitration and Conciliation in 1868 was due largely to the efforts of M.D. Hollins, who was chairman of the Potteries Chamber of Commerce.[135]

If the early nineteenth-century northern coal and pottery industries represent arbitration systems largely regulated by owners and management, then the London compositors of the same period offer a glimpse of arbitration devised and regulated by employees. Once again, in the case of the compositors the essential question regarding the success of arbitration relates less to its forms of fairness than to its relation to authority over rule-making. We have already seen how the London compositors frequently resorted to a variety of methods of arbitration in order to mobilize consent to the maintenance of the scale of prices.[136] Indeed the various disputes committees formed by the compositors' unions perceived themselves and understood their function as serving as arbitrators between the masters and men. 'Let not the utility and importance of your Society be questioned', the London General Trade Society of Compositors had once declared. 'The usefulness of an institution which arbitrates between two adverse parties, where one is inclined to have, and the other to withhold, must be so apparent to all reasonable men, as to render any observations from your committee wholly unnecessary.'[137]

In many disputes, distinctly *ad hoc* measures of arbitration were implemented. Such was the case mentioned earlier when the charges for casting up a large broadside were settled by polling thirteen different masters' opinions.[138] Still, in that dispute, the composition of the arbitration panel was less important than who authorized the process. The dispute had begun after a master printer had rejected the union's initial decision on the charges to be paid for printing up a broadside. To resolve the impasse, the union's executive committee suggested that representatives of three of the leading printing houses arbitrate the dispute, an offer that the master printer preliminarily accepted. But when one of the arbitrators failed to give a speedy decision, the compositors then moved to solicit the advice of thirteen other firms in the trade, the majority of which supported the union's case. Despite such meticulousness, the master printer still refused to accept the arbitrators' decision until he had completed his own personal enquiries, only to agree in the end to accept the arbitration of the three master printers initially agreed upon. When these referees also supported the union's original decision, the master finally accepted the charges.[139]

Because it ultimately functioned as a test of rule-making and authority, the prospect of arbitration often served to facilitate informal negotiation and agreement rather than impose a formal settlement upon the parties. In 1833, for example, the charges for composing a Bible became the matter of a dispute that not only pitted the compositors' union against the employer but also the shopfloor work group against the union. All three groups had calculated a different set of charges for the job ranging from an average of £3 to £3 9s 6d per sheet. In the midst of the impasse, the employer suggested that although he 'would not consent to pay more than £3 per sheet; but if they chose to refer it to 2 or 3 master printers, and they decided it was worth more than £3.[,] he might then, perhaps, be induced to pay 2 or 3 Shillings more'.[140] The union immediately decided that 'it was considered expedient to submit the matter to arbitration' and proposed that the dispute be put before a committee of four master printers and four journeymen compositors and that their decision be considered binding upon both parties. Meanwhile, however, more informal shopfloor bargaining continued and the employer eventually offered up to 62s a sheet.[141] Contrary to the union's recommendation, the work group, or companionship, eventually accepted the offer and set to work on the Bible. Several weeks later, the companionship reported to the union that 'the whole of the present companions are satisfied with the price of 62/. Per sheet, and they think they are paid as much as they can demand'.[142]

Such a concatenation of events in which the promise of arbitration preceded an informal shopfloor bargain may not have been all that uncommon. By 1834, the newly founded London Union of Compositors had included an arbitration clause as Article 7 in its *Rules and Regulations* that incorporated the union's earlier desire to arbitrate disputes formally between an equal number of journeymen compositors and master printers.[143] This procedure was followed in the dispute over payment for printing up the paper wrappers to periodicals at the Penny National Library Office in 1834, but again arbitration became the impetus for an informal shopfloor settlement. In July of that year, the compositors had stopped work after they had not been paid for the wrappers on a job. After refusing to negotiate, the compositors received the following note from their foreman: 'Mr. Pickburn informs the Father of the Chapel that the Proprietors *have consented* and will agree to submit the measure in question to arbitration' (emphasis in original).[144] After the father of the chapel, or shop steward, relayed this message to the union, the compositors' executive council quickly tried to surmise the likelihood of their success. Chapel representatives from nearly half a dozen printing firms were quickly canvassed and although not every firm paid for the printing of wrappers many of them did. The union executive, or Trade Council, therefore unanimously adopted the resolution 'that the Trade-Council are willing to submit to arbitration, agreeably to Art. 7 of the Union, the question respecting the charge for Wrappers to the Penny National Library'. As in the Bible dispute, the union's proposal indicated that the dispute be arbitrated by an equal number of compositors and master printers, although in this case the number suggested was five instead of four. As a confidence-building measure, the compositors agreed to go back to work on the condition that they be paid for all the wrappers printed up on the job prior to the arbitration decision. Moreover, in the event that the decision went against the compositors, the union guaranteed to the repay the money.[145]

As in the case of the Bible, however, the employer preferred to reach an informal agreement rather than submit the dispute to arbitration. Thus when the chapel members submitted the union's proposal to their foreman, they eventually received this note in reply: 'P.N.L. Office, July 4, 1834. – The Proprietors of the Penny National Library have, under the peculiar circumstances in which they are placed, and to prevent further loss of time and capital, come to the determination of paying the present demand, of £6. 9s. 6d. made by the Compositors in their employ for wrappers. In doing so, however, they protest against the principle upon which the claim is founded deeming it one of positive extortion and injustice.'[146] Why bow to such 'extortion and injustice'? On the one hand, many employers probably preferred to deal with such disputes in an *ad hoc* and one-off manner rather than risk inscribing work practices in rules, despite the fact that such informal work practices might become accepted as custom-and-practice thereafter.[147] On the other, employers' resistance to such practices was elicited especially when the authority to decide such issues, or even the authority to decide which issues merit arbitration, was shared or ceded to unions or work groups.

The connection between arbitration and authority in printing's industrial relations was highlighted further by later developments in the trade. The compositor union's readiness to include masters on arbitration panels was not solely an attempt to make arbitration more fair. More importantly, it was a response to the growing unwillingness of the master printers to allow the authority of the union to decide pricing disputes and initiate arbitration to go unchallenged. In 1837, the employers combined to form their own Association of Master Printers and immediately established their own arbitration committee to hear disputes. For a time, the union and masters' committees operated without regard to one another, although it is clear from the union's minute books that the compositors were eager to resolve the impasse. Interestingly enough, their attempts to do so involved a redefinition of the arbitration process. The union committee no longer 'invariably considered themselves as arbitrators – and thereby, acting in the true spirit of Justice', as the LGTSC committee had claimed in 1829.[148] Instead, the union had to reposition itself rhetorically. It began to argue that both 'employers and employed have equal rights in the adjustment of the price of labour' and that arbitration had to be jointly regulated and authored in order to gain legitimacy. Thus, the union's Trade Council proposed in 1837 and again in 1838 that 'whenever the decision of the Committee of Masters shall be contrary to the decision of the Trade Council, the employer in whose house the dispute originated shall be at liberty to refer it to arbitration: the arbitrators to consist of an equal number of the Committee of Masters and members of the Trade Council, whose decision shall be binding on both parties'.[149] The connection between the formation of the masters' combination and this new approach to arbitration is also implicit in the union's annual report of 1837. 'Let no Chambers of Commerce as in Staffordshire, or Association of Masters, as in London, prevail', the union reported to its members, 'but, if the rate of wages is to be decided by any tribunal, let it be that kind of tribunal in which labour and capital may each be fairly represented, and in which masters and men may fairly advocate their individual interests.'[150]

Arbitration continued to be an essential element of the industrial relations of compositors and printers through the middle of the nineteenth century. The term itself even seemed to carry a special cache, for it was applied to a series of what might be more properly called collective bargaining sessions in 1847 and again in 1856. The results of the former conference, however, point to a significantly different balance of power in the trade by this time. The so-called general Arbitration Committee of master printers and compositors proposed the creation of a 'Committee of Reference', that old arbitration term again. Similar in many ways to the earlier practices in the Durham and Northumberland coal industry and the Staffordshire potteries, this new committee was to be comprised of a dozen master printers, six of whom were selected by the masters themselves and six others by the compositors.[151] The principle of arbitration, therefore, survived in the London printing trades but the source of its authority was changing dramatically. It is unclear whether this arbitration board ever replaced the older forms of resolving disputes, but arbitration's function as a source of authority apparently had become clear enough to the master printers of the period.

Although it should be quite clear by now that arbitration was commonly practised in several sectors of British industry before the advent of boards of conciliation and arbitration in the second half of the nineteenth century, a brief discussion of the arbitration of the 1861 Clitheroe weavers' strike may serve to bring into relief several of the issues discussed to this point. Our account of this arbitration case comes not from any official source such as a newspaper or union record, but from the diary of one of the strike's leaders, John O'Neil.[152] The strike had its origins in the efforts of the Lancashire weavers to maintain the famous Blackburn List that set the standard for working prices throughout much of the district. Employers outside Blackburn, however, had consistently argued through this period that they required reductions to that list in order to account for the additional transportation costs they incurred when shipping their products to Manchester or Liverpool.[153] This conflict had engendered a series of strikes in the Lancashire weaving districts, including those at Colne and Clitheroe.

The Clitheroe strike was provoked in February 1861 by just such an attempt to lower local weaving prices below the Blackburn standards. Several weeks into the strike, however, an unknown 'friend of the working class' posted placards throughout the town on the night of 15 March urging both the weavers and the manufacturers to each select 'five disinterested persons' to arbitrate the dispute. The next day, a general union meeting was called during which the proposal to submit the case to arbitration was rejected. Union officials argued that the local advantages enjoyed by Clitheroe manufacturers, such as lower building costs, undermined their claim that they needed lower weaving prices to compensate for 'local disadvantages'. Moreover, the union officials argued that if arbitration led to any reductions to the Blackburn List then 'they would also be shut out from every other district in the union'.[154]

A week later, however, four weavers mysteriously arrived in town, two of whom, George Cowell and Mortimer Grimshaw, had been the most prominent leaders of the famous Preston Strike of 1853–54.[155] After arriving unannounced in Clitheroe, they proceeded to convene a public meeting. But before this could happen they were intercepted by the leaders of the Clitheroe weavers, including John O'Neil. According to O'Neil, 'we knew them to be a gang of notorious scoundrels, we were determined to know the reason of their coming here, and who sent them'. In a 'long and stormy discussion' with the union leaders, the 'gang of scoundrels' claimed they were only in town 'to see if the dispute could not be settled by arbitration'. They refused to admit either who sent for them or who paid them. O'Neil assumed they had been called upon 'to help the masters to get up an arbitration and to help the workpeople to a reduction'.[156] The union's response to the intervention of these 'scoundrels' was emphatic. The initial discussions with them were threatened by a crowd of weavers who were 'very impatient and threatened to pull the house down if we did not come out'. When the group emerged from the house and tried to make their way to the union committee room, 'the crowd followed us, throwing stones, pushing them and kicking them, shouting and brawling, telling them they sold the Preston strike and must not come here to sell them'.[157]

Despite the weavers' obvious antipathy to the scoundrels and their mission, two days later the manufacturers put up placards offering to settle the dispute by arbitration and, after a public meeting, the weavers' union appointed a deputation to meet the masters and hear their proposal. After a further public meeting, the offer of arbitration was accepted by the union, although they initially refused to return to work until the arbitration was concluded. When this hurdle was finally surmounted and the mills opened, formal agreements to arbitrate were drawn up by a local solicitor and signed by representatives of the two parties. The local Reverend George Fielding of St James's church was chosen as an umpire and, as was common in civil arbitration cases, it was agreed that his decision would be binding in the event that the arbitrators failed to reach an agreement. On 3 April, the union executive committee selected their panel of arbitrators and on the following day arbitration sessions began at the Swan Hotel.

These sessions soon became deadlocked and on 11 April the umpire was called for. The umpire decided that a reduction was justified by the differences between Blackburn and Clitheroe. However, rather than accepting the owners' demand of a 5 per cent reduction, the umpire declared that he had come to the conclusion that there was only a 2½ per cent difference between the two towns. Moreover, the burden of this difference should be shared by the masters and weavers and thus he decided that a rate reduction of only 1½ per cent was justified. While the masters vehemently protested against the decision, and some of them even went to the extent of victimizing some of the union leaders, the award stood and was accepted uniformly.

It is difficult to identify precisely why the Clitheroe weavers so emphatically rejected arbitration both when the process was initially suggested by the anonymous 'friend of the working class' and when Cowell and Grimshaw arrived, only to accept it several days later. Part of the answer may lie in an understanding of the weavers' perception of the sources of authority promoting arbitration. There appears to have been a pronounced suspicion of the process when its promoters were either anonymous or their interests unclear. In the cases of both the 'friend of the working class' and Cowell and Grimshaw, this form of intervention aroused suspicions that the promoters were in league with the masters and intent upon secretly undermining the weavers' bargaining position. In the words of the French revolutionaries, they lacked 'publicity' and 'transparency' and thus became suspect because the sources of their authority were occluded. However, when the masters approached the weavers directly and expressed a willingness to proceed to arbitration openly and in accordance with law and custom, then the parties jointly authorized the process and the sources of arbitration's authority were unambiguous. Thus the Clitheroe weavers appear to have understood that arbitration was not necessarily neutral or equitable, yet they also believed that it could be when the process was jointly authorized.

Industrial arbitration as test cases

These forms of what might be termed 'collective arbitration' that covered work groups and work sites may not have developed in all trades, and during this period they may not have been present in very many. Yet arbitration in its more traditional individual form nonetheless exerted an important influence over industrial relations in many other sectors. We have already noted the parliamentary attempts to expand the scope of individual arbitration, but both the courts and individuals frequently settled complex trade disputes between masters and workers through arbitration. In some of these circumstances, arbitration hearings came to be perceived as test cases and the award was intended to apply to the entire trade. This certainly seems to have been the understanding in the arbitration case of Messrs. Bevans & Sons, master carpenters, and Benjamin Walrond, one of their journeymen, in 1803. The proceedings were apparently initiated in response to an attempt to secure a rise in piece-rates for the journeyman carpenters during the difficult war years. The dispute was arbitrated under the terms of the 1800 Combination Act and was initially heard before two arbitrators. Upon the failure of the arbitrators to agree on an award, the dispute was then referred to an umpire, in this instance a Middlesex JP named Joseph Moser, for final determination, or, to use the modern term, binding arbitration. It is likely that both sides were represented by legal counsel at the final hearing, but it is certain that the magistrate understood this individual submission to apply to the trade generally. He spoke of the impact of the case in the broadest possible language: for example, applauding 'the Masters, who certainly, both collectively and individually, are of the highest respectability; and it gave me great pleasure to find (in the course of this ardent and important disquisition) no single instance which indicated a desire in them to withhold from the men a proper, just, and let me add, a generous remuneration'. He similarly commended the 'other class of applicants, the Journeymen Carpenters', whose 'conduct, as far as it has come to my knowledge, has been quiet, regular, and orderly'. After considering the effect of contemporary price rises on both masters and journeymen, as well as the potential effect of a rise in wages on 'that spirit of enterprize in the masters', the magistrate pointedly awarded a modest rise in wages to the journeymen carpenters as a whole and not the individual claimant. 'Founded upon a full consideration of the evidence adduced on both sides', the final order read, 'and combining it with collateral circumstances, I am of the opinion that the wages of Journeymen Carpenters ought to be in future rated at the sum of TWENTY-FIVE SHILLINGS PER WEEK, PER MAN, which standard in this case I accordingly order.' Thus, what had initially been adjudicated in the form of the umpirage of an individual arbitration case had been elided into a general settlement of a trade dispute incorporating the magistracy's summary jurisdiction over wages.[158]

Even when the application of arbitration awards was not specifically directed at the general trade, workers often circulated the results of arbitration cases precisely because they were understood to act as precedents in future disputes. A letter in *The Trades' Newspaper, and Mechanics' Weekly Journal* from one of the arbitrators in an 1826 case announced the award of nearly

£2 to a Macclesfield silk-weaver who was forced to go without work because the silk masters could not provide him with weft for his loom.[159] More than a decade later, a pamphlet appeared in Macclesfield publicizing a similar arbitration case, *Gent v. Broome*, which reprinted the testimonies and evidence of over thirty witnesses as well as the final decision.[160] In 1837, the arbitration case of *Poyton v. Robinson* was reported at length in *The Spitalfields Weavers' Journal*. As in the Macclesfield dispute, this case involved a weaver whose employers had failed to provide work for him. The initial arbitrators failed to agree on an award and the matter was referred to a London alderman who found in favour of the weaver. The masters appealed, however, and won on the ground that the City magistrates had no jurisdiction over the weaver who was a resident of Bethnal Green. The weavers immediately recognized that such a decision would effectively render arbitration useless and they mounted a persistent and successful campaign to amend the 1836 Master and Workmen's Bill.[161]

Workers' interest in arbitration was also sometimes born out of desperation. Several failing unionization efforts sought to establish arbitration tribunals in the desperate hope of defending themselves from the effects of falling wages and unemployment. Perhaps it was these difficult circumstances that most strongly evoked the equity promise of arbitration among workers. John Doherty's plea to local magistrates, and then later to churchwardens, to arbitrate the 1828–29 Manchester cotton-spinners' strike was made at a time when the union's solidarity was crumbling and the employers' resolve was stiffening.[162] In 1823, Gravener Henson published his approval of the arbitration clauses of the Combination Acts, and his hope that they might help save not only the troubled Nottingham framework-knitters but the British working class generally.[163] In 1853, the Preston cotton operatives offered to refer their dispute to arbitration about a week and a half after the masters announced their plan for an indefinite lock-out.[164] In all of these cases, the equity promise of arbitration stemmed from the belief that, as Gravener Henson put it, people of good faith would not let the Devil take the hindmost.[165]

Conclusion

In conclusion, arbitration was well known to the British working class long before the craze for such systems in industry was begun by A.J. Mundella's Nottingham Hosiery Board or Sir Rupert Kettle's arbitration in the Midlands building trades. Arbitration commonly interceded in everyday commercial transactions and was a typical remedy for family and community disagreements. By the end of the eighteenth century, Parliament had begun to take an increasing interest in the adoption of systems of arbitration to resolve industrial disputes, even though the application of arbitration by statute to an entire industry or trade was apparently at odds with a more profound defence of the individuality of the employment contract. The Cotton Arbitration Act, for example, foundered on this contradiction. There nonetheless does appear to have been significant legislative effort toward expanding the scope of arbitration among the working class in particular in order to provide at least a simulacrum of access to a justice system that was otherwise denied them.

More importantly, however, arbitration systems began to appear autonomously in several industrial sectors during the first third of the nineteenth century. By 1850, many of the principal features of the role of arbitration in British industrial relations were already well established. A bifurcated system had appeared by this time in which government policies aimed at sponsoring arbitration were complemented by autonomous arbitration agreements covering individual industrial sectors. Indeed, as the late H.A. Turner observed to be the case in the twentieth century, the former was largely moribund while the latter exhibited a greater degree of vitality, if not necessarily success.[166] Turner also suggested in his brief study of arbitration in twentieth-century Britain that the success of arbitration was 'conditional upon the agreement of workers generally' and, therefore, understanding the conditions implied in workers' acceptance of arbitration was fundamental to understanding the system itself. For him, the workers' acceptance of arbitration depended upon whether the decisions accorded to their sense or standards of 'fairness'. In different sectors this operated according to different criteria. In some, the fairness of arbitrated settlements was determined in comparison to the cost of living – a 'subsistence' principle, he called it. In others, fairness was determined by the extent to which the settlements maintained wage-differentials either within or between industries. This was the 'fair wages' principle.[167]

While some such fairness principles did indeed operate and can be made to apply to a history of earlier arbitration, it has been suggested here that systems of arbitration were not neutral but that they were both the results and reflections of struggles for authority in industry. The authorship of these arbitration schemes and the subsequent authority granted by them were well understood at the time. This is almost certainly what Thomas Winters, Secretary of the National Association of United Trades for the Protection of Industry, had in mind when he told a parliamentary committee that while workers of his organization were bound and willing to accept other workers as arbitrators, there was a noted unwillingness to accept masters in a similar capacity.[168] This may also have been on the minds of the striking Clitheroe weavers who stoned, pushed and kicked the group of visiting weavers who were suspected of being behind the employers' effort to initiate arbitration. Certainly, during the early nineteenth century, the success or stability of arbitration systems was in part dependent upon the implied or explicit conditions workers placed upon the settlements or awards, as Turner wrote. However, the acceptance of these conditions was based less upon an unarticulated equity promise than it was upon an understanding of who was implementing the system and who was writing the 'rules of the game'.

Notes

1 Quoted in Stewart Macaulay, 'Non-Contractual Relations in Business: A Preliminary Study', *American Sociological Review*, vol. 28: no. 1 (February 1963), p. 61.

2 Francis Place, *The Autobiography of Francis Place (1771–1854)*, ed. Mary Thale (Cambridge: Cambridge University Press, 1972), pp. 225–6.

3 This phrase is taken from Robert Ellickson, *Order without Law: How Neighbors Settle Disputes* (Cambridge, Mass.: Harvard University Press, 1991).

4 The recognition that the British system of industrial relations before the middle of this century was uniquely characterized by such 'voluntarism' is largely due to Otto Kahn-Freund. See, for example, his 'Legal Framework', in A. Flanders and H.A. Clegg, eds, *The System of Industrial Relations in Great Britain* (Oxford: Blackwell, 1954).

5 This is how the term 'informal' is used, for example, in Ellickson, *Order without Law*, pp. 71 *et seq.*

6 On the disciplinary state, see V.A.C. Gatrell, 'Crime, Authority and the Policeman-State', in F.M.L. Thompson, ed., *The Cambridge Social History of Britain, 1750–1950*, vol. 3 (Cambridge: Cambridge University Press, 1990), pp. 243–310.

7 Patrick Joyce, 'Refabricating Labour History; or, From Labour History to the History of Labour', *Labour History Review*, vol. 62: no. 2 (Summer 1997), pp. 150–1.

8 For a contemporary example, see Ellickson, *Order without Law*, pp. 40–81.

9 Edward Powell, 'Arbitration and the Law in England in the Late Middle Ages', *Transactions of the Royal Historical Society*, 5th ser., vol. 33 (1983), pp. 53–5; William S. Holdsworth, *A History of English Law*, 16 vols (London: Methuen & Co., 1964), vol. xiv, pp. 187–204; on contracts, see A.W.B. Simpson, *A History of the Common Law of Contract* (Oxford: Clarendon Press, 1975), pp. 173–7; on commercial and maritime arbitration, see Carole Rawcliffe, '"That Kindliness Should be Cherished More, and Discord Driven Out": The Settlement of Commercial Disputes by Arbitration in Later Medieval England', in J. Kermode, ed., *Enterprise and Individuals in Fifteenth-Century England* (Stroud: Alan Sutton, 1991), pp. 99–117, and L.S. Sutherland, 'The Law Merchant in England in the Seventeenth and Eighteenth Centuries', *Transactions of the Royal Historical Society*, 4th ser., vol. 17 (London, 1934), pp. 164–5.

10 Rawcliffe, '"That Kindliness Should be Cherished More"', *passim*.

11 Peter Earle, *The Making of the English Middle Class: Business, Society and Family Life in London, 1660–1730* (Berkeley: University of California Press, 1989), pp. 104, 242.

12 Alan Macfarlane, ed., *The Diary of Ralph Josselin, 1616–1683* (London: British Academy, 1976), p. 278; Craig Muldrew, 'Interpreting the Market: The

Ethics of Credit and Community Relations in Early Modern England', *Social History*, vol. 18: no. 2 (May 1993), p. 179.

13 Joan Thirsk, ed., *Chapters from the Agrarian History of England and Wales, 1500–1750, Volume 4, Agricultural Markets and Trade, 1500–1750*, rev. edn (Cambridge: Cambridge University Press, 1990), p. 125.

14 J.S. Cockburn, *Western Circuit Assize Orders, 1629–1648: A Calendar*, Camden Fourth Series, vol. xvii (London: Royal Historical Society, 1976), p. 85.

15 Cockburn, *Western Circuit Assize Orders*, p. 8.

16 Cockburn, *Western Circuit Assize Orders*, p. 16.

17 Cockburn, *Western Circuit Assize Orders*, pp. 12, 19, 28.

18 Cockburn, *Western Circuit Assize Orders*, pp. 54, 55.

19 Cockburn, *Western Circuit Assize Orders*, p. 70.

20 Cockburn, *Western Circuit Assize Orders*, p. 116.

21 Cockburn, *Western Circuit Assize Orders*, p. 256.

22 Martin Ingram, *Church Courts, Sex and Marriage in England, 1570–1640* (Cambridge: Cambridge University Press, 1987), pp. 50, 8–9. See also Ralph Houlbrooke, *Church Courts and the People during the English Reformation, 1520–1570* (Oxford: Oxford University Press, 1979), pp. 43–4: 'it was the duty of the ecclesiastical judge to encourage the peaceful settlement of most types of dispute by compromise or arbitration. In the consistory courts of both dioceses [Norwich and Winchester] far fewer cases were pushed as far as the expensive formality of final sentence than were settled by peaceful agreement.'

23 Ingram, *Church Courts, Sex and Marriage*, pp. 207, 307–8; Houlbrooke, *Church Courts and the People*, pp. 67, 137.

24 Cockburn, *Western Circuit Assize Orders*, pp. 55–6, 183.

25 Cockburn, *Western Circuit Assize Orders*, pp. 67, 109, 145, 159.

26 Cockburn, *Western Circuit Assize Orders*, pp. 3, 131, 138.

27 Cockburn, *Western Circuit Assize Orders*, pp. 7, 55–6.

28 Simpson, *History of the Common Law of Contract*, p. 174; Henry Horwitz and James Oldham, 'John Locke, Lord Mansfield, and Arbitration during the Eighteenth Century', *Historical Journal*, vol. 36: no. 1 (1993), pp. 140–1; Holdsworth, *History of English Law*, vol. xiv, p. 189.

29 Cockburn, *Western Circuit Assize Orders*, pp. 159, 181.

30 Horwitz and Oldham, 'John Locke, Lord Mansfield, and Arbitration', pp. 137–59; Holdsworth, *History of English Law*, vol. xiv, pp. 196–8.

31 Horwitz and Oldham, 'John Locke, Lord Mansfield and Arbitration', pp. 158–9; see also Bruce Mann, 'The Formalization of Informal Law: Arbitration before the American Revolution', *New York University Law Review*, vol. 59 (1984) cited in *ibid*.

32 Horwitz and Oldham, 'John Locke, Lord Mansfield and Arbitration', p. 145.

33 Stewart Kyd, *A Treatise on the Law of Awards*, 2nd edn (1799; Philadelphia, Pa.: Farrand & Co., 1808), p. 12.

34 *Tatersall* v. *Groote*, 1800, 2 Bos. and Pull. 132. I have tried to modernize the punctuation.

35 *Kill* v. *Hollister*, 1746, 1 Wils. 129 in Basil Montague, *A Digest of the Law of Partnership; With a Collection of the Cases decided in the Courts of Law and Equity upon that Subject*, 2 vols (London: J. Butterworth and Son, 1822),

vol. i, p. 64n. was a prevailing case concerning arbitration in insurance disputes; see also Horwitz and Oldham, 'John Locke, Lord Mansfield and Arbitration', pp. 145–6; P.S. Atiyah, *The Rise and Fall of Freedom of Contract* (Oxford: Clarendon Press, 1979), p. 421.

36 A. Bartholomew, *Specifications for Practical Architecture*, 2nd edn (London, 1846) cited in M.H. Port, 'The Office of Works and Building Contracts in Early Nineteenth-Century England', *Economic History Review*, 2nd ser., vol. 20: no. 1 (April 1967), p. 107.

37 *The Grosvenor Estate in Mayfair, Part I* (Survey of London 39, London, 1977), pp. 15–16, cited in Horwitz and Oldham, 'John Locke, Lord Mansfield and Arbitration', pp. 145–6.

38 A.W.B. Simpson, *Leading Cases in the Common Law* (Oxford: Clarendon Press, 1996), pp. 145–54, and 'The Origins of Futures Trading in the Liverpool Cotton Market', in P. Cane and J. Stapleton, eds, *Essays for Patrick Atiyah* (Oxford: Clarendon Press, 1991), pp. 179–208. See also H.W. Arthurs, *'Without the Law': Administrative Justice and Legal Pluralism in Nineteenth-Century England* (Toronto: University of Toronto Press, 1985), pp. 65–7.

39 Simpson, *History of the Common Law of Contract*, p. 174.

40 Kyd, *Treatise on the Law of Awards*, pp. 10–11.

41 Kyd, *Treatise on the Law of Awards*, pp. 52–3, 63–4, 68–9; see also J.S. Caldwell, *A Treatise of the Law of Arbitration* (London: Butterworth & Son, 1817), pp. 1–6.

42 Lord Eldon noted in 1800 that 'no man, I apprehend, ever heard of a suit in equity to compel the specific performance of a covenant to refer disputes to arbitration'. *Tatersall* v. *Groote*, 1800, 2 Bos. and Pull. 135. See also Montague, *A Digest of the Law of Partnership*, vol. i, p. 65n, and Kyd, *Treatise on the Law of Awards*, pp. 29–34, on powers to revoke arbitration agreements. The legal historian H.W. Arthurs aptly remarks that 'the Achilles' heel of arbitration was the extent to which it depended upon voluntary compliance with both the promise to arbitrate and the award itself'. See *'Without the Law'*, p. 69.

43 Montague, *A Digest of the Law of Partnership*, vol. i, p. 65.

44 Kyd, *Treatise on the Law of Awards*, p. 30.

45 *Halfhide* v. *Fenning*, 1788, 2 Bro. 336.

46 *Street* v. *Rigby*, 1802, 6 Vesey 817, 821. See also Montague, *A Digest of the Law of Partnership*, vol. i, p. 67. Such an attitude appears to be in line with Holdsworth's analysis of the courts' view of arbitration, although, as Horwitz and Oldham have shown, Holdsworth misunderstood several important early rulings and failed to recognize the degree to which the courts supported arbitration. Such support, it might be noted, may have been more forthcoming either when the cases for arbitration were enrolled by the courts under the terms of the 1698 act or when they did not specifically attempt to forestall actions at law. See Horwitz and Oldham, 'John Locke, Lord Mansfield and Arbitration', p. 155.

47 Kyd, *Treatise on the Law of Awards*, pp. 27–34.

48 Rawcliffe, '"That Kindliness Should be Cherished More"', pp. 101–2.

49 F.L. Wiswall Jr, *The Development of Admiralty Jurisdiction and Practice since 1800* (Cambridge: Cambridge University Press, 1970), p. 10; Marcus Rediker,

Between the Devil and the Deep Blue Sea: Merchant Seamen, Pirates, and the Anglo-American Maritime World, 1700–1750 (Cambridge: Cambridge University Press, 1987), pp. 119–21.

50 See generally, Wiswall, *Development of Admiralty Jurisdiction*, pp. 8–19.

51 Indeed eighteenth- and nineteenth-century commentators recognized that proceedings in admiralty were nearly identical to summary causes in ecclesiastical courts.

52 This is only a bare outline. For a full explication of the procedures *in rem*, see Arthur Browne, *A Compendious View of the Civil Law, and of the Law of Admiralty*, 2 vols (London: J. Butterworth, 1802), vol. ii, pp. 396–430, and for a more succinct discussion of the same see Wiswall, *Development of Admiralty Jurisdiction*, pp. 12–16.

53 Wiswall, *Development of Admiralty Jurisdiction*, p. 18, although the author's complaints against the contemporary description of these procedures as 'summary' are not fully warranted. Browne, for one, was quite clear that admiralty proceedings were 'summary' only in the sense that the term was used to denote a certain type of proceeding at ecclesiastical law.

54 Alfred Conkling, *Admiralty Jurisdiction, Law and Practice of the Courts of the United States* (Albany, N.Y.: W.C. Little & Co., 1848), p. 312, cited in Wiswall, *Development of Admiralty Jurisdiction*, pp. 24–5.

55 Wiswall, *Development of Admiralty Jurisdiction*, pp. 25, 45–6.

56 William Hay, *Decisions on the Poor Law of Scotland in the Court of Session, and Awards by Arbitration* (Edinburgh: T. & T. Clark, 1859), pp. 145–61.

57 On the expansion of the summary jurisdiction of the magistracy, see Norma Landau, *Justices of the Peace, 1679–1760* (Berkeley: University of California Press, 1984), p. 246; David Lieberman, *The Province of Legislation Determined: Legal Theory in Eighteenth Century Britain* (Cambridge: Cambridge University Press, 1989), pp. 14–15.

58 James Moher, 'From Suppression to Containment: Roots of Trade Union Law to 1825', in J. Rule, ed., *British Trade Unionism: The Formative Years, 1750–1850* (London: Longman, 1988), pp. 78–9.

59 13 Geo. III, c. 68 (1773) and 32 Geo. III, c. 44 (1792).

60 J.V. Orth, *Combination and Conspiracy: A Legal History of Trade Unionism, 1721–1906* (Oxford: Clarendon Press, 1991), pp. 45–9.

61 Moher, 'From Suppression to Containment', pp. 74–82; M. Dorothy George, 'The Combination Laws Reconsidered', *Economic Journal* (Supplement), Economic History Series, 2 (May 1927); Orth, *Combination and Conspiracy*, pp. 57–60.

62 Orth, *Combination and Conspiracy*, p. 60. The relevant wage-fixing sections are XV of 39 Geo. III, c. 81 (1799) and XIV of 39 & 40 Geo. III, c. 106 (1800). While Moher notes that a 1796 act against combinations among journeymen papermakers intentionally dropped proposed wage-fixing clauses, a 1799 bill against combinations among journeymen millwrights, which was an immediate precursor to the general Combination Act, specifically tied the expansion of magistrates' jurisdiction over combination to the more effective regulation of wages by those same justices. See Moher, 'From Suppression to Containment', p. 81; *Journals of the House of Commons*, vol. 54 (1798–99), pp. 412–13, 613.

63   Moher, 'From Suppression to Containment', p. 82; Orth, *Combination and Conspiracy*, pp. 45–6.

64   C.R. Dobson, *Masters and Journeymen: A Prehistory of Industrial Relations, 1717–1800* (London: Croom Helm, 1980), ch. 6; Moher, 'From Suppression to Containment', p. 82; Orth, *Combination and Conspiracy*, pp. 45–6

65   Orth, *Combination and Conspiracy*, p. 58.

66   On the intent of act, see John Rule, 'Trade Unions, the Government and the French Revolution, 1789–1802', in J. Rule and R. Malcomson, eds, *Protest and Survival: Essays for E.P. Thompson* (London: Merlin Press, 1993), pp. 119–21; for examples of workers' petitions against the act, see *Journals of the House of Commons*, vol. 55 (1799–1800), pp. 645–6, 648, 665, 706–7, 712, 770–1.

67   Moher, 'From Suppression to Containment', p. 83.

68   Moher, 'From Suppression to Containment', p. 83; Orth, *Combination and Conspiracy*, pp. 50, 156–61.

69   39 & 40 Geo. III, c. 106 §18–22. See also Lord Amulree, *Industrial Arbitration in Great Britain* (London: Oxford University Press, 1929), pp. 26–9.

70   Orth, *Combination and Conspiracy*, pp. 55–6.

71   39 & 40 Geo. III, c. 90. On the acts generally, see J.L. and Barbara Hammond, *The Skilled Labourer*, rev. edn (1919; London: Longman, 1979), pp. 49–54; Paul Mantoux, *The Industrial Revolution in the Eighteenth Century*, rev. edn (1961; Chicago: University of Chicago Press, 1983), pp. 458–62; E.P. Thompson, *The Making of the English Working Class* (New York: Vintage Books, 1963), p. 541; Robert Glen, *Urban Workers in the Early Industrial Revolution* (London: Croom Helm, 1984), pp. 148–50.

72   See §10.

73   *Report of the Select Committee on Petitions relating to the Act for settling Disputes between Masters and Workmen in Cotton Manufacture* (hereafter *Select Committee on Petitions*), Parliamentary Papers (hereafter PP), vol. viii (1802–3), pp. 3, 33; Hammond and Hammond, *Skilled Labourer* , p. 50.

74   *Select Committee on Petitions*, pp. 33–4; Amulree, *Industrial Arbitration*, pp. 30–2.

75   Glen, *Urban Workers*, pp. 148–9.

76   44 Geo. III, c. 87.

77   The act also introduced a ticket system whereby each manufacturer was obliged to give out with the work a detailed note of the quantity, price and nature of the work-bargain. Many aspects of the law were curiously revived in the 1845 Ticket Act that applied to silk-weavers. Generally, see Amulree, *Industrial Arbitration*, pp. 33–5.

78   For a concise review of the 'diametrically opposite rules' in the common law and Chancery courts, see Joan Perkin, *Women and Marriage in Nineteenth-Century England* (London: Routledge, 1989), pp. 10–19.

79   Kyd, *Treatise on the Law of Awards*, p. 35.

80   Caldwell, *Treatise of the Law of Arbitration*, pp. 8–9.

81   *Bateman v. Countess of Ross*, 1 Dow's Rep. 235, also cited in Caldwell, *Treatise of the Law of Arbitration*, p. 11.

82   See Sonya Rose, *Limited Livelihoods: Gender and Class in Nineteenth-Century England* (Berkeley: University of California Press, 1992), pp. 8, 50–

75, and 154–84 on gender relations among Lancashire cotton-weavers in the fourth quarter of the nineteenth century, and Anna Clark, *The Struggle for the Breeches: Gender and the Making of the British Working Class* (Berkeley: University of California Press, 1995), pp. 18–24, 131–9.

83 Hammond and Hammond, *Skilled Labourer*, pp. 53–4; Glen, *Urban Workers*, p. 150.

84 Amulree, *Industrial Arbitration*, p. 44.

85 1 & 2 Geo. IV, c. 75.

86 5 Geo. IV, c. 96; Amulree, *Industrial Arbitration*, pp. 46–7.

87 It should be noted as well that Parliament was concurrently expanding the summary jurisdiction of the magistracy over the wage nexus. In 1819, the authority of justices to decide disputes and order the payment of wages was formally extended to cover seamen (59 Geo. III, c. 58), then to the wages of 'any Servant in Husbandry or any Artificer, Calico Printer, Handicraftsman, Miner, Collier, Keelman, Pitman, Glassman, Potter, Labourer or other Person' in 1823 (4 Geo. IV, c. 34), and subsequently to the hat, linen, fustian, cotton, iron, leather, fur, hemp, flax, mohair and silk trades by 10 Geo. IV, c. 52.

88 Alexander Macdonald, *Handybook of the Law Relative to Masters, Workmen, Servants, and Apprentices in all Trades & Occupations* (London: W. Mackenzie, 1868), p. 269. I owe this reference to Marc Steinberg.

89 Place Papers, British Library Additional Manuscript (hereafter BL Add. Ms.) 27800, f. 21.

90 Place Papers, BL Add. Ms. 27799, f. 160.

91 Amulree, *Industrial Arbitration*, pp. 50–1.

92 On savings banks, see 9 Geo. IV, c. 92 §45 in which disputes between depositors and the bank were settled by compulsory arbitration. Similarly, in the Friendly Societies Act of 1829 (10 Geo. IV, c. 56), §27 requires a society's rules to include whether disputes are to be settled by the summary jurisdiction of a magistrate or the appointment of arbitrators. Arbitrated settlements of salvaged ships was also reinforced by 1 & 2 Geo. IV, c. 75.

93 The relevant statutes are 3 & 4 Wm. IV, c. 42; 9 & 10 Vict., c. 97; and 17 & 18 Vict., c. 125. See also Arthurs, 'Without the Law', pp. 67–77.

94 Simpson, *Leading Cases in the Common Law*, p. 212.

95 Arthurs, 'Without the Law', pp. 99–103.

96 M. Miles, '"Eminent Practitioners": The New Visage of Country Attorneys, c. 1750–1800', in G.R. Rubin and D. Sugarman, eds, *Law, Economy and Society, 1750–1914: Essays in the History of English Law* (Abingdon: Professional Books, 1984), pp. 495–7.

97 James Losh, *The Diaries and Correspondence of James Losh, Volume I, Diary, 1811–1823*, ed. Edward Hughes, Surtees Society vol. 171 (Durham and London, 1962), pp. 13, 131; C.W. Brooks, 'Interpersonal Conflict and Social Tension: Civil Litigation in England, 1640–1830', in A.L. Beier, D. Cannadine and J. Rosenheim, eds, *The First Modern Society: Essays in English History in Honour of Lawrence Stone* (Cambridge: Cambridge University Press, 1989), pp. 380–1.

98 J. Chitty, *The Practice of Law in all its Departments; with a view of Rights, Injuries, and Remedies, as ameliorated by recent Statutes, Rules, and Decisions*, 2 vols (London: Henry Butterworth, 1834), vol. ii, pp. 73–4. Con-

sidering this energetic defence of trial by jury, it is likely that this is the same 'Mr Chitty' who assisted Samuel Shepherd in the defence of T.J. Wooler on charges of seditious libel in 1817. On Mr Chitty, T.J. Wooler, and the significance of trial by jury in radical rhetoric, see James A. Epstein, *Radical Expression: Political Language, Ritual and Symbol in England, 1790–1850* (New York: Oxford University Press, 1994), pp. 29–69.

99 See Sidney and Beatrice Webb, *The History of Trade Unionism*, new edn (1894; London: Longman, 1920), pp. 337–8; E.H. Hunt, *British Labour History, 1815–1914* (London: Weidenfeld and Nicolson, 1981), pp. 281–6.

100 See, for example, E.J. Hobsbawm, 'Custom, Wages, and Work-Load in Nineteenth-Century Industry', in Asa Briggs and John Saville, eds, *Essay in Labour History* (London: Macmillan, 1960), pp. 113–39; John Belchem, *Industrialization and the Working Class: The English Experience, 1750–1900* (Aldershot: Scolar Press, 1990), pp. 169–70; and Hunt, *British Labour History*, pp. 282–6

101 Place Papers, BL Add. Ms. 27800, f. 21.

102 Modern Records Centre, University of Warwick Library , National Graphical Association, London region: London Society of Compositors (hereafter MRC, NGA), Mss. 28/CO/1/1/2, London General Trade Society of Compositors Minute Books (hereafter LGTSC Minute Books), 5 May 1829.

103 *The Weavers' Journal*, 1 March 1836.

104 Place Papers, BL Add. Ms. 27803, ff. 358–63, *Articles and Regulations of the West Riding Fancy Union, for the Protection of the Trade of the Fancy Manufacturer* (Huddersfield, 1824).

105 Place Papers, BL Add. Ms. 27803, f. 338v., James Digby, 'A Poor Framework-Knitter's Last Appeal, and Best Advice'.

106 This, of course, is a distillation of a lengthy and complex debate. For a concise introduction to the problem as it applies to labour history, see Dave Lyddon, 'Industrial-Relations Theory and Labor History', *International Labor and Working-Class History*, no. 46 (Fall 1994), pp. 122–41. The debating points are clearly laid out in Eric Batstone, *The Reform of Workplace Industrial Relations: Theory, Myth and Evidence*, rev. edn (1984; Oxford: Clarendon Press, 1988), pp. 1–32. Also by way of introduction, the issues in the debate are perhaps best brought out in articles by two of its major contributors: Allan Flanders, 'Industrial Relations: What is Wrong with the System?', in *Management and Unions: The Theory and Reform of Industrial Relations* (London: Faber and Faber, 1970), pp. 83–128, and Richard Hyman, 'Pluralism, Procedural Consensus and Collective Bargaining', *British Journal of Industrial Relations*, vol. 16: no. 1 (March 1978), pp. 16–40.

107 Flanders, 'Industrial Relations', pp. 94–5; Hyman, 'Pluralism', p. 34. Such a perspective was most clearly elaborated by the 'pluralist' Hugh Clegg in *Trade Unionism under Collective Bargaining* (Oxford: Blackwell, 1979).

108 I follow here in part the Weberian distinction between 'authority' and 'power' elaborated by P.J. Armstrong, J.F.B. Goodman and J.D. Hyman, *Ideology and Shop-floor Industrial Relations* (London: Croom Helm, 1981), in which 'power' denotes the objective ability to impose one's will upon another, while 'authority' indicates the extent to which the use of power is perceived as legitimate.

109 Michael W. Flinn, *The History of the British Coal Industry, Volume 2, 1700–1830: The Industrial Revolution* (Oxford: Clarendon Press, 1984), pp. 349–58; Hylton Scott, 'The Miners' Bond in Northumberland and Durham', pts 1 and 2, *Society of the Antiquaries of Newcastle-upon-Tyne*, 4th ser., vol. 11: nos 2 and 3 (1947), pp. 55–78, 87–98; Robert Colls, *The Pitmen of the Northern Coalfield: Work, Culture and Protest, 1790–1850* (Manchester: Manchester University Press, 1987), pp. 45–51, 64–73; James Jaffe, *The Struggle for Market Power: Industrial Relations in the British Coal Industry, 1800–1840* (Cambridge: Cambridge University Press, 1991), ch. 5.

110 Flinn, *History of the British Coal Industry*, p. 353.

111 Scott, 'The Miners' Bond', pt 2, p. 90. Similar sections can be found in later bonds including the 'typical' one published by the miners in *A Candid Appeal to the Coal-owners and Viewers of the Collieries on the Tyne and Wear* (Newcastle upon Tyne, 1826), the bond from Killingworth and Burraton Collieries from 1837–38 also published in Scott, 'The Miners' Bond', pt 2, p. 94, and the 1841 Monkwearmouth Colliery bond published in *Reports from Commissioners: Children's Employment (Mines)*, PP, vol. xvi (1842), pp. 536–8.

112 On bargaining over changing conditions, see Jaffe, *Struggle for Market Power*, pp. 105–16.

113 Durham County Record Office (hereafter DCRO), T.Y. Hall Papers, NCB I/TH/20(10). Other bonds provided for the presence of miners' and viewers' representatives while the tubs were measured, but no arbitration of the dispute as such. See *Reports from Commissioners: Children's Employment (Mines)*, PP, vol. xvi (1842), p. 538.

114 *A Candid Appeal*, p. 16.

115 Newcastle Central Library (hereafter NCL), Matthias Dunn's Diary, 23 February 1832.

116 Flinn, *History of the British Coal Industry*, p. 65.

117 DCRO, T.Y. Hall Papers, NCB/I/TH/20(9).

118 *Newcastle Chronicle*, 10 March 1832.

119 Hepburn's strike was eventually defeated in the following year. On the strike generally, see Colls, *Pitmen of the Northern Coalfield*, pp. 88–98, 248–56; Jaffe, *Struggle for Market Power*, chs 7 and 8.

120 NCL, Matthias Dunn's Diary, 24, 25, 28 January; 2, 8, 13 February 1832.

121 Scott, 'The Miners' Bond', pt 2, pp. 94–8

122 J.H. Porter, 'Wage Bargaining under Conciliation Agreements, 1860–1914', *Economic History Review*, 2nd ser., vol. 23: no. 3 (1970), pp. 460–75; more generally, see Roy Church, *The History of the British Coal Industry, Volume 3, 1830–1913: Victorian Pre-eminence* (Oxford: Clarendon Press, 1986), pp. 607–701.

123 W.H. Warburton, *The History of Trade Union Organisation in the North Staffordshire Potteries* (London: George Allen & Unwin, 1931), pp. 70–9, 140–67; Robert Fyson, 'Unionism, Class and Community in the 1830s: Aspects of the National Union of Operative Potters', in Rule, ed., *British Trade Unionism*, pp. 200–19; Richard Whipp, *Patterns of Labour: Work and Social Change in the Pottery Industry* (London: Routledge, 1990), pp. 154–6.

124 Compare the descriptions of the pottery trades provided by Warburton, *History of Trade Union Organisation*, pp. 44–9, and Whipp, *Patterns of*

Labour, pp. 145–61, with Jaffe, *Struggle for Market Power*, pp. 96–119.

125   J. Boyle, 'An Account of Strikes in the Potteries, in the Years 1834 and 1836', *Journal of the Royal Statistical Society*, vol. 1 (1839), pp. 37–8.

126   Boyle, 'An Account of Strikes in the Potteries', p. 39; Fyson, 'Unionism, Class and Community', pp. 212–13; Staffordshire Record Office (hereafter SRO), Letter Book of Samuel Allcock, MF 49/13.

127   Boyle, 'An Account of Strikes in the Potteries', p. 39; SRO, Letter Book of Samuel Allcock, MF 49/13, although Fyson suggests that the board's failure was due to the manufacturers' lack of faith. See 'Unionism, Class and Community', pp. 212–13.

128   SRO, Letter Book of Samuel Allcock, MF 49/19.

129   Boyle, 'An Account of Strikes in the Potteries', p. 39.

130   Quoted in Boyle, 'An Account of Strikes in the Potteries', p. 40.

131   British Library of Political and Economic Science (hereafter BLPES), Webb Trade Union Collection, Section A, XLIV, ff. 252–3. Thanks to Marc Steinberg for this reference and Emma Taverner for the transcription.

132   An American observer sent by the State of Pennsylvania held the potteries up as an example of the successful operation of arbitration; see Joseph Weeks, *Report of the Practical Operation of Arbitration and Conciliation in the Settlement of Differences between Employers and Employees in England* (Harrisburg, Pa.: L.S. Hart, 1879), p. 3. The *Royal Commission on Trades Unions*, Final Report, PP, vol. i (1869), p. xxvii also referred to the potteries' arbitration boards in quite favourable terms.

133   Warburton, *History of Trade Union Organisation*, p. 114.

134   *Report from the Select Committee on Masters and Operatives (Equitable Councils of Conciliation)*, PP, vol. xiii (1856), pp. 49–50.

135   BLPES, Webb Trade Union Collection, Section A, XLIV, f. 297; Warburton, *History of Trade Union Organisation*, p. 151; see also Hollins's testimony before the *Royal Commission on Trades Unions*, 10th Report, PP, vol. ii (1868), pp. 86–9.

136   See above, Chapter 6.

137   MRC, NGA, Mss. 28/CO/1/1/1, LGTSC Minute Books, 6 May 1828.

138   See above, pp. 191–2.

139   MRC, NGA, Mss. 28/CO/1/1/2, LGTSC Minute Books, 12, 15 and 26 October; 16, 20 and 23 November 1829; 2 and 8 February 1830.

140   MRC, NGA, Mss. 28/CO/1/1/3, Union Committee Minute Books, 20 August 1833.

141   MRC, NGA, Mss. 28/CO/1/1/3, Union Committee Minute Books, 17 September 1833.

142   MRC, NGA, Mss. 28/CO/1/1/3, Union Committee Minute Books, 5 November 1833.

143   See *Annual Report of the Trade Council to the Members of the London Union of Compositors ... to which are added the Rules & Regulations of the Union, as amended to February 1837* (London,1837), p. 38.

144   MRC, NGA, Mss. 28/CO/1/1/5, London Union of Compositors (hereafter LUC) Trade Council Minute Books, 3 July 1834.

145   MRC, NGA, Mss. 28/CO/1/1/5, LUC Trade Council Minute Books, 3 July 1834.

146 MRC, NGA, Mss. 28/CO/1/1/5, LUC Trade Council Minute Books, 8 July 1834.
147 Employers' resistance to formal agreements was noted by the Donovan Commission and re-emphasized by K. Sisson and W. Brown, 'Industrial Relations in the Private Sector: Donovan Revisited', in G.S. Bain, ed., *Industrial Relations in Britain* (Oxford: Blackwell, 1983), pp. 149–53.
148 MRC, NGA, Mss. 28/CO/1/1/2, LGTSC Minute Books, 5 May 1829.
149 MRC, NGA, Mss. 28/CO/1/1/6, LUC Trade Council Minute Book, 27 December 1837, 20 February and 25 April 1838.
150 *Annual Report of the Trade Council to the Members of the London Union of Compositors* (London, 1837), p. 6.
151 MRC, NGA, Mss. 28/CO/1/10/1, *Proceedings of Arbitration Committee, or Conference of Masters & Journeymen. Freemason's Tavern. Friday, July 9th, 1847*; Mss. 28/CO/1/1/10/1, Minute Books: 1846–1849, 16 November 1847.
152 The following account is taken from John O'Neil, *The Journals of a Lancashire Weaver, 1856–60, 1860–64, 1872–75*, ed. Mary Brigg (n.p.: Record Society of Lancashire and Cheshire, 1982), pp. 112–22.
153 See the Introduction to O'Neill, *Journals*, p. xviii and pp. 113–14.
154 *Preston Guardian*, 23 March 1861, quoted in O'Neil, *Journals*, p. xxii.
155 On the Preston Strike, see H.I. Dutton and J.E. King, *'Ten Per Cent and No Surrender': The Preston Strike, 1853–1854* (Cambridge: Cambridge University Press, 1981).
156 *Preston Guardian*, 30 March 1861, quoted in O'Neil, *Journals*, p. xxiii; see also pp. 118–19.
157 This diary entry is noted by Dutton and King, *'Ten Per Cent and No Surrender'*, p. 206 although it is attributed to 'John Ward'. The author of these journals had initially been identified by this name but subsequent research has identified O'Neil as author.
158 Place Papers, BL Add. Ms. 27799, ff. 119–21.
159 Place Papers, BL Add. Ms. 27803, f. 424v.
160 *Capital Arraigned Against Labour; or, The Hand-loom Weaver contending for his Right* (Macclesfield, 1837).
161 *The Spitalfields Weavers' Journal*, no. 3 (October 1837), pp. 19–22; no. 4 (November 1837), pp. 28–31. This particular act apparently sparked several important arbitration cases, many of which were widely reported. A further arbitration case from Kilmarnock (Scotland) is reported in *The Weavers' Journal*, no. 5, 1 March 1836, p. 37. In addition, such jurisdictional issues had a relatively long history of settlement by arbitration. A report in *The Times* from 1 September 1817 describes a similar case that the City magistrates referred to arbitration.
162 R.G. Kirby and A.E. Musson, *The Voice of the People: John Doherty, 1798–1854, Trade Unionist, Radical and Factory Reformer* (Manchester: Manchester University Press, 1975), pp. 73–5; A. Fowler and T. Wyke, eds, *The Barefoot Aristocrats: A History of the Amalgamated Association of Operative Cotton Spinners* (Littleborough, Lancs.: George Kelsall, 1987), p. 28.
163 George White and Gravener Henson, *A Few Remarks on the State of the Laws, at Present in Existence, for regulating masters and work-people ...* (London, 1823), pp. 101–2, 139–40.

164 *Report from the Select Committee on Masters and Operatives (Equitable Councils of Conciliation)*, p. 20; H.I. Dutton and J.E. King, 'The Limits of Paternalism: The Cotton Tyrants of North Lancashire, 1836–1854', *Social History*, vol. 7: no. 1 (January 1982), pp. 68–9.

165 White and Henson, *A Few Remarks on the State of the Laws*, pp. 101–2, 139–40; see also Roy A. Church and S.D. Chapman, 'Gravener Henson and the Making of the English Working Class', in E.L. Jones and G.E. Mingay, eds, *Land, Labour and Population in the Industrial Revolution* (London: Edward Arnold, 1967), p. 148; Malcolm Thomis, *Politics and Society in Nottingham, 1785–1835* (Oxford: Blackwell, 1969), pp. 105–7.

166 H.A. Turner, *Arbitration: A Study of Industrial Experience*, Fabian Research Series no. 153 (London: Fabian Society, 1952–53), pp. 2–9.

167 Turner, *Arbitration*, pp. 18–19.

168 *Report from the Select Committee on Masters and Operatives (Equitable Councils of Conciliation)*, p. 11.

Conclusion

From the preceding details may be gathered the fact of the constant operation in the contract for wages, made by large masses of lowly-skilled artizans, of influences which have been little elucidated, and are wholly unrecognized by economical science. (Joseph Fletcher, Assistant Handloom Weavers Commissioner, 1840[1])

During the nineteenth century, English contract law generally came to be expressed in the language of a free market economy. 'The model of contract theory which implicitly underlay the classical law of contract', P.S. Atiyah has written, was 'the model of the market'.[2] In this model, parties to a contract freely negotiated and bargained over its terms, primarily relied upon their own judgements to evaluate offers and other information, gave their consent voluntarily, and bound themselves to the terms of contract upon pain of pecuniary damages. In law, as in political economy, the nature of the bargain itself became irrelevant. The role of the courts in contracts, like the role of the state generally, was 'to ensure procedural fair play' not fairness or justice.[3] Therefore, substantive intervention was at best unnecessary, for competition would naturally rectify any undue advantages; at worst, state intervention would prove to be detrimental because it violated the autonomy of the market.

As Joseph Fletcher, the Assistant Handloom Weavers Commissioner whose quote opens this chapter, realized in the 1840s, the market model of the wage contract was ill-suited to explain satisfactorily the ways in which wage bargaining functioned in practice.[4] That by this date he did not even consider the applicability of an alternative model derived from the status relationships prescribed in the master and servant acts is in itself revealing. Still, for Fletcher, the primary failure of both legal and economic theory was the inability to recognize and account for the role of public opinion in the determination of wages and employment. 'We see a powerful *public opinion* among the great body of employers, and of the community at large', he wrote, 'that it would be uncharitable and unwise to allow the competition of numbers for employment to take its full course, and reduce large masses of a lowly-skilled population to a demoralizing state of misery, in the midst of wealth. And among the workmen themselves we see combination to express their *public opinion*, on the subject of reductions, towards those who under-pay, and who are underpaid, in modes not always within the limits of the law.' Nevertheless, while Fletcher recognized that 'on both sides, the strict letter of the law has been systematically though almost unconsciously vio-lated', he was baffled as to how to harmonize either the prescriptions of the law of contract with the operation of community standards of justice or political economic theory with everyday practice. In the end, he was forced to conclude his *Report* with a question rather than a recommendation: 'Are these proceedings unjust and immoral in their object, as well as unsanctioned by the law in practice, – or are they not?'[5]

Fletcher's obvious confusion may serve to illustrate the prescriptive power of the doctrines of law and classical political economy even upon this excep-tionally insightful and observant individual.[6] His puzzlement should not lead us to ignore his identification of the important function public opinion had to play in wage bargaining. As we have seen, in many communities public opinion played a significant regulatory role in the process of indus-trial relations. However, Fletcher's observations are especially useful because they provide a view of the shadows that lay over the landscape of industrial relations in early nineteenth-century Britain. These observations throw into particularly sharp relief the process whereby the comprehension of the char-acter and operation of industrial relations was filtered and shaped by as-sumptions and expectations. It was precisely this contradiction between observation and expectation that generated Fletcher's confusion. Yet Fletcher's bewilderment is in part our own as well, for our understanding of industrial relations during this period has often been determined, perhaps over-determined, by many of these same grand theories or master narratives that obscure as much as they reveal. The object of this book certainly has not been to replace these grand theories, but it has been to bring into question their explanatory value and to test alternative perspectives on the past.

Thus it has often been argued that the importance of wage bargaining in Britain's social and economic history was coeval with the stage of 'mature' capitalism when labour had learned the 'rules of the game' and capitalists expressed a readiness to seek social reconciliation rather than confrontation. However, as we have seen, wage bargaining was an essential feature of Brit-ish industrial culture long before that. Shopfloor bargaining was an intrinsic element of the work experience during the late eighteenth and early nine-teenth centuries. Its presence in the workshop, on the factory floor, and down the pits cut across levels of skill, occupational specializations and regional diversities. Moreover, it could occur informally and cover a wide range of issues, including piece-rates, occupational hazards and managerial prerogatives, but it was also provided for in a more formal sense, as in the contracts of compositors and coal-miners, that left several important issues to be resolved on the shopfloor. Indeed the prevalence of shopfloor bargaining was reflected in the great cultural significance it expressed as well. For some, the ability to bargain was a signal of adulthood and thus marked a rite of passage; for others, bargaining became the idiom through which social and political ideals, such as reciprocity or mutuality, were articulated.[7]

Shopfloor bargaining exhibited a dynamic of its own that can be best revealed through an understanding and appreciation of the importance of reciprocity within an asymmetrical work relationship. Such a view does not seek to deny the ultimate authority of employers to hire and fire their workers, or the support employers often received from the state to suppress strikes or other forms of industrial unrest. It would be ludicrous to do so. However, work did get done within this unequal social relationship and this needs to be explained as well. After all, even in the most strike-prone of British industries, coal-mining, it has been calculated for a later period that most strikes were confined to a single workplace, were of extremely short duration (a week or less), and were heavily concentrated at a relatively few highly strike-prone locations.[8] Thus people's lives were shaped by the quotidian compulsion to work as much as, if not more than, the strike and its consequences. How these 'forces of circumstance' worked themselves out in the everyday lives of labouring people has been the ultimate reference point of this work.

Moreover, for this period, it is possible to overemphasize the autonomy artisanal workers possessed on the shopfloor, as some historians have done. There were obvious limits to this autonomy that did not necessarily emasculate them. However, the 'frontier of control', one common explanatory tool, is not perhaps the most appropriate metaphor to describe how many of these limits were set. While theories of conflict and confrontation may be suitably deployed to analyse strike activity and some aspects of the work experience, alternative analytical tools are equally necessary to excavate the working relationships that developed on the shopfloor. Foremost among those used in this book have been the notions that Marcel Mauss gave expression to in the term 'gift relationship', that E.P. Thompson identified as a 'field of force', or that have been variously described as games and bargains.

The value of these terms and the perceptions that support them lay in their ability to help explicate the network of reciprocities and obligations which inhere in an unequal relationship. Of course, many have sought to express similar perceptions in a variety of ways, or have expanded upon these notions in the context of different academic disciplines. Yet when viewed from the broadest perspective, these authors, and among them I would situate George Akerlof, Wilhelm Baldamus and Robert Wilson, have sought to explain work as at least in part an exchange relationship. In this exchange, the 'commodities' are sometimes tangible, as is the case when an employer pays the worker or when an 'implicit contract' exchanges extra output for job security or time off. However, it is equally true that these exchangeable 'commodities' are often intangible as well. Thus the stability of the ongoing work relationship often comes to depend upon the exchange of expectations and reputations to provide work, pay wages regularly, or complete tasks in a timely manner. Therefore, the work relationship also involves cultural notions of honour, respect or fairness. Certainly, the least tangible and most variable element of the work relationship is retained by workers in the form of the effort they choose to exert on the job. This 'effort bargain' lies at the core of workplace industrial relations and is frequently the focus of shopfloor bargaining.[9]

Of equal significance to the recovery of shopfloor bargaining for our understanding of British social and economic history during the early industrial period is the recognition that bargaining in a more formal and collective manner was more common than has frequently been acknowledged.[10] Again, the existence of collective bargaining during this era contradicts some commonly held notions of the manner in which capitalism and industrial relations matured simultaneously. Fletcher's observation that public opinion played an important role in the conduct of industrial relations is certainly borne out by the experience of many of those who went out on strike during this period. It is also evidenced by community efforts to initiate and enforce collective bargaining negotiations. Of greater importance, however, is the extent to which collective bargaining was practised in a wide variety of industrial sectors during this period, the flexibility of its forms of bargaining and negotiation, and the sophisticated theatre of the collective bargaining sessions themselves that is apparent so early on. This would seem to suggest that the filiation of collective bargaining and mature capitalism is questionable at best. Moreover, while the economic antecedents of collective bargaining remain of fundamental importance, the particular forms and practices of collective bargaining that developed during this period were equally rooted in British political culture. Thus we can see that such important elements and issues of that culture as formal petitioning, public meeting and approbation, representative government, and parliamentary procedures were all replicated within the collective bargaining process.

In a manner similar to that of the analysis of collective bargaining, the consanguinity of industrial arbitration and mature capitalism has been called into question. Here, however, the patrimony of this element of industrial relations lay in the realm of British legal rather than political culture and practice. Indeed arbitration was of medieval lineage and was quite well known to the British labouring classes of the early nineteenth century. Its apparent invisibility during that era may be due in part to the often informal nature of its proceedings, but Parliament's evident failure to successfully legislate its manifestation had a similar effect upon the recognition of its presence. Like collective bargaining, the forms of arbitration were quite flexible.

It equally could be adapted to collective bargaining situations or, using its more traditional form, to individual disputes which themselves often then set standards and precedents. Yet arbitration's equity promise was often more apparent than real and this was well understood by both employers and workers during this period. Rupert Kettle's insertion of the 'authority of masters' clause into the Wolverhampton building workers' arbitration agreements during the late 1860s only made obvious what many workers and their employers had long understood.[11]

From these perspectives, one may also be able to gain a fuller appreciation of the many sources and affinities of trade union ideas. Undoubtedly, visions of a moralized economy that were built upon largely Christocentric notions of justice and fairness were extremely important, as were the influences of contemporary political radicalism. However, there were also ready at hand a pervasive set of ideas that sanctioned the recognition of a 'transactional universe' and the 'civilizing process', two elements that may well have given expression to both the experience and projections of trade unionists. Other 'elite' ideas also became common currency among trade union and other working-class leaders, if not through their own autodidacticism then indirectly through the works of Thomas Hodgskin, William Thompson and many others. The populist element of trade union ideology may in fact be overdrawn to the detriment of the full recognition of the sources deployed for the didactic function of trade unionism. Yet it is equally true that from these sources could be derived elaborations and justifications of concepts of mutuality, obligations and reciprocities that were vital to the movement. Such ideas both constructed and reflected workers' understanding of the nature of the bargains they regularly struck on the shopfloor, an understanding that connoted a shared vision of society but not at the cost of subservience.

While the notion of England's Industrial Revolution has been subject to important questions and revisions over the past decade from the unlikely marriage of econometricians and postmodernists, the late eighteenth and early nineteenth centuries continue to elicit a wealth of research from scholars. Researchers resolutely adapt new analytical techniques and perspectives that reveal new fissures and faults in the terrain of British economic and social history during this period. The work you have just read may give some solace to both sides, or to neither. The view of this era as seen through the lens of industrial relations reveals many continuities both over time and across industrial sectors. The caesura that for some marked the end of early industrialization and the onset of mature capitalism, and which was accompanied by a pronounced transformation of social and economic relations, was not necessarily a feature of shopfloor industrial relations. The deep texture of these relations retained a vitality and longevity that was remarkable indeed. Moreover, the fractured experience of industrialization that at one point in the debate appeared to characterize workers' encounter with this transition to a modern economy may have been less profound than once thought. Not only were the 'modern' and 'traditional' sectors 'inseparable and mutually reinforcing', as two prominent economic historians have written, but the patterns of industrial relations retained a surprising degree of coherence across rural putting-out industries, extractive industries, artisanal workshops and factory shopfloors.[12] The organizational and competitive pressures of the era were in large part responsible for the growth of collective bargaining practices, which themselves were often associated with the growth of piece-work and the elaboration of price lists.[13] Pressures to construct and regulate these lists emanated equally from the local magistracy, employees and workers, but the developing forms and practices of collective bargaining nonetheless do seem to have been new, if not always successful, to this era.

In the end, these observations present a complicated view of this era and its relation to industrialization. It is one that looks both backwards and forwards, recognizes both continuities and change, and sees the persistence of old forms, the development of new ones, and the coexistence of both. While the focus may have been largely on the shopfloor and the bargaining session, these images are important reflections of how labour came to be constructed in Britain and how it assumed the role it did in British industrial relations.

Notes

1 *Reports from Commissioners: Handloom Weavers*, pt iv, Parliamentary Papers, vol. xxiv (1840), p. 241.

2 P.S. Atiyah, *The Rise and Fall of Freedom of Contract* (Oxford: Clarendon Press, 1979), pp. 402–4.

3 Atiyah notes, however, that there were many statutory enactments that simultaneously eroded the market principles of contract law. See *Rise and Fall of Freedom of Contract*, pp. 506–61.

4 The reliability of contracts generally as a model of economic relations is seriously question by Stewart Macaulay, 'Non-Contractual Relations in Business: A Preliminary Study', *American Sociological Review*, vol. 28: no. 1 (February 1963), pp. 55–67. For a more recent perspective, see Robert C. Ellickson, *Order without Law: How Neighbors Settle Disputes* (Cambridge, Mass.: Harvard University Press, 1991).

5 *Reports from Commissioners: Handloom Weavers*, pt iv, p. 241. Emphasis in original.

6 Duncan Bythell describes Fletcher's work as 'much the best in the series published at the end of the 1830s by the Royal Commission on the handloom weavers'. See *The Sweated Trades: Outwork in Nineteenth-Century Britain* (New York: St Martin's Press, 1978), p. 62.

7 See, for example, Robert Gray, 'The Languages of Factory Reform in Britain, c. 1830–1860', in Patrick Joyce, ed., *The Historical Meanings of Work* (Cambridge: Cambridge University Press, 1987), pp. 150–1.

8 Roy Church and Quentin Outram, *Strikes and Solidarity: Coalfield Conflict in*

Britain, 1889–1966 (Cambridge: Cambridge University Press, 1998), pp. 74–94.

9   A valuable survey of Baldamus's work has recently been provided by John Eldridge, 'A Benchmark in Industrial Sociology: W.G. Baldamus on *Efficiency and Effort* (1961)', *Historical Studies in Industrial Relations*, no. 6 (Autumn 1998), pp. 133–61.

10   Many excellent works on early trade unionism, including C.R. Dobson, *Masters and Journeymen: A Prehistory of Industrial Relations, 1717–1800* (London: Croom Helm, 1980) and the contributions to John Rule, ed., *British Trade Unionism, 1750–1850: The Formative Years* (London: Longman, 1988), tend to emphasize the longevity of combination. Richard Price's *Labour in British Society: An Interpretative History* (1986; London: Routledge, 1990) offers a brilliantly cogent analysis of these developments anchored in industrial relations theory, although that analysis obviously is quite different from the one offered here.

11   On arbitration and the building trades during this period, see Richard Price, *Masters, Unions and Men: Work Control in Building and the Rise of Labour, 1830–1914* (Cambridge: Cambridge University Press, 1980), pp. 116–28.

12   Maxine Berg and Pat Hudson, 'Rehabilitating the Industrial Revolution', *Economic History Review*, vol. 45: no. 1 (February 1992), p. 31.

13   These organizational changes are well described by Price, *Labour in British Society*, pp. 15–27.

Select bibliography

Manuscript sources

British Library
Francis Place Papers

British Library of Political and Economic Science
J.F. Bray Papers
Webb Trade Union Collection

Corporation of London Record Office
London Sessions Papers (Gaol Delivery and Peace), 1648–1833
Orders of Quarter Sessions and Orders upon Appeal, 1793–1826
Court of Requests:
    Warrant Books
    Precedents, 1799–1801
    P.A.R. Book 12

Durham County Record Office
Londonderry Papers
National Coal Board Records:
    John Buddle Papers
    T.Y. Hall Papers

Lambton Estate Archive
Lambton Mss.

Modern Records Centre, University of Warwick Library
National Graphical Association, London Region: London Society of Compositors
Union of Construction, Allied Trades and Technicians: Friendly Society of Operative
    Stone Masons

Newcastle Central Library
Matthias Dunn's Diary

Northumberland Record Office
Bell Collection
Delaval Papers

John Watson Papers
Minutes of the Committee Meetings of the Coal Owners of the Rivers Tyne and
    Wear
Minutes of the General Meetings of the Coal Owners of the Rivers Tyne and Wear

Oxfordshire Archives
Mayor's Court Proceedings, 1768–88, 1805–32, 1841–53

Staffordshire Record Office
Letter Book of Samuel Allcock

Parliamentary Papers

Journals of the House of Commons.

Reports from commissioners:
*Report of the Royal Commission on the Practice and Proceedings of the Courts of
    Common Law*, vol. xxv (1831–32).
*Returns of the Number of Causes, Officers, Jurisdictions and Committals of the
    Courts of Requests*, vol. xliii (1839).
Reports from Commissioners: Handloom Weavers, vol. xxiv (1840).
Reports from Commissioners: Children's Employment (Mines), vol. xvi (1842).
*Report of the Commissioners appointed to inquire into the Organization and Rules
    of Trades Unions and other Associations*, vol. xxxii (1867–69).
Royal Commission on Trade Unions and Employers' Organizations, Research
    Papers, nos 1–6 (1967).
*Report of the Royal Commission on Trade Unions and Employers' Associations,
    1965–1968* (1968).

Reports from select committees:
Report of Select Committee on the State of the Laws between Masters and Servants,
    vol. iii (1801)
*Report of the Select Committee on the Petition of the Woollen merchants and Manu-
    facturers in the County of York*, vol. v (1802–3).
*Report of the Select Committee on Petitions relating to the Act for settling Disputes
    between Masters and Workmen in Cotton Manufacture*, vol. viii (1802–3).
*Report of the Select Committee on more effectual modes of adjusting differences
    between Masters and Workmen in Cotton Manufacture*, vol. v (1803–4).
Report from the Select Committee on Silk Ribbon Weavers Petition, vol. ix (1818).
Report from the Select Committee on Framework Knitters Petition, vol. v (1819).
*Report from the Select Committee on the Recovery of Small Debts in England and
    Wales*, vol. iv (1823).
Report from the Select Committee on Artizans and Machinery, vol. v (1824).
Report from the Select Committee on Combination Laws, vol. iv (1825).
Report from the Select Committee on the State of the Coal Trade, vol. viii (1830).
*Report from the Select Committee of the House of Lords on the State of the Coal
    Trade*, vol. viii (1830).
Report from the Select Committee on Manufactures, Commerce, and Shipping,
    vol. vi (1833).

Report from the Select Committee on Masters and Operatives (Equitable Councils of Conciliation), vol. xiii (1856).

Periodicals

Advice to Labourers
The Advocate, or, Artisans' and Labourers' Friend
The Associate
The Associate and Co-operative Mirror
The Birmingham Co-operative Herald
Bookbinders' and Machine Rulers' Consolidated Union Friendly Circular
The Bristol Job Nott; or, Labouring Man's Friend
British Association for Promoting Cooperative Knowledge
Gorgon
The Labourer's Friend and Handicraft's Chronicle
Lancashire Co-operator
Leicester Chronicle
Manchester Gazette
Manual of the Association of all Classes of all Nations
Mechanics' Chronicle
The Mechanics' Magazine, Museum, Register, Journal and Gazette
The Mechanic's Oracle
The Merchants & Manufacturers Magazine of Trade and Commerce
Midland Counties Standard
The Mirror of Truth
The Monthly Liberator
The Monthly Messenger
The Morning Star
The National
Newcastle Chronicle
Official Gazette of the Trades' Union
Operatives Free Press
Scottish Trades Union Gazette
The Spitalfields Weavers' Journal
The Times
The Voice of the People
The Weavers' Journal
The Working Bee, and Herald of the Hodsonian Community Society

Books and pamphlets

Annual Report of the Trade Council to the Members of the London Union of Compositors ... to which are added the Rules & Regulations of the Union, as amended to February 1837 (London, 1837).
Articles and Regulations of the West Riding Fancy Union, for the Protection of the Trade of the Fancy Manufacturer (Huddersfield, 1824).
Brown, Thomas, *Sketch of a System of the Philosophy of the Human Mind*, ed.

Daniel Robinson (1820; Washington, D.C.: University Publications of America, 1977).

—— *Inquiry into the Relation of Cause and Effect*, 4th edn (1835; Delmar, N.Y.: Scholar's Facsimiles and Reprints, 1977).

Browne, Arthur, *A Compendious View of the Civil Law, and of the Law of Admiralty*, 2 vols (London: J. Butterworth, 1802).

Caldwell, J.S., *A Treatise of the Law of Arbitration* (London: Butterworth & Son, 1817).

Chitty, J. *The Practice of Law in all its Departments; with a view of Rights, Injuries, and Remedies, as ameliorated by recent Statutes, Rules, and Decisions*, 2 vols (London: Henry Butterworth, 1834).

Gent, H., *Capital Arraigned against Labour; or, The Hand-Loom Weaver contending for his Right ...* (Macclesfield, 1837).

Hale, William, *An Appeal to the Public, in Defense of the Spitalfields Act: with Remarks on the Causes which have led to the Miseries and Moral Deterioration of the Poor* (London, 1822).

Hay, William, *Decisions on the Poor Law of Scotland in the Court of Session, and Awards by Arbitration* (Edinburgh: T. & T. Clark, 1859).

Hodgskin, Thomas, *Labour Defended Against the Claims of Capital* (1825; London: Labour Publishing, 1922).

—— *The Word BELIEF Defined and Explained* (London, 1827).

—— *Popular Political Economy: Four Lectures delivered at the London Mechanics' Institution* (1827; New York: Kelley, 1966).

Hutton, William, *The Courts of Requests: Their Utility and Powers* (1787; Edinburgh, 1840).

Kyd, Stewart, *A Treatise on the Law of Awards*, 2nd edn (1799; Philadelphia, Pa.: Farrand & Co., 1808).

London Union of Compositors, *The London Scale of Prices for Compositors' Work: Agreed upon, April 16th, 1810, with Explanatory Notes*, 2nd edn (London, 1837).

Losh, James, *The Diaries and Correspondence of James Losh, Volume I, Diary, 1811–1823*, ed. Edward Hughes, Surtees Society vol. 171 (Durham and London, 1962).

Macdonald, Alexander, *Handybook of the Law Relative to Masters, Workmen, Servants, and Apprentices in all Trades & Occupations* (London: W. Mackenzie, 1868).

McCulloch, J.R., *A Treatise on the Circumstances which Determine the Rate of Wages and the Condition of the Labouring Classes*, 2nd edn (London, 1854).

Malthus, Thomas R., *Principles of Political Economy*, pt 1, 2nd edn, ed. E.A. Wrigley and David Souden (1836; London: William Pickering, 1986).

Marx, Karl, *Capital: A Critique of Political Economy*, vol. i (1867; New York: Vintage Books, 1977).

Mill, John Stuart, *Principles of Political Economy*, ed. Sir William Ashley (1848; New Jersey: A.M. Kelley, 1987).

Miller, Samuel, *Small Debts: Three Letters ... showing the Manifold Advantages of Enlarging the Powers of the Court of Requests* (London, 1830).

Montague, Basil, *A Digest of the Law of Partnership; With a Collection of the Cases decided in the Courts of Law and Equity upon that Subject*, 2 vols (London: J.

Butterworth and Son, 1822).

O'Neil, John, *The Journals of a Lancashire Weaver, 1856–60, 1860–64, 1872–75*, ed. Mary Brigg (n.p.: Record Society of Lancashire and Cheshire, 1982).

Owen, Robert, *Selected Works of Robert Owen*, ed. Gregory Claeys, 4 vols (London: Willliam Pickering, 1993).

Parkes, Joseph, *The State of the Court of Requests and the Public Office of Birmingham* (Birmingham, 1828).

Place, Francis, *The Autobiography of Francis Place (1771–1854)*, ed. Mary Thale (Cambridge: Cambridge University Press, 1972).

Poulett Scrope, G., *Principles of Political Economy* (London, 1833).

Report adopted at a General Meeting of the Journeymen Broad Silk Weavers (London, 1828).

Ricardo, David, *On the Principles of Political Economy and Taxation*, ed. Piero Sraffa (Cambridge: Cambridge University Press, 1962).

Rules and Regulations, for the Formation of a Society to be called the United Association of Colliers, on the Rivers Tyne and Wear (Newcastle upon Tyne, 1825).

Rules and Regulations of the Coal Miners' Friendly Society in the Counties of Northumberland and Durham (Newcastle upon Tyne, 1832).

Senior, Nassau, *Three Lectures on the Rate of Wages* (1831; New York: A.M. Kelley, 1959).

—— *An Outline of the Science of Political Economy* (1836; New York: A.M. Kelley, 1965).

Smith, Adam, *An Inquiry into the Nature and Causes of the Wealth of Nations*, ed. Edwin Cannan (1776; Chicago: University of Chicago Press, 1976).

Thompson, William, *An Inquiry into the Principles of the Distribution of Wealth Most Conducive to Human Happiness* (1824; New York: A.M. Kelley, 1963).

[Thompson, William], *Labour Rewarded: The Claims of Labour and Capital Conciliated, or How to Secure to Labour the Whole Product of Its Exertion* (1827; New York: A.M. Kelley, 1969).

Torrens, Robert, *On Wages and Combination* (London, 1834).

United Collieries Association, *A Candid Appeal to the Coal Owners and Viewers of the Collieries on the Tyne and Wear* (Newcastle upon Tyne, 1826).

A Voice from the Coal Mines; or, A Plain Statement of the Various Grievances of the Pitmen of the Tyne and Wear (South Shields, 1825).

Weeks, Joseph, *Report of the Practical Operation of Arbitration and Conciliation in the Settlement of Differences between Employers and Employees in England* (Harrisburg, Pa.: L.S. Hart, 1879).

[White, George, and Gravenor Henson], *A Few Remarks on the State of the Laws, at Present in Existence, for Regulating Masters and Work-People* ... (London, 1823).

Secondary literature

Books

Allen, V.L., *The Sociology of Industrial Relations: Studies in Method* (London: Longman, 1971).

Amulree, Lord, *Industrial Arbitration in Great Britain* (London: Oxford University Press, 1929).

Armstrong, P.J., J.F.B. Goodman and J.D. Hyman, *Ideology and Shopfloor Industrial Relations* (London: Croom Helm, 1981).

Arthurs, H.W., *'Without the Law': Administrative Justice and Legal Pluralism in Nineteenth-Century England* (Toronto: University of Toronto Press, 1985).

Ashton, T.S., *Iron and Steel in the Industrial Revolution* (Manchester: Manchester University Press, 1924).

—— *The Industrial Revolution, 1760–1830* (1948; Oxford: Oxford University Press, 1980).

Atiyah, P.S., *The Rise and Fall of Freedom of Contract* (Oxford: Clarendon Press, 1979).

Bailey, F.G., ed., *Gifts and Poison: The Politics of Reputation* (Oxford: Blackwell, 1971).

Baldamus, W., *Efficiency and Effort: An Analysis of Industrial Administration* (London: Tavistock, 1961).

Batstone, E., *The Reform of Workplace Industrial Relations: Theory, Myth and Evidence*, rev. edn (1984; Oxford: Clarendon Press, 1988).

Batstone, E., I. Boraston and S. Frenkel, *Shop Stewards in Action* (Oxford: Blackwell, 1977).

Behagg, Clive, *Politics and Production in the Early Nineteenth Century* (London: Routledge, 1990).

Belchem, John, *Industrialization and the Working Class: The English Experience, 1750–1900* (Aldershot: Scolar Press, 1990).

—— *Popular Radicalism in Nineteenth-Century Britain* (New York: St Martin's Press, 1996).

Belchem, John and Neville Kirk, eds, *Languages of Labour* (Aldershot: Ashgate, 1997).

Biernacki, Richard, *The Fabrication of Labor: Germany and Britain, 1640–1914* (Berkeley: University of California Press, 1995).

Blaug, Mark, *Economic Theory in Retrospect*, 3rd edn (Cambridge: Cambridge University Press, 1978).

Burawoy, Michael, *Manufacturing Consent: Changes in the Labor Process under Monopoly Capitalism* (Chicago: University of Chicago Press, 1979).

Child, J., *Industrial Relations in the British Printing Industry: The Quest for Security* (London: George Allen & Unwin, 1967).

Church, Roy and Quentin Outram, *Strikes and Solidarity: Coalfield Conflict in Britain, 1889–1966* (Cambridge: Cambridge University Press, 1998).

Claeys, Gregory, *Machinery, Money and the Millennium: From Moral Economy to Socialism, 1815–1860* (Princeton: Princeton University Press, 1987).

—— *Citizens and Saints: Politics and Anti-Politics in Early British Socialism* (Cambridge: Cambridge University Press, 1989).

Clapham, J.H., *An Economic History of Modern Britain: The Early Railway Age, 1820–1850* (Cambridge: Cambridge University Press, 1959).

Clark, Anna, *The Struggle for the Breeches: Gender and the Making of the British Working Class* (Berkeley: University of California Press, 1995).

Clegg, Hugh, *Trade Unionism under Collective Bargaining* (Oxford: Blackwell, 1979).

—— *The Changing System of Industrial Relations in Great Britain* (Oxford: Blackwell, 1979).

—— *The Oxford School of Industrial Relations*, Warwick Papers in Industrial Relations, no. 31 (1990).

——, Alan Fox and A.F. Thompson, *A History of British Trade Unions since 1889, Volume I, 1889–1910* (Oxford: Clarendon Press, 1964).

Cockburn, J.S., *Western Circuit Assize Orders, 1629–1648: A Calendar*, Camden Fourth Series, vol. xvii (London: Royal Historical Society, 1976).

Colls, Robert, *The Pitmen of the Northern Coalfield: Work, Culture and Protest, 1790–1850* (Manchester: Manchester University Press, 1987).

Cuthbert, Norman H., *The Lace Makers' Society: A Study of Trade Unionism in the British Lace Industry, 1760–1960* (Nottingham: Amalgamated Society of Operative Lace Makers and Auxiliary Workers, 1960).

Dobson, C.R., *Masters and Journeymen: A Prehistory of Industrial Relations, 1717–1800* (London: Croom Helm, 1980).

Dutton, H.I. and J.E. King, *'Ten Per Cent and No Surrender': The Preston Strike, 1853–1854* (Cambridge: Cambridge University Press, 1981).

Edwards, Paul, ed., *Industrial Relations: Theory and Practice in Britain* (Oxford: Blackwell, 1995).

Ellickson, Robert, *Order without Law: How Neighbors Settle Disputes* (Cambridge, Mass.: Harvard University Press, 1991).

Epstein, James, *Radical Expression: Political Language, Ritual and Symbol in England, 1790–1850* (New York: Oxford University Press, 1994).

Flanders, Allan, *Management and Unions: The Theory and Reform of Industrial Relations* (London: Faber and Faber, 1970).

Flinn, Michael W., *The History of the British Coal Industry, Volume 2, 1700–1830: The Industrial Revolution* (Oxford: Clarendon Press, 1984).

Fowler, A. and T. Wyke, eds, *The Barefoot Aristocrats: A History of the Amalgamated Association of Operative Cotton Spinners* (Littleborough, Lancs: George Kelsall, 1987).

Fox, Alan, *History and Heritage: The Social Origins of the British Industrial Relations System* (London: George Allen & Unwin, 1985).

Friedman, Raymond A., *Front Stage, Backstage: The Dramatic Structure of Labor Negotiations* (Cambridge, Mass.: MIT Press, 1994).

Glen, Robert, *Urban Workers in the Early Industrial Revolution* (London: Croom Helm, 1984).

Goffman, Erving, *Frame Analysis: An Essay on the Organization of Experience* (New York: Harper & Row, 1974).

Goldthorpe, J., D. Lockwood, F. Bechofer and J. Platt, *The Affluent Worker: Industrial Attitudes and Behaviour* (Cambridge: Cambridge University Press: 1968).

Goodrich, Carter L., *The Frontier of Control: A Study in British Workshop Politics* (1920; London: Pluto Press, 1975).

Gospel, Howard F. and Gill Palmer, *British Industrial Relations*, 2nd edn (London: Routledge, 1993).

Gray, Robert, *The Factory Question and Industrial England, 1830–1860* (Cambridge: Cambridge University Press, 1996).

Green, David R., *From Artisans to Paupers: Economic Change and Poverty in London, 1790–1870* (Aldershot: Scolar Press, 1995).

Gunn, J.A.W., *Politics and the Public Interest in the Seventeenth Century* (London: Routledge, 1969).

Halévy, Elie, *Thomas Hodgskin*, ed. and trans. A.J. Taylor (London: Ernest Benn Ltd, 1956).

Hammond, J.L. and Barbara, *The Skilled Labourer*, rev. edn (1919; London: Longman, 1979).

Harrison, J.F.C., *Robert Owen and the Owenites in Britain and America: The Quest for the New Moral World* (London: Routledge and Kegan Paul, 1969).

Hilton, Boyd, *The Age of Atonement: The Influence of Evangelicalism on Social and Economic Thought, 1785–1865* (Oxford: Clarendon Press, 1988).

Hirschman, Albert O., *The Passions and the Interests: Political Arguments for Capitalism before its Triumph* (Princeton: Princeton University Press, 1977).

Hont, I. and M. Ignatieff, eds, *Wealth and Virtue: The Shaping of Political Economy in the Scottish Enlightenment* (Cambridge: Cambridge University Press, 1983).

Howe, Anthony, *The Cotton Masters, 1830–1860* (Oxford: Clarendon Press, 1984).

Howe, Ellic, ed., *The London Compositor: Documents Relating to Wages, Working Conditions and Customs of the London Printing Trade, 1785–1900* (London: Oxford University Press, 1947).

Howe, E. and H.E. Waite, *The London Society of Compositors: A Centenary History* (London: Cassell and Co., 1948).

Huberman, Michael, *Escape from the Market: Negotiating Work in Lancashire* (Cambridge: Cambridge University Press, 1996).

Hudson, Pat, *The Industrial Revolution* (London: Edward Arnold, 1992).

Hunt, E.H., *British Labour History, 1815–1914* (London: Weidenfeld and Nicolson, 1981).

Hyman, Richard, *Industrial Relations: A Marxist Introduction* (London: Macmillan, 1975).

Jackson, Michael P., *An Introduction to Industrial Relations* (London: Routledge, 1991).

Jaffe, James A., *The Struggle for Market Power: Industrial Relations in the British Coal Industry, 1800–1840* (Cambridge: Cambridge University Press, 1991).

Joyce, Patrick, *Work, Society and Politics: The Culture of the Factory in Later Victorian England* (Hassocks: Harvester, 1980).

—— ed., *The Historical Meanings of Work* (Cambridge: Cambridge University Press, 1987).

—— *Visions of the People: Industrial England and the Question of Class, 1840–1914* (Cambridge: Cambridge University Press, 1991).

—— *Democratic Subjects: The Self and the Social in Nineteenth-Century England* (Cambridge: Cambridge University Press, 1994).

Kaye, Harvey J. and Keith McClelland, eds, *E.P. Thompson: Critical Perspectives* (Philadelphia: Temple University Press, 1990).

Kirby, R.G. and A.E. Musson, *The Voice of the People: John Doherty, 1798–1854, Trade Unionist, Radical and Factory Reformer* (Manchester: Manchester University Press, 1975).

Lazonick, William, *Competitive Advantage on the Shop Floor* (Cambridge, Mass.: Harvard University Press, 1990).

Lupton, T., *On the Shop Floor: Two Studies of Workshop Organization and Output* (Oxford: Pergamon Press, 1963).

Macfarlane, Alan, ed., *The Diary of Ralph Josselin, 1616–1683* (London: British Academy, 1976).

McCarthy, W.E.J., *The Role of Shop Stewards in British Industrial Relations*, Research Paper No. 1: Royal Commission on Trade Unions and Employers' Associations (London: HMSO, 1967).

Malmgreen, Gail, *Silk Town: Industry and Culture in Macclesfield, 1750–1835* (Hull: Hull University Press, 1985).

Mathewson, Stanley B., *Restriction of Output among Unorganized Workers* (1931; Carbondale: Southern Illinois University Press, 1969).

Mauss, Marcel, *The Gift: The Form and Reason for Exchange in Archaic Societies*, trans W.D. Halls (1950; New York: W.W. Norton & Co., 1990).

Mokyr, Joel, ed., *The British Industrial Revolution: An Economic Perspective* (Boulder, Colo.: Westview Press, 1993).

Orth, J.V., *Combination and Conspiracy: A Legal History of Trade Unionism, 1721–1906* (Oxford: Clarendon Press, 1991).

Palmer, Bryan D., *Descent into Discourse: The Reification of Language and the Writing of Social History* (Philadelphia: Temple University Press, 1990).

Pocock, J.G.A., *Virtue, Commerce, and History* (Cambridge: Cambridge University Press, 1985).

Postgate, R.W., *The Builders' History* (London: National Federation of Building Trade Operatives, 1923).

Prest, John, *The Industrial Revolution in Coventry* (Oxford: Oxford University Press, 1960).

Price, Richard, *Masters, Unions and Men: Work Control in Building and the Rise of Labour, 1830–1914* (Cambridge: Cambridge University Press, 1980).

—— *Labour in British Society: An Intrepretative History* (1986; London: Routledge, 1990).

Prothero, Iorwerth, *Artisans and Politics in Early Nineteenth-Century London: John Gast and His Times* (1979; London: Methuen, 1981).

Putnam, Linda L. and Michael Roloff, eds, *Communication and Negotiation* (Newbury Park, Calif.: Sage Publications: 1992).

Randall, Adrian, *Before the Luddites: Custom, Community and Machinery in the English Woollen Industry, 1776—1809* (Cambridge: Cambridge University Press: 1991).

Randall, Adrian and Andrew Charlesworth, eds, *Markets, Market Culture and Popular Protest in Eighteenth-Century Britain and Ireland* (Liverpool: Liverpool University Press, 1996).

Reddy, William M., *Money and Liberty in Modern Europe: A Critique of Historical Understanding* (Cambridge: Cambridge University Press, 1987).

Rose, Mary B., *The Gregs of Quarry Bank Mill: The Rise and Decline of a Family Firm, 1750–1914* (Cambridge: Cambridge University Press, 1986).

Rose, Sonya, *Limited Livelihoods: Gender and Class in Nineteenth-Century England* (Berkeley: University of California Press, 1992).

Rowe, J.W.F., *Wages in the Coal Industry* (London: P.S. King & Son, 1923).

Rule, John, *The Experience of Labour in Eighteenth-Century English Industry* (New York: St Martin's Press, 1981).

—— *The Labouring Classes in Early Industrial England, 1750–1850* (London: Longman, 1986).

—— ed., *British Trade Unionism, 1750–1850: The Formative Years* (London: Longman, 1988).

Sabel, Charles F. and Jonathan Zeitlin, eds, *World of Possibilities: Flexibility and Mass Production in Western Industrialization* (Cambridge: Cambridge University Press, 1997).

Schumpeter, Joseph A., *History of Economic Analysis*, ed. Elizabeth Boody Schumpeter (New York: Oxford University Press, 1954).

Schwarz, L.D., *London in the Age of Industrialisation: Entrepreneurs, Labour Force and Living Conditions, 1700–1850* (Cambridge: Cambridge University Press, 1992).

Scott, James, *Weapons of the Weak: Everyday Forms of Peasant Resistance* (New Haven: Yale University Press, 1985).

Scott, Joan Wallach, *Gender and the Politics of History* (New York: Columbia University Press, 1989).

Sewell, Jr, William H., *Work and Revolution in France: The Language of Labor from the Old Regime to 1848* (Cambridge: Cambridge University Press, 1980).

Simpson, A.W.B., *A History of the Common Law of Contract* (Oxford: Clarendon Press, 1975).

—— *Leading Cases in the Common Law* (Oxford: Clarendon Press, 1996).

Sisson, Keith, *The Management of Collective Bargaining: An Interactive Comparison* (Oxford: Blackwell, 1987).

Stack, David, *Nature and Artifice: The Life and Thought of Thomas Hodgskin (1787–1869)* (Woodbridge, Suffolk: Boydell Press, 1998).

Stedman Jones, G., *Languages of Class: Studies in English Working Class History, 1832–1982* (Cambridge: Cambridge University Press, 1983).

Stirati, Antonella, *The Theory of Wages in Classical Economics: A Study of Adam Smith, David Ricardo and their Contemporaries*, trans. Joan Hall (Aldershot: Edward Elgar, 1994).

Sweezy, Paul M., *Monopoly and Competition in the English Coal Trade, 1550–1850* (Cambridge, Mass.: Harvard University Press, 1938).

Thomis, Malcolm, *Politics and Society in Nottingham, 1785–1835* (Oxford: Blackwell, 1969).

Thompson, E.P., *The Making of the English Working Class* (New York: Vintage Books, 1963).

—— *Customs in Common* (London: Merlin Press, 1991).

Thompson, Noel W., *The People's Science: The Popular Political Economy of Exploitation and Crisis, 1816–34* (Cambridge: Cambridge University Press, 1984).

Turner, H.A., *Arbitration: A Study of Industrial Experience*, Fabian Research Series no. 153 (London: Fabian Society, 1952–53).

—— *Trade Union Growth, Structure and Policy: A Comparative Study of the Cotton Unions* (London: George Allen & Unwin, 1962).

Vernon, James, *Politics and the People: A Study in English Political Culture, c. 1815–1867* (Cambridge: Cambridge University Press, 1993).

Wallas, Graham, *The Life of Francis Place, 1771–1854*, 4th edn (1898; London: George Allen & Unwin, 1951).

Warburton, W.H., *The History of Trade Union Organisation in the North Staffordshire Potteries* (London: George Allen & Unwin, 1931).

Webb, Sidney and Beatrice, *The History of Trade Unionism*, new edn (1894; London: Longman, 1920).

—— *Industrial Democracy*, new edn (London: Longman, Green and Co., 1902).

Whipp, Richard, *Patterns of Labour: Work and Social Change in the Pottery Industry* (London: Routledge, 1990).

Wiswall, Jr, F.L., *The Development of Admiralty Jurisdiction and Practice since 1800* (Cambridge: Cambridge University Press, 1970).

Articles

Akerlof, George A., 'Labor Contracts as Partial Gift Exchange', *Quarterly Journal of Economics*, vol. 97: no. 4 (November 1982), pp. 543–69.

Arthurs, H.W., '"Without the Law": Courts of Local and Special Jurisdiction in Nineteenth Century England', in A. Kiralfy, M. Slatter and R. Virgoe, eds, *Customs, Courts and Counsel: Selected Papers from the Sixth British Legal History Conference, Norwich 1983* (London: Frank Cass and Co., 1985), pp. 130–49.

Bailey, P., '"Will the Real Bill Banks Please Stand Up": Towards a Role Analysis of Mid-Victorian Respectability', *Journal of Social History*, vol. 12: no. 3 (Spring 1979), pp. 336–53.

Behagg, Clive, 'Narratives of Control: Informalism and the Workplace in Britain, 1800–1900', in O. Ashton, R. Fyson and S. Roberts, eds, *The Duty of Discontent: Essays for Dorothy Thompson* (London: Mansell Publishing Ltd, 1995), pp. 122–41.

Belchem, John, 'Reconstructing Labour History', *Labour History Review*, vol. 62: no. 3 (Winter 1997), pp. 318–23.

Boyle, J., 'An Account of Strikes in the Potteries, in the Years 1834 and 1836', *Journal of the Royal Statistical Society*, vol. 1 (1839), pp. 37–45.

Brooks, C.W., 'Interpersonal Conflict and Social Tension: Civil Litigation in England, 1640–1830', in A.L. Beier, D. Cannadine and J. Rosenheim, eds, *The First Modern Society: Essays in English History in Honour of Lawrence Stone* (Cambridge: Cambridge University Press, 1989), pp. 357–99.

Brown, W., 'A Consideration of "Custom and Practice"', *British Journal of Industrial Relations*, vol. 10: no. 1 (1972), pp. 42–61.

Canning, Kathleen, 'Feminist History after the Linguistic Turn: Historicizing Discourse and Experience', *Signs*, vol. 19: no. 2 (1994), pp. 368–84.

Church, Roy A. and S.D. Chapman, 'Gravener Henson and the Making of the English Working Class', in E.L. Jones and G.E. Mingay, eds, *Land, Labour and Population in the Industrial Revolution* (London: Edward Arnold, 1967), pp. 131–61.

Clapham, J.H., 'The Spitalfields Acts, 1773–1824', *Economic Journal*, vol. 26: no. 104 (December 1916), pp. 459–71.

Dutton, H.I. and J.E. King, 'The Limits of Paternalism: The Cotton Tyrants of North Lancashire, 1836–1854', *Social History*, vol. 7: no. 1 (January 1982), pp. 59–74.

Edwards, Paul, 'Industrial Conflict: Themes and Issues in Recent Research', *British Journal of Industrial Relations*, vol. 30: no. 3 (September 1992), pp. 359–403.

Eley, Geoff and Keith Nield, 'Starting Over: The Present, the Post-modern and the Moment of Social History', *Social History*, vol. 20: no. 3 (October 1995), pp. 355–64.

Ewing, K.D., 'The State and Industrial Relations: "Collective Laissez-Faire" Revisited', *Historical Studies in Industrial Relations*, no. 5 (Spring 1998), pp. 1–31.

Finn, Margot, 'Debt and Credit in Bath's Court of Requests, 1829–39', *Urban History*, vol. 21: pt 2 (October 1994), pp. 211–36.

Fox, Alan, 'Collective Bargaining, Flanders, and the Webbs', *British Journal of*

Industrial Relations, vol. 8: no. 2 (1975), pp. 151–74.

Hay, Douglas, 'Patronage, Paternalism, and Welfare: Masters, Workers, and Magistrates in Eighteenth-Century England', *International Labor and Working-Class History*, no. 53 (Spring 1998), pp. 27–48.

Hobsbawm, E.J., 'Custom, Wages, and Work-load in Nineteenth-Century Industry', in Asa Briggs and John Saville, eds, *Essays in Labour History* (London: Macmillan, 1960), pp. 113–39.

Hollander, Samuel, 'The Post-Ricardian Dissension: A Case Study of Economics and Ideology', *Oxford Economic Papers*, vol. 32: no. 3 (November 1980), pp. 370–410.

Hont, I., 'The Language of Sociability and Commerce: Samuel Pufendorf and the Theoretical Foundations of the "Four-Stages Theory"', in A. Pagden, ed., *The Languages of Political Theory in Early-Modern Europe* (Cambridge: Cambridge University Press, 1987).

Horwitz, Henry and James Oldham, 'John Locke, Lord Mansfield, and Arbitration during the Eighteenth Century', *Historical Journal*, vol. 36: no. 1 (1993), pp. 137–59.

Huberman, Michael, 'Piece Rates Reconsidered: The Case of Cotton', *Journal of Interdisciplinary History*, vol. 26 (Winter 1996), pp. 393–417.

Hunt, E.K., 'Value Theory in the Writings of the Classical Economists, Thomas Hodgskin, and Karl Marx', *History of Political Economy*, vol. 9: no. 3 (1977), pp. 322–445.

—— 'Utilitarianism and the Labor Theory of Value: A Critique of the Ideas of William Thompson', *History of Political Economy*, vol. 11 (1979), pp. 545–71.

Hyman, Richard, 'Pluralism, Procedural Consensus and Collective Bargaining', *British Journal of Industrial Relations*, vol. 16: no. 1 (March 1978), pp. 16–40.

Jaffe, James A., 'The Origins of Thomas Hodgskin's Critique of Political Economy', *History of Political Economy*, vol. 27: no. 3 (1995), pp. 493–515.

—— 'Authority and Job Regulation: Rule-Making by the London Compositors during the Early Nineteenth Century', *Historical Studies in Industrial Relations*, no. 3 (March 1997), pp. 1–26.

Joyce, Patrick, 'Labour, Capital and Compromise: A Response to Richard Price', *Social History*, vol. 9: no. 1 (January 1984), pp. 67–76.

—— 'Languages of Reciprocity and Conflict: A Further Response to Richard Price', *Social History*, vol. 9: no. 2 (May 1984), pp. 225–31.

—— 'The Imaginary Discontents of Social History: A Note of Response to Mayfield and Thorne, and Lawrence and Taylor', *Social History*, vol. 18: no. 1 (January 1993), pp. 81–5.

—— 'The End of Social History?', *Social History*, vol. 20: no. 1 (January 1995), pp. 73–91.

—— 'Refabricating Labour History; or, From Labour History to the History of Labour', *Labour History Review*, vol. 62: no. 2 (Summer 1997), pp. 147–52.

Kahn-Freund, Otto, 'Legal Framework', in A. Flanders and H.A. Clegg, eds, *The System of Industrial Relations in Great Britain* (Oxford: Blackwell, 1954), pp. 42–127.

—— 'Blackstone's Neglected Child: The Contract of Employment', *Law Quarterly Review*, vol. 93 (October 1977), pp. 508–28.

King, Peter, 'Edward Thompson's Contribution to Eighteenth-Century Studies: The

Patrician–Plebeian Model Re-examined', *Social History*, vol. 21: no. 2 (May 1996), pp. 215–28.

Lawrence, Jon and Miles Taylor, 'The Poverty of Protest: Gareth Stedman Jones and the Politics of Language – A Reply', *Social History*, vol. 18: no. 1 (January 1993), pp. 1–15.

Lis, Catharina and Hugo Soly, '"An Irresistible Phalanx": Journeymen Associations in Western Europe, 1300–1800', *International Review of Social History*, vol. 39 (1994), supplement no. 2, pp. 11–52.

Lyddon, Dave, 'Industrial-Relations Theory and Labor History', *International Labor and Working-Class History*, no. 46 (Fall 1994), pp. 122–41.

Macaulay, Stewart, 'Non-Contractual Relations in Business: A Preliminary Study', *American Sociological Review*, vol. 28: no. 1 (February 1963), pp. 55–67.

McCord, Norman, 'The Government of Tyneside, 1800–1850', *Transactions of the Royal Historical Society*, 5th ser., vol. 20 (1970), pp. 5–30.

Mayfield, David and Susan Thorne, 'Social History and its Discontents: Gareth Stedman Jones and the Politics of Language', *Social History*, vol. 17: no. 2 (May 1992), pp. 165–88.

Maza, Sarah, 'Stories in History: Cultural Narratives in Recent Works in European History', *American Historical Review*, vol. 101: no. 5 (December 1996), pp. 1493–515.

Miles, M., '"Eminent Practitioners": The New Visage of Country Attorneys, c. 1750–1800', in G.R. Rubin and D. Sugarman, eds, *Law, Economy and Society, 1750–1914: Essays in the History of English Law* (Abingdon: Professional Books, 1984), pp. 470–503.

Muldrew, Craig, 'Interpreting the Market: The Ethics of Credit and Community Relations in Early Modern England', *Social History*, vol. 18: no. 2 (May 1993), pp. 163–83.

Offer, Avner, 'Between the Gift and the Market: The Economy of Regard', *Economic History Review*, vol. 50: no. 3 (1997), pp. 450–76.

Oliver, W.H., 'The Labour Exchange Phase of the Cooperative Movement', *Oxford Economic Papers*, new ser., vol. 10 (1958), pp. 354–67.

Phelps Brown, E.H., 'The Labour Market', in Thomas Wilson and A.S. Skinner, eds, *The Market and the State: Essays in Honour of Adam Smith* (Oxford: Clarendon Press, 1976), pp. 243–59.

Port, M.H., 'The Office of Works and Building Contracts in Early Nineteenth-Century England', *Economic History Review*, 2nd ser., vol. 20: no.1 (April 1967), pp. 94–110.

Porter, J.H., 'Wage Bargaining under Conciliation Agreements, 1860–1914', *Economic History Review*, 2nd ser., vol. 23: no. 3 (1970), pp. 460–75.

Powell, Edward, 'Arbitration and the Law in England in the Late Middle Ages', *Transactions of the Royal Historical Society*, 5th ser., vol. 33 (1983), pp. 49–67.

Price, Richard, 'The Labour Process and Labour History', *Social History*, vol. 8: no. 1 (January 1983), pp. 57–75.

—— 'Conflict and Co-operation: A Reply to Patrick Joyce', *Social History*, vol. 9: no. 2 (May 1984), pp. 217–24.

—— 'Postmodernism as Theory and History', in John Belchem and Neville Kirk, eds, *Languages of Labour* (Aldershot: Ashgate, 1997), pp. 11–43.

Putnam, Linda L., Shirley A. Van Hoeven and Connie Bullis, 'The Role of Rituals and Fantasy in Teachers' Bargaining', *Western Journal of Speech Communication*, vol. 55 (Winter 1991), pp. 85–103.

Rawcliffe, Carole, '"That Kindliness Should be Cherished More, and Discord Driven Out": The Settlement of Commercial Disputes by Arbitration in Later Medieval England', in J. Kermode, ed., *Enterprise and Individuals in Fifteenth-Century England* (Stroud: Alan Sutton, 1991), pp. 99–117.

Reid, Alastair J., 'Old Unionism Reconsidered: The Radicalism of Robert Knight, 1870–1900', in Eugenio F. Biagini and Alastair J. Reid, eds, *Currents of Radicalism: Popular Radicalism, Organised Labour and Party Politics in Britain, 1850–1914* (Cambridge: Cambridge University Press, 1991), pp. 214–43.

Roy, Donald, 'Quota Restriction and Goldbricking in a Machine Shop', *American Journal of Sociology*, vol. 57: no. 5 (March 1952), pp. 427–42.

—— 'Work Satisfaction and Social Reward in Quota Achievement: An Analysis of Piecework Incentive', *American Sociological Review*, vol. 18: no. 5 (October 1953), pp. 507–14.

—— 'Efficiency and "The Fix": Informal Intergroup Relations in a Piecework Machine Shop', *American Journal of Sociology*, vol. 60: no. 3 (November 1954), pp. 255–66.

—— '"Banana Time", Job Satisfaction and Informal Interaction', *Human Organization*, vol. 18: no. 4 (Winter 1959–60), pp. 158–68.

Rule, John, 'Trade Unions, the Government and the French Revolution, 1789–1802', in J. Rule and R. Malcomson, eds, *Protest and Survival: Essays for E.P. Thompson* (London: Merlin Press, 1993), pp. 112–38.

—— 'Against Innovation?: Custom and Resistance in the Workplace, 1700–1850', in T. Harris, ed., *Popular Culture in England, c. 1500–1850* (New York: St Martin's Press, 1995), pp. 168–88.

—— 'Proto-Unions?', *Historical Studies in Industrial Relations*, no. 2 (September 1996), pp. 139–52.

Samuel, Raphael, 'The Workshop of the World: Steam Power and Hand Technology in Mid-Victorian Britain', *History Workshop Journal*, no. 3 (Spring 1977), pp. 6–72.

Schon, Donald and Martin Rein, 'Frame-Critical Policy Analysis and Frame-Reflective Policy Practice', *Knowledge and Policy*, vol. 9: no. 1 (Spring 1996), pp. 85–105.

Scott, Hylton, 'The Miners' Bond in Northumberland and Durham', pts 1 and 2, *Society of the Antiquaries of Newcastle-upon-Tyne*, 4th ser., vol. 11: nos 2 and 3 (1947), pp. 55–78, 87–98.

Sisson, K. and W. Brown, 'Industrial Relations in the Private Sector: Donovan Revisited', in G.S. Bain, ed., *Industrial Relations in Britain* (Oxford: Blackwell, 1983), pp. 137–54.

Steinberg, Marc, '"The Great End of All Government ...": Working People's Construction of Citizenship Claims in Early Nineteenth-Century England and the Matter of Class', *International Review of Social History*, vol. 40 (1995), supplement no. 3, pp. 19–50.

—— '"The Labour of the Country is the Wealth of the Country": Class Identity, Consciousness, and the Role of Discourse in the Making of the English Working Class', *International Labor and Working-Class History*, no. 49 (Spring 1996), pp. 1–25.

Sykes, A.J.M., 'Trade-Union Workshop Organization in the Printing Industry – The Chapel', *Human Relations*, vol. 13 (1960), pp. 49–65.

Thompson, E.P., 'The Moral Economy of the English Crowd in the Eighteenth Century', *Past and Present*, no. 50 (1971), pp. 76–136.

—— 'Patrician Society, Plebeian Culture', *Journal of Social History*, vol. 7 (1973–74), pp. 382–405.

—— 'Eighteenth-Century English Society: Class Struggle Without Class?', *Social History*, vol. 3: no. 2 (May 1978), pp. 133–65.

Tiratsoo, Nick and Jim Tomlinson, 'Restrictive Practices on the Shopfloor in Britain, 1945–60: Myth and Reality', *Business History*, vol. 36: no. 2 (1994), pp. 65–84.

Vernon, James, 'Who's Afraid of the Linguistic Turn?: The Politics of Social History and its Discontents', *Social History*, vol. 19: no. 1 (January 1994), pp. 81–97.

Wilson, Robert, 'Reputations in Games and Markets', in Alvin E. Roth, ed., *Game-Theoretic Models of Bargaining* (Cambridge: Cambridge University Press, 1985), pp. 27–62.

Winder, W.H.D., 'The Courts of Request', *Law Quarterly Review*, vol. 52 (July 1936), pp. 370–7.

Index